LOGOS AND LIFE:

CREATIVE EXPERIENCE AND THE CRITIQUE OF REASON

ANNA-TERESA TYMIENIECKA

The World Institute for Advanced Phenomenological Research and Learning
Belmont, Massachusetts

INTRODUCTION TO THE
PHENOMENOLOGY OF LIFE
AND OF THE HUMAN CONDITION

Book 1

Logos and Life:
Creative Experience and the Critique of Reason

Book 2

Logos and Life:
The Three Movements of the Soul

ANNA-TERESA TYMIENIECKA

The World Phenomenology Institute

LOGOS AND LIFE:

CREATIVE EXPERIENCE AND THE CRITIQUE OF REASON

Published under the auspices of
The World Institute for Advanced Phenomenological Research and Learning
A-T. Tymieniecka, President

KLUWER ACADEMIC PUBLISHERS

DORDRECHT / BOSTON / LONDON / TOKYO

BD
431
.T9
1987
v.1

Library of Congress Cataloging-in-Publication Data   C̄IP̄

Tymieniecka, Anna-Teresa.
    Logos and life.

    (Analecta Husserliana ; v. 24)
    "Published under the auspices of the World Institute for Advanced
Phenomenological Research and Learning."
    Includes index.
    Contents: v. 1. Creative experience and the critique of reason – v. 2. The three
movements of the soul.
    1. Life. 2. Phenomenology. 3. Creative ability. 4. Reason. I. World
Institute for Advanced Phenomenological Research and Learning. II. Title.
III. Series.
    B3279.H94A129   vol. 24   142′.7 s [142′.7] 87–28428 [BD431]
    ISBN 90–277–2539–X (v. 1)
    ISBN 90–277–2540–3 (pbk. : v. 1)

_____

Published by Kluwer Academic Publishers,
P.O. Box 17, 3300 AA Dordrecht, The Netherlands.

Kluwer Academic Publishers incorporates the publishing programmes
of D. Reidel and Martinus Nijhoff.

Sold and distributed in the U.S.A. and Canada
by Kluwer Academic Publishers,
101 Philip Drive, Norwell, MA 02061, U.S.A.

In all other countries, sold and distributed by
Kluwer Academic Publishers Group,
P.O. Box 322, 3300 AH Dordrecht, The Netherlands.

Also published in 1988 in hardbound edition by Reidel
in the series Analacta Husserliana Volume XXIV

Dedicated to my brother
Bohdan Zaremba-Tymieniecki
who has never ceased to inspire me

BY THE SAME AUTHOR

Essence et Existence, Etude à propos de la Philosophie de Roman Ingarden et de Nicolai Hartmann, Editions Montaigne, Aubier, Paris, 1957.

Phenomenology and Science in Contemporary European Thought, Farrar, Straus and Giroux, 1961.

Leibniz's Cosmological Synthesis, Royal Van Gorcum/Humanities Press, 1966.

Why is there Something rather than Nothing? Prolegomena to the Phenomenology of Cosmic Creation, Royal Van Gorcum/Humanities Press, 1966.

Eros and Logos, Nauvelearts, Louvain, 1972.

Monographs in the Analecta Husserliana Books Series, D. Reidel, Dordrecht.

"Beyond Ingarden's Idealism—Realism Controversy with Husserl," Vol. IV.

"Poetica Nova: At the Creative Crucibles," Vol. XII.

"The Moral Sense in the Foundations of the Social World," Vol. XV.

"The Moral Sense, the Person, and the Human Significance of Life," Vol. XX.

"Tractatus Brevis: First Principles of the Metaphysics of Life Charting the Human Condition; Man's Creative Act and the Origin of Rationalities," Vol. XXI.

TABLE OF CONTENTS

THE FIRST PANEL OF THE TRIPTYCH
THE EROS AND LOGOS OF LIFE
WITHIN THE CREATIVE INWARDNESS

THE CENTRAL PANEL OF THE TRIPTYCH

(PANEL TWO)

THE ORIGIN OF SENSE

The Creative Orchestration of the Modalities of Beingness within the Human Condition

CHAPTER ONE
THE CREATIVE CONTEXT AS CIRCUMSCRIBED BY THE CREATIVE PROCESS — ITS ROOTS "BELOW" AND ITS TENTACLES "ABOVE" THE LIFE-WORLD:
Uncovering the Primogenital Status of the Great Philosophical Issues

CHAPTER TWO
THE TRAJECTORY OF THE CREATIVE CIPHERING OF THE
ORIGINAL LIFE SIGNIFICANCE:
The Resources and Architectonics of the Creative Process

CHAPTER THREE
THE CREATIVE ORCHESTRATION OF HUMAN FUNCTIONING:
Constructive Faculties and Driving Forces

ACKNOWLEDGMENTS

Now that this book is going to print, I wish to express my warmest thanks to Miss Rebecca Ramsay, Cambridge, Mass., who has used her many talents and great expertise to faithfully transcribe its handwritten version.

I am also thankful to Mr. Robert Wise for the attentive copy-editing and proofreading of the text, and to Mr. Louis Houthakker for his help with the index.

Selected translations of the poetry and criticism of Paul Valéry from *The Collected Works of Paul Valéry* are quoted with the permission of The Princeton University Press.

Extracts from *The Virginia Woolf Diary* are quoted with the permission of the Estate of Virginia Woolf and The Hogarth Press.

Part of the first panel of the triptych is a translation from A-T. Tymieniecka, *Eros et Logos*, 1972, Nauvelearts Publishers, Louvain, and is printed here by permission of the publishers.

ANNA-TERESA TYMIENIECKA

FOREWORD

It is rare that we feel ourselves to be participating in history. Yet, as Bertrand Russell observed, philosophy develops in response to the challenges of socio-cultural problems and situations. The present-day philosophical endeavor is prompted not by one or two, but by a conundrum of problems and controversies in which the forces carrying life are set against each other. The struggles in which contemporary mankind is fiercely engaged are not confined, as in the past, to economic, territorial, or religious rivalries, nor to the quest for power, but extend to the primary conditions of human existence. They undermine man's primogenital confidence in life and shatter the intimacy of his home on earth.

Philosophical reflection today cannot fail to feel the pressure of the current situation within which it unfolds. Since this situation now involves the ultimate conditions of human existence, its demands have at last given to philosophy the impetus and direction needed for conceiving that the *first* and *last* of its concerns should be life itself.

INTRODUCTION

THE PESSIMISM—OPTIMISM CONTROVERSY CONCERNING THE HUMAN CONDITION AT THE ROOTS OF THE MALAISE OF OUR TIMES

1. TOWARD A RE-EXAMINATION OF THE CRISIS OF MAN: A QUEST FOR PHENOMENOLOGICAL GUIDELINES FOR THE INVESTIGATION OF MAN AND THE HUMAN CONDITION

The so-called "crisis of culture," a focus of interest since Spengler's *Der Untergang des Abendlandes*, and which was reappraised in relation to transcendental phenomenology by Husserl in his *Crisis*, has finally reached a culmination. The crisis now involves not only man's cultural and social modes of life, but extends down into the very core of the human being. It underlies not only man's conduct and way of thinking but his innermost tendencies in approaching the *evaluation* of life phenomena, his tasks, prospects and aims, and the meaning of his existence. All these are, in fact, permeated by the attitude of *radical pessimism toward the human condition*.

Let us leave to sociological inquiry all the phenomena of cultural life and technological progress which, in their vicissitudes, have to a large degree disclosed the implications of their reductionistic empiricistic assumptions. These are assumptions which have been denounced by Husserl in his diagnosis of the crisis, and fought against, but not overcome, by phenomenological research. Now, at the stage in which the most intimately human dimensions of the human being are at stake, we may recognize them as a specific task left for philosophy. To begin with, we have to ask how the human mind traveled toward, and on which assumptions naively reached, this pessimistic view of the human condition.

Pursuing this question we hope to differentiate the specific issues that are involved in the pessimism-optimism controversy which philosophical research is called upon to clarify and — through this clarification — offer to man a ground for commitment.

Classic phenomenology, in both its Husserlian and post-Husserlian phases, offers the most elaborated anthropological inquiry yet available. But to undertake this task it will have to renew its investigations into the origins of man and his *life-world*. To this end we propose to replace the *constitutive* by the *creative research framework*. Our inquiry will culminate with the outline of such an investigation.

Two key notions that will emerge in this proposal, which develops further my work on the phenomenology of creativity, are: *initial spontaneity* and the *experiential modalities of life*. In my subsequent remarks it will appear that not only is the *pessimism-optimism* anti-thesis the crucial form of man's crisis, but that its investigation reveals the way in which philosophy is called upon to perform its fundamental task.

2. THE RATIONAL ENLIGHTENMENT: THE SELF-AWARENESS OF MAN AND THE QUESTION OF THE HUMAN CONDITION

Having in our time realized Descartes' dream of man's becoming the master of nature instead of its slave, man now believes that he has reached the peak of his powers and found the Archimedean point from which he may estimate the prospects of all humanity as well as his own individual human condition. We see the practical man analyzing the natural resources of the world and forecasting the course of economic development. We see him preoccupied with planning the future use of his resources. Similarly, he conjectures about the prospects for development of the human life-style or modes of existence, and deliberates about plans for the survival of the world's population. Unlike in previous ages when the human world was only partly accessible to man's knowledge and the course of humanity a matter of wonder and mystery, contemporary man believes he has definitively uncovered the mechanisms of both organic and social evolution. Because of the seemingly exhaustive knowledge of the world and of human behavior accessible to him, he no longer wonders about the mysterious and unforeseeable forces guiding the destinies of nations. All "mysteries" appear to him to be, if not resolved, then at least resolvable by his infallible reason. There seem to be no barriers to reason's searching and nothing to resist its grasp.

However, man does not end his inquiry with nature and society; he seeks also to understand himself. There is nothing new in this concern. Man has always wondered about the meaning of life, destiny, and the human condition. However, contemporary man goes about this investigation in the same way he goes about inquiries into nature. He approaches every aspect or dimension of life with the same thoroughness and intrepidity. Man aims to reach a final answer, and he believes he has found it. Indeed, in opposition to traditional man, who, as Valéry puts it, cherished as his greatest treasure the mystery of his being — "de ne rien comprendre à son sort" — contemporary man believes that he has the ability to understand himself essentially, to find out "who he is," "how he operates," and "where he is going"; in brief, he questions himself until he is convinced that he has arrived at a complete self-awareness that yields total knowledge of himself and his being.

Contemporary literature, the mirror of contemporary man's concerns and the witness of his struggle, shows us how man irremediably is led to search into himself and the human condition, and also, what he finds.

In fact, we find in the images of man which that literature offers, three dominant guidelines in this search.

(1) The prevailing approach to this investigation of himself requires that man scrutinize all actions, reactions, and relations to others in the conventional and familiar situations of life in order to find their hidden motivations and thereby arrive at an understanding of himself. Most often inspired by psychoanalysis, this self-understanding reduces the whole richness and complexity of life and experience to some rational pattern of a mythological nature.

(2) Man, however, may not be satisfied with his discoveries concerning a given life situation; he will endeavor to locate the deeper self that must be hidden behind these virtual manifestations. Thus he "experiments" with his sensibilities, capacities, and feelings, believing that this "self" or its features hidden in current life will reveal themselves in extraordinary circumstances and in extravagant actions.

(3) Man's quest for the discovery of himself and his condition may go even deeper. He may attempt to reach the virginal state of manhood beneath the supposedly falsifying sedimentations of inheritance, cultural conditioning, and conventional attitudes that progressively clothe him in the course of life. Behind them man hopes to discover his "authentic" aim and "ultimate allegiance."

What is the result of this search? What answer do we find along these lines to the question of the significance of human life and of the *human condition*? Let us start with the last-mentioned, truly philosophical issue as it is treated in the literature of our day.

Kafka's approach to the understanding of the human condition in *The Castle* depicts man as aware both of the accidental status of his station in life and of the tenuous character of his situation, while, at the same time, incessantly engaged in the discovery of his own unique "assignment" in existence. All man's endeavors culminate in unceasing efforts to establish "contact" with a "higher instance" that is responsible, man believes, for the distribution of higher instructions that would invest man with the role he has to assume in the haphazard and shadowy play of existence, as well as indicate to him the final aim that would bestow meaning upon it. But the contact always eludes him. The assignment is never given to man.

In *Finnegan's Wake*, James Joyce, taking another approach, seeks the authentic human self by scrutinizing the modes of man's participation in his ancestral inheritance, those cultural molds created by individuals throughout the history of humanity and passed from generation to generation. What would we in the end find along these lines?

It is precisely here that Beckett takes up the search. Upon reaching the end of his earthly course, his hero reviews his past in all its lived dimensions, seeking what there was that really mattered for his "true" being. Was there anything in his life that so captivated his unreserved allegiance that he would consider it as an expression of his "very self"? Was there no feeling of attachment, ambition, success or failure, or faith that would reveal him to himself as possessing intrinsic significance? Alas, after going through all the phases, incidents, emotions, and hidden motivations of his life, he reaches only a self-awareness of a void and of the futility of his being — every element of his life appearing arbitrary, circumstantial. In *Waiting for Godot*, men, stripped to their bare vital essentials — like an onion of which nothing remains upon the removal of its skins — hang merely upon a thread of compassion for each other, in a tenacious waiting — waiting for someone or something that would bring some direction or open a perspective; but, in the end, they are left in endless suspense.

The Polish *Theater of the Absurd* shows life as an endless comedy played by men enacting ever-recurring schemes (*Tango* by Mrozek); Cesare Pavese shows man as essentially a foreigner, an eternal emigré on earth, who sinks no roots there. Unlike a tree he does not inscribe himself by his deeds in its history, does not participate in anything essential and lasting, but leads a marginal and fleeting existence.

Examples of this search are innumerable. It is enough to mention Sartre's *Flies*, in which the human condition is shown to be a form of slavery in which we are caught by our own impulses and tendencies (as well as by the tyranny of others). Orestes, who has freed himself from all these constraints — even from such a primitive one as filial piety — and who eventually gains his "human freedom" from all seemingly arbitrary conditions, nevertheless discovers only a total emptiness, a life without any purpose and consequently one impossible to continue.

In brief, we are bound to ask:

(a) "What is the net result of man's investigation of himself and his condition?"

(b) "What are the guidelines for this scrutiny and its precritical assumptions?"

(c) "Should we consider this rational self-awareness a gift of the gods or their curse?"

From the very style of these investigations, in which priority is given to certain phenomena of existence while others are overlooked, we may conclude that the ENLIGHTENMENT which they bring to man has been arrived at by giving absolute priority to the rational functions of man as opposed to others. In fact, it is THE SOVEREIGNTY OF REASON, pervading the empirical realm of man's nature, life, and his world that has been the guiding principle of this search. Empirical psychology and psychoanalysis, promising to open man's complete existence to the lucidity of rational inquiry, have been from the start unwittingly accepted as valid points of reference in deliberation upon life-phenomena and as an approach to their mutual entanglements.

The results obtained by these investigations entail loss of aspiration and hope for the future of humanity, which appears doomed to moral disintegration and pending extinction. Far from revealing a hidden meaning, these sciences portray man not as a sphinx but as the disarmed, helpless victim of the play of nature and of social conditions.

Finally, all attention is directed away from the individual to the social as if it were society that makes man. While the scientific legacy has seemed to glorify the individual right to freedom, self-determination, progress, etc., in fact, the way in which these "humanitarian" approaches are interpreted empty man of personal value, self-orientation, and all the *specifically* human privileges, and subordinate him to social conditions.

Seen merely as a natural mechanism, man becomes transparent in his rational array of functioning. And what does this transparency seem to show? Indeed, according to this one-sided line of inquiry, it seems that man's life is nothing other than a course of animal survival, a play of circumstances.

This means life's complete *devaluation*. Indeed, if everything is to be brought down to the level of human survival, all the ideals and values (fairness, patriotism, self-sacrifice, family inheritance, loyalty, disinterested satisfaction from a well accomplished work, great deeds, heroism, truth, justice, etc.) which have led mankind through the ages, inspiring, giving meaning to actions, pursuits, and struggles seem to have been emptied of any intrinsic and transcendent value.

The "enlightened" man, who takes into account only the course of natural life, sees justice in practice defiled or fallible, fairness seldom rewarded, patriotism leading to nationalism and conflicts, and the degradation of great deeds by publicity. The only value remains the preservation of life. And what significance has this day-to-day living?

The most recent witnesses to this view — such as Kurt Vonnegut — deprive even the typical simple life of contentment and satisfaction of the senses. Vonnegut wants to unmask all the natural aspirations and joys of youth, of community life, social roles and national ambitions, whether naive, scientific, or humanitarian, as pretenses, believed in because men lack the intelligence and the perspicacity to see that these experiences are futile and ultimately mean nothing.

Investigated exclusively from the standpoint of his natural, empirical resources man does not reveal a "secret message," a "sign" that would answer to the yearning of the search. Hence, the radically pessimistic conclusion drawn is that human ambitions and pursuits are nothing but expressions of our vital drives for survival; all values are invented for the purpose of survival and are relative to our basic self-interests. And since, as most of the literary images demonstrate, there is a basic "*mal de vivre*" essential to life — life is not a smooth pleasure-ride but a weary struggle and drudgery —, what point would there be to living?

If, instead, such an inquiry were conducted in an unprejudiced way, it would show how limited these scientific methods are and how new vistas on human life have still to be considered.

Indeed, let me venture the diagnosis that the major and most profound issue upon which the destiny of humanity depends is the *controversy between the pessimistic and the optimistic assessments of man and life*. Basically, it is this issue which divides humanity into two camps — the one struggling and enthusiastically building a social future for man though within restricted empirical bounds, the other, losing faith in the purpose of human life, deteriorating at its roots, corroded by *ennui*, apathy, and captive to the spirit of defeat.

From the above, it goes without saying that the crucial target of the present philosophical quest is this center: the Human Condition. However, Bertrand Russell was right in claiming that philosophical interrogation and preoccupation always originate with some poignant questions concerning life itself.

What are the questions which concern us so that we cannot call a halt to our questioning before we question the very condition of man, of the human, and of man's humanity? These will soon be brought forth.

FOREGROUND

PART I

THE CREATIVE ACT AS THE POINT OF PHENOMENOLOGICAL ACCESS TO THE HUMAN CONDITION

1. THE RADICAL OVERTURN OF THE PHENOMENOLOGICAL PERSPECTIVE

The crucial philosophical issue decisive for the path which a theory or a philosophical system takes to explain the human universe is that of its means of access to the real. Philosophical query stems from the desire to encompass the totality of what there is, to differentiate it appropriately, and to discover its order and modes of operations in order to discover the reasons of its origination, as well as its direction or scope. Seeking this, the philosophical point of view entails the consideration within its scope of the place and role of man. This effort at a "philosophical point of view" entails the consideration within its scope of the place and role of man. Moreover, intrinsic to this effort at a "philosophical reconstruction" of the human universe is the postulate of certainty with which it is to be established. Every great philosopher in the history of Occidental thought, no matter what his starting point, has sought a "uniquely" appropriate way to approach the reality of the human being, life, nature, and the cosmos. However, it is not (1) the choice of criteria, according to which such or some other type of cognition, empirical or intellectual, is approached (since, unanimously, the criterion is the specific evidence which the type of cognition has to carry with itself), but (2) to what this evidential criterion is being applied, and (3) how this object of investigation is preconceived, that not only diversifies the various philosophies, but also determines their respective starting points.

Phenomenology sets out to avoid all biases by facing "things in themselves." Yet, although (1) its choice of criteria offers absolutely valid postulates for philosophy, its antithetic position — cognition/ reality — led it astray. In a vicious circle the choice of the privileged type of cognitive experience, mode of existence, or type of action presupposes already the option for such or other "absolutely valid" reality. Can this vicious circle in the orbit of phenomenology be

3

avoided? Ingarden, who proposed to leave this vicious circle by (2) a cognitive "insight of genius," never found it. He tried then to seek it in moral action — in vain. For a good reason: there cannot be a type of cognitive experience or action which is not bound by a restrictive apparatus separating it from the whole in an arbitrary way according to the modes of reality it yields. In contrast, for an authentically radical founding of philosophy, which Husserl calls for, we need indeed to find a truly "Archimedean point" from where everything finds its proper place.

In our investigation it came to light that neither cognition, in any form, nor human behavior, conduct, or action (with all their evidences: intellectual, intuitive, morally emotive, pragmatic, etc.) may open an access to the essential state or nature of human knowledge, or to man's essential status and his role within *the unity-of-everything-there-is-alive, of which he constitutes an inextricable segment.*

Phenomenology, being among Occidental philosophies unique in its recognition of all types of experience, inasmuch as each in its own objective region offers a perspective upon the human cognitive system, has enormously enlarged our perspectivistic assessment of the human life-world expansion. However, access to the *basic unity* of these experiential perspectives — eidetic, emotive, aesthetic, intentional — and the corresponding regional ontologies of the social, aesthetic, ontic, transcendental, etc. realms — spheres of human expansion — remains extant. Husserl sought vainly to bring nature, body, soul, and spirit under the aegis of transcendental intentionality; Ingarden left us merely ontologically unintegrated "regional" fragments; Maurice Merleau-Ponty did not succeed in bringing together flesh and the world, flesh and nature, the infinite logos and human destiny.

In the focus either on the givenness of the human factor or on the ways in which this givenness is established, the crucial point has been overlooked — namely, that this givenness of man within his world is not only of a *process-like nature* but, moreover, indicates a specific type of CONSTRUCTIVISM.

Classic phenomenology has been oriented by the search for the patterns, forms, principles, and rules according to which givenness is constructed, and it has made a monumental contribution to our knowledge of what givenness is made of as well as of the ways in which it is constituted with reference to transcendental subjectivity. This search culminates in Husserl's unsurpassable attempt to bring together the

constitution of "reality" by referring ultimately to the theory of objectivity and logic — ontology — on the one hand, and to the constitutive
structuration of experience in the theory of consciousness — or of
knowledge — on the other. Yet the ontologically approached theory
of knowledge (Ingarden), which proceeds from the assumption that
"reality," man's universe, may be adequately grasped in terms of parts
interrelated in wholes, that is by isolating artificially elements within a
cogent complex as if they contained within themselves — individually —
the clues to their interconnectedness within the whole, has failed to
account for the vast spread of givenness in its discrete and yet minute
cogent interconnectedness. The truth of the fact is, that all that an
individual or any abstractly isolated element of givenness may contain
is only in its *virtual* state and is suspended in its actualization upon the
entire complex in which it is existentially woven.

Through this stress upon the autonomy of abstractly isolated structures which seeks the ultimate principles of "reality" through a more
and more advanced isolation of the elements of which it is composed,
we accomplish nothing more than the loss of their crucial feature: the
specific significance which they may assume in their virtual interplay
with other elements within a cogent complex. To find the clue to the
vast, seemingly dispersed and yet cogent macrocosm of the human
universe in flux, we can rely neither on any ever-more-precise scrutiny
of the cognitive constructivism — constitution —, nor upon the rational
nuclei of ontic structurations of objectivity. If we presumed that reality
in its "womb" may correspond to the organization of a jigsaw puzzle the
parts of which can be separately discovered with the certitude that they
will ultimately fall all together in place, we would get lost, as has classic
phenomenology, in an ever expanding game played by the speculatively
reconstructing mind. I propose instead to strike at the heart of given-
ness-in-becoming where all differentiates from the *virtual* powers.

First, the constructivism of the human givenness is foremostly not
only that of the *development of his life-course*, but also, and secondly,
the human being is not merely (as Husserl proposed) a meaning-
bestowing agent, the maker of his life-world; what comes first is that *his
very life in itself is the effect of his self-individualization in existence
through inventive self-interpretation of his most intimate moves of life.*
Thirdly, although the aspect of man's evolution as a living being has
already been acknowledged by Max Scheler, yet Scheler misses the
critical point: he believes that self-constructivism through invention and

creativity closes life's possibilities. We intend to show, to the contrary, that *it expands them into possible worlds of life.*

In brief, I propose that the access to the Archimedean point from which, alone, the unity of all the possible perspectives on man's experience can be explained, and the key to the Human Condition be obtained, lies in the creative act of the human being which makes him "human" — the creative act of man where the differentiating factors of the macrocosm of life differentiate.

2. DISCOVERY AND APPROPRIATE ASSESSMENT OF THE ARCHIMEDEAN POINT FROM WHICH THE UNITY OF BEINGNESS IS TO BE EXFOLIATED

The search after the origin of forms, the origin of order, the unity of cognition and praxis within the human being, calls for a privileged access to the springs of life where the universal Logos differentiates itself. Raising these issues again in a new attempt at a philosophical reconstruction of our universe of life, I take up again the root-principles of Husserl, but free them from his interpretation of this unity stemming from the assumption that the world-order and the order introduced by cognition be sought in the origin of cognition itself, which then converts restrictively into the origin of the objective order. As we well know, this direction encounters its limits in the boundaries of intentionality beyond which it cannot reach; it misses the entrance to the constructive arteries of life and the source of life itself. The present work originated from dissatisfaction with the deficiency of the Husserlian intentional approach, the sovereign rule of intentionality that is assumed from the start narrowing the context of research as well as giving it a misleading focus: human consciousness. This latter cannot legitimately function as the central point of reference for a radical investigation of the universe of *human existence in the unity of all.* We raise here the Husserlian question of the origin of knowledge in a larger framework than his, that is, instead of beginning the inquiry with the question of the origin of order within the orbit of human involvement with the world and nature, we ask first after the *origin of forms of this involvement, that is, of life itself.*[1]

However, being faithful to the fundamental assumptions of Husserlian phenomenology, namely that it is the human being who is the agent of meaning-bestowing upon his orbit, and, having raised the question of the origin of order *before* and not conjointly with that of cognition, it appeared that it is not cognition (and the intentional network of its highest rational manifestations) but the *essential ways in which the human being enacts and delineates the enactment of his life-course that gives us cornerstones for searching out the origin of the order which he bestows upon the life-world and his social world.* It is thus proposed that cognitive meaning-bestowing and life-course enactment cannot be separated or even sharply distinguished in their life-meaning function. As a matter of fact, they are one: *while delineating by response, deliberation, selection, choice, imaginative invention, planning, etc.* and their enactment, his life-route, the individual living being is *performing his self-interpretation-in-existence.* In other terms, the apparatus of enactment of life and that of cognition mingle in the essential work of life-meaning establishment. They are separable only at the fringes of abstraction, at the one extreme, and at the abyss of life's origins, at the other. The leading factor, however, of life-progress lies in its enactment for the needs of which cognition is projected; it is the performance of this enactment which entails the principles of the cognitive emergence and of its nature. Indeed, both life-enactment and cognitive function of the human being meet in the crucial device which life-progress entails: the prototype of human action which resides in the CREATIVE ACT OF MAN.

With the creative act of man as a focal point, a complete overturn within phenomenology itself is effected; not only does the phenomenology of creative experience reveal the reverse perspectives of the "objective" ontological structures as well as those of "subjective" constitutive forming, but the entire span of man's questioning emerges in its full extent with a pristine appearance in which all the lines of life's assumed progress gather in order to receive their significance.

PART II

THE STRUCTURE OF THE PRESENT WORK

1. PLURIVOCAL CORRESPONDENCES OF COHERENCE: JUXTAPOSITION OF DESIGN PATTERNS

What in the actual workings of Nature and life unfolds is either in simultaneous (yet distinctive), or successive (yet intertwining) events (which partly cooperate and partly advance over each other's phases) or in fusions, which enact each other's propensities. The discovery process of the human mind, in contrast, first follows the whims of the spontaneous, intrinsic processes of Nature, yet diverges in the ways of their plotting organization into expository presentation, and second, has, in the traditional discourse in which philosophical visions of Nature, life and man are presented, followed the strictly delineated pattern of the temporal succession in which our reading-cognizing process works.

Why, instead of following this usual way of composing a learned work, did I choose to make this presentation in such a form that no forcible direct continuity of the rational argument is projected, but the three parts into which the first two books of this treatise are divided appear in the guise of three different "tableaux?" Their unity is, in fact, not that of a continuing argument, but that of numerous significant threads which, being subjacent to the direct themes of presentation, maintain interconnections among various issues, various analytic complexes, and various dimensions which are projected by the great themes in question. In this inter-connectedness resides that which we aim to reveal: *the workings of the creative condition of man.*

This is why these three parts are called a "triptych," a term borrowed from plastic visual reconstruction of a segment of life's fullness, which, limited to a one-dimensional presentation of its topic may, within one of the panels, bring to life merely one phase of the development of the objective sense of the work, as well as only one "sphere" of its inner workings, the revelation of the complete significance of which necessitates and indicates its innermost links to an ulterior as well as a preceding phase (either in temporal genesis or in spatial extension, or, lastly, in thematic expansion).

8

Thus a medieval "retable" of the nativity which has, in its center, the nativity scene situated at the cross-section of several spheres — a real babe in a manger, a historical situation, and a transnatural message — functions in its fullness only by having at the right the scene of the shepherds heading for Bethlehem to make their discovery and, on the left — bringing both to the culminating point of significance — the homage of the wise men of the Orient in its full dimensions as the recognition of the mysterious message at the center. This artistic answer to the question of the unity of various spheres of life brings us back to the problem of philosophical exposition. When dealing with a subject matter which involves the phenomenological recognition of, on the one hand, *all* types of experience as well as of *all* the ways of making "objectivities," operations, forces, dynamisms, virtualities, etc. present which these types of experience may entail or postulate, and, on the other, recognition of the modalities in which the making "present" may take place (evidence, presumption, conjecture, etc.), we do not want to introduce either a forced connectedness, or dubious speculative nets of unity. But we must also avoid unwarranted conclusions as to the non-existence of merely evoked facts on account of their ungraspability in one perspective when they delineate themselves in their own unique fashion within each other. Lastly, aware as we are that discreteness and discontinuity on one level do not mean chaos — that tracks that vanish in one modality might be traceable in another —, instead of following the traditionally established patterns of exposition of ideas that are assumed to be attuned to a strictly rational, cogent, intelligibly graspable unity of the universe, we realize that we have to proceed according to a different pattern; a pattern that the originating reality, in acquiring its sense, projects.

We know that the path of discovery which our mind follows so that we may come to grips with some elements of *reality-in-becoming* and "understand" it is so tortuous, disrupted, and takes in complete obscurity so many by-ways of our entire human functioning, that there are contemporary thinkers who are led to identify its tortuous progress with the nature of reality itself.

Yet that which we call the "reality of life," however tortuous progress in approaching and "understanding" it might be (for it is certainly fluid, infinitely expansive, and, as such, ungraspable in its fullness), it progresses in a harmonious—disharmonious unfolding which is just the opposite of the chaotic ways of our discovering process; reality in becoming indicates a harmony, the networks of which are woven on so many looms, with such infinitely varied types of warps and woofs, in so infinitely changeable a variety of patterns, that no direct passage from one segment of its weaving to another — with each segment extending into both infinitely simpler and more complex designs — can be established by analyzing it through a certain selected number of modalities.

Neither may we begin our "reconstruction" of the vision of reality, that is, of natural life, the passional abyss of the soul and the human universe which unfolds on the wings of the creative consciousness, by beginning, with Pascal, in fixating on the "infinitely small," for it leads us precisely into infinitesimal dimensions that are beyond our discernment. Nor may we begin this "reconstructing" endeavor, which of necessity has to keep to the main lines, the "essential" complexities, and the primordial arteries of forces, within the horizon of the infinitely expanding, because that lies beyond our embrace, and, diving into its flux, we will of necessity go astray. This means that neither descent into the origin of consciousness, which leads us into the vital realm but leaves us at a loss in finding a "beginning," nor reaching toward the life-world genesis, which escapes our grasp, is the way to find the harmony of the "reality of life."

To strike the right chord, which echoes and resounds from all the roads of the human universe-in-the-making, we have to begin at the center of all differentiation. We have to begin by evincing the human creative experience, in which all the forces which carry the meaningfulness of natural life play upon the strings of the passional soul and are gathered and transmuted, filtered, and untied and tied again into new networks, bringing new, unprecedented, and unique *specifically human significance to life*. Indeed, the emergence of creative experience, creative consciousness, and the human creative act means the establishment of a unique condition for life. *With their orchestration the natural life is lifted to a level* of novel significance. Instead of the field of the life-world assumed as the ultimate ground, even by Merleau-Ponty, yet seen as the expansion of the constitutive, objectifying consciousness which is being restricted to the intellectual surface of life, we gain, within the "creative context," a full-fledged field of philosophical inquiry into Nature, life, its specifically human meaningfulness and the sense of the human orbit, in which human functioning is not cut off at source points but stretches in all directions and into all dimensions — is not dwarfed as some or other modality, rational or sensuous, but comprises them all.

The central panel, then, gathers all the strings from the knots which analysis of poetic creativity reveals and follows them in their intricacies through analytic evidence, allusive surmising, conjectural inference, and evocative correspondence in order to investigate the crucial complex of the origin of meaning. The *creative process* proper opens the Pandora's box of the source of all the meaningfulness with which the human individual's circumambient conditions are endowed: the life-world, the social world, and the world of culture emerge.

The new division of human faculties, in which the supreme role passes from the intellect to the *Imaginatio Creatrix,* and sensory perception cedes primacy to the *will*, emerges as the cornerstone of a renewed critique of reason.

2. EVOCATIVE SYMMETRIES/ASYMMETRIES, ANTICIPATORY PRESUMPTIONS, ETC. OF GRAPHIC CORRESPONDENCES

There is also a special role which the seemingly "plastic" design of our triptych presentation of a philosophic work plays. No doubt the graphic presencing of meaning is a forceful mode of language; it causes its eluding bodily signs to reverberate throughout our experiential system, seeking for an appropriate chord to resound. What within the turmoil of experience of every instant seeks to surface into the limelight of attention as fully significant, has to be completed with innumerable other instances of feeling, affect, thought, sense, etc. If it succeeds for an instant in making its message "known," in imprinting it on the canvas of our self-interpretative script, it is in the next carried away while the turmoil proceeds.

Yet these instances of experience which assert their significance fully are not the most significant within the entire picture of our self; nor simply by surfacing with a clear signal, sign or meaning, can they be considered the essential factors within the great game of life that is being converted from a mute, neutral, one-voiced play of Nature into a uniquely human polyphonic symphony. On the contrary, this gigantically intricate performance is carried at its crucial joints by the experiential elemental strivings, bends, passions, whims, willings which do not surface with a clearly determined signal; they play "en sourdine" their decisive roles. We may not sort them out distinctly, but merely evoke an allusion to them, not by direct experiential association, but by artfully assembling against each other entire segments of meaningful data from the different phases in which the life symphony constructs itself. From the fragments of their juxtaposed designs, from their plastic symmetries/asymmetries, anticipatory emptiness in one phase versus plenitude in another corresponding phase, develops the constructively progressing design, in view of its presumed coherence which projects itself; and there appear corresponding experiential evocations, bringing what has been mute and absent from the limelight into its proper structural places and significant roles.

As is obvious from the above description of this endeavor, the infinitely complex and differentiated web in which the meaningfulness of what is being presenced as the human universe of life, comprising the "world," originates in the *on-going process of man's self-interpretation-in-existence.* This meaningfulness begins to acquire significance in subjacent areas of reality that remain unexplicated in the shadowy network of significant linkages of the inner meaningfulness of the merely sketched (but alluded to, and present in the background) contents of both panels: direct intellectual connections between problems here — in the first tableau — raised poetically, and there — in the central one — treated further in a scholarly fashion; discrete but unfailingly obvious correspondence between different types of intuitions brought forth first there, and then expounded rationally, in full, within the "creative context" of the scholarly analysis; indeed experiences alluded to and forcefully insisted upon in the poetic sphere of vision find correspondences that are unmistakable in the intellectual insights and intuitions. In fact, all these seemingly alien moments are, as seen in the central panel, united by the lived experience within our own flesh. An entire symphony of human life and human creative endeavor is meant to be brought forth for the reader to evince for himself. In this fashion the authentic ideal of Husserl that phenomenology be not a "science," operating by ratiocination, but an evincing of the "anti-predicative," which, in our perspective, means "pre-experiential evidences," in which the "state of things," — in our new radicalism understood as the genesis of "thinghood" — would be brought forth in its evocative present ("in its bodily selfhood"), is at last fulfilled.

Yet in this investigation of the origin of the meaning-of-all, to which the entire phenomenological endeavor of Husserl, Heidegger and Merleau-Ponty was geared, with the new *filum Ariadne* of our conception of *man's self-interpretation-in-existence,* we do not center upon consciousness, with its special sphere of thought, but focus on the all-coordinating functional complex integrated in the unity of everything in a unique configuration which we call the "human person." As emphasized above, we conceive of it as an element within this primeval unity. And our quest, which carries on the effort of pursuing our vital, as well as our *specifically human, self-interpretative course of life to its furthest*, does not stop at human destiny to be devised as fulfillment of life's meaningfulness. It continues beyond it, propelled by the longing for an encompassing understanding of "what is it all about?"

As a matter of fact the passional soul, which, in the center of the creative orchestration of human functioning, plays the role of the galvanizing and dynamic complex from within which all the other functional segments of the creation of meaningfulness draw promptings, propulsions, passional stirrings, etc., may from its abysmal depth surge into its own aspirations and engage in a passional pursuit of its own. At that point it forsakes all the self-interpretative schema of life and asks for the *ultimate answer to All*. And thus, from the very heart of the creative orchestration, while using all available constructive and self-interpretative configurations, the human being embarks upon an ulti- mate quest of which his soul is the instigator and the judge.

This ultimate quest, or the genesis of the spiritual life, is in fact the subject of the third and left panel of our triptych. Using all of the self-interpretative schema, and yet rejecting each and every means as falling short of its aim, the soul in its pursuit is, in fact, rejecting every schema meaningful to its existence; reaching an apex the soul is using all the creative devices of the laboriously conquered arsenal of the creative system of the human being precisely to dismantle all its constructive works. The soul is seeking to free itself from every "meaningful" attachment, aim, perspective: it rejects all *sense*.

Indeed, making its way through the tortuous meanders of the creative ciphering progress, the soul takes the reverse course and, in a creative fashion, despoils itself while seeking its *ultimate fulfillment*.

Within the third panel we find, thus, a double reflection: one, of the creative work operating at its peak toward the destruction of its very context; the other, this work itself, at the highest proficiency of the creative endeavor directed toward freeing the human being from its meaningfulness, from all significant entanglements of his beingness he has accomplished during his life-course at the very core of his inter- worldly existence. This twofold creative reflection illuminates the indef- initeness of the entire life enterprise. What we think to be our very self

could all have been otherwise; that in which we have invested our
dreams, longings, and love could have been altogether different. And
what about our very "sense of life," then? At the one extreme, in the
third panel's reflection, the center — the unique vertiginously complex
and rich, inventive and free game of creation and of the Human
Condition — appears in its right proportion as just a marvellous "game
of life."

At the other extreme, however, as we stand on the brink of being de-
molished by our own deepest wish, carried on by our innermost longings for the ultimate, the vertiginous beauty and greatness which is ours
at last reveals itself!

3. THE STYLE OF EXPOSITION: EACH TYPE OF EVIDENCE MEANT TO APPEAR IN ITS PRIMEVAL OPERATIVE SURGING AND ENACTMENT

In the light of the foregoing, it is already obvious that there are three
major styles in which the triptych is conceived. Indeed, each of the
panels presents a special type of the human experiential life pursuit
and, consequently, in order to present each of them with its proper,
lively evidence, "in its bodily selfhood," or, in our frame, "primeval
operative surging," we have to forge a proper form and language for
each. While the first part, the analysis of poetry, has at times to use the
evocatively fluctuating language of poetry itself, the third, which deals
with the seemingly disperse fragments of reflection within the continuity
of our everyday existence, in which a "sense" opposing the objective
reality is forged, calls for a special expository device. Those poignant
quasi-experiences that are without immediate follow-up and appear as
seemingly disconnected fragments of human relations and events, etc.,
cannot have a discursive inter-connectedness imposed upon them
without losing the very gist of the specific role that these fragments play
within the genesis of the spiritual soul. It happens too often in learned
dissertations "about" this genesis that we rationalize what cannot be
grasped and project bridges between unbridgeable experiences.

Thus, an effort has been made to present the quest in a "natural"
sequence of reflective-experiential material itself, in order to *evoke* and
suggest that which cannot be rationally grasped because its very
intention is to divest itself of the objectifying sense.

It is the central panel which gathers all the threads from both sides and treats the philosophical issues in a philosophical and intellectual — that is, scholarly — fashion.

Yet this would be a flattened surface from which all the vibrating evocative fullness would be gone had we not conceived of it as reworking with appropriate sensitivity the polyphonic wealth of insights, associations and intimate allusions to the material of the two other panels. Life is full: discrete, disharmonious, seemingly inconsequential, and, nevertheless, it is an ever-expanding creative coherence that surpasses itself at every instant.

The fact is that discursive reason, being just one instrument — and, for that matter, one that can dominate only at the expense of listening to and being attuned to others — for introducing and establishing meaningfulness within the brute elementary forces of life, cannot do justice in reconstructing the architectonic blueprint of this gigantic edifice; on the contrary, discursive reason is bound to overlook the most powerful, that is, most complex and subtly coinciding, designs of forces, because they do not follow a rational pattern; and in its ordered striving discursive reason may just cut through the great, innermost nerves of the life-designs, emptying the polyphonic synapses of their creative spontaneities. Yet, because it possesses only one "voice," that of the intellect, for expressing itself, it does not follow that this gigantic polyphonic game of life that moves incessantly onward and surpasses itself at each of the stages by the new creation of forms, experiences, etc., has to be otherwise considered incoherent or chaotic or altogether ungraspable. *To the contrary, it is precisely the authentic vocation of phenomenology to make philosophical inquiry attentive to all the "voices of sense" other than intellect; to be open to all the avenues of life's constructive meandering; courageous enough to oppose all the traditional prejudices, codes, established patterns of argumentation, rhetorics, etc. — all the paraphernalia of the rational limitations of our mind — and to use all the means at our disposal in order to elucidate this gigantic game of human creation.*

4. THE NEW CRITIQUE OF REASON

In reconstructing the pluri-evidential, pluri-vocal, plastico-graphic Polyphony of the Great Architectonics operative within the pulsating spontaneities in the workings of life, we must, however, ultimately raise two great questions: *First, what are the crucial and decisive sources of "sense"*? We will, in fact, distinguish *three factors of sense within the Human Condition as operative within the creative orchestration: moral, poetic,* and *intellectual* sense. Second, what is the thread of the coherence among the discrete, disruptive, randomly enmeshed or dissolving fragments such that they meet spontaneously in the great constructive phases of the self-interpretative game of life in which to "live" means to *delineate a self-individualized path of constructive advance while simultaneously endowing with significance each step of its articulation and progress*?

What is, in brief, the primeval *Logos of Life* from which the creative endeavor draws its disconnected, yet somehow cohering, manifold and multiple rationale?

In his enthusiasm for the constructive power of the intellect the Occidental philosopher, beginning with the Greeks, has engaged upon grasping reality by forging intellectual forms and concepts, the variation of which can go *ad infinitum* as the marvelous game of the intellect proceeds on its own, and has been seeking through the instrument undeservedly considered as privileged, namely the human intellect, a solution or solutions to the multiple problems of the infinitely expanding plenitude that is man's life in the simplest and most alien — because abstract — constructs of the rational mechanisms of the human being (in the principles and rules referring to an abstract entity or ideal forms), and has thus abused his privileged position as philosopher. Even so, contemporary philosophers, disabused of the domination and power of rational order and language, have proposed no definitive justification for rejecting the quest after the ultimate principles seen by them as antiquated presumptions. The truth of the matter lies elsewhere than in such a one-sided opposition between *reason* and *anti-reason*. Like the seeker after underground water, we first have to strike the right source for all the controversies about the legitimacy of questions concerning ultimate principles and reason. And we find it, obviously, in the Archimedean point: the creative orchestration of the specifically human existence. There it is that all the cords of significant arteries and articulations of life are tied together; there it is that we will find the source of the multiple rationalities wherefrom we may proceed further in our quest, wherever the philosophical Daimon prompts us to go.

5. THE PHILOSOPHICAL "ARGUMENT" IN OUTLINE

The above-sketched triptychal disposition of the present investigation is devised with the aim of revealing the *creative orchestration of man's self-interpretation-in-existence*. It focuses upon the crucial role of Imaginatio Creatrix, the surging of which, out of the vital complex of life's virtualities, marks the emergence of the *specifically human significance of life*, at the one extreme, and of the set of *primogenital elemental virtualities* that, being simultaneously activated, set up and circumscribe its basic platform within the incessant progress of *life's constructivism*, the Human Condition, at the other extreme.

The triptychal disposition takes into account the differentiation — and still constructively complementary, distinctive and yet interdependent intergenerative and mutually reflective, cooperation — of the *three major modes of the logos/antilogos currents in the generatively constructive lines by means of which the three major avenues of the uniquely human self-interpretation-in-existence* — *man's creative self-constructing* — advance. These are: first, the "poetic logos," which presides over the creative work of man proper, and through which man establishes the cornerstones of his human existence; third (the third tableau), in extreme opposition to the poetic logos, the "spiritual" *anti-logos*, which, in a swing contrary to man's highest self-creative aspirations, seeks to discover/invent the "ultimate reality" in a process of dissolving the ties projected by the first; and centrally, the tableau that is in the middle, the second, where the works of the creatively orchestrated intellect transmute the plurivocal insights, project syncretic unities, and establish the outlines of its plurirational operational system with a skeleton of structures, regulations, and principles. It is this discursive modality of the intellect's works that allows us to re-construct the mechanisms of *man's self-interpretation-in-existence*, with its central spine, the *creative apparatus*, and to appreciate with proper distance, and yet from within, its powers. It allows us, as well, to locate *from the center* the bearings of the *specifically human existence* upon the very playground of existence and within the system of life, with the expanse of meaningfulness at the one extreme, and with the aspiration to reach beyond that at the other extreme; it is along the axis which these directions form that the philosophical quest stretches in trying to "understand the truth" of the meaningfulness of everything there is, the pursuit of which gives to our life its own destiny.

PART THREE

MAN-THE-CREATOR AND HIS TRIPLE *TELOS*

1. THE REGULATIVE *TELOS* OF THE REAL AUTONOMOUS INDIVIDUAL: *TELOS* AND ENTELECHY

The eidetic intuition instrumental in both the ontological and the transcendental phenomenological analysis gains its clarity and apodictic evidence by focusing upon the object in its intentional, that is, strictly rational, ideal skeleton in which it "appears" within constitutive consciousness. Although we may retrace the steps of its transcendental constitution, that is, the progress of its origin within intentional consciousness, yet these origins — or "appearances" — themselves are repetitive. This "repetitiveness" — as opposed to the uniqueness of the actual origination in existence of the real individual being — is the very condition upon which the phenomenological retracing of the intentional constructive progress of the object rests. Indeed, it seems, first, that we may intentionally follow only the genesis of an object preconceived as having been already accomplished in its constructive process. Second, if in doing so we find an intersubjective consensus it is because what we do follow is beyond the *hic* and *nunc* of the concrete existential genesis: what the intentional analysis pursues consists merely of the rational itinerary of its articulations insofar as it retrieves segment by segment the phases of its structures as *reproduced*. In this perspective it becomes even clearer what I mean by claiming that the phenomenological analysis of transcendental constitution is only the *formal "reconstruction"* of the universal structures of the constructive mechanism, insofar as the *construction* has reached already the clearly objectifying level. The *actual existential genesis* of the concrete individual in its *material process of construction* does not reach to the surface of the formation which "appears" as, or is embodied in, the intentional objectivity. It is then the repetitiveness of the object, in its ontological "universality," preconceived as already completed that, on the one hand, allows for the eidetico/intentional analysis and imparts to it its methodological privileges. On the other hand, however, while taking into consideration merely this phase of the actual genesis of the existence of the individual being, at which its genetic progress has already taken the shape of the structure that "appears" objectified within consciousness, it pays the price of missing the principles of the actual existential origin of that being.

These origins are not to be found in the final stage identifiable by a repetitive, universal model representative of the role of human consciousness in assimilating givenness, categorizing and establishing the universal interconnections of an intersubjective *life-world*. Even if, as seems undeniable, the individual real being progresses by ultimately falling into a universal category of objective structures, yet his origination in existence by *individualizing himself from the otherwise anonymous Elemental Nature* is a unique and unrepeatable instance.

Indeed, if instead of severely narrowing the field of intuition to the sphere in which the already categorized forms appear, we open it, we need not plunge into a precritical attitude. The indubitable evidence of consciousness which was instrumental in their final shaping belongs only to a stage at which they are already individuated from the whole of the elementary processes of Nature, and their appearance within intentional reflection completes the process of severing them from the same elementary processes. By opening the expanse of intuition and losing its absolute evidence of consciousness, however, we may make a gain on the part of being. In fact, in the attempt to follow the real individual being in its emergence from the primitive forces as he progressively stands out as an autonomous factor of the whole which then becomes the "world," we gain the evidence of his *beingness*.[2] With his beingness in focus, we discover that the real individual makes his route as an *autonomous agent*. That is, he differentiates himself as a singular being from the rest of Nature by virtue of his own regulative devices.[3] He enters the self-constitutive progress endowed with the nucleus of his own material endowment; together with it goes virtual operational equipment ready to be triggered into action should the external conditions allow it. In this way he may direct from within his constructive differentiation the unfolding of his potential material as well as the using to this effect of matter external to his very own field.

This *inside/outside direction* of his inner workings not only establishes him progressively as a self-directing agent but makes him assume the role of a constitutive factor with respect to the entire realm of Nature. It makes him exercise an impact upon the circumambient forces of Nature and to become a center in which these forces of the hitherto

anonymous Nature converge. While unfolding in his outer/inner directed constructive processes, the agent of the real individual develops
his operational mechanisms, and by dealing with outer elements
strengthens his very own, unique position. In short, he projects his own
itinerary, establishing himself in existence, countering or evading some
of the cross-currents he encounters, and assimilating others for his own
benefit.

Accomplishing in this way step by step the constructive individualization of his being from within his own inwardly unfolding rule and
on the basis of his own initial resources, he establishes himself within
his context of actual existence, which reaches as far as the radius of his
operations.[4]

Our perspective upon the constitution of the real individual being,
which we have labeled elsewhere "cosmological," retains as its system
of reference both the eidetic and the transcendental systems of interrelated rational networks, but it rises above them on its own wings. As
Eugen Fink has observed, the philosophical significance of phenomenological analysis postulates indications from its findings on how to
proceed further, leaving analysis itself behind. Verified by these systems
of references, the *context of the actual existence* of the real individual
yields, indeed, evidences of its own. These corroborate partly those of
classic phenomenological inquiry; partly they enlarge upon them and
make some essential corrections. First of all, the real individual within
the context of his actual existence bridges the gap, otherwise insurmountable in Husserl's thought, between the empirical functioning of
the human being and intentional consciousness. As we know, Husserl
struggled in vain with this problem until the end of his quest and seems
to have been ready to give up the initial project of the total hegemony
of intentionality. Without it, however, that is, without bringing the
empirical zone of functioning within the intentional system, no unity
between the two realms can be maintained.

Secondly, by starting with a focus upon the real individual in his
hazy, changeable, blurred contours from which we may nonetheless
"conjecture" the outline of his actual existential process, we avoid with
this one initial stroke the Ingardenian predicament.

In fact, Ingarden has, in his ontological analysis of the fundamental
types of things and beings, given an eidetic skeleton of the real
individual. He has attempted to supply the Husserlian transcendental
conception of the real individual being with an ideal intrinsic structure.

In the Husserlian conception we see the real individual constituted in his character as a transcendent real object by a series of noematic glimpses (*Abschattungen*) with which the perceptual process of consciousness fills the spaces appropriately left empty within a preposed model. As close as this investigation may come to the ways of coalescing and accounting for the features in which the object "appears" within transcendental constitutive consciousness, it does not reveal its essential intrinsic structure, showing what he is in his own right. On the Ingardenian analysis complementing that of Husserl, it is then the complex ideal structure governed by a nucleus of an essence which contains a constitutive nature that should account for the real individual's existential distinctiveness from other types of beings and his autonomy. To the degree to which the intrinsic essence of the being would indicate the necessary coexistence of structural mechanisms which allow for the exchange of externally conditioned properties, internal processes with external outlets are founded in the structure itself. Thus motion, action, and interaction are "ideally possible."

The differentiated structural mechanisms explain the existential status of the real being. That is, they allow him to be a center of action and the foundation for the causal network of the domain of the world. In other words, the temporal spread of his existence is accounted for. However, there is an important difficulty which Ingarden's analysis entails without solving it. The individual cannot remain in a stationary stage; in order to maintain his identity in the temporal spread of existence, the individual could not enter indiscriminately into action undergoing haphazard transformations. To exist one and the same throughout a succession of temporal occurrences, to be an "individual," means to organize *actio* and *passio* into a developmental process. The question then emerges whether the Ingardenian ontological structure of the real autonomous individual provides us with the *principle of his intrinsic development*.

This question has to be answered in the negative. Neither the question of the progress of the real being's development nor that of his itinerary is raised in the framework of Ingarden's ontology. Hence it is easy to see why the idea of the *telos* seems to Ingarden altogether irrelevant. But can the conception of the real individual do without it?

Furthermore, I consider the incapacity of pure eidetic analysis to find the internal principle of the development of the real individual being as the reason that ultimately prevents Ingarden from establishing existential bonds among the various types of objects that he categorizes. Disconnected, as it were, they cannot function as a base of the universal order. The existing world asserts itself to be perpetually evolving, and its process-like progress in its continuity has to be accounted for step by step. However without a principle not only of order but also of the dynamic progress intrinsic to the individual — the foundation of the real world —, its systematic progress cannot be grasped; progress and systematic development fade away; and the origin and point of extinction of the individual being fail to be explained.

Could Husserl have provided a plausible formulation of the problem of teleology after having assumed that, while the *eidos* does not hold an intrinsic principle of development, it yet serves as a conduit of the individual object's transcendental constitution? Would the framework of research that he has set for himself allow an adequate formulation of the issues involved? Although he with time expanded considerably the methodological framework of his research, he never abandoned its eidetico-intentional assumptions which determine the analytic possibilities of the investigation.

In contradistinction to these two approaches of phenomenology, Husserlian and Ingardenian, I have proposed elsewhere that it is the element of *entelechy* which, within the individual structure of the living individual's autonomous being, asserts itself as a decisive factor in the cosmological perspective. The *entelechial factor* of the living individual being appears as the material nucleus of his existential mechanism, as absolutely his own, and as that which carries out the progress of the being's particular identification.[5] While containing a whole project of its cyclic development, the entelechial factor presides over the overall orchestration of vital processes that allows an individual being to unfold, on the one hand, and appropriate ontological structures and the corresponding biologico-psychic "programs," on the other. It is only upon the assumption of an *entelechy* inherent to the development of the real individual that we can give an account of the emergence of the individual real being into existence, as well as of his cyclic progress which leads not merely toward an unavoidable extinction, but primordially aims at a constructive attainment. In fact, while both the eidetic and the transcendental perspectives emphasize either the universal type as such or the universal progress of the constitutive function, it is this latter that implies an orientation. Without this orientation, would there be a life-unfolding which advances from one constructive step to the next? Without progress would there be an order of events? And without order, would life and real existence be at all possible?

At this point, however, a new question emerges: "In order to achieve its fundamental existential role with respect to the real individual, should not the *entelechy* comprise a foreshadowed principle of its final attainment, the *telos*, the development of which the entelechy is planning and to which it would aspire?" With this question, which pinpoints the *conjectural* postulate of individual becoming, referring it to its intrinsic prerequisites, we project the *common network of the existential agent of real being which extends between his entelechy and its telos.*

Concerning the nature and the significance of this established *telos*, we must ask: "Does it comprise the final explication, the sufficient reason for the being of the real individual object?" When I approached this subject in the Leibnizian fashion elsewhere, that is to say, through the bias of the question, "Why is there something rather than nothing?",[6] I noted that conceived in the cosmological perspective, the real autonomous individual does not contain in the framework of his being his sufficient reason for being; his individual *telos* is custom-made to deal within temporal, contingent, and natural-existential conditions, therefore it is subjected to various circumstances and is partly predetermined by the total life-process. The reasons ordering his origin, those accounting for the emergence of the means to deal with both his existential conditions and those of his having been selected as such a being from other possible beings, remain foreign to him. Asked to account for them, his *telos* refers to the concrete *universal order of things.* This, in turn, refers to the *architectonical plan of the objective constitution* of the universe of things and beings.[7] Once there, the thread of the cosmological analysis, that is to say, of *conjecture* established on the basis of the eidetic and intentional data, breaks down before leading us to a terminus.

These questions remain unanswerable despite our having begun with the consideration of the primitive initial dynamism: we must accordingly approach them from another angle.

2. MAN-THE-CREATOR AND HIS SPECIFIC *TELOS*

The consideration of the development of the real individual oriented toward the *telos* of his natural accomplishment encounters a particular problem in regard to the progress of the specifically human being. But we may wonder whether there is something "specifically human"?

However, in contrast to all empirical-reductionist tendencies, any philosophy of phenomenological inspiration seeks to claim and establish a specifically human aspect of this real and autonomous individual being that is man.

In this connection it suffices to mention Dilthey, who had already defined Man by his capacity for self-experience; Jaspers, who saw the specifically human element in man's ability to transcend himself; Husserl, who perceived the specifically human factor in the full expansion of transcendental consciousness; and Paul Ricoeur and Ingarden (in his last years), who seem to point to moral consciousness.

Aside from Ricoeur, Husserl as well as Ingarden conceive of man's freedom as an integral factor of moral consciousness, which is on their analysis confined to the exercise of human faculties within the intentional configuration. This position makes us wonder whether, restricted to the basic constitutive system, man would be capable of a complete moral life. Would he be altogether capable of the socio-cultural development recognized in the phenomenological conception of the *life-world*? Furthermore, does not the progress of this development presume a renewal of structures? If man remained closeted in the categorical jurisdiction, all the possible variables of forms would be quickly dried up; as progress becomes stifled, all life would be snuffed out. The successive stages of our constructive progress, according to the variability of the preposed set of categories, arrive at a limit at which a new reshaping is necessary. In the postulate of a new reshaping *is included* the request for the renewal of the *types of objects*. As to moral freedom itself, if limited in its exercise to the framework prescribed by an unchangeable set of categories, it would be governed by corresponding preestablished ideal values. What meaning would it have to the ethical man to move solely in the closed circle of preestablished ideal values? The central question here is: "Could man-in-his-world unfold completely through the productive and reproductive functioning of intentional constitution alone?"

And yet, throughout the entire span of phenomenological reflection, this assumption of the very possibility of *life-world-constitution*, that is, the assumption of the *total renewal of the forms* underlying its conception, has been ignored. Indeed, this conception appears to have neglected, literally without exception, the *genuine originality* and *exemplary uniqueness* of the masterpieces of artistic creativity and of revolutionary scientific and philosophical theory, which have manifest themselves in the present phase of the constituted *life-world* and slowly establish themselves and gain "citizenship rights", although at first they meet with distrust or lack of understanding, often having to wait a long time until man fashions new crucibles in which they can be assimilated.

Although in his aesthetic investigations Ingarden established varied forms of "transcendence" of the structural forms of objects with respect to each other — in contrast to the all-embracing homogeneity of the constitutive process in Husserl —, he did not acknowledge the unique status of the "exemplary" Work of Art in the world. On the contrary, following Husserl, he accepted explicitly the total domination of the categorical system with "*die oberste Gattung*," and insisted that no new and original object could be introduced into the world. Husserl, in contrast, reserved the privilege of bringing forth and introducing into the constitutive genesis a new and original proto-element to the *Urimpression* alone. Once introduced, the constitutive genesis molds and reproduces it into endless variations in its preestablished and universal forms.

Thus, neither of these at least partly correlative conceptions of *man-in-the-world*, takes into consideration this need for the complete reshaping of types of objects on which very existence within the *life-world (Lebenswelt) in progress* seems to depend. On the contrary, both of them seem to have erected obstacles to its recognition.

In approaching the world through these two mentioned channels, we are bound to ignore the issue which appears to us to concern the main condition of man's existence in the world. It is obvious that we must then seek to enter directly the path leading to it, that is to say, the analysis of the *creative function of the human being*.

We cannot forget that Bergson was conscious of the necessity of the renewal of forms; yet, having identified too quickly this need of the *constituted world in progress* with one of Nature's strivings, he perhaps overlooked some conditions found at both levels of phenomenological consideration. In the final analysis, the two should undoubtedly rejoin each other, although in appearance they rest on two opposed poles: the one of the elementary conditions (blind Nature), and that of the human freedom to go beyond the limits of objectivity. We will now attempt to investigate these poles separately and bring them together precisely by means of an analysis of the human creative process.

Our first step involves the discovery that the *creative function*, guided by its own *telos*, generates *Imaginatio Creatrix* in man, as the means, *par excellence*, of specific human freedom; that is, freedom to go beyond the framework of the *life-world*, the freedom of man to surpass himself.

In the second place, by following on the opposite side the networks and elements of its synchronization, we enter into *Elementary Nature*. While recognizing the creative function as a basis of the fundamental human condition, we shall discover, then, that *to be human means to be creative*.

The creative act, which we have analyzed elsewhere, emerges within the *human-being-in-conflict*, in man rebelling against the interpretation of the Real that the present phase of the constituted world gives us. Then, in orienting himself during his first set of operations to the direction to be taken in giving a new shape to his personal and intimate vision of the Real, man finds out that the perception of reality which through habit became the surrogate of experience is disintegrating. Whether it be in poetry, painting, visual art, etc., or in the pursuit of an idea, a thought, a color in response to our aspiration for a meta-morphosis, the constitutive perception of the object of our attention disintegrates in all its aspects. It falls into pieces, leaving, however, a half-open door through which this searching impulse, unshaped but rallying all our being's faculties, we may glimpse a passionate, emotional depth, which fuses all together within a *spontaneity* which puts to work all that is within us. This *spontaneity* offers the vision of a new universe. Indeed, starting with disintegrating constitutive consciousness, our efforts do not fall into inertia as is the case in the pathological disintegration of consciousness. On the contrary, all our energies are mobilized in the discovery of means, ways, and materials, and the channeling of them into a constructive apparatus capable of concretiz-ing this vision. A line of progress is thereby delineated, a path of constructive advance. This path must emerge from a gathering of the faculties of universal and anonymous constitution that we have unveiled as such. And yet, meanwhile, we pursue a unique and personal objective, within a new *orchestration* of our faculties which become organized under the pressure of a *spontaneity* directed at its own *telos* as foreshadowed by its vision. Is it possible that this *spontaneity*, comprising the blind and dynamic passion of our being, may be itself blind — as Husserl has argued concerning the "passive synthesis," that is, the unfolding of the intentional constitution about which man does not *decide* but with which he flows *nolens volens* onward, or like Kant's

Einbildungskraft? In such a case, could it be capable of giving direction to this progress? In what way then could the *telos* of the vision toward which the creative process aspires be attained?

As we have shown elsewhere, it is, on the one hand, in the work of art, of scientific invention, philosophical doctrine, etc. — that is, in an intersubjective object — that the vision will crystallize. On the other hand, this new *orchestration* would not be able to fulfill its role without acquiring its own constructive rules and directives, that is, rules and directives which establish it in its own right, outside the categorical system that controls the eidetic and intentional structurization. Thus it must *create its proper forms.*

In this connection it is appropriate to consider the nature of the vision, emphasizing those features that allow it, on the one hand, to fulfill its function of aiming at a specifically creative *telos* and, on the other, to have intimate bonds with the *particular type of spontaneity* which it may prompt from the specifically human condition.

In fact, the vision of a "new universe," in contrast to the shape granted to the Real by the present phase of the constituted world, glimmers upon the horizon of every creative impulse. We identify in it again our yearnings disabused by the actual *life-world*, yearnings for the "authentic" in contrast to the "fictitious" in this world, a desire to surpass it while undergoing a corresponding transformation of ourselves. This vision, nurtured and carried by the very passion, the emotive forces, and the inner pulsations and impulses of the interior of our being, crystallizes our volitions into a definite objective. It aims at finding or inventing a new form for grasping the Real more adequately and embodying it in the form of an object that can enter into the present phase of the constituted world — provisionally suspended — in order to transform it. In this way the vision foreshadows the *telos* of the creative process, a process which it guides while prompting it into action.

Prompting the process, the vision appears to stand for that *elementary spontaneity* carried silently by the elementary forces we have mentioned. A doubt still arises: While rising from those blind depths, could not this spontaneity generate itself in a totally "neutral," that is, aimless, outpouring, which may be mute and blind, such as *Einbildungskraft* or the *vital impulse?* If it were the case, how could we explain the nature of the emerging vision which not only seeks an outlet for constructive fulfillment but also proposes its goal?

Indeed, the deep-seated remaking of our operative faculties in the *creative orchestration*, which the vision initiates and brings about, and the nature of the progress of the creative process into which its dynamism flows and which it leads, bear witness to the contrary. Already at the point of its taking off from the *initial spontaneity*, the vision carries in it the seeds of this creative tendency and outlines the scope of the creative process and its significance for man: man in his quest for a form in which to embody his vision *is seeking to acquire his own form for his self-explication in existence.*

Thus, man's *elementary condition* — the same one which Husserl and Ingarden have attempted in vain to break through to, by stretching the expanse of his intentional bonds as well as by having recourse to prereduced scientific data — appears to be one of blind nature's elements, and yet *at the same time*, this element shows itself to have virtualities for individualization at the vital level and, what is more, for a *specifically human* individualization. These latter virtualities we could label the "*subliminal spontaneity.*"[8]

However, does the specific human *telos* embedded in the mechanism of the creative vision rest in itself? Does not its own genesis indicate other conditions to be fulfilled in order that man's creative self-inter-pretation may acquire its specific significance? As to the creative freedom which appears to be the source of *specifically human* freedom, is it not necessarily bound to another form of freedom, equally inherent to the human being? The question arises: Is it enough for man to go beyond the boundaries of the *life-world* (*Lebenswelt*) in its present preestablished phase, surpassing himself by *self-explication within a work unique and original* in relation to this world, in order to satisfy his primitive yearning? Does creative self-explication bestow upon human existence its final significance? Is the transcending creative impulse carried by the vision fulfilled in its concrete completion in a work of invention: art, theory, social life, world-development?

We may conclude this discussion of the *telos* which presides over the enactment of the creative function by stating its crucial role in three major points:

(1) It allows the human agent to break with his imposed survival-oriented patterns and advance toward the orchestration of *Imaginatio Creatrix*. Thus it opens up an exit from the closed horizon of Nature (and of the transcendental circle, for that matter) for specifically human freedom.

(2) Leaving behind the preestablished regulative principles of the intentional system (subservient to Nature), the creative *telos* guides the origin of new forms as fruits of human invention. Thus it leads man from *natural determination* to *creative possibility*.

(3) Finally, the creative vision offers us the much sought system of reference for thematizing the preintentional dimension of human functioning as its "subliminal" resource: it appears as the *specific endowment of the real, human individual basic to his human condition*.

THE FIRST PANEL OF THE TRIPTYCH

THE EROS AND LOGOS OF LIFE WITHIN THE CREATIVE INWARDNESS

Translated from the French by Philip Lawton

THE OUTLINES OF AN INQUIRY

1. IS CREATIVE ACTIVITY A DISTINCT PHENOMENON?

What is there more mysterious, more unfathomable than man's creative activity? Must we simply avoid the philosophical question it poses by attributing a supernatural character to it, by analogy with divine creation? In the effort to adopt a rational approach, must we emphasize the creator's personality (which raises the problem, difficult to unravel, of the complexity of the psyche), or must we insist on the primacy of inspiration (which raises the problem of transcendence)? Finally, doesn't the historical, economic, and social situation of the epoch suffice to explain the creative act?

However we pose the problem, don't we necessarily envision creative activity relative to another reality considered more fundamental?

A more decisive question: Is creation a distinct phenomenon? Plunging its roots into the infinite variety of human activities and experiencing the repercussions of life's variations, wouldn't creative activity simply be one of those activities among others? In effect, if by creation man seeks to surpass his natural self and the world of ordinary life, the final goal of the creative act is to place the fruits of creation back in the framework of this world and of the ordinary functions of men.

Nonetheless, this very paradox discloses the crucial character of that tension toward a surpassing: Man seeks to go beyond himself, to go beyond the framework of the world in which he lives and which lacks many objects, forms, sentiments whose possible existence he vaguely senses. He seeks to go beyond the limitations that the world — which he finds before him — imposes upon his existence as it appears to him according to his faculties of feeling, thinking, acting, the flights of his imagination and his nostalgias for the absolute. Thus, in forcing back the limits of the exterior world, the creative impulse responds to an interior drive toward the surpassing not only of the limits which the world fixes as a framework of our experience, but before all else of molds which we have forged for ourselves by our ways of feeling, seeing, evaluating, and which we passively perpetuate as the forms of

33

our participation in the world, in others, in our own interiority. In introducing the objects of creation into the world, we introduce in reality new forms of experience, whether aesthetic, ethical, affective, or intellectual. In seeking to surpass the world it is the world at which the creative act aims; but in aiming at the world it is, by ricochet, to the self that it returns, precisely to that interiority from which we have set forth.

A new paradox: Created objects return creation to the world, yet the creation of new objects and their introduction into the world is possible only in a subjective, interior act. Since creative activity is engaged in a spontaneous and snared way of living and feeling, would the creative act be reducible to a function of our psyche? It seems not. As Kant saw, with the creative act we come into possession of all our latent possibilities, of new and unsuspected resources and forces which suddenly burst forth alive, free, active. For these forces, which remain in the state of virtuality within the established framework of our ordinary life, to cooperate in a creative task means: to go out from that framework, to blow it up in order to return to a first state of power, establishing a new framework.

Whatever its complexity, it seems that the phenomenon of creation is summarized in this synthesizing act which makes us live a quasi-complete, unique, and intoxicating possession of our power tending toward the infinite. We suddenly find ourselves ready to undertake vast projects replete with obstacles which we feel ourselves up to conquering thanks to the virtualities which are revealed in us, and nothing, it seems, could hinder us from obeying their injunctions. By that, the creative act is radically distinguished from every normal and established activity.

Finally, the distinct creative phenomenon presents itself as a process which appears, develops, and is achieved in what we customarily consider "subjectivity." Could it, however, be reduced to individual or collective subjectivity? Would the nature of the subject be a closed vessel, or on the contrary a being-in-the-world? Conversely, one could question the validity of an analogy between man's creative activity and the generation of new forms as accomplished in the incessant progress of living nature.

This is certain: The paradoxes which the idea of creation conceals send us back to classic pairs of concepts — soul and body, sensibility and intellect, objective world and subject, nature and spirit, order and chaos. Doesn't this mean that the problem of creation involves aesthetics, epistemology, ontology and metaphysics at the same time? But it shatters the narrow formulations of these disciplines.

Under what aspect will sensibility and intellect, nature and spirit, world and subject appear in the particular optic which the creative problem imposes upon us?

To the extent that they enter into creative activity and confer its distinct reality upon it, how are these elements articulated, on what plane, according to what configuration?

2. THE ITINERARY OF THE POET

Isn't the phenomenon of creation, arising from the human aspiration toward a surpassing, situated then at the limit of philosophical investigations of the world and the self? Rather than pursuing it on the basis of established data, is it not appropriate to interrogate the laws of *the unrepeatable, of the unique*? Does this interrogation not lead beyond the beaten paths of our faculties toward the *conditions of the ultimate powers of consciousness*?

Artists and poets understood this long before philosophers. While philosophy questioned the consciousness of man in order to find its discursive, universal, almost static rules, a Leonardo, a John Donne, a Valéry were aware of the fact that in understanding the nature of the sentiment of love they transformed, by that grasp, the quality of the emotion, and that to satisfy the longing for a new and unique work it was necessary to abandon the tracks already traced and to question the mind on the original operations of which it is yet capable. For the appearance of original works is not contestible. But would that appearance be explainable if the mind had to limit itself to schemas that are always identical? How would the almost radical leap from the cultural forms of one epoch to those of the next take place if the constitutive activity of the mind, working according to constant laws, alone assured human progress? Artists have understood the need for a conversion which the vocation of creator requires: to *confront* the world, then to *transform* it. But to get hold of that love which steals away, it does not suffice to continue on one's way; it is necessary to cross over to the other bank of the Styx which separates us from our natural existence.

Thus, to circumscribe the phenomenon of creation concretely in the *interiority of the creative subject*, can we do better than interrogate the latter in action? And we could not follow a more revealing interior itinerary of a creator than that of a poet; it exhibits most clearly the "inward" phases of creation. We will outline such a "typical" itinerary of the creative conversion in the philosophical perspective. Yet not abstractly. In effect, it has seemed to us that the analysis of poetic texts of Valéry might help to illuminate the nature of the creative phenomenon and to make its philosophical meaning evident. In its turn, as every passage from a lived intuition to an intelligible and synthesizing formulation is solidary with a frame of reference, it has seemed to us that by re-attaching poetic intuitions to the philosophical framework they suggest we could hope to renew the interpretation of the central philosophical questions that Valéry's work which represents the poet-creator's concerns at their peak poses.

3. CREATION VERSUS CONSTITUTION

However, creation is necessarily tributary to knowledge. Is it not by its progress that creation progresses? Is knowledge not its criterion? We must unravel its links with the problems of knowledge in order to illuminate its specific and irreducible nature. Contemporary philosophy, in particular *constitutive phenomenology*, has placed the problem of knowledge at the center of its preoccupations. Having devoted profound and incomparably extensive investigations to knowledge as tributary simultaneously to the nature of the knowing subject and to that of the world, constitutive phenomenology has proposed to us a conception of man who "knows" his universe to the extent that he makes it "arise" in its own forms by *constituting* it.

To the first questions: "What can we know?" and "How can we distinguish between adequate and delusive knowledge?", phenomenology has replied with a supreme effort to find and establish for them a certain and unshakeable basis. Husserl, following Descartes, is not satisfied with verification, with exterior testimony on the validity of our observations concerning the world, other persons, and ourselves; he transports the "Archimedean" point into our own interiority. The mind itself should account for its proceedings, for their foundation, for the legitimacy of its operations. To find this crucial point is to wrest it, by a radical and sustained effort, from the intimacy of our life; it is to convert our natural ways of seeing, feeling, envisioning beings, things, and ourselves by bringing them back to their original source: our mind. For that mind, which has never ceased to lavish sensations, reflections, ideas, desires, enchantments, judgments and fantasies upon us, remains nonetheless veiled, submerged in the true nature of its functioning by layers of acquired habits. Thus, at the first stage of phenomenological work, we are exhorted to clarify the complex totality of our conscious life by distinguishing what belongs to the mind pure and simple from all that which is only the result of the mind's necessary intimacy with the natural, empirical, animal man. The exigency of the Husserlian pheno-menology of the *Ideas* and the *Cartesian Meditations*, an exigency which is however maintained in the rest of his later work and which may be apperceived as an unavowed residue in the ensemble of phenomenological inquiries, lies in effect in the acceptance of pure consciousness, stripped of empirical psychology, as the sole valuable domain of knowledge.

To the fundamental questions concerning the being of man and of his world: "Who am I?" and "What are others and this world in me and around me?", the answers are given by phenomenology simultaneously with those concerning knowledge, for consciousness as the source of knowledge proves to be "constitutive," that is, generative and formative of the self and of the human universe in all its amplitude. Seized at the root of its functioning, lived experience is revealed as setting itself up in being by the forms it establishes in the self which experiences, as well as by the forms of the objects it projects. In effect, there is no question of the mind itself "discovering" a reality, a world, such as they would be or would become "in themselves," for knowing and being arise in the same genesis of the constitutive consciousness.

Once these determining points have been assured, Husserl and phenomenological thinkers apply themselves to the pursuit of the genesis of the complete constitutive consciousness, which should at the same time signify the genesis of the human world, the world of sensations and of familiar objects, the social, cultural, scientific world, of which conscious man is the agent. Under the name of constitutive phenomenology, we have henceforth a perspective of philosophical research which — conceiving man fundamentally as being-in-the-world and having thus surpassed the dichotomy: being and knowledge — devotes itself to discovering the laws and the mechanisms of conscious-ness in accordance with whose exercise the human world arises, while consciousness fashions itself in relation to the world.

It is remarkable that the interior drama of Valéry — the man seeking his poet's way — shows a parallelism of problems, exigencies, and obstacles between the creative vocation and that of the mind assuming its phenomenological task. Both demand the transformation of the inner man and both must confront the exigencies of natural man which oppose those of the pure mind. Both call for and go together with a provisional "suspension" of the natural world.

However, doesn't this parallelism necessarily cease once the pure mind is placed in the service of a *reconquest* of this world, in the pursuit and explication of the *universal* laws and structures of constitutive consciousness, to the extent that it assures the continuity, stability, and familiarity of a shared universe of men? On the other side, doesn't it cease with an *individual* assumption of our unforeseeable, singular, "unrepeatable" powers which arise as a function of an original work whose appearance blows up the habitual frames of the world?

To introduce new forms into this familiar world, shouldn't the poet, the artist, forge a new apparatus for which the acquisitions of ordinary, universal consciousness would serve only as material? Doesn't creative activity necessarily acquire the support of a *configuration of human consciousness truly different from that which characterizes constitutive consciousness in its universal functions*?

To the contrary, whatever the nuances, a deeper examination shows, on the one hand, that the constitutive analysis of consciousness applies itself and limits itself to the discovery of rules and laws which may be observed in comparison with the formed world *such as it actually is* — rules which should be valuable for each individual and whose evolution may be deduced from the logic proper to their functioning. More than that, faithful despite itself to the description of essential structures, which alone lend themselves to a purely descriptive analysis, constitutive phenomenology, like Newtonian physics, limits itself to phenomena which can be observed to reproduce themselves as established types. Its vocation seems to be bound to *indifference, indeed to scorn with regard to the spirit of invention in advance of its own conclusions*; thus one avoids reaching conclusions by going from the behavior of phenomena to their causes.

In this function of witness to a universal genesis, the mind takes distance with regard to itself, to its development, and to its singular existence in a particular individual: Identifying with its universal, descriptive functions, stripped of all contingency, it thus remains at the surface of phenomena.

On the other hand, existential thought, in its revolt against the primacy of knowledge, has put forth the individual man against universal, theoretical consciousness. However, hasn't existential thought, whether devoted to the individual existence of man or to the nature of contingency itself, conceived both in their universal aspect, common to all human beings?

From now on, while adopting from the beginning the principal acquisitions of constitutive phenomenology, we must seek to define our own attitude toward the phenomenon of creative activity by *contesting* that of constitution, *for the creative activity of man is outlined in its distinct specificity in contrast to the constitutive activity of consciousness.*

Guided by the fundamental difference in point of departure between the two activities: the one starting from the most universal condition of man, which is to be in the world, the other starting from the *conflict which issues from the aspiration to surpass this world,* we shall throw ourselves into the pursuit of the sources and resources of creativity by passing from the common to the unique, from the universal view to the singular, from the spontaneous to its bounds, from the opaque to the significant. *from Eros to Logos, whose union presides over the passage from a present life-world to possible worlds.*

PART I

THE EMERGENCE OF THE PROBLEM OF CREATION: THE POET-CREATOR VERSUS THE PHILOSOPHER

1. HUMAN LIFE AS CONFLICT

There is nothing more ancient in the cultural heritage of humanity than the awareness of a conflict at the very heart of man's life. For the ancients, it is the drama which lacerates the tragic hero constrained to choose between noble laws, bound to values which surpass human life in giving it a meaning, and the current rules of social life, the former radically opposed to the latter. Think of Orestes, Antigone, or many others. From the classics, we have inherited an analogous vision: If great passions, sublime sentiments make us equal to the gods, they engender at the same time — and inevitably — a discord, a conflict in the world. Thus it is that for Racine the virtue of Junie is safeguarded, certainly, but is not victorious over the baseness of the world: she conserves her purity by taking refuge outside the world. As far as Andromache is concerned, her final victory is due only to the defeat of Hermione's passion, a passion which touches upon the sublime and which is the stake of the drama. The testimony of the Romantics also goes in the same direction. From them we know that spiritual peaks, "the blue flower" which alone can illuminate the earth, can be attained only at the price of life itself, which is consumed in the pursuit of the absolute. The modern epoch, whose art is based upon the grasp of fugitive impressions, on the quest for a "veritable reality" hidden to our eyes, has cruelly illuminated the essential conflict: every enthusiasm of man, which makes him rise above the baseness of everyday life, is opposed to the latter, seeks to transform it and finally to destroy it.

No testimony, however, has taken a form as lucid and decisive as that of Paul Valéry. His poetic work emphasizes precisely the origin of the work of art as the result of a conflict between the superior vocation of man and the natural laws which govern existence, that is, between the sublime enthusiasms of man and the natural conditions of his life, between the spirit and the senses, in a word between "creative man" and "natural man." More than that, the Valérian debate reveals to us the essential dilemma of creation as an extreme case of this initial

40

conflict. Thus, the vocation of the spirit pushed to the extreme demands first the exploration of oneself, the deepened knowledge of our physical as well as our mental mechanisms; and, once the laws of our nature have been grasped, it is a question of learning to use them in order to become one's own master. That mastery, the result of an indefatigable work upon oneself, does not proceed without exactions. On the one hand, one must concentrate totally on that task; on the other, one must maintain the criterion followed with intransigence and analyze the results obtained or expected with a critical eye (so much so that it's a betrayal to direct one's attention to something other than the conquest of one's spirit). Thus the creation which is complacent with an effort whose results are achieved only in appearance (for no human work can attain a definitive perfection, since the progress of the creator himself is in evolution as long as he has not attained his complete mastery — perhaps impossible to attain) is merely a betrayal of the principal task, an inexcusable vanity.

Truly great beings, Valéry tells us, have not "confessed," whereas so-called great men have, each one, started with an error. By vanity, by weakness, they have delivered an imperfect work, incomplete and provisional. Valéry, disciple of Mallarmé, haunted by the exigencies of the perfect work, places us at the heart of a dilemma. Creation is a vocation of the spirit. But to take that vocation seriously — the only way of escaping animal turpitude —, is to be chained to ourselves; it imposes upon us such exactions that we end up abandoning every effort other than that of our own perfection, a task forever unachievable. And creation becomes impossible.

2. THE CONQUEST OF THE MIND AND THE NEUTRALIZATION OF NATURAL LIFE. SOLIDARITY BETWEEN PHILOSOPHER-PHENOMENOLOGIST AND POET

The vocation of the spirit, in our epoch, finds its expression in two radical forms: on the one side, it is, in the second stage of Husserlian phenomenology (notably that of the *Ideas*), the pursuit of the field of pure consciousness; on the other side, it is, for the poet Valéry, the conquest of pure mind. It is remarkable that the philosopher and the poet aim, in appearance, at the same goal: to arrive at a certain knowledge of oneself, of the self grasped in the entirety of its manifestations. Whatever the difference between their final objectives — where

the difference between the domain of phenomenology and that of
creative research will be revealed —, they submit to the same methodological demand. In effect, phenomenology, in order to arrive at a certain
knowledge, must treat with mistrust all knowledge acquired in a
"natural" way, with a "naïve" and not a critical attitude; because it has
discovered — and this is what counts before all else — that all
knowledge, insofar as it is an expression of the life of the mind
imprisoned in the body, is concealed, warped by the laws proper to
corporeal life. It is the same for the poet. In order to see his quest
through, following the laws which govern his mental activity, he should,
like the phenomenologist, effect a division in himself by opposing
rational man to natural man, mind to body. Thus, the mind delivers
itself directly neither to the poet nor to the phenomenologist; it must *be
conquered*. And in this conquest resides the very life of the mind that
opposes itself to the natural life of the senses.

In sum, the phenomenologist is defined as the one who, having no
other goal but the conquest of certain and unshakeable knowledge,
hopes to find its source in the field of his mind disengaged from its
corporeal links, and therefore disengaged from the natural world of
sensible life and thus purified of everything accidental, opening itself in
its essence to the contemplative gaze. This separation is entirely
provisional, of course, yet nonetheless it is significant in its definitive
results and even when unavowed is found at the basis of all phenomenological work.

This field of pure consciousness can, however, be attained in its
"purity" only in the course of a long process, since that purity is
obtained only when all the forms are unraveled from their ties with the
complex of nature in which they normally remain buried. We must, in
effect, remove from the field of our attention all the elements (causes,
aspects, forms) relative to the context of natural life, that is, all the
physical aspects, psychological aspects, voluntary aspects, etc., which in
the habitual state of our thought influence our judgments and disclose
cause-and-effect liaisons. Only what remains of our knowledge of
things, of our own states, when we have progressively "suspended" all
"natural" factors slanting our judgment is that which we will know in a
clear, immutable, and necessary way. Once this suspension is accomplished, an entire field of the mind will open itself to our eyes, a field in
which we ourselves in our corporeity and the world will be rediscovered, but in the *essential* and *universal purity* proper to the human
individual as such. That suspension is not a simple intellectual game,

but rather an *ascesis* mobilizing for its employment all the interior resources of man (insofar, it is true, as the analysis of our conscious acts is not enough for attaining the "essences" in their virginity if we have not to a certain extent become masters of the very functioning of consciousness, which allows us to mechanize certain acts, certain habits so that the "suspension" may find support in its progress). Yet, all the same, that partial mastery of the mind remains a secondary thing, whereas, the role of consciousness, in suspension as well as in the grasp of the field of pure consciousness, remains purely observational. What is most important is our becoming aware of the disengaged structures, their analysis, the establishment of valuable foundations, and finally the extension of knowledge. All are ends which are attained only at the deliberate price of the neutralization of natural life.

It does not belong to the poet to develop theories. Thus Valéry, who more than anyone has written about art, has not left us a theory of creative conflict. He has however brought a witness to life: Monsieur Teste. M. Teste, whose story may appear to us to exemplify a man's life given over to the vocation of the spirit, seeks, like the phenomenologist, to attain "total" and "certain" knowledge of his own functioning.

M. Teste devotes all his attention to dissociating the elements of his life and of his being from their natural and social context in order to examine their absolute validity apart from all relativity. In all our behaviors, he seeks to recognize all that which is not restricted to expressing our deep being, all that which is only a sign of our participation in nature or in the world of conventions and social habits. Everything relative to nature and to human conventions is contingent, moving, fictive. Our deep self, that is, the permanent laws of our own functioning, alone is essential, alone authentic.

M. Teste fulfills the habitual functions of man. He obeys the indispensable physiological demands; he breathes, eats, sleeps, suffers, makes love. He also has his place in the social web; he occupies an apartment, earns a living, frequents public places (theatre, stock exchange, restaurants, etc.). He has a wife, a friend, and enjoys the general esteem of his parish. In short, he does not seem out of the ordinary in anything. But one must not be deceived. M. Teste, Valéry tells us, eats "as one purges himself," and "as soon as the arms of a Bertha assume importance, he withdraws." For it is an indispensable condition for the proper functioning of the mind to remain a being ordinary way; the body is an indispensable base. And yet all these living in an apparently ordinary way; the body is an indispensable base. And yet all these natural functions do not make a life. In the pursuit of the laws of the mind, one has had to liberate himself from the constraints of the body. What is love, Valéry tells us in *The Method of Leonardo*, if not the license to behave like animals together? The mind is opposed to the beast. It is not a question of suppressing the body, impossible thing, it is a question only of mastering it in suppressing the beast. To master the body is to strip it of all that which belongs to what we call human life. In opposition to the existence led by M. Teste, we see clearly to what point that life is woven of emotions, of feelings, of habits, fruits of the natural abandon to emotivity or to imagination, as well as of commerce with those others who become the pieces for eking out this "weaving," the conducting wires of emotive transformations always alive. In the eyes of the pure mind, Madame Teste is now just "a thing," now just "an oasis"; a friend is only a witness; a mistress, an instrument for the exercise of sexual functions.

His own pain does not surprise him; he foresaw it, awaited its arrival, and not being caught short he can master it. He masters his sensations as much as his inclinations or his desires. Neither his body nor others have a hold on him. He is reserved.

In reality, parallel to the effect of the phenomenological suspension, M. Teste has conquered his natural self. He has made the entirety of his intellectual, sensorial, emotional, volitional functioning pass through the filter of the critical mind, dissociating the essential from the acquired, the necessary from the conventional, the authentic from the imitated, the free act from the social convention. Having accomplished that dissociation, he gradually detached himself from all active participation in that which belongs to natural dimensions: the blind pleasure of the senses, the weakening chains of sentimental attachments, friendship, brotherhood, the conventional social relations of the member of a group, of a milieu, of the heir to a tradition, finally the surprise and the violence of the emotions.

Thus liberated from all natural constraints, having "killed the puppet," M. Teste, just like the philosopher, has succeeded in grasping the mechanism of his mind. Or rather of his complete being, body and mind. Having attained his goals, M. Teste, like the philosopher, concentrates on the discovered domain of the pure mind; but he does not seek, like the philosopher, a total knowledge of the world, he lets himself "mature."

However, *Monsieur Teste*, in which an attempt to conquer the mind with a perfect logic pushed to its extreme consequences is presented to us, is at the same time the trial of "the case of M. Teste," where M. Teste also appears as the accused.

Although he does not reproach him, Valéry shows us his way of living, his individual attitude in the world, as doubtful, unrealistic, even impossible. Once again, the comparison between the Valérian attempt and phenomenology, driven to its extreme limits, is imposed here. It is appropriate, in effect, to ask ourselves now what qualities more sublime, more essential than those of natural life have been offered to us in compensation by the conquest of the pure mind. But M. Teste remains mute on this subject. The pure mind, discovered and limited to itself, has only been able to reveal states of despoliation, silences, "zero points," entirely negative qualities of the experience. M. Teste's freedom, like that of the Sartrean Orestes, an application of the phenomenological pursuit of analysis of the mind to life, is reduced to choosing oneself, to exulting in the exercise of one's choice as a pure spectator. One has freedom which one cannot apply to enlarge the field of human activity or experience, freedom which has no other goal than its own exercise: the self sufficing unto itself.

That freedom is in addition exempt from morality: Like Sartre's hero, M. Teste is beyond good and evil. The life of pure mind is purified of every quality. It is also somehow extricated from the temporal framework of natural life: It reposes entirely in the present, comports with no hope, therefore with no future. M. Teste's life is not, in reality, involved in any temporal pursuit, it does not follow any development. No horizon of possibilities opens up before the pure mind thus attained and practiced: the body is mastered, the blows of sickness and pain do not count. No change in social situation will ever reach the summit in which the source of his cares resides; he does not abandon himself to any weakness, and nothing can reach him.

In fact, nothing perhaps has shown us what human life is more poignantly than the existence of Monsieur Teste, because it is not a human life. Having submitted all the movements of his body and his soul to his will, being exposed to nothing unforeseeable, he is like Sartre's hero who takes part in life only in spite of himself and in an accidental way, since he has taken sides in advance. What of significance can therefore happen to them, death? But, one will object with reason, the discovery of the pure mind has, for Husserl, no goal other than the analysis of knowledge; one seeks therefore to approach the sources whence arise intelligence and knowledge, and not at all the sources of life. But, in the case of the Sartrean hero, we see exactly how absurd it is to take the strict nature of consciousness as the final point, the only absolute, at once source and arbiter, whose ultimate "nothingness" resembles the "zero points" of Valéry only too much, but which is however nothing but a lived state.

Let us still try however to justify M. Teste. Perhaps his interior privation has made of him an ascetic, a being comparable to the Christian mystics, or a Zen adept, as has recently been suggested. Having abandoned all constructive aspirations in the domain of life, he may turn toward a "spiritual" construction.

But neither M. Teste nor Sartre's hero constructs anything at all. In effect, M. Teste is far from being a mystic, and the ascetic life he leads has not made an ascetic of him. For the Christian saint or the Hindu sage, the important thing is the transcendental orientation of their way of living, and asceticism is only a path, a condition for attaining this goal. Although Valérian asceticism and Husserlian suspension are likewise paths, means, these means are no less integral parts of the goal; the goal fashions them as much as they themselves fashion it. The silence of St. John of the Cross and that of a Zen disciple, have meaning and a reason for being only as a function of the transcendental values in which one and the other want to make us participate. To the contrary, the silence of the pure mind stops with itself; the mind is the only justification of that silence which reposes in itself in enjoyment of the discovered mind. The pursuit of the pure mind at the price of an asceticism is therefore only a rigorous consequence of a particular vocation which is defined by its object. This is a vocation however which should justify itself by its own exercise, for the pure mind does not reveal any source of values superior to itself. Thus, whereas religious asceticism conserves for man the indispensable perspectives of waiting and hoping, the asceticism of the pure mind offers no hope other than itself and in that way renders life "inhuman."

3. SEPARATION OF THE TASKS: DESCRIPTION OF THE
CONSCIOUS MECHANISMS OF PHENOMENOLOGY, IN
OPPOSITION TO THE GRASP OF THE OPERATIVE RULES
OF CONSCIOUSNESS IN THE CREATIVE EFFORT

The phenomenologist and the poet have, it seems, followed up till now the same path toward the examination of the pure mind. The analogy is however less complete than one at first believes because for the phenomenologist total knowledge is the final objective, the conquest of pure consciousness being only a transitional stage; once pure consciousness is attained (and by that very fact the foundations of a certain knowledge are laid), the philosopher will pursue, across his analyses of the life of consciousness, goals other than consciousness itself. And although for the phenomenologist every object of knowledge remains in the transcendental precincts, that is, takes up the laws of consciousness anew, it is nonetheless the entire man and the universe that he will seek to grasp in their immutable forms. Certainly, mastery of the mind is necessary in order for the phenomenological reduction to be employed, in order for it to continue to be exercised in the discovery of the field of intentional objects as well as in their subsequent analysis, in which the phenomenological investigation of universal knowledge truly consists. But that mastery leads one to apply oneself to certain types of acts of consciousness; once that habit of automation is acquired, the mastery of the mind may disappear from the field of preoccupations; it has been an indispensable means only for founding and exploiting a certain knowledge. In virtue of this, it is limited to the functions of universal consciousness, and it leaves intact the functions which make up the intimately personal life of man, emotion, desire, all things individual and "unrepeatable," etc. In reality, as Bergson stressed in *Matter and Memory*, conscious activity, from the moment of its emergence from motive functions, is already oriented toward a task which is incumbent upon it. In seeking to accomplish this task, conscious acts first improvise certain regulations which they then follow as rules. Conscious activity, progressively forging itself, acquires at the same time rules and habits for its mode of acting. We can attempt to go further in suggesting that in discovering, by success, the appropriate ways of reacting in certain circumstances, consciousness itself arises as a system of functioning appropriate to the circumstances and to the goal whose pursuit it assures. It is therefore established as a stable and recurrent system of functioning thanks to regulation of its activities as it assents to take up the same forms again and again and to acquire in consequence a facility which requires a minimum of effort. Rather than making each of its acts follow that first spontaneous route, whose path is cleared by a staggering, painful effort, consciousness quickens and sets itself up as a network of forms and molds, while spontaneous acts take shortcuts, reproducing themselves as they prove useful. It it precisely thanks to that "automation" of our conscious process that we find a basis of stability and organization for our experiences. It is thanks to the system of conscious life and to the automation of conscious processes and acts that we ourselves are organized beings, individuals who bear in ourselves a center of reference, a benchmark of stability, and that we are in a world which is also relatively stable; thanks to this same system of recurrent order, we are not fragments dissolved from chaos.

In reality, our own constitution and that of the world around us proceeds to the extent that certain acts of consciousness which already arise in certain molds are organized in certain types of activity, whether in a process constituted by certain types of an object or in one constituted by certain types of emotion in our communion with others, in our lived experience in general. It is as the work proceeds that these acts become spontaneously organized, ready to be recast without hesitation into their molds on the basis of previous apprenticeship, the basis of the past acquired under the form of a synthesizing power of learning, in which we constitute the world and our own self. Without that automation of its procedures, consciousness could not progressively establish itself as that agent which makes man and the world arise as a common order.

On these automations of conscious life reposes the meaning of the progressive genesis both of the self and of the world. The self which is supported by these progressively acquired ways of feeling, of evolving, of wanting, advances toward more and more complex tasks and aspirations as its universe simultaneously becomes richer, more vast, better formed.

On that woof of the progressive acquisitions of constitutive consciousness is woven a pluridimensional self and a pluridimensional world; every progress is pursued unceasingly on the initial model to which lived experiences incessantly adjust and which thus assumes a unique universality.

This simultaneous genesis of the self and of the world in conscious constitution is the object of phenomenological investigations. The phenomenologist seeks to take a step back from knowledge only in order to grasp and describe the rules and procedures of consciousness, such as it is offered to his gaze in its activities as an established constitutive system. In describing conscious phenomena as they appear in the phenomenological attitude we are describing acts which follow the universal order common to the constitution of the universal self and of its actual world. We grasp the conscious acts and procedures to the extent that they belong to that great constitutive synthesis, guarantor of stability and continuity in the genesis of the self in its world, a synthesis which is itself founded in one of its first powers, that of learning, that of the automation of its acts.

Whether it be Husserl, who distinguished between a "naïve," pre-critical level of human life and the "critical" and transcendental level of phenomenological inquiry, or existential philosophers who devote themselves precisely to lived auto-predicative experience, there is always the question, on the one hand, of consciousness operating according to the universal constitutive system. On the other hand, the distinction between the natural self and knowledge bound to rules clarified on the basis of their universal nature remains present.

Thus it is on two planes that the activities of the philosopher will henceforth be pursued: search for knowledge on the critical plane, and "naïve" life on the pre-critical plane.

For the poet-creator, to the contrary, it seems that the demand for knowledge, taken rigorously, is identified with the demand for mastery of his personal being.

We are here approaching a capital difference. It seems, in effect, that in order to grasp the pure mind in its laws, *such as the poet understands them*, it does not suffice to dissociate certain aspects of our mental activity from others, nor to separate, in an entirely provisional abstention, the natural habits of thought from the transcendental habits which do not vary as a function of corporeal conditions. More than that, it suffices not at all to follow the established procedures of ordinary constitutive consciousness.

To satisfy the exactions of a poet, one must, it seems, attain a *radical transformation* of the functioning of all conscious faculties. Following M. Teste in his particular way of approaching pure mind, one has the impression that as pure mind discloses its own life to him, he descries new obstacles in it, and he must conquer again to go further. Thus, it is first necessary that nothing remain of the natural man, bound by physiological and social constraints. A step further on, and we see M. Teste also combatting interior motivations, aspirations, ambitions, ideals, insofar as they are bound to "mundane" tasks, that is, tasks sanctioned by convention.

In reality, among the motivations of our acts, he applies himself to distinguishing those which respond to concern for our "essential" and

solely valuable task — namely our interior development — from those
which, in comparison with that supreme task, seem to lead only to vile
complacencies. Thus it is needful to eliminate from the life of the mind
all motivation mixed with ambition, with vanity, with "mundane" pride,
which can lead only to socially conditioned — thus relative and
transient — acts, as well as to the production of mediocre works
characteristic of simple mortals. For Valéry, as we have seen, truly great
beings have not allowed themselves to be seduced by the ephemeral
glory of imperfect witnesses, they have not "confessed." He has nothing
but scorn for the so-called "great men" who have purchased their
mundane success with an essential infidelity to themselves.

Thus, for the poet, the conquest of the mind first demands a total
mastery of the mind, and it consists, it seems, in the exercise of that
mind transformed in its discursive function as well as in the entirety of
its functions which are life itself.

Let us now attempt to specify how the conquest of the pure mind is
conceived differently by the poet and the phenomenologist. What is
most striking in M. Teste's progression toward "asceticism" is that at no
stage does the mind reveal itself as it is sought. One would say that
none of the habitual levels of the operations of the mind is of interest in
itself, that they should thus be surpassed toward a final point of mastery
to be acquired. In other words, one does not seek to grasp the laws of
the pure mind in its usual functioning even if these are not dependent
upon the laws of nature and possess their own autonomy. One tries to
the contrary to disarticulate the habitual mechanisms of the life of
consciousness in order to arrive at the laws of *consciousness in the
primordial state*, those from which its actual way of being exercised
proceeds as well as *all the other possible ways* which have not been able
to mark out a path for themselves.

It is clear from then on that the objectives of the poet and those of
the phenomenologist diverge fundamentally.

The first motto of Husserlian phenomenology, that to which this
phenomenology in all its forms has remained faithful, is that pure mind
is of interest in that it is conceived as the source and the depositary of
the human universe, under its fluctuating aspects but above all under its
stable, established aspects: our universe, in sum, such as man has
projected it, and which he assents to transform according to the rules
he has posed.

The contribution of the field of "absolute consciousness," or the transcendental field, is that there one can immediately observe and describe in their direct and unimpeachable presence all the phenomena contributing to the structure of the world. The certitude of phenomenological knowledge is based precisely upon that evidence of the presence of the objects of inquiry. In examining the rules of the functioning of consciousness, phenomenology links them essentially to the objects that they construct and which in their turn construct the human world, our world.

It is thus that phenomenology, in its pursuit of knowledge, finds itself chained to the world *such as it is*. It remains entirely sheltered from the disquieting concern of Leibniz who, in seeking the constitutive factors of our world, was equally preoccupied with finding the factors valuable for every possible world as well as for the world actually created.

The classical phenomenologist approaches consciousness only insofar as it is narrowly correlative with the world as it has created it, the unique world whose structures indicate the laws of the functioning of consciousness. All that which would go beyond that grasp, all that which would show the mind not in it particular mechanisms, linked to that unique world, but in its first rules indicating the possibility of other mechanisms, is inaccessible to him. The search for these primordial factors is, by definition, what cannot be an object of actual consciousness. What could be evident — that is, present to the surface of the field of consciousness — but whose indices are too well hidden, and thus indescribable, is beyond the vocation which phenomenology, in all the forms elaborated up to this point, has prescribed for itself.[1]

Very much to the contrary, the poet, as a matter of principle, does not seek the established world. What leads the creator to the problems of the mind is not the desire to know the world which surrounds him and for which he is not responsible; it is rather, at a first stage, his concern for the possibility of the work, the will to open a new track to the experience of the world by attempting to enlarge the acquired and to surpass the ordinary. Thus he has little to learn from the constituted mechanisms of the mind; their immutable functioning, dependent upon the established world, interests him only in a secondary way.

At a second stage, his inquiry on the subject of the mind is bound to his concern for the perfection of the work, the first vocation of the artist. Thus when the creator encounters the secret of the mind and tries to resolve it, what he seeks to attain is the secret of *new and rare operations* capable of leading to a "perfect" work. Thus he cannot stop at the level of the acquisition of knowledge or content himself with discovering the modes of operation of consciousness in its ordinary functioning.

At the same time, since the secret sought touches upon the hidden nature of the mind, and is not at all expressed in the habitual forms of the mind, and is one which ordinary consciousness is in any case incapable of expressing, the radical transformation of ordinary consciousness as the phenomenologist describes it appears to the creator as an imperious necessity.

Thus a new path is indicated to us. In affect, in his concern to go beyond the constituted world, the poet makes this truth appear: *the ordinary mechanisms of the mind are relative to the constituted world.* From that point on a question arises, not for the poet, but for the philosopher: is that relativity "absolute"? Should we, in admitting the fundamentally transcendental aspect of our world, consider this world to be the only one possible? In other words, are the powers of consciousness limited to the constitutive mechanisms of the world as they are familiar to man? Doesn't the very possibility of creation, no matter whether artistic or scientific, indicate that the dimensions of the mind are more vast? Aren't the mechanisms constitutive of our world only a particular aspect of the mind, and isn't an infinity of other aspects possible? In reality, the mind is not at all exhausted in these particular mechanisms. It is a question to the contrary of discovering the *modi operandi* which constitute its true nature. For what the poet seeks to discover, reeling at first to secure them later, are these *modi operandi*, to the extent that they hide the secret of a perfect and unique operation confronting that world that is the fruit of habitual mechanisms.

If the ultimate vocation of the philosopher is to answer not only to the objective form of the existing world, to the nature of existing man, but also and above all to that man and that world taken in their deep nature (that is, *that he must explain their origin and the reason for their existence*), then beyond the habitual mechanisms relative to our form of the world we should seek the mind in its first rules, capable of responding to *every possible world*. It is in effect toward an investigation as fundamental as that, that our inquiry into creative experience will be oriented; thus we will have a new basis for philosophical reflection proceeding from a new examination of the relations of consciousness and the world, of knowledge and experience, of man and nature.

4. THE RECONQUEST OF THE BODY, OF FECUNDITY, AND OF THE WORLD IN THE CREATIVE EFFORT: CREATIONAL PHENOMENOLOGY

We have seen that the creator's quest for the laws of pure mind encompasses the whole man. Paradoxically, he started out on a search for the conditions of the perfect work, but the exigencies of his pursuit have led him to the laws of the mind, have created involvements and necessities for him such that first creation appears to him as a vain arrogance which he should renounce in order to consecrate himself to the mastery of the mind, and then life itself becomes impossible. It seems, however, that if the phenomenologist who arrives at absolute consciousness as unique source of knowledge can live in a "natural" manner, it is only by a subterfuge. Those who, like Sartre, have wrongly drawn the rigorous conclusion from this show us human life as a nightmare, impossible to conduct to the end. The subterfuge consists in proclaiming that it is possible to divide man in two: on the one side, the rational activity of a discursive mind "illuminated" in the light of the discovery of absolute consciousness, on the other side, the naïve life of natural man.

However, that separation at the heart of man applies only to a transitory stage of Husserlian research, that of the *Ideas*, a stage which was to be surpassed by what followed. Once again, poet and phenomenologist take the same road. In effect, Husserl like Valéry began by "suspending" the contingent side of the world, of human life: they both wanted to envision the world and life not as existing, but simply as possible. And they both collided with the same obstacle which threatens the logical consequences of their attitude with absurdity. Thus they picked themselves up again by making a radical leap toward a new stage of their inquiries. From *M. Teste* to *The Young Fate*, there is a distance comparable to that which separates the phenomenology of the *Ideas* from that of the *Cartesian Meditations* and of the *Crisis*.

For Valéry it is the passage from an intransigent and unrealizable exigency of perfection to creative activity conceived as the only possible way to reconcile the antagonism which opposes the quest for the perfection of life.

For Husserl, it is, in the same manner, the passage from phenomenology as the description of static and ideal forms to the constitution of the life-world.

In effect, at the moment in which the exploration of immutable and static forms threatens to lead to sterility, to a rupture with the living world, the phenomenologist amplifies his task by introducing the world into the field of his investigations. Not, this time, that of the absolute forms of pure consciousness, but that of "natural" life, not "illuminated," that is, "naïve," contingency and change itself. The constitutive phenomenology of the *Crisis*, and the contemporary movement to which it has given impulse, is actually an investigation of pre-theoretical life, of the natural world, of particularity and contingency. It signifies, if not the return of the philosopher to the cave, at least the return to the natural world which was at first "suspended," and the search for the ultimate key to the mysteries of man in what was at first abandoned. Thus we assist at a quasi-complete reversal of current.

As far as M. Teste is concerned, symbol of a total intransigence in the pursuit of what the vocation of the mind is, he could never have existed. For the sole reality whose existence is incontestible is life. The meaning of *The Young Fate* is in this avowal: the vocation of the mind is made for man, but *in order to be man, one must take up life*. Against the pure translucent Logos-intellect we have to vindicate the opaque realm of Eros.

That being admitted, how can we maintain ourselves in one track while travelling toward another when they seem to be mutually exclusive?

What is incompatible on one plane is not necessarily incompatible on another. *The Young Fate* shows us, in effect, that there is no question of simply denying life; envisioned from the point of view of the higher vocation of man, life has not been shown to be impossible, it has only been revealed under a new aspect: not as a preordained system of human actions, but as a reality whose *essence is conflict*.

There is thus no question of denying life, but, after having rejected it, of taking it up again on a higher plane, of accepting it as having a conflict at its center. ". . . The sea always begun anew . . . ," what else is it but the deployment of this conflict? Falls, recoveries, more falls and partial victories trace the new path which is projected before us. Once vegetative existence conditioned by amorphous conventions and habits has been rejected, it is a question of taking up a new form of life. But that life does not offer itself gratuitously, it does not come naturally. "One must try to live . . . ," for one must find, perhaps invent, a new mode of existing, the only one thenceforth acceptable. Thus this resumption of life on a new plane, illuminated by a prior inquiry into the mind, is found at the center of the preoccupations of creator and phenomenologist. However, here as elsewhere, philosopher and poet separate from one another in their manner of envisioning the final objective of their search.

Although the phenomenologist thenceforth refuses to stop with the static skeleton of things but envisions the world in the dynamism of its becoming, and consequently seeks the mechanisms of the world's genesis, he nonetheless applies himself to the immutable rules of the consciousness which produces the world. Once again, he seeks as first evidence the rules which allow themselves to be observed in constituted acts or objects; thus he tacitly admits the supremacy of constitutive consciousness as it is actually observable, as it is determined in the present world, and he supposes it to be absolute in its functions and the only one possible — so much so that at the same time our world, as it is and can become, is likewise supposed to the alone possible.

Finally, the philosopher-phenomenologist identifies this world and that constitutive consciousness with mechanisms universal in their application, chosen because they are incontestible and because without them our world risks disintegration. This means that constitutive consciousness, insofar as it is a system of mechanisms, does not admit any spontaneous change at its heart, that is, it is impossible that a development not motivated by the ensemble, not foreseen, not conditioned, should intervene. All the past genesis of consciousness which constructs itself in its world forms, together with the virtualities of that constitution, a "horizon." In principle, God cannot be integrated into the life of consciousness without being explainable in its genesis, proceeding from its horizon. The linking of the elements of this system is such, its hostility toward the unforeseen so complete, its functioning so invariable and so perfect that we have to do with a veritable system of automated mechanisms. It is in effect consciousness which, in its constitutive activity, is responsible for the automatism of natural man, for the fundamental stability of nature, for the identity of the world.

However, aren't the progress of humanity and the interest of individual life due precisely to a margin of indetermination, to all that which in the eternal cycle of nature escapes its laws? Poets like T. S. Eliot or Rilke seek to break the chains of this cycle, to see the life of man not as irremediably determined by this cycle but as liberated from it. Cézanne, Van Gogh try to see further than the forms of the world constituted and common to all. Contemporary art, we would say, has gone much further than philosophy, which can pride itself on having been able to discover that thought is bound to linguistic and logical forms, those forms merely being the sedimentation of men's ways of living and thinking at certain epochs. In effect, poetry and painting have attempted to burst the chains which our ways of living and seeing had imposed upon the world, to disintegrate the forms of that way of seeing which appeared to be essential, and finally to sense the authentic and unconditioned content of experience by going out to seek the mind in its more supple, spontaneous, improvised and unforeseen functions.

When the artist, after his initial revolt against the blind submission which natural existence imposes, accepts life, he accepts it only in rediscovering himself there in his individuality; but then he has discovered life on another plane where, by the search for his own originality, he is opposed to the automatisms of the established system. The life he accepts is then that of a conflict: *the conflict between the present condition of man* — the choice common to the species — and that which he himself wants to undertake — *a choice which is individual, unique, and cannot be repeated.* He seeks what is neither pregiven nor preordained, but what must be won, conquered in an entirely personal struggle against the amorphous and passive resistance of established rules.

This aspiration of the mind to surpass the rules, to surpass itself for a more authentic task, is perfectly conscious, and the effort to which it gives birth, far from being caught up in the natural current of spontaneity, is conscious of itself. For the artist's goal is not only to grasp the immutable with impassibility; he seeks above all to penetrate to the ultimate laws governing consciousness, hidden laws whose grasp demands that he forge new means of investigation. In seeking a more profound vision of man and the world, the artist should mark out for himself an access *to the foyer of every possible vision.*

If phenomenology, in reconstituting the world of first experience, reconquers it in its lived virginity, before the schemas imposed by the theoretical mind pervert it, nonetheless it grasps it only in the schemas of "phenomenological constitution," which is universal and proper to the species.[2]

The artist, to the contrary, takes up life in the hollow of his own particularity; he carves out his individual nature in order to escape the universal circle, in order to break loose. If he accepts life, it is not by submitting to the universal rule but by imposing his own conditions.

What then are those conditions? What is the *modus vivendi* which arises from them? What are the terms to reconcile?

This resumption of life in the terms enunciated is possible only in the creative effort; this new mode of life is situated at the level of *creative reality*. The analysis of Valéry's *The Young Fate* is the best illustration of it. For, remarkably, for the poet the reprise of life signifies to me the return to creation. Having abandoned poetry with *M. Teste*, Valéry returns to it twenty years later with *The Young Fate*, conceived as an attempt to found a new mode of life in which natural man and body are conquered again.

Established phenomenological researches also bear on the modalities of human life. We find there probing descriptions of lived experiences taking up the forces of individual as well as of social life: habitat, work, fecundity, love, social rapports, social functions and institutions. However, as penetrating and as nuanced as they may be, these structures of human experience rise up invariably from one and the same fundamental system of constituting consciousness such as responds to our actual world and which transcendental analysis aims at insofar as it is a universal common to man.

Contrary to the life which issues from constitutive analysis, the life reconquered in the analysis of creative reality is the fruit of *free choice* and of *voluntary effort*; personal and original, it is neither foreseeable nor interchangeable and advances by a series of choices which are not restricted by objective structures but operate by weighing the infinite variation of possibilities.

It is a question, all told, of seeing how the rules of the consciousness which creates surpass those of the constitutive consciousness by explaining how and in what way the frameworks of living humanity always blow up the rational frames of the world, by showing that a subterranean current boils beneath the world as well as in man as all philosophies envision him and as the theoretical mind accounts for him.

5. THE PROBLEM OF CREATION ARISES IN THE FORM OF A MUNDANE CONTEXT

Those are the outlines of the problems in whose center arises the problem of creation. These problems concern, directly or indirectly, the quasi-totality of human life. However, the problem of creation arises at a level where man, life, and the world appear under a radically new aspect.

Man, who is first of all oriented toward action aiming directly at the world and permitting him to extend himself beyond his limits, is led by the exigencies of that action itself to return into himself. It is within himself that he must seek to resolve the problems, by his particular manner of participating in the exterior world, by his creative participation. This participation, which is defined by the *desire to surpass the actual framework of the world*, collides with two obstacles. The one is posed by convention, habit, the automatism of the established world, world of things, of beings, and of nature; the other is the interior obstacle encountered by the man who tries to accede to that which is most fundamental and who, turning all his faculties of participation in the world back toward himself in order to find a solution there, meets exigencies and apparently irreconcilable oppositions. Thus man finds himself doubly rent, in conflict with the world whence he arises and in conflict with himself.

If this conflict ends up being resolved in the return to creative activity, it's that this activity, in provisorily suspending the relations between elements which are factors of man's participation in the world, projects new connections, establishes new rapports and thus creates a complete system of relations wherein the antinomies are surpassed.

The system takes up the functions by which man participates in the world but it gives them a new form. There the body and mind are harmonious parts which have undergone an essential transmutation. Man is there present under all his aspects: natural man who fulfills physiological functions, social man in the bosom of the human community, as well as the man who feels, who loves, or who hopes and who, so doing, transcends himself and wins his freedom by breaking the chains of natural man. This system which knots harmonious bonds between man and the world does it on a different basis, issuing from man's conquest of himself. The transformation of intramundane rapports, thanks to the creative act, is accomplished in the interior of man, in the zone of his being which, far from being able to be "mundanized," is on the contrary a condition of his participation in the world, as well as the agent of all his activity and finally the central point from which arise the networks of relations which re-attach him to the universe. In effect, in starting from "mundane" relations and from functions which create our world, and in seeking to transform them by an original work, we are led to *creative inwardness*. The latter, without exhausting them or shackling their automatism, is nonetheless their center and their point of departure. It is consciousness — agent of the constitution of the world — which here assumes another function. It operates differently in order to lead no longer to an opaque, hardened form of reality and one which is interposed like a screen between the deep self and the world but to *a dynamic reality consisting in its very exercise and transparent in its forms.*

To the extent that consciousness, in its creative function, totally transforms our mode of apprehension of man, of nature, and of the world, the creative problem — placed at the level of the operations whose constellation we call "creative" — arises from our motive operations, affective operations, passions of the soul and communion with others, as well as intellectual activities of every order, in its most intimately individual, personal, and singular expression. The network of its improvised operations, which interlace with one another, is governed by its own internal logic and remains autonomous with regard to its basis in the universal system of man's functioning as such. It is this autonomous system, from which the creative act seems to hang, that we are going to call the "creative context." We will see that it is a question here of a two-sided context. The first facet indicates the extent and the import of the problems of creation taken as a "mundane" phenomenon; it is the objective facet. But, in investigating the laws of creation, we must penetrate to the very source of that objectivity, well beyond all reality. It is at this level that the other "facet" of the creative context is revealed, as a "loom" — equipped with a system of rules for weaving — on which consciousness, operating according to the rules of construction in the creative context, makes a new form of nature and of man arise.

PART II

CREATIVE REALITY

1. THE CREATIVE DEBATE BETWEEN THE MIND AND
THE BODY OPENS

We would say that all poets, have lived in the acute awareness of a conflict between the mind and the body. We might perhaps add that poetry arises from that opposition. We might finally say that this tension is the very condition of poetry. However, what side should the poet take in this conflict? Assuredly not that of natural life. It would submerge him, and it is precisely against natural life that the conflict arises; he becomes a poet only in claiming his rights against the amorphous dominion of that life. As far as the misadventures of the pure mind, taken exclusively, are concerned, we have shown them in the example of M. Teste. At the same time, all too much has been said about the "evasion" of reality adopted by romantic poets, surrealistic poets, etc., as well as about their refuge in dreams. Mallarmé, whose powerful demands traverse the entire effort of his great disciple, was not satisfied with the ephemeral region of dreams and erected an ideal kingdom with its own laws, an artificial sphere supporting itself like Aristophanes' "Cloud-cuckooland," a kingdom built by the birds halfway between the earth of men and the heaven of the gods and separated from each. If Valéry refuses this solution, it is because he refuses to seek a refuge in poetry. Escaping also means that one admits defeat, that one turns his back to an essential point.

In the conflict of the mind and the natural man, the sides are almost even. Each has its merits. To find a solution, we must lend an ear to both. There is no question of dismissing them back to back and escaping toward the open sea. The only choice rather is to reconcile them above their contradiction, in a *tertium quid* attempting to pass through a narrow door. We have already spoken of the reconciliation which Valéry undertakes. But Valéry does not content himself with taking up again what generations of poets have always attempted to do. His effort being more aware, his methods more effective because they are based upon a true philosophical reflection, he gives us the most fully elaborated and the most original example of that reconciliation. For creation is nothing else but the mode of reconciliation between the pure mind and the natural self.

The poet who escapes into ideal constructions, who wraps himself in dreams, forever cuts himself off from reality. Creation is a resumption, not an abandonment of reality. It is not a definitive desertion, but a conscious and desired reconquest of that which, passively accepted, threatened to submerge us. Therefore it is a question of reconquering natural reality by pure mind under the form of a *poetic reality*.

The body and nature are the first stakes in this rebirth of man to himself; it is in becoming aware of them that the Young Fate reaches her first station on this road. *The Young Fate* opens with an implicit avowal: "a rumor of lamentation and self-constraint," "the thirst for disaster," "the shadow of a reproach," which draw tears from her and yet are nothing but the beginnings of a temptation — the serpent has "just" stung her. The temptation infiltrates the train of a state of soul which is unexpected but finds its reason for being in the Young Fate's present state of mind, the sign of an insufficient condition and, let us say it right away, the sign of an entirely negative virtue of the mind. For it is a question of a critique of the mind; while lavishing gifts, while spilling over, the mind does not satisfy. It opens an emptiness of solitude: the Young Fate finds herself "alone with ultimate diamonds." The kingdom of the mind is here revealed as an arid earth: its "heap of marvels" has the cold and compressed beauty of precious stones, the beauty of a desert without vegetation and without life, where only the serpent can live. Must we be so astonished that he has chosen it for his home? What surprises Corneille can only be natural and necessary in Valéry's eyes. The latter broaches the debate by revealing the fault at which the life of the pure mind, henceforth vulnerable, will be attacked. He indicates the actual situation.

> . . . gradually dividing from my other destinies
> For the purest to enlighten a broken heart in silence [3]

while suggesting that the primacy of the "purest" is not always certain. This division in the heart of the Young Fate cannot be welded, it is the stake of the drama which is foreshadowed. It is, in effect, at the very heart of consciousness. The "watchful opposite," bearing on herself the weight of the pure universe, is encompassed by an unequalled solitude; she confronts the "pure," the "supernatural" in its "sovereign rays" and the "shooting glances of eternity," but she must do it alone, without support, without counsel, without witness, and accept the full responsibility: "I am alone with you, shivering." Each instant requires an extreme effort and each instant stretches on indefinitely to bear up that universe of mind, effort that only a total conviction can sustain. And that conviction itself entails a solitude without return.

Solitude, in reality, becomes grievous:

> God! In my loaded wound a secret sister burns
> Who loves herself more than her watchful opposite.[4]

The bifurcation in the self is accentuated at the very heart of its exercise. It is a self consisting entirely in effort, will, mastery, which opens the universe of the mind to us. And in the aridity of the mind, this self suddenly appears as a desert, its sudden purity recalls death. A battle is then engaged between the effort sustained by the will and the natural self formed by abandonment to tendencies born of a vast context more sensed than known. This abandon is encroaching, it requires no effort, and asks rather that one draw more tightly to oneself the lines of concentration, of that ultimate attention limited to one sole point. This abandon draws toward a complicity, a contact, an opening of the "walls of its gloomy tomb" by the attraction of an "animal dream." From that battle the mind emerges "pale, a thing of wonder . . . uneasy and yet supreme," but not without some regrets. It trembles at losing a "divine sorrow" that the breath of nature, carnal stirrings, the thirst for complicity brings into its "rich deserts." The serpent has offered the bait. Temptation has entered from the purity of non-being, and it will germinate. Up to this point, the mind is defined in terms of extreme power; it operates by a supreme concentration of will and reflective power:

> . . . me entire, mistress of my flesh . . . .
> And in my own tender bonds, hung on my blood,
> I saw me seeing myself, sinuous, and
> From gaze to gaze gilded my innermost forests.[5]

By what is the temptation defined and how is the natural self manifested?

The mind is a call toward eternity, the absolute, the true; the natural self, to the contrary, is submission, the changing course of a dream to which one is abandoned, inscrutable, fugitive and factitious.

"Thing of harmony, ME" differs from a dream which is imposed, from a dream governed by a law, because the mind has chosen; the dream disappears without a trace, whereas the mind has the power to direct its own course, to sustain itself in the eternal. "Mortal me, sister, falsehood," these are passing forms, ungraspable and delusive.

In return, the movements of the mind correspond to higher aspirations, and can accord with the vanity which is the definitive judge, and consult "the slightest stirrings of my visions between night and the eye . . . ." The delusive promises of "natural dreams" can only be "foul." Foul, for they are manifested by the first stirrings of our being which, like the first stirrings of the earth before springtime, presage the renewal of life, a course that nothing could stop in its development onto its final decrepitude. The mad and fugitive passion for life, which allows itself to be disclosed and tries to arrange an entry for itself, will have to be established on the "distances," the bases painfully acquired by the mind. These first stirrings, so profound, presage an upheaval similar to childbirth; it is the subterranean advance of life seeking to burst forth in the nature which plays in us. Hidden forces buzz, dormant energies re-animate the body, and behold, the first concrete form of the temptation: the feeling of our own corporeal force. The feeling sets us ablaze like a rapture, suddenly seizes us in our innermost heart. It reveals to us a dynamic extension across the new awareness of our limbs: "Burningly I moved, pressed the solid ground, Binding, unbinding my shadows beneath the linen." The mind suddenly discovers itself identified and, moreover, buried in the body: "The arc of my sudden body reveals me pronounced . . . ." It is by an analogous upheaval that the earth, just before springtime, suddenly kindles and is transformed under the magic stroke of life.

The mind still has the possibility of arising "erect," but soon it is gasping for breath. A dialogue is born: it is the dialogue between life and death, and that, before the Immutable. With it appears the seductive privilege of doubt. Radical doubt, sparing nothing, establishes itself sovereign in the dialogue of the two "me's" who are thus presented in equal terms. The stirrings of the world, of an earth swirling in the reborn self, dizzies that self to the point of giddiness and introduces it to the heart of nature: "The newborn year To all my blood foretells secret impulses . . . ." And whereas "rueful the frost relinquishes its last diamonds" — of a sublime but insensible beauty —, the natural self is manifested in an *overture of sensation*.

This time, not only by the dynamic extension of our limbs but by an upheaval of our identity, spring comes to our corporeal substance, to that which is nature in us: "Spring comes to break the sealed-up fountains: Astounding spring, laughing, raping . . . ." But since it is the whole man who is engaged in that spontaneity which is released, could sensation, involving only a part of ourselves, be maintained on the surface for long? It is transformed into emotion. On the horizon, like an exterior dominating the pure foyer, nature suddenly appears; but it's an exterior provisorily separated, for the trees which "brandish against the sun their resounding fleeces," "leaves in myriads," the woods, enter into us by all our open senses, impregnate us, and we there discover ourselves, feeling swollen up again with the same new fluids, vibrating with the same designs aborning. Then this interior spectacle is immolated in a universal emotion: ". . . Its frankness brims with speech So soft, earth's entrails are seized with tenderness." Is emotion anything other than the union of the interior and the exterior in a sensation which renders us master of ourselves and makes us open forth to a zest, to a fullness without limits?

However, our opening in sensation to ourselves *qua* nature and the emotive bursting forth which immerses us in a unique whole, only prepare the terrain where the phenomena of nature may arise and expand. Becoming imperious, in effect, the appeals of vital forces raise up the entire body like sap which becomes the agent of generation. The flesh arises like a flower bearing in itself the promise, the germ of a fruit which all the combined forces of the plant impel to be born. This emotive complex makes the drunkenness of a heart which beats, of a bosom which burns, of the thirst and infinite desires which contact with beings raises in us.

> Dear dawning phantoms whose thirst is one with me,
> Desires! Bright faces! . . . And you, love's lovely fruits,
> Have the gods shaped me this maternal contour
> And these sinuous verges, folds and hollows,
> So that life might hug an altar of delight
> Where, mingling the alien soul's continual changes,
> Fertility, milk and blood forever flow?[6]

This time, the temptation of the natural self does not only concern the compass and the powers of the body, the spontaneous world of nature being reborn in us; it goes so far as to participate in the generative work of nature. The flesh is thus no longer simply animated and open to the world, it is in addition felt under the form of its powers; it is extended in the "networks" of our being, by the desire which transports us further than the flesh toward the azure of the mind. But that is accomplished only at the price of a return from the azure to the altars where the pure and the absolute are mixed with the ephemera of eternal returns. The lover's flesh, however, will have no victory. Let us follow the debate.

The natural self is going to be amplified again. But the spirit reprimands:

> No no breaths, sighs, tender gazes . . . my fellows,
> Race all athirst for me, begging you may live,
> No from me you will not have life . . . .[7]

The spirit emerges victorious, but only halfway. For if one has avoided being submerged by carnal enthusiasms, there remains no less a drama issuing from this refusal. It is a more subtle drama; the adversary has indeed withdrawn in person, but he has appropriated a part of the terrain. There remain gaps, remorse, doubts. Certainly, there are moments in which the mind finds its absolute limpidity anew, in which one believes it capable of drawing forth "divinities in virtue of the rose and the salt," but these recoveries are transient. The battle is partially won, but it is now clear that independent terrain, belonging exclusively to the mind, is forever lost. Of course, the mind retains an important place; its voice remains that, perhaps, which dominates the dialogue:

> Amid all possible moments you touched on the ultimate . . .
> — But who could win mastery over the very power
> That is greedy, through your eyes, to contemplate
> The day which chose your brow for its tower of light?[8]

Remarkable thing! One would say that at present the pure mind is likewise moving in an emotional and psychological context relevant to the natural self. Isn't the threat of the pure mind thus averred to be a link between the two selves? It is the thread of the mind by which "night restored you to day from among the dead . . . ." The body has not triumphed; the pure self has stolen toward its domain. And yet a grave transformation has been accomplished, whose terms will occupy us in the future, for we will apply ourselves to disengaging them. At present it is appropriate to gather together the results of the debate itself, before its acute phase is arrived at.

The last phase has made us penetrate fully into a psychological climate. The reflection conducted by the pure self is bathed in an awareness of self more complete than it was before the combat. The self now speaks of itself by identifying with the two selves at the same time; no more brusque, insurmountable separation. Only a distinction of accent is perceptible:

> My body desperate stretched its naked torso
> Where the soul, crazed with self, silence, and glory
> Ready to faint away from its own memory
> Listens, in hope, to this heart knocking against
> The pious wall, with a secret, self-destroying beat,
> Till only from sheer compliance does it keep up
> This thin quivering of a leaf, my presence . . . .[9]

How are body and mind defined in this interior debate?

First of all, the mind is characterized by the perfect clarity, the transparence, of its articulations; it appears entirely determined in its structures, its causes, and its consequences like a domain over which the reflective self has complete mastery. Its perfect intelligibility renders it immutable, and it draws a supreme pride from its aspiration to the absolute. Moreover, it is revealed as the agent who organizes, establishes connections, and who, thanks to its transparence, concentrates reflective action. For the mind appears as reflective activity itself which, while being a cognitive activity, has this, in particular, that its object, whatever its structural extension — that can be the entire universe —, is reducible to a unique core, to an acute point totally graspable in its causes and its consequences. It is absorbed by the reflective function and experienced in complete identification with the act of reflection: those are the silences, the peaks of the pure mind! This domain of transparent reason, of pure rationality is arid and exigent: "I am the reward of effort," says the Young Fate who personifies it.[10] It reposes in a complete folding-back upon itself, which explains its solitude. Solitude however which is not the passive solitude of an abandoned being, but the solitude of one who, aware of his power, means to use it like a demiurge taking full responsibility for it upon himself. We have shown that the virtues from which the mind draws so much pride, and which consist principally in a directed spontaneity, an active mastery, and in the function of unification which is property, remain negative.

To the mind thus conceived is opposed passivity, the initial inertia of the body. For what is the feeling of our vital forces if not the awareness, all told disaggregating, which possesses itself of our will in order to unbind it? What is the opening out to sensation if not a passive sensation (for it has long since been shown that there is no sensation without the active cooperation of the mind)? — at least if one considers prereflective sensation, that is, sensation abandoned to confused and unsorted regions where the awareness of the flesh is primary. Emotion and sensation are born in the moment in which we become conscious of our flesh, in which we identify ourselves with our body; in virtue of this, they disperse us in an opaque consciousness whose density is such that we live it without attempting to reduce it or to order it. The carnal stirrings which provoke emotion — some of them are what we call erotic feelings — put an end to the arrogant isolation of the mind and lead to a spontaneous union with the rest of nature. Thus are abolished the contours which the mind jealously traces around its domain. We are then led toward the anonymity of sovereign nature, where our place is nothing more than that of a link without autonomy in the impenetrable cycle of life. Emotion attracts us for, in unbinding us, it gives us the illusion of being liberated; in submitting us to anonymity, like a cog in a mechanism, it seems to open to us an immense horizon because in it we escape examination.

2. THE UNDERGROUND CABLE AND THE FACTORS OF CREATIVE TRANSFORMABILITY

It is remarkable that already in the initial phase when the debate between the pure mind and the body has hardly been outlined an unexpected index appears. It is however appropriate to underline that the debate already analyzed in the case of M. Teste takes a particular form. In effect, its form indicates the manner of its resolution. It is now no longer a debate between the mind and the body taken in their objective forms in the bosom of a mundane conflict. To the contrary, we have since then withdrawn from the objective world and its habitual forms; the world, the body, nature appear as they are experienced by an individual consciousness. We are therefore assisting at an interior drama, at a dialogue of the self with itself in which the protagonists are reduced to what they represent for consciousness: they are present in their lived qualities.

But what must be noticed most particularly is that the protagonists in this conflict, who seem to be separated by an abyss if one considers the lived qualities they represent, are not at all opposed in a radical way. For the peculiar trait of this form of our debate is that both appear in the field of consciousness, as objects of reflection. That which appears irreconcilable in its mundane forms is not necessarily irreconcilable on another plane.

The debate is possible only because the pure self is presented as the harmonious self, source and agent of all organization, of all unity. There is manifestly a link, an underground passage connecting the antagonists who can one at a time become objects of reflection. If this passage seems buried too deeply under the sedimentations of constitutive consciousness, it can be disclosed in the field of consciousness during conflict. Like a Fate who spins the chain of our destiny from disparate elements, the "harmonious" self produces a thread "whose fine-spun trace is blindly followed." In reality, this thread of the pure self, the agent of relation which renders objects translucent, is also what surreptitiously connects the pure self to the natural self. Thus it is the guarantor of possible commerce. Beneath forms, beneath layers of constituted forms, we are here touching upon the nature of the mind itself. To the extent that this thread is the conductor of a conscious activity, it becomes the guarantor of conscious activities which, in the light of the mind, transform the lived forms of the body — and thus the guarantor of a new form of life. Once more the Young Fate indicates a way. But, once indicated, that way is lost. Valéry never explained it. We must discern it in his work.

Yesterday, the insidious, the masterful flesh Betrayed me . . . .[11]

is the plaint of the Young Fate. That betrayal was not however the realization of the "dream" against which she defended herself; it was not the realization of one of those desires whose attraction is almost irresistible and which the pure self had, all the same, vanquished. Nonetheless, at the heart of the combat, the raptures and retreats, the desires and refusals, the doubts have not at all been detached and annihilated into oblivion. The thread, "whose fine-spun trace blindly followed to this shore" of the flesh, has carefully rejoined them. By it, the two "me's" are bound together and "amid my own arms, I become another . . . ." Always erect, at this second stage of the debate, the pure mind surveys a transformed empire — an empire which is not that of "brute" life. For one has escaped nature in its common and fugitive form. The thread of the pure self is guarantor of the absolute: "My night's delirium thought to snap your moorings, But all I did was rock with my laments Your sides thronged with day and created things!"[12] In reality, why have we been so frightened? "The dark is not so dark," the flesh was not the death of the mind. The latter remains sovereign, it has appropriated the flesh. One can open one's eyes upon the universe and feel with one's feet a sea of life shuddering, and come

> To this edge, unafraid, inhaling the high foam,
> My eyes drinking the immense salt laughter,
> My being into the wind, in the keenest air
> Receiving the sea's challenge on my face . . . .[13]

That temptation of life has an attractive familiarity, it is no longer endowed with dangerous qualities. What detour has made this change possible? How has the embittered adversary been able to be so totally disarmed? Was it simply to discover that he was fighting a windmill that M. Teste in Paul Valéry imposed twenty years of silence upon himself?

We therefore find ourselves before a rebirth, but manifestly it is not quite simply a rebirth to nature, for there is a condition to that acceptance of the body's appeal:

> If the intense soul snuffs and furious swells
> The sheer on the shattered wave, and if the headland
> Breaker thunders, immolating a snowy monster
> Come from the open sea to vomit the deeps
> Over this rock, whence leaps to my very thought
> A dazzling burst of icy sparks . . .
> Then, even against my will, I must, oh Sun,
> Worship this heart where you seek to know yourself,
> Strong, sweet renewal of birth's own ecstasy . . . .[14]

"The intense soul" which "snuffs" is this cable between the two otherwise irreconcilable sides. This thread leads toward the carnal extreme, but it brings back from it something other than passive submission to the dream, abandon to the eternal return. The nature which is revealed in us is entirely transformed by the reflection which forms it to its very blooming; it has left behind its inert opacity, and its elements, when they arise, are already bound by the thread of the mind to the reflective life. It is thus a *nature born in the effort, the supreme effort, of the mind.*

To the dilemma born of the impossibility of creation, the Young Fate has succeeded in finding a solution by adopting a mode of life in which creativity's adversary, conceived in objective terms, is found to be transformed. After her interior conflict, the battle she wages, which is no longer that of a natural existence abandoned to its orders, is revealed to be other than a battle whose stakes would be simply winning or losing. It is to the contrary a struggle in which the loser wins. Of the two apparently distinct terms, neither has proven to be definitively determined; for in a slow transformation invisible to consciousness, the two terms have been transfigured.

This conflict, with its unexpected outcome, outlines the combat of the creative process in a rough draft for us. For, as we speak of consciousness in its discursive function, or in its constitutive function, so we can without any doubt speak of *consciousness in its creative function.* What essentially characterizes it is that it is borne by a dramatic unfolding: it acts through conflict, across a dynamic and active dialectic. Far from being a refusal of life, it is placed at life's very heart, not to undermine it, not to explode it or to lead it to defeat, to the inertia of elementary static forms, but to transform it into a complete life, made of games and efforts, consciously directed toward an end which surpasses the established current. The artist, the scholar, the philosopher have often discovered for themselves a tragic existence, like that of Socrates; but without considering that existence a defeat, they have to the contrary conceived of the creative effort as a means of resolving their own tragedy while contributing to the liberation of humanity.

3. THE CREATIVE PROCESS AS AN ACTIVE SYSTEM OF
TRANSFORMATION: SENSIBILITY, NEW SOURCE OF
MEANING AT THE ORIGIN OF THE WORLD

If creation can reconcile the two extremes — on the one hand the immutable forms founding the identity of that which incessantly evolves, on the other hand that which variability itself is and which each form can only congeal and betray —, that action should bear on the whole extent of the conflict. Because it is a question of finding a point of contact between the extremes, we must try to grasp what essentially concerns both. Apart from its secondary aspects, the created work is only a *new opening toward an original experience* for by its form it blows up the framework of the constituted world and by its content it bursts the provisory limits that consciousness imposed upon forms previously projected.

But it is by sensation that we will find the world again, not at all the Kantian myth of the world as it is "in itself," but the world as it is projected on the basis of its autonomous laws, and man as he is crystallized in himself in relation to the rules of operation of consciousness in their nascent state.

But exactly what do we mean by "sensation"? The term is one of the most ambiguous, and each current of thought has charged it with different presuppositions. Let us leave to one side the physiological aspect of the problem, however important it may be; the natural sciences study constitutive mechanisms in a particular perspective. That reservation made, it is, we think, appropriate to see in sensation the germ of the human world.

Sensation has been shown, in effect, to lay the foundations of that world, insofar as it is a sensed world, an affective world, a meaningful world. For our emotions, our sentiments, our value judgments make our world just as much as do the structural lineaments around which are organized the forms of bodies, of other beings, etc. Moreover, just as our affective stages, far from being "blind" (that is, qualifiable only by their intensity and their duration), are to the contrary organized, formed by their connection to objects, in sum drawn into the net of objects and the attitude of the feeling subject with regard to them, so the objects and beings which compose in our eyes the world called "objective" — that is, that world which does not belong to our affective complex as subjects — are never shown to us in their "objectivity" except under the conditions of the psychological laboratory when we abstract from the natural state in which we see them in ordinary life.

In ordinary life, in effect, objects, structures never appear to us as abstract forms, but always in an affective fullness in which their very form is crystallized. We are not thinking of the apple in its *eidetic* structure — fruit of an affective abstraction —, rather we see it as an object of taste, corresponding to our gustatory sensibility, aesthetic sensibility, etc. For the objects of nature, as Bachelard discovered with rare penetration, are neither simple, vital utilities nor abstract structures. They are the correlatives of our emotions, the sensations which we incubate in the depths of our being. Everything is at the same time emotion and form (an entirely academic distinction anyway); everything that man senses has a meaning in relation to the lineaments of the whole, everything he distinguishes is sensed or connected to the sensed. In short, sensation marks the origin of this world which is lived and sensed, but lived insofar as it is meaningful.

From that point on, if we consider sensation as the root of meaning because it makes a world simultaneously sensed and signifying arise in us and around us, then meaning becomes an encounter of the intelligible and the sensible. In the constitutive process, the forms of sensibility seem to be preestablished: their extent is transmitted to them, imposed by the molds and automatisms of consciousness.

The creative act, to the contrary, reveals itself to be that which institutes new forms of sensibility. Consciousness in its creative function can therefore be considered as a transformer of sensible forms, as a forge of new sensibilities.

Sensation thus understood as a "signifying root" should first of all account for what we are accustomed to considering related to the body, to the "sensorial," in short, to the physical.

In reality, if we observe sensibility in its changes of possible forms, it is manifest that what we call our body is "ours" and "body" only to the extent that we become aware of it by sensation. The most primitive forms of sensation or those most directly linked to our passive being are precisely those which make the awareness of our body in its articulations arise. The body as hands, head, internal organs becomes "ours" only by the consciousness we have of them as the extent of our sensations, by the mastery we have over the movements of our limbs, by the attention the functioning of our organs demands of us. Our stomach or our liver would never be "ours" except by interference and indirectly — like the parts of a system — if they were not directly manifested, at certain moments of life, by a sensation.

Becoming aware of certain stirrings of our body, of its rhythms and exactions, discloses "nature" to us in certain of its aspects.

At a higher level, sensibility mobilizes more extensive faculties of our being and gives birth to emotion. The latter, which makes us become aware of our natural powers, as for example in erotic emotion, reveals nature to us in its functions and in its works. On all emotive levels, thanks to sensation, an entire universe is sketched for us in the objects of our desires, of our judgments, of our joys and our sufferings. For, as

Poe noticed so well, the plan of the universe finds its symmetrical replica in the structure of the mind; both meet in sensation. The body is their intermediary. It becomes the measure of the universe, being itself an awareness of the extent of our forces.

To return to our subject, we can only speak of creation if, as we have seen, in transforming the forms of sensibility we enlarge the field of experience, and if, in accomplishing a new crystallization of man, we burst, by new objects, the limits of the constituted world. The creator is on the track of original forms and that pursuit obliges him to begin again dialogue with diverse aspects of the human being. He cannot hope to reach his goals except by a new synthesis of those aspects, synthesis which he alone can achieve. Creation is therefore placed at the level of conscious functions, superior to those of sensation as such. However, the process of creation is — we have indicated why and we hope to have demonstrated it concretely — strictly and inevitably bound to the process of transformation of the forms of sensibility and of affectivity; more than that, it is a question of establishing a new relationship between the mind and the body, and between man and nature, the world, and others.

At present it is a matter of showing that the advent of the creative process reverses at once the reality of the life which was, thanks to the automatism of the constitutive process, guaranteed as a foreseeable and established reality, a public place of security and stability. That is because creation totally upsets and remodels the generation of the universe by man. At a higher stage, for he provisorily leans upon the constituted world, the creator penetrates into a vertiginous process: before him lay an infinity of possibilities, an interminable road of choices. It is a universe that he reconstructs in constructing a limited work. Each station on his road is marked by an act, not by the nearly passive act of the constitutive automatism, but an act resulting from a choice, that is, an act of will as much as of knowledge. A creative act knows itself, and knowledge is not separated from will nor from action. Thus this progress of conscious transformation becomes a new form of life which encompasses natural life and is erected above it. It is crystallized in a new reality, *creative reality*, that which the Young Fate indicates to us.

In the analysis of creative reality the poet becomes aware of his weaknesses, mutation, forces, whereas the philosopher seeks to discover the rules of "transformability" of sensation, the ultimate possibilities of the mind.

But it is at present appropriate to incarnate our theoretical considerations.

4. THE NEW FORM OF LIFE BEING REBORN IN CREATIVE REALITY

The creative function of consciousness reveals itself to be essentially transformative of that which was pre-given — understanding by "pre-given" here what was already constituted or what ranks in the system of possible constitutions. The philosopher will seek the procedures, the rules of consciousness' transformative operations. Valéry himself speaks of the mind as the "inexhaustible creator and transformer." In effect, rebirth to the world, to life is a question of the first conditions of sensation, of emotion, of sentiment. The creative conflict has made us penetrate as far as the hidden depths of consciousness, whence arises the possibility of transforming these first conditions. Therefore, it is seemingly behind the scenes of the creative function that we are entering. Let us first specify these universal conditions in opposition to the particular conditions of constitution.

In its new form, life appeared to us, through the Young Fate, to be insinuating itself surreptitiously, thanks to our becoming aware of our body, and then to be spreading by a more ample, more open sensation which unites us to what is not our body. Nature as well as the body, as they are ordinarily understood — that is, when they are not fundamentally grasped in relation to the notice that we take of them, remain brute and mechanical notions. In relation to lived experience, they are endowed with a sense. And this sense is indispensible in order that physical and mechanical concepts, like the concept of numbers, not remain empty before one applies them to a qualitative content. Only too much has been said of consciousness as the source of quality. And the effort of the constitutive function is precisely to grasp the world at the instant of its genesis before its forms congeal and are emptied of their lived content. If it is true that life clothes itself with sensed qualities and thus becomes their source for the discursive mind, it should equally be true that "quality" is not identical to "quality."

It is no longer in vogue to think of "sense data" as Locke's entirely simple qualities. Husserlian phenomenology has made us aware of the fact that a quality which would be totally isolated in its distinct nature, in its "purity," if we may so call it, would have to be an "ideal" quality.

It may be that one should, on the basis of all the shades of red, of blue, admit the ideal existence of a "pure" red, a "pure" blue, but primordial experience, the most primitive sensation is not simple; it is necessarily complex. One can admit, at the bottom of the ladder of consciousness, at the level of organic functioning — of which we receive only vague and indistinct echoes in the form of pain, uneasiness, sexual excitation — the existence of simple forms, of purely sensitive reactions. It is a significant thing that these forms are equally indistinct, confused, and do not arrive as such at the level of lived consciousness.

Socrates was already intrigued by the interval which separates the physical blow given the foot, whose reaction is no doubt instantaneous, and the pain felt by us which we attribute to the blow as its cause. Such an interval seems necessary to allow the instantaneous reaction of the foot to run across the ensemble of the nervous, physical, and psychic mechanism, to reorganize itself there in order to produce a phenomenon different from that which is purely mechanical — the shock of one body against another — which is attributed to it as its cause. As Heidegger has justly noticed, the most minute sensation when it arises from the confused pit of functional mechanisms to penetrate into the field of consciousness already forms a complex.

Moreover, and this goes against the empiricists, it arises not as a witness, spokesman of virgin truths, but in function of reference points already established. M. Piaget has shown us at length how one constructs the framework in which new sensations come to be placed as the work proceeds. However, these reference points are neither entirely subjective — submitted to the rules of consciousness which must transform them to appropriate them to itself, as lived experience —, nor are they entirely objective — conforming to a world already constituted and exterior to consciousness. They are at the same time one and the other. Constitutive phenomenology has in effect shown that the world is constructed in relation to the consciousness which penetrates it everywhere. From that it follows that the individual destiny of man is the result of his subjective dispositions and of the world he has created for himself. However, as in the process of the constitution of the world, there is a "natural" assimilation, a quasi-automatic organization of the new sensation in comparison with the pre-existing context of the individual world. In the case of poetic creation, the equilibrium is reversed; each phenomenon of one's own body which attempts to arise in the field of consciousness passively undergoes a sort of milling, which is opposed to the as yet unqualified spontaneity that it bears with it. There is something astonishing in that.

In effect, whether a landscape not yet seen, a symphony never before heard, or the first song of the birds in springtime brings us something new, or merely comes to be added to the inert mass of our current knowledge, should depend only on our own dispositions at the moment. In certain states of stagnation of the senses and the intellect, one believes himself never to see, never to hear, never to read anything new: The world seems to have forever exhausted its resources. Evidently, in the case of constitutive genesis, everything that comes to us through the intermediary of the consciousness of our own body is received automatically as into a mold, itself inert, which plays the role of a screen between the nascent sensation and the self, the ultimate point of reference. This self itself has limited its functions to the automatism of natural constitution and remains hidden behind this mold that it has given itself as a screen, thus creating for itself a peacefully formless existence. But the creative conflict scorns that factitious peace. It throws man into a struggle which demands the participation of that which is most specific to him, of that by which he is most essentially himself. Neglecting intermediaries, he should expose himself directly and undertake the combat in plain daylight. For Valéry, the pure self is always an absolute point of reference. And all his work leads back to the search for the laws of the mind, to an exercise which has as its goal either to make them disclose themselves or to master them.

A theoretician before being a poet, Valéry left us more considerations on the mind, on poetic creation, than he did poems. Surprisingly, we are going to seek, not in his theories but in the analysis of his poetic effort, the *unavowed explanation* of his poet's work — rather than referring to his reflections or limiting ourselves to explaining what he does by what he says. The poet's reflections, interesting and most often ingenious, are, the great majority of them, responses to questions which were readily posed in his time, answers adjusted to the particular formulations of those questions. Considerations abound there on inspiration, work, pure poetry, etc. But few of these reflections, while they seek to be universally valid, touch upon the particular condition of creation, to which Valéry bears witness of a unique acuity.

When the Young Fate is shown to us, arising from a battle with the forces of nature on her return to a natural world after having lived apart in an absolute world, this natural world is no longer apart, it is other. It is not a passive world, a simple place of habitation, but a world which speaks and moves us like an entirely new phenomenon. In reality, the world of art is always so new, so different in comparison to that of natural life that those who lack poetic initiation hardly find their way there and must translate it into the terms of the ordinary world.

Would there then be two worlds superimposed? The constituted world is entirely one of thoughts, of ideas, whereas the artist "speaks" in terms of sensibility.

Would there then be two sensibilities, one ordinary, the other created? Or, in opposition to ordinary sensibility, aren't there as many forms of sensing as there are great artistic movements?

These suppositions are false. There is only one world, and only one life, subject to universal rules. They leave room only for one sensibility: it begins with the awareness of our body which is revealed in our awareness of the forces which animate it. Every life begins only with that. However, counter to the constitutive mechanism which jumbles the paths, there arises the effort, the creative inspiration which returns to the mind its active role, clears the paths, and takes up everything anew. In reality, in Valéry's work, we penetrate to the level where there arises in the field of consciousness a double current of the sensible which becomes a resource for the development of life's phenomena. This new form of life is woven on the basis of a direct commerce between carnal consciousness and activity, on the one hand, and lucid choice and pure mind, on the other. In everything the body has as its point of reference the mind in its absolute lucidity which weighs, chooses, and decides for it. It would be hard to find an expression of ideas more sensual than Valérian poetry. But the most sensual emotions are not uniquely felt in relation to the natural system that is obedient to the laws of the eternal return of generation and corruption; the sensation which arises from consciousness of vital forces enters into a less passive and more reflective system. The natural mechanism of constitutive forces is broken up in advance. Sensation is directly related to absolute mind and the latter examines, compares, and chooses anew each time. And sensation is thus found to be introduced into a system where ideas are likewise found, for the mind mixes what is necessarily united in the natural context with what belongs to separate systems. Narcissus is conceived in this mixture:

> I see you there, my soft body of moon and dew,
> Form compliant, still adamant to my wishes![15]

To the primitive sensation of the body are linked ideal and universal

notions in order to make a complex sensation arise, one in which the
ideal is wed to the sensual:

> How beautiful the vast and vain givings of my arms!
> My slow hands weary in the adorable gilt
> Of enticing that captive bound among the leaves . . . .[16]

Related to the world of ideas, the primitive emotions of the body are
interiorized, transformed under the hold of reflection and become
translucent to the eye of the mind. The other Narcissus speaks to us:

> Dear *Form*, I yield me only to your grace:
> My arms are open, drawn by the still pool
> In a pure vertigo I cannot rule.
> What can I labor if my Beauty grieves?
> For this I trod my shadow amid leaves
> With precious footsteps in the forest cool.[17]

Interiorized, the sentiment of the body retains its savor and its
spontaneity. The body is liberated from the objectivating forms which
constituting consciousness impose upon it and are incarnated in other
forms, those of the mind. Thus, far from being opposed to the mind,
one furnishes it with a body, a place where it can act and be completed.
Escaping the hardened schema of "physical" interpretations which
sealed it off from the mind, sensation comes to be embellished with
attributes the mind has chosen for it. The latter, which is itself thus
placed in another context, cannot turn away from it:

> What and how keen and mortal soever
> Your sting may be . . .
> Over my tender basket I've thrown
> Only a mere dream of lace.[18]

That "lace" is a nerve of sensation, and across it a filtration is produced.
The sentiment of summer passes through the filter of a "rock of pure
air," love through the filter of an "ardent hive." By these unexpected
"mixtures" new systems of sensation can arise which unite, on the level
of ideas, the sensibility of the flesh and the current of the mind.

The thread of the Young Fate creates in effect a unique current, a
"filtered," quasi-spiritual sensibility which becomes the line of encounter
between the two:

> Withstanding the Sun's all-powerful laziness
> Soaring and self-surrendered to the thinking eye,
> Gaze! . . . I am drinking heaven's wine, caressing
> The mysterious texture of the uttermost height.[19]

What in the nascent state was destined to enter into a certain series of the constitutive system is grasped by the mind and led into a series of another order. That order is part of another system little by little being realized on the plane of the unity of the flesh and of ideas. Each of these systems is governed by its own laws.

The new system, which the mind seems constantly to invent and reinvent, retains nonetheless its filiation with regard to the constitutive system. Even the means of translation from one to the other are preserved, for one and the other are in fact in constant commerce thanks to the magic thread of the mind which runs from end to end across all the systems and all the series.

In this process of transformation every human factor has its own function. The senses find there a double employment, "exterior" and "interior"; what one loses to the eye in detaching it from brute "reality," one gains for "inner use," by the "inner eyes" of which Mme. Teste speaks and which with the aid of imagination fashion common products by drawing forms and qualities from the world of ideas. Thus, on the level of creative sensation, the constitutive distinction between what is and what is not vanishes.

An inverse current, that of the "exterior," also collaborates in this transformation. For it is equally at the level of sensation that the interior is incarnated in the forms of the real world. Let us see how in "Palm" and "The Plane Tree" natural functions, buried in unconscious material, are re-animated by the mind, how the mind rediscovers itself in an entirely invented sensation, that of mounting sap, of the plant's natural refusal to the sun.

> You lean, great plane, and proffer yourself stripped,
>   White as a young Scythian,
> But your candor is trapped, and your foot held in
>   By the strength of its site.
>
> Reverberating shadow where the selfsame blue
>   Transporting you, grows calm,
> The dark mother constrains that pure and native foot
>   Heavy with the loam.[20]

Here is the refusal to be bound by the chains of nature in its course, the refusal to be enchained by its laws. The poet shows the plane tree as nature's prisoner, in its attachment to the soil, in the movement of its branches. He identifies these facts with those analogous facts that man discovers in his mind. Thus there is a servitude there, common to all the beings in nature:

> Sense all about you the lives of others bound
>   By the venerable hydra;
> Your equals are many, from the pine to the poplar,
>   From ilex to maple.[21]

But this bondage which, within the system of nature, is only a natural condition, assumes an entirely different meaning when the poet sees its extension in the human condition. The sentiment, peculiar to man, of being bound by the bonds imposed by the very laws of nature, and of being unable for that reason to take flight with the mind alone, penetrates the opacity of the brute facts of nature and is made explicit by them. Thus the facts of nature which appear first of all in narrow framework are thereby seen to be relocated in a more extensive whole. For this parallelism reserves a place in nature for the mind and thus institutes a universal system in which the natural fact ceases to be a brute fact because it participates in cosmic laws.

Conversely, man ceases to be imprisoned, in his aspirations to flight, by the natural condition as well as by the "unconditional freedom" proper to the mind in its closed circle; these aspirations being found reflected in natural facts, the mind sees itself extended in a series of phenomena no longer directly "brute" but thenceforth cosmic. This series is not in the order of pure subjectivity, it is in an objective order, that of the processes and laws in which the mind as well as nature participate. In being incarnated, the mind throws a bridge across the abyss which separated it from nature. Natural being, like the mind, cannot escape the laws of the cosmos, which limit both in the same sense if not on the same order:

> That brow can only accede to those luminous heights
>   Where the sap exalts it;
> Grow you may, candid one, but never break the knots
>   Of the eternal halt.[22]

Mind and nature are found to be in an analogous situation if we consider both in relation to an ultimate framework which encompasses them. The plane tree, the beech, just like the mind, "Beat without ceasing on a heaven forever closed, Armed with their oars in vain"[23]; they cannot break the bonds of nature which made the trees grow separated from each other, which created man apart from his neighbor:

> Separated they live, they weep altogether
> Blended in a sole absence;
> And their silvery limbs are cleft all in vain
> At their tender birth.[24]

A complete communion of the beings of nature is forever impossible. And yet — Plato sensed it — it seems that in the beginning beings were created for complete communion. But the laws of nature have limited this first grandiose plan which allows itself to be divined by poets.

Like the mind which cannot rise above its own domain, a domain where it can at most penetrate to the bottom of its own creative activity, to the roots of its own functions, so the plane tree can only participate in its own germination, in the passage of its own powers to action. As a natural fact, that sap would only be a mechanical and biochemical operation; but the poet, transposing his creative power into a natural process, transposes both of them into their common framework, that of the universal designs of the cosmos. By incarnating the meanings of his interiority in the natural fact of growth, he gives a soul to a natural being. That soul remains entirely sensitive but it is raised to a level parallel to his own, to the spiritual level.

Thus, in the first movement, the corporeal is led toward the mind and interiorized by reflection, and in the inverse movement the inwardness of the poet goes toward the natural in its most primitive functions and is incorporated there.

The mind is incarnate in living nature, finds in its processes and its generative forms a destiny parallel to its own. Thus arises a network of connections, which assigns its place to each phenomenon after having orchestrated all of them in the same symphony, to use the image dear to Leibniz. Living nature and fabricated nature bear the stamp of universal designs and have a role in the cosmic symphony.

In this context, we cannot fail to mention "Palm," so often analyzed, so much discussed. The pure mind struggling with the despair born of sterility, of its seeming impotence to master its powers, sees its analogue in the natural existence of a palm and finds there a higher wisdom applicable to its own case.

> If at times there is despair,
> If the adorable strictness,
> For all your tears only labors
> Under the guise of languors,[25]

then you must seek to be enlightened by analogy with the wholly organic existence of a plant, apparently passive and inert but in fact not so at all. "Image of a sibyl," its sleep is only a sign of wisdom. In appearance entirely passive, not measuring its effects at all, it is not inert:

> Every day as it still shines
> Compounds another mite of honey [26]

for new sap. Compared to the apparent inertia of the mind, that natural impassivity which is revealed to be a generative process assumes the meaning of a subterranean maturation. The moments when the sap does not yet take body are comparable to the silence of the mind; it is a slow germination. By reflection the mind buries itself in the natural process, spiritually vitalizes it, and so draws from it a lesson. Just like "Her wisdom as it prepares So much gold and so much power," so "These days that seem to you void And wasted for the universe Have their roots of eagerness That put the deserts to work." [27]

The palm has not lost precious hours in its apparent lethargy:

> Now you are left so light
> After such lovely yieldings:
> Image of a thinking mind
> Where the spirit spends itself
> To be increased by what it gives.[28]

These then are the conditions of the mind's creation illuminated by the conditions of natural growth.

At the same time this analogy between the two series of functions leads us to a universal law, that of subterranean but sovereign germination, in the mind as in the body: "An ever-living hopefulness Mounts towards its ripening," [29] and throws a bridge between the two series.

From then on, starting from the invisible but incontestible maturation of the palm, from the certitude that nature is never a sterile desert, the poet can conclude as to the meaning of the "silences" of the mind:

> Endurance, endurance,
> Endurance, in the sky's blue!
> Every atom of silence
> Is a chance of ripened fruit! [30]

The mind in its deep doings discovers itself, thanks to nature. Once more, still life is not as "still" as one believed. The mind descends toward it, is reflected there, lends it its breath; it divines in nature a dynamic mechanism in which it rediscovers itself making "its soul dream of its secret architecture." Thus nature becomes an instrument in the universal orchestra. Examples of this trajectory are so numerous that we can say of Valéry that he constantly *appeals to "brute" nature in order to rediscover the deep sense of the soul,* the sense they both have in the universal scheme where nature presents itself as a sensitized prolongation of the soul, a terrain of extension for the pure mind.

A column rises toward the heavens like a song. A form, inert and impassible in itself, has however an analogous function: the release of a *force* which is fluctuation, the effervescence of man's vibrating vitality. Under the stamp of the chisel, the birth of columns in their cold beauty, their emergence from the formless stone which held them entombed, resembles an awakening. Arisen from sleep, they appear, to enter into the order of the world, to be adjusted there and to participate: "To stare back at the moon, The moon and the sun, We were polished each one, Like the nail on the toe!" [31] We see then that to "re-animate" nature, which in itself is mobile only in a purely mechanical way escaping our sensibility, it is necessary to impose a rational chain of links upon it, to dissociate its elements and to sew them up again as functions of a new schema; in a word, it is necessary to sensitize nature.

In the whole of the universe, the mind could not be content with the separate forms that constitutive consciousness proposes to it; it seeks therefore to establish parallels, correspondences. Symbolism is a manifestation of that creative search. In creative reality we find a complete reality, universally encompassing, differentiated by degrees but at the same time entirely unified by sensibility.

Thus, thanks to the creative process, the body that first repulsed is reconquered. But it reappears in a new system of sensations. In becoming aware of itself, with the aid of reflection, it reconnects the phenomena arising from the "senses" with those of the mind and integrates both into the order of cosmic laws. And, for him who has examined in depth its organization and its mechanisms, it is the body itself which makes its need for extension seen, and that limitation shows that it is born to function in a vaster scheme. Commenting on the way Leonardo treats the body, Valéry writes: "For such a student of organisms, the body is not something contemptible, a mere rag; it has too many properties and resolves too many problems; *it possesses too many functions and resources not to answer some transcendent need, which is powerful enough to dispense with its complexity.* The body is the creation and the instrument of someone who has need of it, does not willingly cast it aside, and laments its loss as one might weep for vanished power . . . ."[32] Thus the natural finality of the body is not its true finality: it is almost a fiction, for it is oriented toward a differently vast project, a project in which it encounters the mind.

Between these two extremes are projected the laws which constitute as it were the invisible "loom" on which the possible will come to be woven. Their mysterious presence gives a distant horizon to the new possible forms of human reality.

5. "GENERATIVE NATURE" TRANSFORMED INTO EROTIC EMOTION — THE MUTE MATERNITY OF THOUGHT

Once again, it is for us a matter of digging beneath constitutive forms to rediscover the mind in its power.

Let us add to that that the forms of nature — taken in its finalistic laws — are susceptible of variation. The new existence we seek cannot in reality be contented with the primary forms of sensibility, which are tributary to the conformism of constituting consciousness. These forms are only a basis on which arise more complete processes of transformability which are organized into systems. Their unfolding gives force to the new human reality which is in germ. It is with this aid that scattered elements are organized into the unity of "life." Erotic sentiment, which we have in view here, is of a particular type. Like all sentiment it arises from carnal forces, stirrings, pulsations, awareness, but this awareness is specified as "Eros."

Brute nature is constituted in a complex manifesting the mechanism of reproduction; the efforts of nature converge toward this point. It is here that the blooming by which the progress of natural development is measured culminates. Constituted nature, even grasped at its birth, tends to perpetuate itself. This tendency is so essential and so powerful that every individual in his concrete particularity disappears behind his reproductive function, surpassing himself by contributing to the perpetuation of the species. And that natural impulse, which is transmitted across a system of mechanisms adapted to its realization, has been quite properly recognized as one of the dominant drives in animals and consequently also in man. Simone de Beauvoir, not without reason, shows us woman, as a sexual being, entirely occupied with maintaining the conditions for the exercise of her reproductive function. The mind is never more completely subjected to nature than in the woman's cycles of organic and physiological development; it is in appearance a sort of slave, approved only when it can serve that carnal end and those which follow it. Is it therefore necessary, on this basis, to condemn the sexual body and to reject it when one chooses the mind? Or must one admit the primacy of natural finality, that quasi-mystical finality which drives man to propagate *ad infinitum*?

We would first have to see what the sexual body is. The body in full bloom resembles the ripe cluster of grapes ready for gathering; the limbs, which form the natural mechanism, are ready to go into action and only await an impulse in order to expand. Speaking of the body, the poet invokes "the force, and the weird gestures That lovers invent so as to kill of love."[33] But aren't these "gestures" explained only by their natural function? The dreaming girl — the reflective consciousness would need a system of meanings which would permit her to translate sexual phenomena into terms intelligible to her.

The natural scheme of human reproduction, made of instincts, of drives, of a mechanism that we are pleased in our epoch to call "sex" is a complex ordering of facts and rules attributed to brute nature. If one follows these drives, if one uses this mechanism so to speak literally, one can expect of it nothing other than an action of the organs involved, that is, finally, muscular contractions. No other effect then than prereflective sensations. Being limited to purely muscular actions and reactions, they hardly help the body to emerge from its isolation. From this we understand why communion cannot be achieved on the natural level, as Malraux has shown in *The Human Condition*. What a sad inventory of sexual phenomena those who refer to phenomenological analysis have presented us! What desolation, what insurmountable solitude, in the novels of Sartre and Simone de Beauvoir! Sex is there merely an instrument for a game between two beings, a game without reason and unreasonable. The solitude proceeding from the isolation of the body is that of man's natural condition, that which he shares with the rest of nature.

Is there not however the possibility of a more ample, more "human" human condition? "Anne" presents to us the protest against brute gestures, against everything which is explainable only in terms of physiology, against a rupture between the mind and the body:

> When, on you, their soul's gaze goes roving,
> Their hearts turn over, altering with their voices,
> For the tender foretaste of their barbaric orgies
> Harries the eager dogs that quiver in those kings . . . .[34]

The rupture between body and soul has become flagrant in today's humanity, which does not cease to produce men of culture who are incapable of finding a bridge to unite their intellectual refinement to the animality of their sensible life. That animality is today proclaimed superior because man believes himself to be liberated from the prejudices of past centuries, in fact, he believes himself to be in a direct line of primates — a superior one of them! But this attitude does not fill the emptiness created in a life thus cut in two, emptiness which waylays Sartrean heroes — whether or not they have reached "the age of reason" — as well as those of Vaillant, of the American novel, etc. Men devoted to the body as physical science conceives it (that is, a natural mechanism on the one hand and pure intellect on the other) exercise two separated mechanisms and make both of them spin out of gear. For the mind alone cannot produce the emotive and sensitive content on which it is exercised, and which is the savor of life; as for the senses, they are emptied of their content in advance if they are reduced to the pure natural mechanism. Is this brusque rupture between the way of the soul and that of the body definitive?

Following Valéry, let us cite Leonardo speaking of carnal love: "'Love in its fury' — he says in almost these words — 'is so ugly a thing that the human race would die out (*la natura si perderebbe*) if those who practice it could see themselves.' Many of his sketches are evidence of that scorn, since for certain things the height of scorn is finally to examine them at one's leisure. Here and there he has drawn anatomical unions, horrible cross sections of love itself. He is fascinated by the erotic machine, the mechanics of living bodies being his favourite domain; but sweat against sweat, the panting of the *operanti*, a monster formed of clashing muscular structures, and the final transfiguration into beasts, all seem to excite only his repugnance and disdain...."[35]*

We have here a succinct analysis of the erotic complex taken in its brute, natural, finalistic form. However, in the margin of that citation, Valéry places twenty years later a commentary which discloses a different conception of nature, in which it is at the same time *first* and *second*, initiating but last, to attain its ends. With this optic, we have by all evidence left the terrain of nature at its animal level in order to move toward its incarnation in a human life. "This cool look at the mechanisms of love," Valéry says, "is, I think, unique in our intellectual history. When love is coldly analyzed, many curious ideas come to mind. What roundabout ways, what a complexity of methods, to bring about fecundations! Emotions, ideals, *beauty*, all intervening as the means of stimulating a given muscle. The essential feature of the function becoming an incidental, its accomplishment something to be feared, eluded .... It would be hard to find better evidence of the degree to which *nature* is *devious*."[36] In effect, in a precise mechanism, self-sufficient, direct and dominating to the point of threatening the autonomy of every other domain, a rupture is avowed, a slackening, an invasion of heterogeneous elements which are however felt to be indispensable to the functioning of this mechanism.

This same natural fact is so much feared and rejected by the Young Fate:

> Menacing my spiritual lot with love ....
> You have no power over me that would not be less cruel,
> Less desirable .... [37]

The mind must defend itself violently against this brute phenomenon which presages submission to the course of nature. Likewise, Semiramis refuses to accept the supremacy of the male, of virility; in its sovereign pride, the mind scorns to assent to the distribution of the roles and privileges of the partners in the games of sex.

> Drunk with voluptuousness, the Lover soon thought himself
>   to be master ....
> But Semiramis is more a man than he!
> Semiramis is pure!
> She has killed! [38]

This pride of the mind weds love and death as two powers of the body;

Semiramis "has but now drained the rich cup of life: Making love, bestowing death."[39] It is not doubtful that love and hate are carnal phenomena. Isn't the most "pure," the most spiritualized of loves modeled on the example of physical forms as seen in identification and the impulse toward the "possession" of a soul? In hatred, the dominant impulse tends on the contrary toward the annihilation of the object, a wholly carnal sentiment! But to say that love, hate, passions are carnal sentiments does not at all imply a causal relationship nor a dependence upon the physical properties of the body. We have just indicated a slackening of the bonds of the physical mechanism, opening the way to a new interpretation of the body different from those that physicists and phenomenologists give of it.

In effect, poets offer us a gamut of examples testifying to their acceptance of the phenomenon of love in all its amplitude, uniting the carnal and the spiritual. On what conditions is this resumption of what had at first been rejected with scorn accomplished? And above all what, in this new alliance, becomes of love as a natural phenomenon?

What we have agreed to call "Eros" arises as an emotion, as a specific sort of complex sensation. At its origin, rather than entering into a natural scheme which would progress toward a definite end, the sensation enters into different schemes, themselves rough, open. Thus of the caress:

> My hot hands, bathe them
> In your own . . . . Nothing calms
> Like love's undulating
> Passing pressures of a palm.[40]

The heat of our hands, which in the beginning is that of nature, calls for contact, but this contact is not going to be concretized in a direct tactile or sensorial quality. The determining analogy which is invoked is that of the undulation of the waves of the sea whose harmonious and repeated movement allies itself with the undulated swinging of a palm-tree's branches. Thus the joining of hands, at first a sensorial fact, is transformed in lived experience into an emotion similar to the undulating vibration of peace, of a peace which passes through our being like the waves over the sea, of a peace which is interiorized in us as the perfect harmony of our being with gentleness. This undulation is accompanied by an unqualified sensation, a sensation unqualifiable in its acuteness. The whole being is seized with a shiver, and the very rings of the hand which caresses are animated:

> Familiar as their touch may be,
> Your rings with their long jewels
> Melt away in the shiver
> Persuading the eyelids to close.[41]

This shiver, close to instinct by its qualitative privation, inferior to sensation itself, does not for all that become the *causa proxima* of a later carnal function. Its sharpness is clothed by a sole determination which is identified with the whole being: It is pain,

> And the pain thins out, to where,
> As a sheet of stone is polished,
> A caress diffuses it
> To the brink of melancholy.[42]

That shiver does not therefore set in motion the expected function, it has its own function. In that penetrating friendship limited to the present instant become eternal and infinite, all particular emotions (desires and thoughts present to the field of consciousness) lose their validity, their meaning — drawn from the specific perspectives in which they were conceived — and are projected toward a new, indefinite perspective which the eternity of the present instant outlines. It is only a factitious eternity, however. It suffices to plunge into it to see it dissipated in duration like fog in space. In our awareness that the apparent absolute of the instant escapes in duration, we transcend ourselves in melancholy. Thus erotic emotion, in this case that of a caress, bound in its emergence to a carnal awareness, has however mobilized all our resources in order to set itself up in a system which is not that of the natural mechanism. Thus, by definition, eroticism does not only relate to a spiritual climate, to a horizon of ideas, it also relates to invention. For its advent, it mobilizes the resources of sensibility and the mind. But above all it undoes the articulations of the finalistic process of nature: It can change the duration, the intensity, the order of time as it pleases. It accelerates or slows (and takes the abridgments of one order to precipitate other orders):

> O Windings, meanders,
> Wiles of the deceiver,
> What art more tender
> Than this in its slowness?[43]

Eros arises as a phenomenon guided by a lucid, prepared, and in

part constructed consciousness. Instead of blind submission to the
cunning release of instinct, we have there at least partial domination by
the mind, domination which is not exercised on the sensible content —
which remains sensible — but on the nature and genesis of the quality
and on its course:

> I know when I go
> To where I will take you,
> My wicked designings
> Will do you no harm . . . .[44]

In the crystallization of erotic emotion that we have just outlined,
analytic reflection brings its collaboration to bear. It calculates its
effects, it makes the choice of its means and of their application. To the
mad course of instinct, it substitutes waiting:

> O Windings, meanders,
> Wiles of the deceiver,
> I must hold in suspense
> The word the most tender.[45]

In the reflective work collaborating in the transformation of natural
instinct, the role of the functions of consciousness transforming lived
experience is revealed. These functions will be analyzed. With conscious
transformability, it is freedom which comes into play — against instinct.
Eros arises as creator.

Must we believe however that in this mixture of the mind and the
flesh Eros definitively turns away from natural instinct? Would the
essential finality, interrupted, be eliminated? Such would be the opinion
of spiritualists desirous of separating love from the flesh. It is also what
one would think if he applied himself to emotion alone, such as it is
expressed in "The Footsteps." This incomparable poem so exalts the
exquisite wait, the almost purely spiritual languor of a loving "communion," that finally it raises the climate of beauty and tenderness so
high that one would believe this climate to be a closed vessel, detached
from its sensual context by the force of its intensity and fullness. Love
there is pure:

> Pure one, divine shadow,
> How gentle are your cautious steps!
> Gods! . . . all the gifts that I can guess
> Come to me on those naked feet!

If, with your lips advancing,
You are preparing to appease
The inhabitant of my thoughts
With the sustenance of a kiss,

Do not hasten the tender act,
Bliss of being and not being,
For I have lived on waiting for you,
And my heart was only your footsteps.[46]

It is instructive thus to see the primitive play of instinct supplanted
by a vaster erotic phenomenon, encompassing in its complexity the
mind and sensibility with their acquisitions and their habits. One must
nonetheless be undeceived. Eros is not disincarnate, nor is it a simple
"sublimation of instinct." It introduces a new, original, and autonomous
configuration of the entirety of conscious data. It dwells on creative
consciousness as we have discovered and specified it to be, and
completes it by indicating the transformability of generative nature.

The dénouement of the lover's drama is in effect suspended. Does
that mean that the present moment has enough beauty to suffice for
itself? In this sense, love is nourished by the eternal mind; it consumes
the present moment without hastening toward the future. But love
cannot do without a dénouement. Simply this dénouement takes another
form than that of the deliverance by which the wait should naturally
find its end. Thus dismembered, the natural process of love loses its
tyrranical power; its elements are placed in another context which
confers upon them other meanings. It is no longer the slave of finality,
its possibilities are no longer determined but free, open. Natural love
retains its power of domination only in helping the complete being of
man to bloom in amorous ecstasy.

There is still the matter of knowing if that transformation of the
natural context is the work of a functional system of consciousness
similar to that which constitutes the world. Indeed, is there perhaps
only one system which, once established, would proceed automatically?
Nothing more false! The bird of instinct never stops making his
too-high voice heard:

The whole night through, the cruel bird held me
At the sheer climax of the bliss of hearing
That voice directed with such tender fury
At a sky on fire with stars until morning.

> You pierce the soul, decree the destiny
> Of a given look that cannot be taken back;
> Everything that was, you change to ashes,
> Oh too high voice, instinct's own ecstasy . . . .
>
> Dawn in the shadow outlines the face
> Of a lovely day: nothing to me already.
> One day more is only an empty landscape,
>
> What is a day without that face of yours?
> No! . . . My mind, turning back night-wards,
> Rejects the dawn, and the youthful day.[47]

That voice can be modified, but its effect is incessant and always taken up anew. It contrives to set off the natural mechanism, is translated by the mind and is heard in the very depths of man. Nature is neither scorned, therefore, nor rejected; but voluptuousness has no other end than its own exercise. On the other hand, most precious are the loves

> Which a long toil of the soul and its desire
> Leads to their delectable ends.
> Deeper hearts are not satisfied
> With a glance, overtaken by a kiss,
> Leading at once to the core of a fleeting affair . . . .[48]

Explaining herself in the "Preface to the Commentary of Alain,"[49] the Young Fate does not simply refuse love. After having striven against the natural exigency of submission, the mind augments its role and tightens the rigidity of its bonds; the pure self and the natural self enter into an alliance which determines both of them. Without losing any of its vigor, instinct with its spontaneity is mingled with the mind, with pure thought:

> . . . A thing truly loved is enhanced by your torments
> Your eyes see it in diamonds of tears,
> The night of bitterness paints it in the tenderest colors.[50]

These elements which have arisen heterogeneously in the schemes of constitution are now placed on the same plane in the context where emotion and erotic sensation arise. Together they pass through the filter of acquired sedimentations and receive from the pure self a chain of new articulations in the process of its becoming aware of their complexity. And now we are finally before an Eros in which nature recovered by the filter of the mind is seen to be reconciled with it in an original and autonomous reality. The articulations of the mind replace natural chains, and natural finality is seen to be deflected if not overthrown by the *mute maternity of thought*. One more step remains to be taken in our inquiry. In effect, the example of the transformation of instinct into Eros illuminates a fundamental trait of the workings of consciousness in its creative function.

Instinct, initial drive, original spontaneity, all that engenders the movement, activates the process which is going to take place, all that is *given*, as the "first verse." But it then belongs to the mind to receive, to fashion this given. Thenceforth, it's a matter of *effort*. The thread, so fine, which links the mind to the senses, which allows their interpenetration and spiritual fecundation, is not an unimportant consequence: "I am the reward of effort," the Young Fate says. Submission to nature is replaced by freedom, passivity by invention:

> My heart requires force, and rejects you, Lovers,
> Who are put off by the knottings of my lovely girdle.[51]

The mind, without losing any of its power, becomes "sensible," becomes life itself. "As a matter of fact, we are interested only in the sensibility. If we also worry about the intelligence (a scholastic distinction, I grant), basically that is only because of the many varied effects it has on our sensibility."[52] Valéry adds in the margin to *Note and Digression*, a remark which for our account we may consider conclusive.

The fissure at the heart of man between the higher self and the lower functions of nature cannot be surpassed otherwise than by a conscious and lucid effort. The creative reality by which we reconcile the terms of this dilemma is the exercise of effort. The terms of this effort announce the definition of the creative function of consciousness. The creative effort which first seemed impossible appears in fact as the very solution of the dilemma which was supposed to imply its suppression. By the effort of the mind there is produced a transfusion of vital forces into the forms of the mind which had remained sterile; thus is achieved the transmutation of those "deserts" where the serpent alone could exist.

Moreover, on the basis of transformed sensation, there is an original fecundation and a reconquest of nature. And it is not for nothing that Valéry, for whom the poet is identical to the man who lives, tells us what is valuable for both: ". . . it is the part of us that chooses, the part that organizes, which must be exercised at every moment. The rest depends on no one, and we invoke it as we pray for rain."[53] In effect, Valéry knew how to interpret that identification, he for whom the analysis of Leonardo's genius was to provide the key to his own unfinished work, scattered as "fragments of a great game." What interests him is not the creator's personal history; and the theoreticians who are partisans of the "objective" analysis of a work, as opposed to the interpretation of a work as a function of biography — that is, novelistic episodes and *facts* —, only touch upon the surface of things: "The author's life is not the life of the man he is . . . ." The man, for Valéry, is not the cause of the work, but rather the effect. What interests him is "the intimate law of this great Leonardo." This intimate law directs that slow and laborious underground task of "conscious internal modification,"[54] from which hangs the work but sketches at the same time the inner itinerary of the man, his true biography.

THE FACTORS IN THE NEW ALLIANCE
BETWEEN MAN AND THE WORLD

1. EXPERIENCE AND KNOWLEDGE, ANTENNAE OF THE MIND

Phenomenology and poet's thought meet once again on the subject of the world. One of the great teachings of phenomenology is that the world in which we passively live is a hardened, petrified world. In our natural abandon, we do not understand that the natural milieu is only a series of sedimentations of our past experiences, of ideas accepted by chance, of secondary attitudes. In order to apperceive it, the distance that the phenomenological attitude gives is first necessary; we can thus rediscover beings and objects, their relationships and their developments, stripped of their vital force. Constitutive phenomenology was then needed to penetrate to the roots that these elements formerly had in our consciousness, and which at present are atrophied, in such a way that the world is no longer anything, even in *fact*, but a dead world which persists as an immutable shell. The same procedure is followed by the creator: to the pure mind, the world shows itself to be empty of vital savor and beings and objects appear not as existing but as possible. Pure consciousness "does not know that it was born or that it will perish," it exalts in the lucidity of its presence to itself, believes itself "quite easily . . . exempt from loss or change."[55]

It is not, however, the opacity of the natural world which acts as a screen for the translucent dynamism of consciousness. The mind itself, under its aspect of discursive intelligence, has prepared a screen separating it from the world. In ordinary life, the use we make of intelligence is before all else the employment of concepts — the inert and interchangeable shell of concrete lived experience. "Most people," Valéry tells us, "see with their intellects much more often than with their eyes. Instead of colored spaces, they become aware of concepts. Something whitish, cubical, erect, its planes broken by the sparkle of glass, is immediately a house for them — the House! — a complex idea, a combination of abstract qualities. If they change position, the movement of the rows of windows, the translation of surfaces which continuously alters their sensuous perceptions, all this escapes them, for their concept remains the same. They perceive with a dictionary rather than with the retina; and they approach objects so blindly, they have such a vague notion of the difficulties and pleasures of vision, that they have invented beautiful views. Of the rest they are unaware." [56]

The passivity of consciousness, allied with the finalism of nature, orients us toward survival, toward the propagation of life. Everything is thus oriented and organized — without fear of simplification — to clear the way for the vital mechanism. It is somehow the economy of nature. We discover in effect that our consciousness, following its natural paths, is not spontaneously oriented toward its own good (which would be the development, the deepening of knowledge); to the contrary, its natural course seems to be subjected first to the interests of survival, and goes that way by the most efficacious, that is, the most direct, paths. Thus knowledge parches the world for the weakness "existing in all branches of knowledge is precisely our choice of *obvious* standpoints, our being content with definite systems that facilitate, that make it easy to grasp." [57] But before the conceptual structures which establish and classify the commonplace, "even these beautiful views are more or less concealed from ordinary observers; and all the modulations so delicately contrived by little movements, changing light, and tiring eyes are lost to them, neither adding to nor subtracting from their sensations." [58] Sensation, which, in effect, is the root of the world, has withdrawn to the background, ceased to renew itself, falling ever like fresh water in the old fonts of the conceptual classifications which have taken its place. In this hardened world, the conservation of subtlety and sensorial insta-bility becomes a revolutionary virtue. As a task, it is incumbent upon artists. Valéry declares: "A modern artist has to exhaust two-thirds of his time trying to see what is visible — and above all, trying not to see what is invisible." [59] Significant, this vocation of the artist in relation to humanity! We will return to it. For the poet, as for the phenomenolo-gist, the same good exercise: "The deeper education consists in unlearn-ing one's first education." [60] Thus, in revolting against enslavement to the body, consciousness directed to the phenomena of life attains the world at the same time. For the world is only the milieu of natural life. It is not consciousness which, as constitutive phenomenology would have it, should correspond to the world, being governed by parallel rules; it is the human life, spontaneously natural, which arises at the same time as the world in which it develops. These are functions one of the other, both being born on the same level, *natural spontaneity*, like two branches from the same trunk. This common trunk is manifestly the body. Thus, when M. Teste rises up against the elements which enslave the mind, he is preoccupied with chasing away the social puppet as well as mental habits and with excluding the indolence of the mind immersed in passive psychological life as well as the indolence of our social self. One would say that in suspending natural life, one breaks at the same time the circuit which feeds the external and social world; for M. Teste, the latter loses all meaning, all vitality, and disappears, as anonymous as his dwelling or his stock-market operations.

That disappearance of the world is shown in a yet more radical way in *The Young Fate*, with the back-and-forth of carnal temptations and the extinction and resurgence of life: "Thing of harmony, ME, unlike a dream, Firm, flexible, feminine, whose silences lead To pure acts!"[61] and "To the light; and on this bosom of honey Whose tender nativity was heavens's fulfillment,"[62] the inner silences, the "deep forests" of the mind, cede to another universe and behold, "There came to lull itself the shape of the world."[63]

It is therefore on the basis of the body that life and the world are animated or extinguished: For both, the body is the nerve center. As we have shown it to be for life, so we must now show it to be for the world.

2. THE INTERMINGLING OF CONSCIOUSNESS AND BODY IN THE CREATIVE FUNCTION, AN INEXHAUSTIBLE SOURCE OF POSSIBLE WORLDS

In the relations of consciousness to the body, within our creative weaving, we find the Archimedean point. In itself, consciousness "judges itself to be deeper than the very abyss of animal life and death."[64] This look at its condition cannot react upon consciousness itself, "so far has it drawn aside from all things, so great are the pains it has taken *never to be part of anything it might conceive, or of any answer it might find.*" Being consumed in its own activities, consciousness rejects in itself the forms of sensibility, the modes according to which connections are made and continuities arise. It discovers "fields of force in which we follow strange circuits between the poles of fear and desire ... non-Archimedean realms that defy movement ... surfaces that cave in ... ." In itself again consciousness finds "abysses literally of horror, or love, or quietude ... ." The true matter of these constructions comes from consciousness: it is time. Consciousness sees vibrating and holding together the skeleton and the substance on which "the pattern of this world" comes to be sketched. To the gaze of consciousness which penetrates to these depths, they seem neither real nor unreal. Valéry says insistently that the person who has not traversed these dimensions, who has not grasped the hidden system of consciousness, "does not know the value of natural light or of the most commonplace surroundings; he does not recognize the true fragility of the world." However, while the world thus pierced in the light of day appears to consciousness to be accidental, fragile and so to speak degraded, that separation, if it is sufficiently examined, leads consciousness, which considered "its body" and "its world" as "almost arbitrary restrictions imposed upon the scope of its functions," to rediscover a juncture, a common framework, a remedy to the opposition to the world that it has raised up itself. In effect, there can no longer be any question of the being or non-being of the world and things once one has discovered their crucible; "the wonder is not that things are, but that they are *what* they are, and not something else." For "consciousness comes to suspect that all accustomed reality is only one solution, among many others, of universal problems." It discovers in itself many more possible solutions, more internal combinations that practical occasions require. The pattern of this world, Valéry tells us, "belongs to a family of patterns of which, without knowing it, we possess all the elements of the infinite group."

Particularizing and particularized constitutive consciousness, however, discovers the necessary mechanisms which prescribe an essentially and universally identical result. That universality is the great privilege of consciousness, for it explains that "so many individual universes can participate in a common, intersubjective world." However, in recognizing itself as author of the world as well as its effect, it is enclosed within the walls of its work, even when projecting beyond that work a closed subjective horizon.[65] Constitutive consciousness can ask *how* things are as they are (it will answer with its constitutive laws, which made things that way); but in the transcendental system it projects, the question *why* has no sense.

Consciousness, naturally englobed in the world it made arise by engulfing in a perpetual resumption *that* which renders the world inert and hardened, suddenly understands in the creative act that it is the engineer of this world. Moreover, it discovers the elements of its employment, the arsenal of instruments and materials, and above all the inexhaustible abundance of architectonic elements and of ideas of planning; it possesses "the secret of inventors." Creative consciousness, while having constructed its own world, "is convinced that things could be *sufficiently* different from what they are without the world being *very* different from what it is."

In Valéry's work we see consciousness reclaiming not only the "discursive" mind, intelligence — a passive faculty constrained to obey rules even when it builds — but also a "poetic" power — that which makes the artist. "It is capable of a greater number of mental combinations than are needed for survival, and of more rigor than any practical situation demands or tolerates," and, considering itself to be beyond nature, with roots deeper than "the very abyss between life and death," it looks at the world it has created as a particular case to which it is bound only by chance, one susceptible of being replaced by a conscious choice. It refuses the solution which would consist in swimming against the current in order to revive a world which would nonetheless remain essentially the same — the sole solution which remains for constitutive consciousness. To the contrary, seeing itself "as responding or corresponding not to a *world*, but to some system of a higher order, the elements of which are worlds," it finds itself capable of reinventing the world, and of passing from the role of impassive blacksmith to that of architect, creator. Thus the artist is given the possibility of fulfilling his role.

3. THE MODE OF THE RELATIONSHIP BETWEEN THE BODY
AND THE MIND: THE ARCHIMEDEAN POINT OF THE WORLD

In the debate between consciousness and body in which human creativity appears to be engaged, the notions "consciousness," "mind" and "body" denote the respective functional complexes that have been distinguished, in post-Cartesian philosophy. This general approach will suffice in the present, preliminary delineation of the main arteries of the philosophical issues which the investigation of the creative effort of the human being involves. In the subsequent systematic analysis of the creative endeavor which will be exfoliated in the central panel of our triptych a far-reaching differentiation of the human functional complexes, forces and faculties with reference to their particular roles will bring us into the creative forge of man's functioning in its full extent.

The relationship between the body and the mind is revealed in the creative function of consciousness as the "Archimedean point" of the world.

How can that be? How can one conceive of a possible world other than that which is given if man seems to be alienated not only by brute nature but also by his own means of feeling and conceiving?

To undo one's acquired education in order to arrive at a deep education, the goal as dear to the phenomenologist as to the poet, is something that cannot be achieved by just any agent of the mind. What will be the modalities of the relations between mind and body, their respective powers, the modes of their encounter in the creative junction which could explain man's possibility of a choice of universes? For to rediscover the first sources of the world is to find once again what lies beneath the commonplace. But constitutive consciousness, just like discursive intelligence, in undoing their links will finally lead us only to the sources of the experience in its universal form, to the laws of knowledge as a process of the formation of objects, relations, and systems, in an abstraction further and further removed from lived experience. Having arrived at these sources, how can one stay there, how reconstruct a world less amorphous and more authentic on the basis of them? All one can do in such conditions is to try to reduce intellectual speculation and to be aware of the *arbitrary* character of the objects that one constructs in relation to experience. That is what constitutive phenomenology is employed in doing; it sweeps away prejudices and reconstructs the world — without prejudgments, certainly, but always following universal laws.

But the poet, for his part, is otherwise exigent. To acquire deep education in a positive manner, to reconstruct an authentic world, he has to recognize past faults, find or forge a mode of knowledge that does not take him away from its source, and a world which in its very essence would remain vibrant and would refuse to be enclosed in an arbitrary form (the lazy solution).

And if there were a deep symmetry between the structure of the universe and that of our mind?[66] We see therefore, and right away, that the mind is solidary with the world in its forms, but these are only ideal forms, empty of content and force like the plans conceived by an architect that correspond to his mind. It remains a vital connection to be found, a manner of animating these plans by giving them a body. Only, the mind is limited. Or even impotent. Concerning Leonardo, Valéry has held forth to us at length on the necessity for the soul to have a body which, far from degrading it, is for it a condition of immortality. Manifestly, there are two different levels on which to examine the relations between the body and the mind, which at one moment seem to us to exclude one another and at the next seem to be inseparable. The mind all alone is therefore powerless. In following the temptation of the mind we will not come up against its positive foundation, the foundation of man and the world. Thought alone, enclosing itself within the framework it weaves itself, is perpetuated to infinity. In giving itself the illusion of progress, it only succeeds in constructing new systems for the transposition of ideas which are emptied of concrete content as thought advances.

One could say with Valéry that from a certain point of view "there is no supreme, final knowledge — a divine point of view . . . and that in consequence philosophy in its entirety, as an enterprise of pure knowledge, would only be an instrument of thought and not a goal."[67]

This verdict of impotence upon the resources of pure consciousness applies to Husserl's conception just as much as to the more complete one of Valéry. The poet even speaks as a phenomenologist: "One could have written abstractly that the most general group of our transformations, which comprises all sensations, all ideas, all judgments, all that is manifested *intus et extra* admits a variant. To limit oneself to seeking that variant is to vow oneself to sterility, it is to condemn the world which arises from it to the anonymity of a despairing universality."

But in the creative function the mind is not separated; it is extended in a system of the body. What — if not the body — could teach us what the spaces which are not of the mind are, and what the continuity which is found only in a formal state in consciousness is? The body, which sensation has opened to contact with nature, is going to be revealed to the mind, thanks to its organization, its organs, and its functions, as "the measure of the world" — of this particular world which surrounds us and of every other world which we could have chosen. "O body of mine, that recallest to me at every moment this tempering of my tendencies, this equilibrium of thy organs, these true proportions of thy parts . . . teach me secretly the demands of nature . . . . Thou art indeed the measure of the world, of which my soul presents me with the shell alone. She knows it to be without depth, and knows it to so little purpose that she sometimes would class it among her dreams; she doubts the sun . . . . Doting on her ephemeral fabrications, she thinks herself capable of an infinity of different realities; she imagines that other worlds exist, but thou recallest her to thyself, as the anchor calls back the ship . . . ."[68] We return here to that reference to the body already mentioned in the *Note and Digression*, and which the poet attributes to Leonardo while giving the impression that he himself subscribes to it: "For such a student of organisms, the body is not something contemptible, a mere rag; it has too many properties and resolves too many problems; *it possesses too many functions and resources not to answer some transcendent need, which is powerful enough to construct the body and not powerful enough to dispense with its complexity.* The body is the creation and the instrument of someone who has need of it, does not willingly cast it aside, and laments its loss as one might weep for vanished power . . . ." Consciousness in its creative function is at the origin of a form of the world that it chooses, but this insofar as it enters into a functional system with the body. Thus, the body — as we know it by constitutive consciousness — appears as a part of a universal system. And although the poet seems here to consider the soul to be the master, one sees nevertheless an open door toward a transcendence which would encompass both of them. From another point of view, it is toward the body that the mind turns when it wants to become aware of the world. How can that be accomplished?

Once again, poetry must precede reflection and furnish it with matter. It is a question in effect of restoring the elements of a new world, which reposes no longer on the illusory certitude of permanence that intelligence imposes but on the unstable, on the vibrancy of sensation — a world which participates in nature without being reduced to physical and mechanical schema — the illusory guarantors of stability — and which draws from nature the vibrant stuff of life, spontaneity. It is a question, in sum, of reclaiming the elements of a new plenitude, the vital atmosphere of man. The Young Fate, who has woven the hidden connection by which consciousness links contraries by including them in a new functional framework gives us another example of that reclamation. The azure of day does not mislead her as before, she has rediscovered an entirely new familiarity with nature which causes her to be born to the world:

> . . . So then — vain farewells if I live — did I only
> Dream? . . . If I come in windswept garments
> To this edge, unafraid, inhaling the high foam,
> My eyes drinking the immense salt laughter,
> My being into the wind, in the keenest air
> Receiving the sea's challenge on my face;
> If the intense soul snuffs and furious swells
> The sheer on the shattered wave, and if the headland
> Breaker thunders, immolating a snowy monster
> Come from the open sea to vomit the deeps
> Over this rock, whence leaps to my very thought
> A dazzling burst of icy sparks, and over
> All my skin, stung awake by the harsh shock . . . .[69]

The sea is no longer a foreign element placed before us like a separate spectacle; it is foam, the element that our whole being comes to inhale. It is the soul itself that finds itself anew, with its élan, its enthusiasm, in the wind that blows, in resisting its thrust. The play of the waves expresses the struggle, the violent gambols deep within the soul; and it is the same depth that is revealed by the return of the waves of the high sea and the return of the waves of the soul which, shaken in its very depths, undergoes disturbances comparable to the violent crash of the elements. We return here to the analogy between the soul and nature, on the condition that we go to the roots of one and the other. Analogy which permits identification, without that traditional identification being reduced to a *licentia poetica*, is a commodious symbolism which makes the beautiful arise. It has powerful roots in the most profound laws which govern the two elements identified:

> Then, even against my will, I must, oh Sun,
> Worship this heart where you seek to know yourself,
> Strong, sweet renewal of birth's own ecstasy.[70]

The "renewal of birth's own ecstasy" finds here its double sense: the first sense of the rebirth of nature vanishes into the second, deeper sense, that of the rebirth of man to the world, which already implies the rebirth of nature in him. We have in the two "Fragments of the Narcissus" the best example of a world incorporated into an entirely fresh, vibrant reality, stirring the soul as well as the waters, forests, and mountains. The soul is there translated by nature to such an extent and

the world is there perceptible across the states of the soul to such an
extent that one believes them to be indissociable, confused in one lived
atmosphere only.

> This evening, the flight towards the pool, like a stag's,
> Has no cease till it drops in the midst of the reeds.
> My thirst brings me down on the very water's edge.
> But, to quench the thirst of this inquisitive love,
> I shall not trouble the mysterious surface:
> Nymphs, you must sleep still, if you love me!
> The merest ghost in air can make you all shudder;
> Even if, in its weakness, unleashed from the shade,
> The bewildered leaf grazes the napaea,
> It is enough to shatter a sleeping universe . . . .[71]

Look at how the woods, their real and imaginary inhabitants, arise
reflecting the sentimental and melancholic state of the soul which is
itself reflected in its disturbances by Nature:

> Even into the deep recesses of self-love.
> Nothing can escape the evening silence . . .
> Night comes whispering on my flesh that I love her.
> Her cool voice tremblingly consents to my vows . . . .[72]

It is one and the same emotion that the vibrant world and amorous
phenomena express. In intense reflection upon his feelings, Narcissus
evokes water, woods, wind. The world and the soul mutually reflect one
another. Haven't they a *common contexture*?

4. EXPANDED CONSCIOUSNESS: VIRTUAL INVENTOR

We have already indicated that common contexture. It is a matter of
seeing how, in the mind-body system which we have just sketched,
consciousness thus expanded plays the role of an "virtual inventor."

It is the mind which, with the body as its instrument, organizes the
world and divides it; we grasp the extension, the continuity, the density
of beings only by our awareness of our body. Our organs, with their
carnal consistency, their pluridimensionality, their functions as instruments, permit us to project an analogous awareness upon the elements
furnished by sensations, to organize them in a contexture which, while
taking a certain distance with regard to us, remains homogeneous with

our awareness of our body. Thus the other beings of nature cease to be separate objects — simple spectacles for intelligence; they become an integral part of our emotive complexes, they constitute a spare universe. While retaining their objective form, they are grasped from within, being in themselves as vibrant as living consciousness and attached to the same frame of reference as it is. It is a framework which transcends both of them, for it involves the laws of the cosmos. The secret networks of the body and those of the mind open themselves in effect in response to these laws, and it is upon this base that they rise up to be completed. What the ultimate designs are, even the architect Eupalinos does not know. Only one thing seems sure: *consciousness is not just an engineer limited by its plans; it is not enclosed by necessity; it disposes resources of its own not yet utilized and perhaps inexhaustible.* From a certain angle, it appears as an *inventor in potency*.

But, in order for that faculty of invention to be employed, it is necessary that the habits of the "consciousness-engineer" be revised. Knowledge, whose role is crucial to the reconstruction in question, must revise its premises. In effect, knowledge — which we know to be only the fruit of constitutive faculties directed by universal laws, or of speculative intelligence — applies itself only to constructing the spectacle of separated objects, to classifying them and to contemplating them as forms become inert. But the poet tells us: "All the labors of the mind can thus no longer have as their object a final contemplation, even the idea of which has lost its meaning (or comes closer and closer to being a theological concept, demanding a contemplator different in essence from ourselves); but on the contrary, these labors appear to the mind itself as *an intermediate activity connecting two experiences or two states of experience*, the first of which is *given* and the second *foreseen*."[73] This function of invention, thus defined, applies just as well to creative reality as it does to scientific invention.

But, what remains to us of the world envisioned in the perspective of the progress of the physical sciences "revealed as it is in a roundabout fashion by a series of relays and indirect effects on the senses, constructed by a process of analysis with disconcerting results when these are translated into common language, excluding any sort of images, ...", thus rendering this world impossible to represent? The changes, hypotheses are like "an ever increasing and incorruptible capital of achievements and modes of producing achievements — in other words, *powers*."[74]

Thus on the scientific plane knowledge ceases to be simple contemplation of the world by the structures of intelligence; it takes on a
regulative aspect. From the search for essential permanences, it passes
on to the invention of improvised rules which allow a certain mechanism
to be grasped, and thus permit the future to be foreseen. Abandoning
the established certitudes of stabilized essences, science attempts to
seize the vital, the quick. Likewise, the poet who comes back to the root
of the world seeks a mode of knowledge more appropriate, more apt to
hold fast the quick. Valéry traces the exigencies of a mode of knowledge susceptible of measuring correctly the interval between two ways
of knowing rather than of stabilizing both of them: "Knowledge of this
sort is never separated from action or from instruments of execution
and control, without which, moreover, *it has no meaning . . . .*"[75]

It must in effect penetrate each act by selected intentions of consciousness — "whereas if it is based on them, if it refers back to them at
every moment, it enables us to deny meaning to knowledge of any other
sort, and specifically to what which proceeds from words alone and
leads only toward ideas."[76]

It seems that here we attain the center of the mind's power, power of
invention as much as of reconstruction. On the basis of this conception
of knowledge, we can make out the *antennae* between the mind, the
body, and the world: antennae whose links are as close as they are
unbreakable, where every experience is transformed into being, every
manner of being into multiple knowledge. The poet becomes *man the
creator*, and the philosopher the witness.

Yet this interplay between the two diversified complexes can be fully
exfoliated only within a new differentiation of function, in which the
soul emerges and within which Imaginatio Creatrix assumes the lead.

We will discover them in our subsequent analysis of the creative
process. (*supra*, pp. 152—166)

5. THE COMMON CONTEXTURE OF THE MIND AND THE BODY

In its organic functioning, the body is "the threshold of capricious
necessities and organized mystery. There the will ceases, and the sure
empire of knowledge."[77] It is the pedestal of life, but in its functioning it
remains outside of knowledge. It is remarkable to see that machine in
action. The man who feeds himself only gives a new impetus to his life;
but he is deaf and blind. He nourishes his goods and his ills. "Each

morsel which he feels melt away and dissipute within him brings new strength to his virtues, but also — indifferently — to his vices. It provides sustenance for his torments just as it fattens his hopes; and is divided somewhere between passions and reasons."[78] One would believe this functioning to be mysterious, so impartial and indifferent it appears. On the other side the soul by itself is disoriented, incapable of sorting out the real from the illusory. Put at the service of life, the props of knowledge have the appearance of falsehood or truth; but life — anchored in the mysterious natural — does not conclude. Truth and falsehood are only, at base, inventions of the mind which serve the soul admirably in defending and protecting itself. The conclusion belongs to the mind which poses limits and establishes contrasts between realities which in life are fluctuating. For life comports all the contrasts; it needs and uses all of them.[79]

The body can however be revealed under an entirely different aspect as a springboard from which the soul derives its impetus, as a means by which the soul becomes coextensive with its ramifications, and interpreter who translates into the language of the soul the muffled workings of nature, and finally the point of incarnation of knowledge. It can be so revealed in an access to complete life. The rebirth of the world is the rebirth of life. But one sees in the analysis of life as a totality that the soul by itself is incapable of reaching a well defined certainty, that knowledge is only an instrument, — and again somewhat arbitrarily — that the body is something other than the hidden mystery of organic functions. But that access to life is opened only through the creative consciousness proper to art. Dance is the most striking example of it.

In effect, we can see "complete" life as being comparable to a dancing woman. It is essentially reduced to "that mysterious movement which, taking the detour of everything that happens, transforms me unceasingly into myself and brings me back, promptly enough, to the same Socrates, so that I may find him again — so that, imagining perforce that I recognize him, I may *be* . . . ."[80] It is in reality in its corporeal limitation that life is comparable to the dancer, who "would cease divinely to be a woman if she could obey her bound up to the skies."[81] Form-movement, spark wholly spiritual, she is that only thanks to the movement of her body. It is the extension of her muscles, their articulation, the function attributed to each of them, and their admirable harmony in concerted play, which makes possible a flight, a succession of flights such that she rejoins the content of the soul. In its orchestration, the movement of the body succeeds in analyzing the world of ideas, in outlining their relations, in inventorying values; descending upon earth, it incorporates the pure forms of the world, the bird, the snowflake . . . . And yet, this movement is only a limit; otherwise the dancer would change into pure mind. It obeys the physical limits — insurmountable — that the limbs from which this movement arises oppose. The same nature which allows the dancer to take flight recalls her and returns her to earth. But her rigor and precision of movement can only be compared to those of the pure mind. The movement is concentrated in a form so perfectly incarnated, so authentic and so "just," so precise, that is seems "absorbed in pure precision." The functions are accomplished with such exactitude that one can believe "that here certainty is a sport . . . ." But this movement is not limited to sketching pure forms; it transmits a content other than itself and transforms it as it pleases; it "borrows" and "restores" elements, ties connections and unties them, varies the elements of sonorous substance and transmits its meaning so perfectly that it is substituted for sonority itself. See, then, that the dance appropriates the functions of the mind, its laws, and the extension of its powers. It is "as though knowledge had found its act, and intelligence on a sudden gives its consent to spontaneous graces."[82] The mind rediscovers itself in its functions, in its substance, and in its ideas within the laws projected by the mobile body. Body and mind are revealed, therefore, as analogous structures. Across a system which obeys physical laws, which is situated in three-dimensional space, the soul translates its own dimensions into those of space and matter. There it finds itself anew; there it is extended, as a soul is extended in *its* body. Constitutive phenomenology has spoken to us at length of the constitution of corporeal phenomena which arise from the awareness of certain physical laws; but it remains for us to discover not only the universal laws, but also the more particular laws which arrange things so that the mind can be moved in its intimacy with the body. That, only art can teach us.[83]

The soul is found again in the movements of the body. Arms and legs in movement now incarnate art itself, the plastic densities of peristyles, trellises, and columns, now nature as art reveals it, now a grove with branches agitated by the breezes of the music, of the torches. By these fluctuating exchanges, by these encounters of forms, the very mind recognizes itself in its own volubility: "I dream of those inexpressible contacts which take place in the soul between the beats, between the whitenesses and passes of those limbs moving in measure, and the strains of that muffled symphony on which all things seem to be painted and transported . . . ."[84] In this mixture of musical scent, of entirely carnal charm, the soul finds itself to be carnal and voluptuous. It is however at the same time a structure of sovereign Reason which is disclosed — and a living structure, all vigilance and all tension, all symmetry and all order, all acts. It is better ordered, more regulated than the real world ever will be, but it is still animated by a self-mastery which the intelligible in itself does not entail, as charming as it must be to create an illusion or a dream. One would say then that the body, transformed by art, becomes the place where "the real, the unreal, and the intelligible can fuse and combine as the power of the Muses dictates . . . ."[85] This spectacle, entirely in images, even makes us surpass the limits of life and of human awareness. Is one not justified in saying that "that infinity of these noble similitudes, the conversions, the inversions, the inexhaustible diversions which answer one another and are deduced from each other before our eyes, transport us into the realm of divine knowledge?"[86]

Dance however shows us still other phenomena of the body in which the soul is rediscovered. The dancer who starts a circular march puts the summit of her art into play: that assurance, that precision, that naturalness is the point of perfection, a second nature, not at all inborn but acquired at the price of immense effort. It is that effort, that mastery of limbs, of the precise play of muscles, that complete self-possession which allows these movements so simple and so *free*. Simplicity and freedom which are also those of the soul, and attained at the same price. Our habitual way of proceeding is so customary that it passes unnoticed. But the dance reveals to us the sense of walking as the relationship between our limbs and the ground, the security of this relationship which is that of the soul in the relations it establishes. Similarly, held in a perfect form, immobility is revealed as a wait, a meditation, the ultimate point of attention: "How can one avoid shouting: Silence!" Silence of the perfect instant, "delicious suspense of breath and of the heart." It is equally the universe of sensations, of emotions, which arises from the mastered body. The expert movements of feet and arms weave an indefinable carpet of sensations. Those toenails, animated by an intelligent fire, which attack, dodge, bind and unbind, are pursued and take flight, those feet which babble, wrangle, and sweep away together — it is a passionate drama which proceeds. The chain of movements is like a dialogue, a series of questions and answers. Let us however return to the fact that all this is only a series of movements of the body, that it is the mastery of bodily mechanisms which produces this strange uprooting of a being in relation to its natural milieu, that this pursuit of an incorporeal form cannot go on to infinity, and that this whole flight, after the rapid exhaustion of natural forces, is beaten down and disappears like an ephemeral apparition. It remains true nonetheless that the profound correspondence of the soul and the body is thus revealed to us wherein the soul finds itself anew as in its own medium, and thus are revealed to us the secret aptitudes of the body to become the natural medium of the soul and to be identified with it. The soul rediscovers itself, as it were in its frolics, at the heart of life: charms, falls, offerings, surprise feints, mysteries of presence and absence, of love and of hate, of avidity, feelings of power and impotence, in a word, "all the hazards of the real."

In the corporeal system, the secret architecture of the world is disclosed. Leaving behind its deaf shell, the body undertakes more ambitious temptations. It tries to be a partner to the soul, and an indispensable partner; better yet, it tries to make itself known by itself; finally, it even seeks to give the soul some light on the problems which concern it and which it cannot unravel. For example, love. And the body dares attempt to present not just any love, not a theatrical personage, a fiction, but the very being of love. How can one paint it?

"Well do we know that the soul of love is the invincible difference of lovers, while its subtle matter is the identity of their desires. Dance must therefore, by the subtlety of its lines, by the divineness of its upsurgings, by the delicacy of its tiptoe pauses, bring forth that universal creature which has neither body nor features, but which has gifts, days, and destinies — that has life and death; and which is even only life and death, for desire once born knows neither sleep nor respite.

"That is why the dancer alone can make love visible by her beautiful acts. Her whole self, O Socrates, was love! . . . She was toyings and tears, and unavailing feints! Charms, falls, offerings; and surprises, and yes's and no's, and steps sadly lost . . . . She was celebrating all the mysteries of absence and presence; she seemed sometimes to be hovering on the brink of ineffable catastrophes! . . . But now, as a thank offering to Aphrodite, look at her. Is she not of a sudden a very wave of the sea? — Now heavier than her body, now lighter — she bounds, as though dashed from a rock; she softly subsides . . . . She is a wave!"[87]

Thus, art has transported us to the heart of these transformations where knowledge discovers the body, where the body is sensitized under the hold of its act, and where both approach and penetrate one another and in a slow transmutation make a more intimate knowledge of the world arise. In the orchestration of that enterprise, each faculty of consciousness is in its proper place. The body and the soul in the search for an analogy of systems put the totality of their resources to work; and, in close quarters with the sequels of that transmutation, they must stay closest to the "quick," to the concrete in their matter. Guided by a lucid awareness of their laws, they recognize themselves in each of their operations: in the supreme creative instant in which they are born in relation to one another in a reciprocal intelligibility, the instant in which they are born together into a life which arises from it. This infinite process in which at every instant every segment recognizes itself by the awareness of its act as well as its power, and of its effects and of the seeds it sows, is knowledge identical to the operation of being, which poets and visionaries speak of but which lay in potency in every consciousness. Very near and very far away, it dozes in us as a Young Fate turned away from life, idle in its absolute silences, unknown. It is the reward of effort to activate it: a near-heroic effort which the poet Hemley tells us may be compared to that of passing the frontiers between life and death.[88] What is required is a change of attitude, of "the central attitude from which the enterprises of knowledge and the operations of art are equally possible; successful cooperation between analysis and action is more than probable — a marvelously stimulating thought."[89] One must go beyond the idle passivity of the body and take possession of its natural course, with its ends, as well as of its opposite, the pure self, sterile, disinterested, inhuman. One must confront their conflict by descending to the roots of both, taking upon oneself the responsibility and the risk of annihilation, and re-ascending victorious, transformed into a creator who on himself bears the weight of the reconquered universe, saved from disaster, This is a universe that one has reconstituted, that one has drawn from oneself with the pains and the fears of childbirth, a universe that one must maintain in life with his faith alone, without encouragement or witnesses. One becomes, oneself, a testimony before the universe.

In this work the body and the soul have found themselves on an equal footing. It is not the mind which projects structures into the matter of the body and which constitutes it as a body by its laws alone; to the contrary, the body has a structure, *an implicit internal harmonization*, identical to the contexture of consciousness, which helps to reveal it.

In return, consciousness is less autonomous, less enclosed in itself than constitutive phenomenology lets us believe; it depends upon the body in order to be exercised in the extension of the world and life. Thus the body and the soul appear to be correlative, like two partners, each one keeping one foot in its particular nature, but integrating itself into a vaster scheme which is alone susceptible of providing a complete explanation.[90] They are merely two fragments of a great mechanism playing their small role in a great play. Knowledge appears to unite contemplation and power, representation and action, disinterest moved by beauty alone and pragmatism in the service of the goals of nature. The appeal it makes to us is that of the higher vocation of man, incarnated in an action, in a work of the reconciliation of contraries, better yet, of their mobilization in a common work guaranteeing the harmonization of all man's resources in a fullness alone worthy of him.

The urgency of this appeal is particularly felt in an epoch in which the situation of man is so "fragmented" and in which the artist, who has always assumed the role of directing humanity, of enlightening it and renewing it by transforming its atrophied branches into healthy branches by making new sap flow, is disoriented before a task of an extreme complexity. He finds himself without a compass and without an anchor in a world which has long since renounced the fullness of its aspects, the orchestration of its powers, to dedicate itself to particular sectors artificially limited. The world has lost faith in the true vocation of humanity, so much has it been inspired by philosophies of action and immediate profit, of life measured by the present alone with all awareness of continuity lost. It is a world finally, in which one finds the effort personal perfection requires repugnant.[91]

Instead of seeking the essence, the artist looks for the shortcut; he is in quest of the striking, the particular, the extraordinary, and no longer of the full, the complete, the profound. Thus is fragmented that grand poetic Reality, which is of value only if it is not mutilated.

That Reality, however, like Great Art, is the reward of the voluntary combination of miracle and effort.

THE THEORETICAL RESULTS OF OUR ANALYSES
AND THE PERSPECTIVES THEY OPEN

In our analyses we have attempted to delve into the "phenomenon" of man's creative activity in its specific nature. It was a question of making that *activity itself speak*, in making its procedures, its preoccupations, its points of support arise in the quick, in the concrete. Thus we have looked at this "phenomenon" as it is immersed in the lived reality of the poet.

It is at present a matter of grasping the ensemble of our intuitions, hitherto scattered, but which yet disclose the interior connections which unite them. In effect, these connections, while having their source in human life, stretching across the whole of man's universe, show themselves to have an entirely specific form. Proceeding from phenomenological intuitions, that form comes to the foreground in detailed concrete investigations; thus it could orient our inquiry. Let us try to interpret the scattered elements of our analyses in order to seize, in an explicit way, the creative phenomenon in this form: as the CREATIVE CONTEXT.

The theory of creative context which is outlined here thus promises an integral way of embarking on a more ample, systematic investigation of human creation unraveling a new, primogenital field in which the great philosophical issues of all times will emerge in their pristine nature before our speculative reflection sets in to distort it.

THE CREATIVE CONTEXT

(a) *The frame of reference*

As we have announced from the beginning, the intuition of the creative context has presided over our inquiry. Although this concept seems to be prior to systematic research, it is itself the fruit of that research which proposes to establish its validity in its concrete substance. While being sketched in the intuition of human creation in its specificity, the concept of creative context allows us to orient ourselves in the ensemble of domains upon which creation leans, to distinguish and reconnect

113

particular elements, necessary constituents of creative activity, which by ricochet are verified as the bundle of fundamental relations inherent in the creative phenomenon. Analysis of the creative act in effect shows that it extends to all the elements of the human world, that it ties them together by a subtle connection after having grasped them at the crucial point of the *birth of the world*, when its form and its existence are decided. It is on the basis of that intuition that the creative context is outlined. We have seen these elements at work; it is now a question of specifying how they are organized into a particular configuration apt to promote and direct physical and psychic activities and form a skeleton in relation to which those activities — which, considered in themselves, pursue fragmentary goals — are articulated in a finalistic manner.

For, this is the principal point, the creative context is by nature subordinated to an end; it is established in function of the objective, distinct, and autonomous work that it serves to realize. It is comparable to a loom on which the work is woven. By the accomplishment of that task, which is separate only in appearance, the creative context bears on the totality of the human universe by introducing a new form of human existence. What then are its principal points, its props, its characteristic aspects?

(b)   *The creative process suspended between two phases of the constituted world*

In the first place, creative activity has its roots in the condition of the individual man; it aims at man as a distinct being occupying a place among other beings of his type — which defines his social condition — as well as man as a being necessarily occupying a place in the assemblage of beings that we call nature. In both cases, he is determined at once by the universal laws of these domains and by the ensemble of relations he entertains with other beings within each sphere. It is that ensemble of relations at two levels that the vocabulary of phenomenology terms "the constituted world." The constituted world is the result of these rapports-relations. Thus therefore the creative activity of which man is at the same time source and agent arises from the *constituted world*. Creative inspiration does not at all emerge in a separated being; it is from the beginning necessarily tributary to the commerce man entertains which other men because he is not only in great part a product of this world but also participates by his functions in its particular *configuration* such as it is lived by him in the instant. The origin of creative inspiration is bound to the lived experience of man in relation to the world and to himself.

The life of the individual takes the form of "mundane" participation; his most intimate emotions and intuitions, even the most individual, are more or less closely bound to "mundane" experiences such as love, social relations, habitation, nourishment. Each of these experiences is lived in a particular form which expresses participation in the constituted world.[92]

It is equally individual consciousness, insofar as it participates in the world, which from its conception guides the evolution of the work in germ. The form that the initial inspiration gradually acquires in order to issue in a work is not constructed in the secrecy of an individual consciousness *closed* upon itself, nor in relation to the isolated elements of a transcendence separated from that consciousness, nor even from a universal consciousness. One has in any case insisted only too much on the influence of the milieu, of the epoch, etc. in the genesis of a work. That of which it is here a question is the work's participation in its creation in the constituted world through the dependence of natural man in relation to the world — of man insofar as he conceives, produces, and fashions the work and who is himself the product of this world that he reflects in miniature as a Leibnizian monad. However, it is remarkable that creation signifies a radical break with the received world.

At the other extreme, the world is also the endpoint of the creative process. The creative act aims indirectly at the world in a movement of revolt in order to transform it. The work whose preparation is pursued in the individual consciousness is destined to penetrate into the world in order to confront it. The direction the artist takes in fashioning his work expresses his constant concern with that encounter between the nascent work and the world, for the finished work erupts into the world by blowing up the framework it had found there.[93]

Thus the creative process, suspended between these two terminal points, is extended by a multiform current to *two temporary phases* of the constitutive world. These two phases become the reference points of the creative context and the dynamic frontiers of this functional network. They correspond to the vocation of the work, which is *to surpass the acquired state of things*. The created work signifies in effect a re-creation of the human world; it invites us to a new form of experience, constrains us to assent to a new synthesis of inframundane alliances, of nature and spirit, body and soul. How these alliances are made, what are their points of support, the factors of their transformation, all that was the object of our concrete analyses. In specifying the idea of a context within which these operations arise, it suffices to point out that between these two terms creative experience reveals the existence of *two currents of sensibility in an unceasing transformation of intensity and quality.* By that very fact is indicated the subjacent existence of an *invisible woof to which the two dynamic currents are referred in the last resort.*

(c) *Creation, a rupture with the constituted world: Toward the emergence of a new contexture of the human world*

That woof on which creative activity labors, on which the work is first woven under the form of *sensibility* and *reflection,* implies the emergence of a *new contexture of the human world.* New, that is, in relation to the world received in the beginning, the constituted world, which, suspended from the operations which constitute it, can only be perpetuated in its established framework without anything fundamentally unforeseeable being able to befall it.[94] *The emergence of the creative context therefore here signifies revolt, a · rupture with the constituted world.* Whereas phenomenological constitution shows us the human mind limited to the constellation of human functions of a particular type repeating themselves to infinity, the *woof subjacent to creative activity presupposes, as its reason for being, the existence of an infinity of possible variants.*

We have shown how this division between constitution and creation, between knowledge, established being, and the being in progress which renews that knowledge, is manifested. There will still be a question of analyzing the creative process in its full extent between the two-phases of the life-world, of doing a theoretical study of it and of showing that division at work. The universality of the constitutive function does not by any means have the last word on the deep nature of human consciousness. If one were to limit himself to its procedures, he could not explain how there is in the world the eruption of novelty, of originality. Many questions have remained thus far in the background, but their solutions are prefigured on the basis of our analyses. They will come to full light in the central panel of our investigation.

Thus we therefore speak of the creative context as an ensemble of antennae suspended between two facets of reality and which a subjacent weft coordinates. It is thus a part of the world under its double aspect, but its relations with the world are referred to a center of transmission, to a source of activity whence these antennae arise not as static relationships but as *active functions* which are returned to their place once their function is accomplished. These antennae which avoid the radical break between the two phases of the constituted world come forth from a dynamic foyer of *will, judgment*, and *choice*, and return there. This foyer is not just human consciousness in its "pure," translucent nature. The latter belongs to the world, but in a particular manner: it appears there as the agent of constitution, the engineer of the human objective world. In appearance delivered to the world, it is in fact extraordinarily folded back upon itself, manifesting itself only in what derives from it. It gives itself to the world, however, without ever abandoning the privilege of being a passionate observer, or a Promethean dreamer. The functional complex discussed here in terms of mind-body is, in its role, which is to project, to choose and to transform the world and itself, in measure like a demiurge with virtual powers to break all connections and to confound all pre-established designs in order to take flight toward a universe of possibilities. Here we see lurking the engine of this flight, Imaginatio Creatrix, which will break into the foreground in the proper place.

(d) Creative inwardness *and the new functional orchestration*

Indeed, the mind is not as impartial and transparent as the pure phenomenological attitude postulates it to be; for it is before all else the agent of a drama. This drama of human life involves it in its depths and places it at close quarters with all the factors of the human condition. Through struggles and tensions, the mind sees its prerogatives but also its limits, for it cannot avoid questioning itself on its universal possibilities, on its origins, on the validity of its rules. Being the foyer of its own progress, whose laws appear in its works, being also the foyer of its own uneasiness and of its aspirations, the mind cannot be satisfied with the given; it cannot renounce the need to seek to rend its temporal limitations, to enlarge its powers, to modify its procedures.

The inquiry it conducts upon itself surpasses the frameworks of direct observation. In order *to transform itself*, the mind must go out from present acquisitions. The mind cannot attain its hidden virtualities in the present, it requires a *conjecture* to grasp them, it must therefore *con-clude* to them. In being discovered to itself in its potentialities the mind is transfigured. Thus it forges its own laws, projecting its own forms and imposing its own restrictions. In short, it becomes *creative inwardness.*

In order for an unforeseen form to be disengaged from the foundation of the ordinary functionings of consciousness, it is necessary that some-thing essential be changed.

A new functional orchestration oriented by the imperious desire for a new form arises from the encounter of our spontaneous acts bursting from the field of consciousness with the constructive sallies of a mind become aware of its powers and of the wealth of its means. Is creative inwardness anything other than the foyer founded by that new alliance of functions which are incarnated in the filters and prisms of a mind become selective which forge molds and project new variants of structures?

All our spontaneous manifestations, from our acts as they appear in the full light of consciousness to the secret pulsations of an obscure natural substratum, acts of intelligence as well as acts of emotion, meet in that inwardness, entering together into the weaving of an original and unique work, of a new universe.

Let us now uncover its primogenital forces, faculties and instruments in their full expansion, which is that of life itself, with the Human Condition at its heart.

CONCLUDING BY WAY OF TRANSITION TO THE CENTRAL PANEL OF THE TRIPTYCH

Let us assess the most salient point of our foregoing investigations, which will serve as the underground cable of our query.

The debate that ensues from our contrasting and opposing the creative and the constitutive functions of the human being has opened up naturally the most fundamental philosophical exploration of all, the *critique of reason.* Immanuel Kant undertook this critique, as we know, on three different levels, but he was trapped by human consiousness, and remained stranded on that island in an uncharted sea. Edmund Husserl, focusing one-sidedly upon the "absolute rationality" of the intellect and clarifying its origin by unraveling the subjacent network of the intentional constitution of objectivity, was fated in his pursuits to never get out from under the shadow of its highest accomplishments. In contrast to both of these great thinkers who paved for us the way into the tantalizing unknown, we, by grabbing the ox by the horns, avoid the traps which they set for themselves. With the creative act revealing itself to be the Archimedean point of the *human enterprise within the constructive strategies of life at large,* we enter the critique of reason full-fledgedly and free from all biases; the individualization of life in its constructive progress alone can give us an opening through which to pursue the ultimate question, an opening vainly sought thus far, — the question of the *origin and differentiation of sense.*

THE ORIGIN OF SENSE

*The Creative Orchestration of the Modalities of Beingness
within the Human Condition*

CHAPTER ONE

THE CREATIVE CONTEXT AS CIRCUMSCRIBED BY THE CREATIVE PROCESS — ITS ROOTS "BELOW" AND ITS TENTACLES "ABOVE" THE LIFE-WORLD:

Uncovering the Primogenital Status of the Great Philosophical Issues

PART I

ART AND NATURE: CREATIVE VS. CONSTITUTIVE PERCEPTION

SECTION 1. THE CREATIVE STIRRINGS

The stage is set for the systematic exploration of the great issues. Human creativity lies at the juncture of all the great philosophical issues. To begin with, when we bring up the question of creativity, then ever since the imitation-theory of Plato and his division between the fluctuating, changeable world of appearances, on the one hand, and the perduring, lasting forms of ideas, on the other hand, we point to the issues of the relation between Art and the "reality" of life — or better, Art and Nature. It is also in this perspective of the distinction between Art and Nature that Pradines, in his classical work, raises the question of the origin of Art, approaching it from the psychologico-genetic point of view.[1] His perspective might be one-sided; nevertheless, his penetrating intuitions go beyond the narrow framework of psychology and meet ours in setting the issue at hand, which makes his thought particularly pertinent to the introduction of our main point.

Pradines pursues his investigation of the origin of Art through the genesis of human functioning within the evolution of the species. There is an intuitive thread which runs through his analysis which makes it most relevant to our own reflection. In his descriptive account of the way in which, according to his intuitive insights, progress in complexity resulting in specific advances in functioning manifests itself, he distinguishes the act of invention as the crucial step by which man differentiates himself from the rest of his species. Its incipient preparatory step consists of the radical change in posture from the horizontal to the upright. Through his vertical posture the human animal liberates his two front extremities which, then used as "hands," allow the "making" of things. Invention/making/*techne* conducts, first, the development of the specifically human life-course. Invention — which emerges together with the liberating development of the means to "make," to "work" — for Pradines, as for Bergson, still follows the rules of life's "adaptation" to circumstance, that is, the rules set by what I call the *vital significance of life*. At a certain point, however, invention separates itself from the tight significant network confined to life's system. It is this point which is of interest for our reflection.

In principle, Pradines' line of thought coincides with our own "evolutive genesis" of the living individual. In the genetic approach to *life's constructive progress* adopted in our work, the *inventive act* appears also as the instance that, in its consequences, differentiates man from among living beings as the founder of a new species. However, in drastic contrast to Pradines, it is not the functional *manifestation of this act* that comes to the front of our attention. As if by a provisory bypass, we delve into its *operational meaning-bestowing specificity.* What merits special attention is, nevertheless, the coincidence between Pradines' and our analysis on the point of *describing how invention sets off on its own, taking a distance from our natural functioning, or, from "Nature."*

In his quest after the origin of Art, Pradines raises the question: What is it that constitutes the difference between the "natural sound" of water in a stream or waterfall, the sound of wind rustling in the leaves, of hail in a storm, etc., and the sound of "music." Opposing the classical theories of the origin of music, he proposes that in nature *there are* only noises; in contrast, what we call "music" or "musical sound" is the fruit of invention. Indeed, while the noises of nature awaken within us meaningful responses to our vital concerns — that is, our hearing enters into an associative web of our concerns with life —, we leave, on the wings of invention, these associative entanglements that tie us down to the earth behind. The swing of invention undercuts the entering into play of the vitally significant concerns, and we replace them by *enchantment* with nature, lofty and "airy" aesthetic and poetic elements, "disinterested" in the vital cares of the moment and beyond the snares of the vital interests, incorporating, so to speak, our sensation into a larger experiential complex. At such a turn Art takes off, leaving Nature behind; it is the incipient moment of Art crystallized in a *pre-perceptual* "sensation." Pradines emphasizes the nature of this "sensation" by giving it a role of "radical mutation" in the sentient circuit of life's functioning. Concern with "adaptation" to the natural — vital — course of life is here suspended and replaced by an "enchantment" with Nature, and the pedestrian everydayness of experience recedes before a novel aesthetic horizon. Pradines' one-sided, psychological perspective precludes his drawing the proper conclusion from this important insight. He fails to make the immediate link between this instance of "radical mutation" and the creative function of man, whereas the radicality of this mutation lies precisely, as we will see in our analysis which follows, in its marking the point at which the life-subservient functional system breaks down and, under the pressures of subterranean forces, and specifically human virtualities begin the work of bringing forth the new, CREATIVE FUNCTIONING.

In what follows we will attempt to isolate precisely this instance of the "radical mutation" from the entire network of the functional systems which intersect with each other in this instance. However, we will not restrict our inquiry to the *manifestation* of evolutionary progress but, on the contrary, seek its *modi operandi.* The great significance of Pradines' intuition came to light once we could identify it as staying in a perfect analogy with the incipient phase of the "creative perception." Creative perception, as I will show, represents, however, a *phase* comprising *the entire self-interpretive operational system of the living individual-on-the-brink* of turning into the specifically human self-construction. This may be witnessed in each characteristic instance of the creative process, whether in the fine arts or in philosophical or scientific creativity.

We will then delve into the operational circuits of the *functional transition from the "vital" to the "creative functioning"* within which the *new system bestowing meaning upon life unfolds.* Its play of forces appears within the field of actual consciousness in the networks of their schematic articulations, partly directly, partly "in profile." Indeed, our functioning appears to us directly in its operations constitutive of the objective forms of life, "presencing" (*Vergegenwärtigen*) then in the field of consciousness in consciousness' fundamental mode, which is perception. We will deal in the first place then with the fundamental, life-subservient perception constitutive of natural phenomena. Constitutive perception, as conceived by Husserl, lies in the full light of the field of consciousness — immediately open to inspection. It is upon its ground that the "radical mutation" takes place. Mutation occurs in opposition to it, and by means of mechanisms which dismember its constructive schema and set the operational forces free to take on new roles within a different constructive system. Its operations lying "in between" the constitutive and the creative systems do not yet "presentify" any objective structure in the actual field of consciousness; we may "see" them only "in profile" as they enter into a new system which, being as yet unco-ordinated, merely lurks on the horizon: *the system of the passage from the constitutive perception of Nature to the "creative perception" of an aesthetic object.*

In our exploration of this "twilight zone," in which at the point of encounter between two different regions of sense we enter into the bowels of life itself, we will follow the lines of the two main contrasting — and yet mutually indispensable — basic functions of the living, specifically human, being, the *constitutive* and the *creative*. Their respective regulative principles and rules will, by this contrast, come clearly to light.

We will embark upon this exploration by contrasting their fundamental modality which is perception as it stands on the brink of its passage from the first to the second. The radius of their respective tentacles will indicate the *creative context*. The groundwork for the philosophical debate will be laid down.

SECTION 2. CREATIVE PERCEPTION AND ORIGINALITY

In evaluating something as "original" we place it in opposition to the totality of human experience in its present state and as we have known it. Something is "original" if it distinguishes itself in this world as a "novel form" in the world's structure and in human experience. Thereby, originality is related to the *living world* (life-world) and to *human experience*, both of which can be traced, in the phenomenological approach, to the constitutive function of consciousness. Furthermore, the essential feature of perception (based on its phenomenological constitution) is to guarantee through its recurrent forms the *intersubjectivity* as well as the *identity* of the experienced world, despite the fluctuations of infinite perceptual instances.

And yet, as the evolution of culture shows, the forms of structure and experience of the lived world relentlessly evolve. We attribute this evolution to man's CREATIVE activity. However, human creativity does not merely emerge from the constituted world, but also remains in many ways dependent upon cognition (constitution). Moreover, upon examination we find a striking resemblance between the creative process itself and the process of constitutive perception. We can, indeed, consider the creative process to be a type of perception, a "CREATIVE PERCEPTION."[2] How, then, could creation renovate forms when constitution obviously follows preestablished patterns?

What is the fundamental difference between constitutive and creative perception that makes novelty and originality possible? With these questions the great debate is opened. We will succinctly set the corner points of the argument which will underlie our investigation of the creative process to follow.

(a) *The analogy between constitutive and creative perception*

As we know, "natural" perception (constitutive of objectivity) is not an instantaneous occurrence producing a ready-made "image" or "sense datum," but a complex process proceeding through a series of instantaneous occurrences of perceptual glimpses. They bring new material into the field of consciousness, the elements of which, after discrimination, coalesce progressively toward the constitution of a coherent, complete, "object." In a parallel manner, in the "subjective" phase of the creative phenomenon, the creative process consists of a series of distinct instances which are carried along by an inherent mechanism, progressing in succession. This mechanism, which "perceives," dismembers, discriminates and reorganizes the material thus coming into focus in consciousness, is oriented toward the construction of the CREATIVE PRODUCT. The PERCEPTUAL GLIMPSES which carry along both processes are confused, fragmentary, inexplicit; they are in need of clarification, they demand completion. Perception, creative as well as constitutive, is progressive clarification, in which discriminated elements are reestablished as significant parts of a new synthesis. We may conclude that these similar features define a formal skeleton of operations or mechanisms which is analogous in both constitutive and creative perception.

(b) *The different regulative principles and frameworks of reference of the two types of perception*: theme *versus* "essence" (eidos)

Furthermore, in both types of perception, clarification advances by "completion" and "verification," and yet the guiding principles and the frameworks of reference for choosing and verifying radically differ. To substantiate these statements we will focus now not upon the formal structure but upon the *network of the concrete operations* in the processes under discussion. In order for any new material (whose announcement to the self signals an incipient phase of perception) to be brought into the actual field of consciousness, the field itself has to disintegrate, its actual pattern has to be dismembered, to permit procedures of discrimination and selection toward a new association of its elements into a new pattern in which the introduced material prevails. In the constitution of the cognitive object such a reorganization is guided by *models of recurrent structural forms* with ultimate reference to one given structural system responsible for the already constituted world. The initial CHAOS of the disintegrated field is RELATIVE, a simple transition between *two different forms of one given system*. This system corresponds to the analytic visibility at the level of what Husserl has called *eidoi* which purposively guide the architectonic operations.

In creative perception, on the contrary, the initial chaos is RADICAL in the sense of an absolute indetermination. Not only are sensations, ideas, images — work of the actual field of consciousness (the integral content) — torn apart and dissociated from their actual net of interconnections, they are also *torn from their frame of reference*, and the *system of laws of their actual coalescence is suspended*. To put it more concretely, the "eye" of an artist or scholar penetrates much deeper than we do in our natural cognitive attitude. It does not stop at the operational level of the cognitive/constitutive system of consciousness. It ignores its "snarls" and seeks to penetrate beneath them. In order to do so the artist or scholar not only has to "pierce" through the meaningful web of objectivity within which he himself is as if "absorbed," but he has to disentangle himself from its ties, which run through his entire functional system. This effort disintegrates the "natural" perceptual context, not only at the analytic level of the given structural system of the constituted world, but in an "absolute" way; that is, at all levels that imagination suggests as possible, so as to make those elements vary freely (as prospective constituents of a new pattern) at any level subsequently and tentatively chosen. Thus artist and scholar often select seemingly quite incongruent elements as those most appropriate for unusual associative links. Indeed, "as an artist," "as a scholar," "as a poet," etc., we "see" the same thing differently from how we normally see it.

To illustrate this disintegrative/reconstructive phase which is essential to *all* modalities of constitutive perception, whether it is of the "real," "fictitious," ("sensory," "intellectual," perceptual) mode of objects, or of that specific mode of "fictitious," and fancied objects, we find the most appropriate and striking example in the incipient phase of representational art: that is, in the incipient instance of the creative process which takes off from the perception of Nature to search out its "representation" in an aesthetic experience. There is a radical difference between the spectacle of nature which we admire and the landscape which inspired its "representation" as a work of art. The layman perceives the spectacle of nature, "re-cognizing" it as an instance of a familiar type of object. In his constitutive process it has been construed with reference to this structural type as its architectonic principle, intentionally orienting its operations. On the contrary, (1) the same scenery, approached as a prospective pictorial landscape, that is with the "searching eye" of an artist, initiates a radical chaos in the actual field of consciousness because there is nothing concrete in the scenery that could even indirectly "enter" into the "landscape," and (2) the *architectonic operations* of the reconstruction ("clarification," "completion") process do not find offhand guiding principles, structural models of a ready-made (given) structural system. From the very beginning the artist proceeds by searching through more and more penetrating dissociations and comparisons, and tentative variations of distinct elements at all possible structural levels, looking for ever new prospective proportions, symmetries and dissymmetries, analogies between colors, intensities, densities, linear shapes, surfaces, etc. From this trial and error procedure there emerges a bare outline of a provisory pattern, a THEME of the prospective landscape toward which the architectonic operations will be directed.

The art/reality relation brings this situation clearly into the light. Indeed, the possibility of a *radical transformation of the field of consciousness is the condition for authentic artistic activity.* Scenery, a human face, a figure, still life, etc., should not appear in a stylized form like the work itself if it is supposed to serve as an "inspiration" for creation. In Henry James' *The Real Thing*, a simple girl of a nearly indefinable type serves much better as the model for a society lady than a highly sophisticated woman who is already quite "stylish." The latter can serve only "reproduction," in which there is no room for any basic change, addition, or transformation, and which consists merely of a quasi-passive reconstruction. And innumerable other examples could be given (e.g., the artistic sterility of the most spectacular Swiss scenery or the fecundity of the hazy light of the French Riviera), in which creation is not a simple process of reproduction, a reconstruction of a given type in a different medium (which is, in principle, the case with copying or photography). In order to inspire art, reality has to appear in a nearly undefined, uncrystallized form. Taking its impetus from features only vaguely outlined, imagination is stimulated by this vagueness to unfold its wings toward the crystallization of a novel "reality." The intrinsic potentialities of this undetermined given material become essential and, scrutinizing them, we try all possible forms and structural systems searching for that most appropriate for this given material, in our movement toward an entirely unforeseeable configuration. Even the most "realistic" artistic representation means transfiguring, regrouping, transforming, adjusting and readjusting toward the progressive crystallization of a novel form. This adjustment and readjustment proceeds with reference to the THEME, which, while regulating the operations, is by these operations itself being transformed. The theme, on the one hand, regulates the architectonic operations of creative perception and, on the other, is (1) essentially indicated by the potentialities of the perceptual material, and (2) transformed by the architectonic operations applied to this material. This TWO-WAY TRAFFIC IS CRUCIAL TO CREATIVE PERCEPTION AND TO THE CREATIVE PHENOMENON IN GENERAL.

With this analogy we have gained a foothold within the network of human/actual/virtual functioning at the point where all its arteries meet. All the freer positions explode from this center: what brings the inquisitive searching "eye" into motion? Where do the natural laws of the constituting consciousness end, and where do the new ones which take over the chaos come from? How is the transition from one set of laws to the other carried out? What is its significance? With these questions we enter into analysis of the creative process and will seek its bearings. They circumscribe the *creative context* of man's functioning.[3] The hooks which the creative orchestration throws into the twilight zone of seemingly chaotic turmoil were already sheathed in crevasses, which hidden presence the above analysis of the origin of creative perception emphasizes.

SECTION 3. THE CREATIVE QUEST FOR "AUTHENTIC REALITY" AND THE FALLACY OF THE "RETURN TO THE SOURCE"

(a) *The quest for the "authentic sense" of reality in the creative endeavor*

What is simplest in experience calls for an investigation of a most extensive life-complex for its philosophical exfoliation. So the matter stands with what we call "reality." An issue which has been an object of discussion since the beginning of Occidental culture — and one could venture that it is so in every culture — lies at the heart of the artistic endeavor. One could say that art and science, as such, are a pursuit of "better" ways to express "true reality." All exemplary works of art and science offer a new perspective upon reality. Each great scientist and artist wrestles with the question, "What is real?" directly. This very preoccupation of the creative pursuit with what is for a simple unreflective mind a "matter of fact" indicates that for the specifically human significance of life's vital course "reality" or the "real" (as *specificum*) is the crux of a controversial wonder. An immeasurable host of essential insights into the nature of reality have been advanced so far, and the ever-renewed attempts of artists, scientists and writers to come closer to reality and go deeper into its heart in their creative efforts by inventing ever-new devices for expression and means of literary transformation of seemingly "external" reality into an "internalized" form indicate that reality in itself is ungraspable — changing with each new perspective we adopt. We will ever be trying to approximate it but never shall we obtain an "essential" view. Only the synergetic nature of the creative act of the writer, painter, scholar, etc., may bring us into vertiginous contact with the generic nature of the real, but reality as such will elude every effort of cognition.

The wide and ever-widening spread of perspectives on the real, which new styles of art, science and technique open, may be seen as variations on the same basic theme of the becoming nature of reality. In each authentic work of art/science reality is present. Each of its new styles enriches and diversifies the perspectives. Yet it is our view, which we will substantiate, that these cannot pretend to bring out something about the real basically other than what other authentic works do, because the real is "real" only insofar as it is an all-embracing whirl of existence — in the making, a primary modality of life. It can only make us attentive to it by refreshing our sensibility of it, and by sharpening our reflection about it.

However, within the creative approach adopted here, in which all the perspectives meet at the point of their diversification as guidelines for meaning unfolding, we may take the plunge into the stream of life and, through the refinements of the creative orchestration, the intuitive sense of both the "reality of life" and of "reality" — in its specifically human significance — may be elucidated. In fact, the transformatory proceedings centered on reality in art/science may teach us not directly what the real is, but what we mean by "reality" as such. Furthermore, within the analysis of the creative process, this research will show us — in contrast with the latter — what reality as an *essential/existential mode of life* is made of. Let us observe that the clearest expression of the real is attempted by the art of literature. Due to its verbal/conceptual forms it also confronts philosophical views most directly. Hence we will take literature to be representative of the creative effort.

We will then address ourselves to the issue of the relationship of reality and literature in creative experience. Since the issue itself raised by philosophers or writers is of a philosophical nature, it calls first for a clarification of concepts used, which are philosophical in nature as well as being fruits of the history of philosophy.

We must, then, ask on the one hand: What do we mean by "reality"? and, on the other: What is the relationship of the literary work to reality? Since this relationship appears in the first place to be a certain way of participating in "reality" through the literary work, we must then ask: How does the creative act in which the literary work originates establish this participation?

This first question must be envisaged, first, from the epistemological point of view. That is, we have to (a) differentiate "reality" from illusion, imagination, hallucination or fiction. Furthermore, it has to (b) be viewed as a global phenomenon of appearance or presence (*Vergegen-wärtigung*) of the human life-world with all that it contains; this appearance we call "objectivity." Second, the question calls for a metaphysical clarification. Do we understand by "reality" the very ground for all the "appearances," in which the human faculties constitutive of them also reside, or, the very conditions of this constitution "external" to man in which, however, he is rooted and which work themselves through his existence, — and which we call "Nature"?

Third, we cannnot overlook the modal aspect of the understanding of "reality." It plays a decisive role in the elucidation of the two previous types. Namely, in the essential function of incarnating the "creative idea," the "real" is usually dialectically coupled with its counterpart, the "possible," on the one hand, and the "actual," on the other. In their existentially significant oppositional character all these points of view and differentiations exercise a leading impact in the creative architectonics.

These issues — too well known, in fact, to necessitate dwelling further upon their role — enter into what, since Aristotle, has been called "mimesis" seen as the royal way by which reality in all its differentiations may enter into art in general and literary work in particular. In its crudest form it has been seen as the mimesis of the "external" reality of the life-world and life; then as the mimesis of the inward reality of the writer. We will approach it neither from the "outside" nor from the "inside" of reality already formed in experience, nor from the side of its already objectified *specificum* of the "real." If the term "mimesis" has to be used, it will find here a new connotation, that of the *inner workings of reality as such.*

The question which predominates in investigating literary creativity along the above enunciated lines is: What does mimesis approached in the *crucibles of the creative act* teach us about the *real* in art/literature and the *possible* in the real life? In its metaphysical formulation this question reads: *What are the conditions of possibility, reality and actuality in the Human Condition?*

The question of "authentic reality" belongs, as mentioned above, to the deepest reflections of artists and poets on their art. Yet this is not a type of objectifying reflection that takes a distance from their work; on the contrary, *this reflection constitutes one of the deepest lines of the creative quest itself.*

We will begin to investigate the issue of reality as seen through the metaphysical interrogation of the poet. As such, it lies at the cross-section of central philosophical issues which preoccupy contemporary philosophical thinkers as well as art critics.

(b) *The "return to the source": Creative destructuring and re-construction; the fallacy of so-called "de-construction"*

We owe first to the reader some preliminary considerations about the philosophical tendency of our times to return to the "source," "origins," or "grounds" — and its futility.

The dominating drive of our age is one of basic renewal through a "return to the source." We have developed an unquestioned belief that the present can be exhaustively understood by probing its genesis, because the forms of experience and expression in life, art, religion and our very own personalities are seen as fruits of the past. They are assumed to be constructs, partly based on man's faculties and partly conditioned by circumstances and intended to hide like a screen the "authentic," the "genuine," the only valid core of "reality" lying there. Empirical psychology claims that what is really "genuine" in man are his primitive drives and strivings. Anthropology in order to find the meaning of our cultural life, in all its aspects, social institutions and habits, religion and its practices, and the orientation of our personal life turns to the myths of the primitive man. Psychoanalysis is founded upon the creed that the most personal, most profound ways of feeling, desiring and evaluating that make our existence are distortions of our "natural" instincts; these should be dissolved, reduced to first elements for the sake of the recovery of our genuine being. Philosophy took the lead in this universal quest for renovation, and the fine arts that followed it devaluated and rejected all the established forms developed through history. They seek, in naive, spontaneous experience the "pure" form of feeling, "genuine" truth or beauty, as if such an instance existed without being formed by an experiential apparatus capable of achieving it. Its capacity means, however, a certain stage has been accomplished in the line of evolution of the living individual which is man. The quest for a radical and *uniquely* valid *beginning of human experience* is most appropriate, but to assume that it corresponds to an already pre-given "reality," "ground," or a basic network of experiences that we could call a "primordial life-world" is not only questionable, but absurd. WE RADICALLY CHALLENGE SUCH A CONTENTION.

The question indeed arises: "Is this claimed return to the source not an illusion? That is, we ask, whether the "primitive," "primordial experience" sought could possibly be such a unique, authentic, genuine, original source of man's "nature"?

It will be shown, first, that there is *no privileged experience free from pre-established structures*; second, that the creative effort through which humanity renovates itself is completely misunderstood when identified with the scientific or philosophical quest after a privileged "authentic reality."

We will then analyze the quest after the "true reality" of the poet and philosopher in which, as poignantly shown by the philosophical pursuits of Jean Wahl, he destructurizes — or as it is now popular to say, "deconstructs" — all the forms. This will bring us to the conclusion that there is no "true reality," or "ground," or "substructure" in which that reality has its roots.[4] On the contrary, it will come to light that reality maintains an existential status of its own, emerging and poised between the workings of the *network of the stream of life and man's creative act.*

On the basis of this realization we will be prepared to investigate the *nature of the creative quest* so as to disentangle it from its relation to the *cultural inheritance of man.*

SECTION 4. THE TRANSCENDENTAL ILLUSION OF THE
RETURN TO THE SOURCE

Whatever may be the reasons for which science and philosophy attempt to disentangle the net of formal constructions which the evolving human mind has established for his own use and man's survival, the reason for which, rightly or wrongly, the contemporary artist also seeks the primitive virginal state of man, is different. The purpose of the artist is not to satisfy intellectual curiosity over what is the basic set-up of the human being, or the original, initial state of human virtualities from which the self-constructing process starts. The purpose of the artist is to find the virginal source of human creative endeavor, not as something geared to man's survival and vital progress, but to artistic accomplishment, to the satisfaction of his nostalgias and higher yearnings. Could the artistic creative endeavor have originated in that functioning oriented strictly toward the promoting of human life? We will show that it does not. To the contrary, the artistic quest stems from dissatisfaction with everyday life. But, first of all, if the artist essentially does not seek to discover the ways of empirical reality but seeks after something which naturally evolving life does not offer, and if his creative endeavor does not serve the aims of life and contribute to the world as it is devised for those aims, can the source of his creative elevations be found in the primitive set-up of the human mind? Can there be a source of the artistic, creative endeavor which would reach beyond the limitations of the established world, which this endeavor is meant to transcend, and that would offer the "virginal ground" of all forms and feelings to be sought in a return to the primitive, undeveloped experience of man and his basic virtualities?

Let us approach this basic question by an investigation of the nature of experience.

If we consider the nature of experience as such we must state its three essential components.

First of all, at every stage of its development — though this is evident principally at the very incipient stage of human reaction, such that it rises to the level of experience — there is the *Initial Spontaneity.*[5] It surges blind and bare as the expression of life itself but is ready to perpetuate life according to its demands and is fitted out for this purpose. If this initial spontaneity acquires the status of human experience, that is if, from its blind stage, it reaches an opening into the light of a self-conscious dimension, this is because its emergence must have activated the various virtualities of the individual being within which it surges. Experience that is basically spontaneous is evidently strictly individual, unshareable. It cannot be transferred from one being to another; its origin, whatever be its roots, which are not directly inspectable, is restricted, as they are, to one specific individual. It is spontaneity only and exclusively insofar as it is his very own, most intimate, force and motor; the spontaneity of an individual in such and such most complex (and in its complexity, ungraspable) conditions, within the natural and social universe of man. This unique concreteness which it shares with individual life alone is, however, complemented at its very emergence by a *universally human system of functioning*. In fact, spontaneity alone would not amount to more than (to use an expression of Dylan Thomas') "the force that through the green fuse drives the flower" had it not simultaneously activized the faculties which account for intelligibility.

The temporal constitution of spontaneity in its entire current of forces, pulsations, etc. initiates, in fact, the activity of the whole system of informing and forms it in both its feeling and signifying aspects: it is something which takes the form of our oneness and simultaneously establishes antennae for expansion beyond it. Spontaneity acquires "significance" simultaneously as a quality of feeling, and as meaning, and as a reflection of the universe with respect to which it is felt as such and no other one.

Indeed, at this very level (at which the initial spontaneity establishes itself within the constitutive molds of experience) there interferes immediately the third factor of its constitution, the world: (1) the *life-world of other men*, and (2) the *world as the prototype of its constitutive orientation*.

In fact, at its incipient stage in human experience, that is, at that instance which opens man to a specific receptivity "within" toward the "without," gathering it within, the whole universally human system of functions — or as we call it, the "constitution" of man — is already oriented toward a final reference point. Only in reference to this point can singular concrete instances of experience emerge as qualitatively specified and as informative; that is, as an interwoven experiential set establishing a precedent with reference to which each further incoming experience is formed. We do not establish, from our infancy on, a "series" or "mosaic" of experiences that stand over against each other within an imposed design; rather, all our experiences are intimately qualitatively familiar with each other and all of them fuse into the homogeneous stream of our inner being, of our own life, of our own universe. But this *felt fusing quality* which, contrary to the atomistic psychology of the British Empiricists, accounts, on the one hand, for the *unity of our inner being* and, on the other hand, for the *unity of the universe as experienced*, which otherwise would be a chaos of scattered pieces, is due principally to the fact that the spontaneous flow gives itself specific qualitative determination — not a random one, at the spur of impulses, but with reference to a prototype of design which each experience enacts in relation to each incoming one.

The other first-mentioned principle which constitutes in a two-way traffic a constant active factor of modeling and remodeling the action-reaction referential system and which operates seemingly on the fringes of the expansive feature of experience, in fact forms and also requalifies the qualitative molding of its very own core. This is the system of the actual, existing, ever-present human world within which the human experiencing being emerges and unfolds.

The surging spontaneity throws out tentacles in its unqualified dynamism. Its projection does not explode into a void but within a milieu of tightly coalescent elements. Its emergence is certainly as much conditioned by this milieu as the natural response to it. The initial spontaneity of our human being emerges at a certain very advanced phase of life's constructive evolution. It surges within the circumambient milieu of the already constructed "world," both as its *new element* and as *one meant to fuse with it*.

It surges always within such a circumambient world. Whether it be the biological, social and cultural world of the man of the Renaissance with its most refined forms, which themselves perpetuated the long progress of the human being that went into the period's structuration, or the world of the cave man with its restricted number of survival values and aims, the human experience emerges always already tuned to and correspondingly *structured with reference to the world in which it appears*. It represents that world's basic, as well as its specific, forms; it appears not as a strictly personal, unique expression of the individual, but as *a participation in and continuation of the collective effort of humanity which designed this circumambient world and, so, has reached at this point its specific structure.*

Being at its very core experience that is already qualified with reference to the universal design of the human world and fused with and within a specific human universe, human psychologico-cultured experience, can never be considered to be anything but representative of some already established pattern of forms. It can never be stripped of them in the way that an "authentic," genuine, uniquely immediate and "pure" experience of reality, if it were in this perspective not a self-contradictory notion, would pierce through its veils. We may say, to the contrary, that *experience itself is the network of the reality of life which we project.* The human world constituted by the collective effort of individual experience is the refinement and corroboration of this network into more subtle and transparent forms of the spirit, whereas return to the primitive types of experience places us before a thick, viscous world that expresses the primitive concern of the flesh with perpetuation, foremost, of physical life and survival. The human universe, being already circumscribed at its incipient individual stage by the design of the mind, is not an experience whose boundaries we can pierce. Leszek Kołakowski has once said: "no matter how deep we dig, all we find is man himself." I would say, in contrast, "no matter how deep we dig into the human experience, *all we find will be human life.*"

Yet, as Edgar Allen Poe, and Paul Valéry after him, expressed it, "the world is already circumscribed within the human mind." We can specify further that, in reverse, it is not only the world as such, but *the specific cultural world of a period that is already circumscribed within the individual experience of man.*

SECTION 5. THE QUEST FOR ILLUSORY "TRUE REALITY" AND
THE DILEMMAS OF INDIVIDUAL AND COLLECTIVE EFFORT

We have attempted to show that, since every individual experience is *inscribed by its quality* into the respective collective effort of humanity within the human world, the "return to the source" cannot then be sought in a supposed "uniquely genuine" experience; if we seek to renew the world, we could never accomplish that by discarding established forms in order to achieve such an experience, which is only fictitious (cf. my critique of Husserl's conception of the "originary experience" in Volume XIV of *Analecta Husserliana*).

However, the creative endeavor in art does undoubtedly contain a quest which is to be interpreted as a quest after an original and hitherto unknown and unprecedented form or quality. This quest itself determines its objective, which we will attempt to unravel and to describe.

Man's creative effort springs from as many sources as there are within himself of promptings to move, to ignite, to awaken and so to transcend the limits of contingency, within which he is caught — that is life, himself and the world.

Unlike the spontaneity of experience, the creative impetus or impulse has not only an individual concreteness but has most *specific personal significances* that are differentiated according to its different sources.

In the turmoil of profound emotions, which invade our being, caught irremediably in a struggle within ourselves between the rage of revolt and the mildness of understanding, passing directly from bitter hate to disarming compassion, after we have fought over and over again the battle between annihilating distress and ardent hope, each of them deepening in us the urge to disentangle the hidden motives at their heart but finding no clues to them, no reconciliation, we feel surging within us an overwhelming compulsion to leave the battlefield. We feel overpowered by forces which emerge within us against our will, which impose disorienting tensions; we feel an impotent rage against the unaccountable surges of emotions that lurk in us each time we attempt to control the situation by reflective evaluation of the forces at play and the significance of the conflicts. We feel an unquenchable yearning to seek another realm where the profound stream of subterranean forces agitating our life and our nostalgia for reconciliation of here irreconcilable opposites could be fulfilled, where unclarifiable discrepancies, and conflicts which tear our inner being apart could be mediated and woven into one harmonious texture. We seek a "higher" level above the irreconciliable crudity of our feelings, above our personal tragedies, a level where the struggle, the feeling, the yearnings are transposed into an all-embracing point that we establish in a poem, a picture, a sonata. In the unity of the creative work our struggle is resolved and transposed to a "higher" (that is, less tangible) interpretation of motives than any the world and life can afford.

We who dart toward this point also transcend our natural life since our impetus engages us in the pursuit of the "unattainable." This impetus is like the consuming fire of a violent passion when our whole being is thrown out of its complacent mold and set on an irresistible course (hope alternating with anguish, burning desire alternating with doubt, enchantment alternating with suspicion) toward a glimmering "light" that, like a firefly, remains always beyond reach. This is a light which springs forth in a sudden flash in the midst of darkness and draws us; but the minute we extend a hand to seize it, it vanishes only to flash again in another place out of reach. We follow it with a tremor from flash to flash, perpetually misled, erring in the darkness of life. Either we drive ourselves toward inward destruction by getting vainly lost in an empirical pursuit of love, of happiness, of glory, of fame or of grandeur, or we turn the search after unattainable earthly illusion into our very longing for it. We elevate ourselves above the limits of the world as well as of our own nature to an attempt to grasp the meaning, the content, of this pursuit by transposing our nostalgias, our yearnings, our plight, into the vision of a work of art. We mold them into a design, projecting it over against us as the prototype of these abysmal strivings, which drove us on our foolish course. This objective, unattainable within the constituted world, futile, perpetually evasive and elusive, is rendered at last motionless and made present in its purest, spiritual form.

In the midst of the current of everyday existence, within that well-defined and tangible stream with its modest and determined aims, we become impatient and exasperated by the monotony of its trivial drudgery. We feel worn out by the necessity to reinvent perpetually new strategies to accomplish these aims which, never realized, go away — but are always there to be taken up again, to counteract elements hostile to our defined line of conduct. We feel abused by the instability and inconclusiveness of our victories, which, with a new turn of events, turn into derision and, by the futility of our particular achievements, which count only as long as they are not surpassed by those of others. A dissatisfaction surges within us with the perpetual vanishing of everything that we strive to establish, with the incompleteness of everything we struggle to make whole and perfect and, finally, with the lack of validity and with the meaninglessness of all our worldly pursuits, which are relevant merely for an instant — whereas we long for perdurance.

We are overwhelmed by an urge to give to this dynamic chaos, this ever-vanishing current, coherence and articulation, to salvage from the fleetingness of life some precious fragments by devising for them a point of reference, a framework of cohesion that something may perdure above the flux of life. We are carried away by our own momentum above the gluey stuff of our everyday emotions, feelings, ambitions. Instead of sinking within ourselves we lift ourselves in a jump above the array of confusion and we pick up its mutilated odds and ends and ruminate on them. Instead of remaining submerged in the flux of the world, we raise these bits we care for to the level of our inward work where an emotional substance rises with fresh sap, and a work originates within which these scraps and bits are restored to their wholeness, unity, order, and we find that justification of our existence we hunger for: *the meaning and purpose to be found within a work of creation.*

But does not this incessant effort to be furnished with the means of life itself release within us a poignant nostalgia to rise higher than life? Do we not, like Sisyphus, pick up the same stone every morning to roll it uphill while every night it rolls down? Do we not have to conjure, after its every downhill trip, new strength, courage, and endurance to pick it up and carry on without being crushed under it, never to rise again? Where do we find a spring of ever-fresh water to refill our reservoir? Is life itself anything other than a chain of tasks to be carried out, so that once we drop our hands we fall lifeless? Do we not, in order to keep raising our hands, have to wring out of ourselves a delirious faith in a task higher than the ever-repeated picking up of that rock — a Promethean task toward which we may rise in spite of having our feet chained to the ground? The hope of such a task lifts our heart, revives and mobilizes our feelings, emotions, yearning. All our virtualities which remained stultified within the dreariness of life, harnessed to the common wheel, now unfold their wings. Is not a creative undertaking such a task that carries us beyond ourselves, breaking the chains of our slavery to the world and life?

Furthermore, can we, closed within the framework of the established world and life as we are, satisfy our higher strivings, our yearning for absolute eternal beauty, our thirst for immortality — all of these to be actualized within a higher level of being than our trivial preoccupations, our everyday actions, thoughts, reactions and stimuli allow us to reach?

Do we not feel wasted and lost until we can rise toward a higher level of existence? And what, then, satisfies more adequately this longing for a higher form of being than to project it toward a transcendent *telos*? Following this projected task our deepest strivings revive, our hitherto atrophied potentialities revive, our virtualities previously unknown sprout and unfold. Transposing these all into the weaving of a web of superior reality, assigning them a superior role, place and value, we make them in turn forge our own being into one more delicate, sensitive and responsive to beauty and sublime texture than before. By rising toward the creative task as a telos, the individual being is transposed to a higher level of existence and fulfillment — our spiritual existence.

However, at the other extreme of our life involvements, does not the rapture, the exalting joy and enthusiasm which bursts into the dullness of faded forms and colors, shed a new light upon everything, heighten our sense of beauty, virtue and innocence, opening us to an all-pervading enchantment, and also carry us beyond ourselves? This exaltation urges us to make translucent all the screens with which current life and the world hide these beauties from the common eye. It spurs us to transgress the limits of the faded, inert, stereotypic, dull, repetitious framework of the world by unveiling all the marvels we believe ourselves to be the first to behold and to witness. Carried away beyond the borders of our present environment, style of life, taste, blinded culture and stagnant humanity, we fly upon the wings of enthusiasm to reach and reveal to all this flower of light and beauty, of magic and elevation, by recreating it upon a canvas, in a musical score, a ballet figure.

Enthusiasm, this exaltation of the soul, is the left wing of creation. The right wing is the unquenchable thirst to surpass the limitations of life, the contingent conditions of the world, the narrow borderlines of our self and to seek the immutable and final, the unrestricted and unconditioned, "hidden behind the veil," of a world we are caught in like a fly within a spider-web. Seeking freedom from the bondage of nature, which runs through our very veins, we elevate ourselves toward the vision of a creative object as toward a point of reference, pure and uncompromising, translucent and unyielding to the treacheries of contingency.

While all subjective, most intimately personal creative *élan* is an act of transcending the narrow limits of the contingent, constituted world, its profound meaning, upon scrutiny, is in its defiance of the fictitious universe of man in an effort to establish contact with the transcendent "ultimate reality," the "true reality," the "real."

While Chekhov on the one hand runs through all the hidden springs of man's passion and desire and longing, which life distorts and stifles by hampering their further unfolding, robbing them of their authentic "true reality", and which the veil of contingency imposes upon man's aspirations, spirit and genius, he, on the other hand, repeats incessantly: "if only we knew" what is the ultimate answer to our plight, what is the sense of our existence, what is the "true reality" behind the screen of life, of the world, of nature.

What is the "real?" Can the artist approach it, since it is to be sought "beyond" or "below" the human world? Does he have to reject or ignore the world as an exponent of the human past, the cultural inheritance of men, altogether?

SECTION 6. THE DILEMMA AT THE HEART OF CREATION: COLLECTIVE HERITAGE VERSUS INDIVIDUAL EVIDENCE

To approach the question of reality in all its forms, we have to envisage it, then, in the perspective of the cultural conundrum in which it appears. Our cultural heritage is constructed upon a great number of contributions, each of which in its own way gave history a turn, transforming or reorienting its course. On the one hand, each segment of human history consists of an accumulation of accomplishments, conquests of adverse conditions of nature, concatenations of relentless human effort. The world we live in is the stage of this effort; it is our historical heritage and the fruit of the collective, continuous work of humanity or of its "creative spirit."

On the other hand, however, the real advance of this incessant line of progress, the steps which gave a new turn to history or led it higher, are the results of personal, individual genius, insofar as a genius steps out of the concatenations of the collective heritage and challenges its course. Each new significant attempt consists precisely in rejecting the previous results, in placing the new endeavor against those of the past. Each attempt glorifies the most intimate and personal effort, with its innermost own, unique evidence prized as uniquely valid. From within its own perspective the creative undertaking of an artist, a thinker, a scientist, a philosopher is absolutely individualized and appears as a singularly personal affair of the individual, that is, confined to his isolated being as if the progress which it introduces into the world could follow the creative laws, conditions and inspiration of an individual consciousness only as they evolve in isolation from the rest of humanity.

What is the relation between these two ways — the one of collective progress, the other of individual quest — which seem to antagonize, challenge and defeat each other? We have already shown that, in order to take advantage of this progress of the creative spirit of humanity, we partake of our own life-world at the point where it is actualized. But it is by rejecting and surpassing this world that our creative elation springs forth and unfolds. Here again we meet the temptation to reject the collective inheritance of the past by ignoring it altogether and to start a strictly personal, genuinely individual effort "at its source" within our individual being alone. A strong temptation, indeed.

At the other extreme, if we follow the course of human culture with historical imagination, understanding sympathetically the intertwinings of influences among individuals, we might get a picture showing us that, although the actual part of creator is played in them, they are themselves only elements of a vast texture in a collective stream into which their limited genius flows and from which it rises.

SECTION 7. CREATIVE DESTRUCTURING IN THE
METAPHYSICAL PURSUIT OF THE POET: A PERIOD OF
PREPARATION FOR THE CREATIVE BREAKTHROUGH

(a) *Life lurking in the media attributed to the illusory*
    "authentic reality"

Indeed, the individual participants acknowledge the great millstones that grind the experience of humanity. He participates with all his functions in the vast process of the life of humanity which proceeds through individual and collective functioning. The individual, as well as the collective, functioning has been established and developed throughout history and takes particular forms in the period in which the individual lives. He, himself, is an organic unity whose feelings, emotions, physiological processes, volitions, actions, and even thoughts, are essentially elements or functions of the same pattern. This pattern itself is a variation on the great collective pattern of the period and time. We are so intimately interwoven within the pattern itself that it appears to us as the portent, the backbone of real life, reality itself, or at least its face.

However, if we consider the fact that various epochs and various cultures developed different patterns which were all accepted in their given times as the reality of the individual life, we may, in the footsteps of artists and poets who sought *new forms of the significance of life*, wonder whether any of them "reveals reality" to us or "disguises" it, "brings forth reality" or "just mediates" it. The function of forms in shaping collective and individual existence cannot be seen as mediating the ultimate, last, "absolute" form of life in an "authentic" configuration, but as *mediating forms of life relative* to the specific configurations into which the forms of our *individual functioning were molded through the inheritance of humanity and by our own initiative and natural cooperation.*

When we then ask "what is the true reality?" and we feel an urge, a longing, to clarify this question — a question which arises in the midst of all endeavors, artistic, scientific, philosophical — then, following poets like T. S. Eliot, but also Jean Wahl, Heidegger, and Rilke, we conclude that "*we are not ready for thought*"; we are moving in a circle like a cat following its own tail. The motor which drives us round and round is the creative longing for a novel "sense" of life. Its guide is the *transcendental illusion that this sense lies elsewhere than in life itself.* By saying we are not ready for thought, *we really mean that we are not ready to initiate a creative endeavor in which, breaking with the vicious circle of an illusory idea, we would aim at a novel significance of our existence.*

Of course, there must be a reason why poets believe that the "true," the "authentic reality has to remain hidden." Nietzsche says that Plato invented the world of essences as an effort to throw a veil over reality, because an artist cannot tolerate the *real*, poignantly concrete, and immediately palpable. In the experience of the creative mind the "real," "true" reality, which is the ultimate target creation aims at, is such that in direct contact with it we become identified with it, our very being is abolished and we are pulled by it into an irreversible flux. It seems to the poets that the creator, artist, poet, philosopher who enters within the creative experience into such consuming contact with the "real" has to avert his eyes and turn himself back to what has been already invented as its various disguises in partial experiences. To come to terms with the palpitating and altogether simple, he introduces distinctions and separations into the indivisible; he fixes in color, sound, form and concept the ever-fluid. We are thus tossed into an array of projected schemes through which reality is envisaged as through a glass darkly and feel, sense and think within their bounds, with their devices and means. Yet to "think" as an original, individual, act would be to come into a direct contact with the "true" reality. But caught irremediably within the various patterns, as in a spider's web, we cannot even know what thought is.

Man, says Eliot, and this is also the thought of Rilke, seems by nature not to be able to stand too much density, intensity, consciousness. His consciousness is already arranged in such a way that he may dilute, extend temporally and spatially, disperse, separate and divide. Man divides because he is divided within himself. By this, concrete, pulsating life is denoted.

To reach "true reality" we do not, as is often thought, have to appeal to privileged moments of the joy of life, of suffering or of the holocaust of self-sacrifice, but have to strive to reach "beyond" the universal pattern of our life and period and further on beyond the very scheme of generations. We have to go behind the scheme of things and to see the real freed from the established cyclic chains of nature like a "spring day in the middle of winter," to quote T. S. Eliot, contradicting the expected and following a more essential, underlying law which remained hidden, one that the human mind hid or buried.

Our thinking is like a Promethean élan in chains. In order to free it and to establish the possibility of its authentic — that is, creative — functioning, we have to reach behind all other functioning (e.g., organic, vital, psycho-physiological, intentionally constitutive).

On his way to discover what "authentic reality" is, a poet, an artist or a philosopher scrutinizes precisely the phenomena of life, birth, suffering, fulfillment, death, love, fecundity, etc., all elements of the natural scheme of things. He discovers then how every action is bound to time which holds it tight in its inexorable laws. Immediately the nature of experience itself is the major barrier. It disindividualizes the content of an individual life because this content belongs not only to the individual, but also to the preceding and coming generations which draw upon it as the actual individual himself draws upon the past. Through necessary obedience to its scheme, experience in its temporal unfolding makes the individual merely a segment in the chain of generations, repeating the same preestablished cycle of birth, growth, suffering, love and death; it makes the individual a mere instance of repetition in a scheme of eternal return. Through its laws and forms within which individual experience is pre-ordained in a way that it establishes what we call "nature," the natural universe correlated to it, as well as the lived world-experience, establishes the universe of phenomena transient and inessential, *yet forming such a consistent system that every new experience at its birth is already "pre-ordained"* to enter into it.

Space and time, the cyclic repetitive scheme of nature, and the entire scheme of forms, life essence, substance, substratum, idea, and concept serve to organize, structurize, relate, separate, divide and form experience at its birth and are thus the basic obstacles to reaching the real.

Thus, in order to reach behind the established *ways of our own response, molds for our spontaneity of volition, cognition, emotion, and to overcome the totality of human tradition* that has infiltrated with pre-ordained forms the very pattern of our functions, *we cannot abandon, discard, or neglect the collective heritage.* We must, on the contrary, enter into a dialogue with it and pierce not only the reservoir of knowledge and forms of thought, but even the preestablished forms of generation down to the cyclic pattern of the natural life and the ultimate web of the temporal and spatial rules which have pre-organized our experience within their molds. Behind them there might be, as Coleridge saw and T. S. Eliot says, a "sacred, indomitable river," breaking instantly into the totality of generations at the cross-section of the temporal and eternal.

This is the basic conviction that the philosopher may share with poets and which would also be essential to the artist and scientist. We must emphasize that *this river is nothing other than the creative process, through which the above quest of the artist proceeds.*

There is, to repeat again, no privileged type of experience that would immediately introduce us into the heart of the real and unveil it. Creation aims at the discovery of "true reality" which we may say, with T. S. Eliot and Jean Wahl, cannot be revealed through a particular experience of a specific quality or intensity; it has its source behind the established schemas; it comes "out of season" as the spring day in the middle of winter, having gained access behind the stage, behind the cycle of nature, where, according to Heraclitus, birth and death are united. In order to reach it we have to seek not a specific way to the real, but must embrace the totality of the given and, *in the synthesis of the creative act, delve into "consuming contact" with life itself* so as to find ourselves face to face with it.

The creative undertaking is essentially an individual quest prompted by our yearning for the new, and guided by the transcendental illusion of an ultimate ground or reality to be discovered. Whatever may be the extent of the cognitive, constitutive material necessary for the individual's creative endeavor, the ways of its use, its evaluation, and its final form is commanded by the basic aim which may be expressed as "How, with what is given, can the true reality be expressed?" Thus the individual creative effort, oriented radically toward the discovery and expression of the "truly real," is essentially a dialogue with the established scheme, a search for the invariant rules underlying changing patterns. The established pattern has to be rejected. Yet if we rebuke it in all its given features as mere media hiding the essence of truth, could we evaluate it for our own purposes?

We can witness in contemporary philosophy itself such self-critical activity of the universal creative mind. The meaning of this term as it is used is basically similar to Nicolai Hartmann's "objective spirit" of humanity as it is carried on by individuals, but simultaneously molds the individual himself. However, the crucial difference in our approach to it (substantiated in the present work) lies in our understanding it *from within the individual's progress that creates and establishes new forms that are re-constructive of reality.*

(b) *Creative conditions seen through philosophy*

First of all, it appears as if the unfolding of the universal scheme of Western thought has completed a cycle and, with thinkers like Bergson, James, etc., a revolutionary suspicion of such basic notions as substance, essence, category, arose; notions which were discovered and progressively established throughout two thousand years of Western culture as constitutive principles of reality and cornerstones of its rational ordering and understanding.

Secondly, from the progress of modern science a simultaneous devaluation of these fundamental notions as basic constituents of reality came to light and their opposites were revindicated. The priority, for instance, of becoming over being, of process over structure, fluid duration over static form, has been established by thinkers like Peirce, Whitehead, and Bachelard.

Let us follow Jean Wahl in his personal philosophical effort.[6] Instead of seeking reality, as is customary, in philosophical practice (that is, within limited particular evidence with its distinctive glimpse), let us engage in our quest from a macroscopic bias taking the totality of the different patterns within which humanity and individuals are caught and from within the process of their incessant transformations, corroborations and refinement.

This macroscopic system itself follows a line of development. In point of fact, individual creative efforts accomplished in different fields carry the main stream of this field in its progress while philosophy, through the reflective, critical aspect of its endeavor leads it onward, remodeling the fundamental molds into which human sensitivity, emotiveness, volition, imagination and mind pour their content by emphasizing some tendencies while discrediting others, by corroborating nuances and redirecting natural bents. Thus philosophical creation assumes also a very specific, unique role, that of guiding progress. But it follows a specific line of development as well.

This reflection is an essential factor of the creative endeavor. To make this progress unfold is to scrutinize the tradition inherited from past stages of growth and to retrace the steps and to unravel the ways of the working of the creative spirit of mankind, the "universal" spirit. Following Jean Wahl, we have first, to grasp the genesis of the entire cycle of realities produced by the genius of history; and then, penetrating into their conditions, and grasping the virtualities of the human genius from which this gigantic game emerges, we might reach the furthest limit concepts, last principles of meanings, ultimate footholds of structuration and rationality beyond which we could not find any more means to express, to structurize anything that would become part of this system along its own lines.

Jean Wahl's metaphysical itinerary is that of each and every creative mind. As individual artists we follow the collective stream in retrospect, discovering the intrinsic workings of its progress; a dialectic of thesis, antithesis and synthesis, of acceptance and negation, of affirmation and opposition, of insufficiency and complementariness, appears to be the intrinsic mode of the development which unfolds new forms and establishes a new pattern: a pattern which articulates the dynamism of progress by setting articulations of forces and molds for experiential evidence and intuitive insights to be poured in and thereby grow, take shape, and create ideas and concepts to be transformed, unfolded, or left behind the main current.

The discovery of the established pattern that simultaneously sustains the constitutive origin of forms and their cognition reveals the depend-

ence and relativity of the constituted universe of man and of the trend
of man's culture, *which could have been different* had the initial molds
and principles of articulation been chosen in a different manner. But we
must also note the dependence and relativity of the singular forms
themselves, in respect to each other and the complete set. Unwrapped
from that which they borrow from the whole set of the constitutive
functioning and their mutual coordinative adjustment, they may serve
as antennae leading to contact with what has remained hidden, what in
itself lies beyond any form, "true reality."

While we follow the whole cycle of the creative spirit of history
correlating, comparing, sifting, distilling the classic ideas, insights and
notions in all the perspectives which philosophical theories may give us,
and discover their validity to be limited to intermediary mediations of
the final and absolute, is the complete universe of our inherited world
going to crumble? Since such cornerstones as essence, idea, being,
substratum, accident, category, universals, etc. are to lose their value
in presenting or structurizing the absolute and, since such ultimate
incipient and truly indispensable notions on the basis of which the
construction of the human universe seems to proceed should be limited
to "relation" and "quality," should the immense reservoir of inherited
experience be then discarded or denied validity altogether?

The critical inventory of the collective philosophical effort of Western
humanity, after being sifted through the sieve of the creative means
of the universal spirit, seems to clear the ground for the individual
endeavor.

Jean Wahl, who was the first to question radically the absolutism of
all forms, including concepts, patterns of thought, habits of seeing
things, experiences, etc., as well as their structural interconnectedness,
and whose philosophical itinerary exemplified step by step the practice
of such a questioning, which J. Derrida made popular under the term of
"deconstruction," shows us that *no reality* is hidden behind the media.
*No life-world as a pristine pattern lies below the networks of experience.
It is experience which establishes it from scratch. The hermeneutics of
culture cannot reveal anything to us. They dismantle, but do not
reconstruct.* Nothing lies behind the dismantled forms which the intersubjective collectivity has not established. To reconstruct, to renovate
the human life-world, to learn about the source, this can only be
accomplished by the creative endeavor of man.

SECTION 8. THE RADICAL BEGINNING: THE LIMIT CONCEPTS AND THE MIND IN A NEW PATTERN

The authentic individual effort may begin after we have, through a double scrutiny — one that shows the relativity of basic cognitive functions and another that shows the relativity of their forms in the constitution of our human universe —, recognized their obscuring role in the effort to establish direct contact with "reality," but found by the same stroke that there is no reality which lies at the core of this endeavor. Yet the universal suspension of basic forms does not leave us in a void. On the contrary, if behind the given forms not reality but the spontaneity of life reveals itself, we will start the quest over again to find a more appropriate form for giving life meaning, a form that would not be felt to be an old screen covering its palpitating core and disguising it to the naked eye, but would be a way of understanding that causes the very springs of life's ramified virtualities in the Human Condition to well up and be transposed and received in the human heart.

We would search for forms attuned both to the vibrant capacities of life and to the human mind; feelings that would express it closest to its transmuted form within man's vibrating being.

The human mind creates these forms precisely to articulate and express life that is transmuted by our being into "reality" and then, by a reverse turn, in its historical advance (which means a sequence of ever-reworked forms), scrutinizes and disproves the validity and efficacy of each for accomplishing the task. And yet these long series of attempts should not be altogether discredited by the individual, who wants to undertake the quest on his own; they are far from being vain. Their creation has forged our virtualities, has developed in us more subtle, acute, experiential, grasping, evaluating instruments and sensitivity to the great question. This creation needed, in fact, this gigantic effort by innumerable individual and collective genius to disentangle the elements of the question and the meaning of our human enterprise that is to be distilled, cornered, and grasped. Finally, it is only through the maze of the merely partial, ephemeral successes and through the unraveling of its limitations that we attain a sharply focused insight.

The criticism and suspension of the validity of the established allows the creator (philosopher) to differentiate some notions as *limit-concepts of the mind itself* in its struggle to work itself for the sake of, through, and within, the real. Furthermore, although behind the screen of constructs no reality emerges to our inner eye, we are not left dispossessed in front of an emptiness as if the horizon were to close in upon us; that would seem to be the situation if we assume beforehand a transcendental view. But the whole course of our dismantling of the sedimentations of human history shows, to the contrary, that there is an objective for our quest; it is out there as the unconditioned, which is independent from the screens of formal structures: as the *reality of life*, on the one hand, and as the *creative endeavor of man*, on the other. The role of limit-concepts is not to throw again the veil of our cognitive media over life, but to assess the very point of contact, discovering the very first medium our mind possesses to serve as the basic subjacent *filum Ariadne* between the unconditioned and its possible manifestations.

There emerges an Archimedean point of encounter between life and the breadth of interrelatedness of the individual human being, through which he is woven into its schema. The individual mind freed from the set of thus denounced molds, and seen through in their inadequate functioning, appears in its essential permeability; it appears transparent to the ever-new patterns of life and virtualities of the Human Condition, and ready to be set into a new pattern of motion in order to meet their challenge.

Thus we have inadvertently arrived at what seems to be the *absolute turning point of the human enterprise*. The "radical beginning" is the point from which human consciousness embarks on the long course of working itself with and through life for the *individual creative undertaking*. The whole heritage of the immense development of humanity, with its uncountable efforts at the same task, is not a waste but rather a long preparation for undertaking ever new creative efforts to work oneself through the real and grasp it ever closer and closer, while fulfilling the *individual's personal virtualities*.

Whereas the creative effort of man in all realms consists chiefly in forging media and approaches to life, and designs a discrete and yet intimately continuous line, its condition is far from taking part in it by simply adding new motives and corroborating the old ones; to the contrary, this means a personal "subjective," "radical beginning." The radicality of clearing the ground instead of its naive acceptance — like that we show in our practical, empirical life attitudes — consists in a critical scrutiny which stops at nothing in order to wring from our most personal, intimate source a point of contact with the "ultimate." The decision to reconstruct this contact in objective forms, the choice of which would come exclusively out of our very own source, responsibility and judgment gives to creation whether artistic, scientific or philosophical its unprecedented, unique character. It is accompanied by an *acute awareness of this uniquely individual task.* A poet struggling to bring about a "new universe" of feelings and unique and unprecedented thought, or a philosopher on the verge of reconstructing a system of the universe more adequate to reality and with all its reasons made more transparent to the mortal eye than those which are already available, stands alone like the demiurge in front of chaos contemplating the scheme he is about to set in motion.

While the same quest — to go beyond the already accomplished, the discovered and established forms of human consciousness, and come to grips with reality — is shared by every artist, inventor, scholar and philosopher, they do not set out with the same instruments nor do they proceed to seek and deal with the same type of expressive media. While the artist, scientist, inventor and poet perform the scrutiny of established forms and make their criticism for the most part intuitively, in the dark, by trial and error, narrowing the perspectives in their specific, particular, very own situation and for the most personal end, the philosopher undertakes the task of a complete and objectively elucidating inquiry in the light of sovereign reason. His investigation not only comprises the collective acquisitions in their totality, but has to probe into their very reasons, clarify their intrinsic laws and the working of the human mind as such.

The creative condition of man is then fundamentally all-embracing and in its very essence aims at the final elucidation of the creative process and its universal and individual condition.

How could we solve any specific riddle confronting us in the nature of the universe around us or within us if we are at a loss to understand, be it dimly, the basic, initial conditions of our own dealing with the ultimate, of which these two "universes" are but the most extensive fruit?

THE BELOW AND THE ABOVE OF CREATIVE INWARDNESS: THE HUMAN LIFE-WORLD IN ITS ESSENTIAL NEW PERSPECTIVE

SECTION 1. CREATION AS THE TRANSITION BETWEEN TWO SUCCESSIVE PHASES OF THE SAME LIFE-WORLD CAUGHT IN THE CONSTITUTIVE PROCESS

(a) *The precarious nature of the creative process*

The nature, source, and conditions of the creative process have always appeared mysterious; creativity is a phenomenon of life, seemingly unpredictable; its existential status as a specific human manifestation is particularly fragile and uncertain. Compared with other human functions which introduce specifically human significance into "Nature" but use man's physical resources as instruments to work directly upon its raw "material," the creative process lacks the solidity of activities like cultivating the soil, ploughing, sowing seed, watering the plants, grafting, and gathering the ripe fruit. It also lacks the concreteness of the processes related to raising cattle, constructing a table, carving a spoon from wood or building a house. These process-like activities have already passed the threshold which differentiates the human functioning that unfolds strictly in accordance with life's scheme. These and many other human "primary" activities stem from man's desire to transform nature according to his vital needs and comfort which themselves are expressions of nature. Mastering the raw material of "Nature," working with instruments which nature, as a system of this significant mediation between the brute forces of life and the *virtualities of the Human Condition* itself, has revealed to man as tools that correspond to their common laws, making use of conditions which also are offered in this same configuration, we express man's "knowledge" and his congenial familiarity *with his own basic situation*. Nature is experienced by man as a solid, "substantial" groundwork that he may grasp and hold on to with his arms and hands, hold on to with his legs, to his breast — simultaneously clinging to it with his whole body —, and it is nature which he transforms through his vital organs, which differentiate its

152

crude force into different elements and articulating them endows the new functional complexes which hence emerge with new significance in the process of life, with force and vigor. Nature is experienced by man as the meaningful network of interrelations which is his "milieu," not only the very foundation of his life, but the realm in which he stretches himself, secure, and almost dormant.

As long as the activities of the human being, who also brings into play his other sort of resourcefulness — that is, his ramified functions of intelligence — are limited to assuring the proper run of the course of the natural unfolding, these activities stay in perfect harmony, enjoying the relative stability and security of nature itself. But the scale goes out of balance when the purpose of activity is no more the continuation of the natural progress itself; when on the side of the purpose, aim, objective, man divorces himself from nature, setting for himself aims which are meant to gratify intelligence alone. The line of demarcation between these two purposive/objective poles goes already through the heart of the cognitive phenomenon which stands out from the natural realm *per se* even if it is in the main serving its purposes.

Already the cognitive process, itself, is much less predictable in its course, much less graspable and certain in the interpretative meaning of its results, and more fluctuating in its orientation than the functional processes of concrete physical work upon "matter," and this is even more the case, if, from the sensuous perception of the physical world we pass to cognition of our inner states, of abstract ideas and theories. Losing foothold in the system of nature, ideas lose solidity, flesh and body, like a ship that has lost its anchor; they leave the ground on the wings of the intellect and float in vertiginous strides in the "pure" emptiness of the "ideal" realm.

The creative process is partly like a vehicle propelled in motion onwards, having lost its rudder and seemingly deprived of a set course to follow, as well as having no station in nature. Yet it does not set off upon a wild, unaccountable course; on the contrary, it projects from within its virtualities an entirely new, unique trajectory.

Poets who have always been puzzled about the source of the creative process have alternatively seen it attached to the profound natural sources of consciousness *below* the level at which the reflexive mind operates. Coleridge presents such a view in "Kubla Khan," in the tale of the "sacred river" which flows in the subterranean caverns of the earth, the very womb and guts of nature, where the stream of the inward life gushes, differentiating itself at the surface of the earth in various activities prepared below. On the contrary, romantic poets, like Novalis, were tempted to look for the sources of poetry beyond, in a realm superior to the human condition, higher, more sublime and transcendent to man, from which — as a special favor of the gods — he may occasionally pick a "blue flower" of an unearthly fragrance.

The process of creation is, indeed, pulled in these two opposite directions, lacking a solid base of nature for its point of departure as well as a secure, solid cable line leading it toward a certain port. Neither does it spring from a concrete strictly pre-determined source — like a chicken from an egg, like a nasturtium from a seed — nor does it terminate in a concrete, individual item of nature like an apple, a potato, a wooden table or a spoon. The creative process stretches on a trajectory between two seemingly equally transient points: the psychological state of the *creative vision*, which appears in an unaccountable way, and disappears, which cannot be either prompted at our command nor retained, and the *creative work*, which once introduced into the life-world does not enter into and continue the chain of natural generation, but stands out isolated above the generative solidity and continuation of nature, seemingly inert and particularly transient but, in fact perduring and fertile in its own way.

(b) *The creative trajectory suspended between two poles*: Creative agent *and* creative object

And yet, as we have seen, this creative process possesses, on the one hand, an iron sequential nature which is its own master carrying with itself its own unalterable rules. On the other hand, this *creative trajectory*, as autonomous in its specific way as it may be, as distinct from the natural process as it may be, does not float in a void.

The creative trajectory is suspended ultimately between two poles: the *creative agent*, on the extreme of its propelling factor, and the *creative object*, on the other extreme, as its destination point. One of them is in itself a concrete, human individual, a part of nature, a segment of the unity of everything there is alive, and an essential factor of the lived world: the other, once accomplished, separates itself from the umbilical cord of the creative agent, breaks off the trajectory, and enters into the same lived world as its new element.

There is, however, a *distance* between the lived world in which the creative agent initiates the creative process and the lived world into which its product *enters*.

To engage in the creative process means for the creative agent/man a differentiation of his naturally exercised functions — their discrimination, selection, reorganization according to a different order of importance. His attention is naturally focused upon his relation with the ambient world and other men in view of the fulfillment of his natural functions, for his vital progress does not leave these points of natural concern entirely behind — we cannot stop living in order to create — but is bent in a different direction. Instead of giving ourselves in a "free" and absorbing passivity to the vital concerns, to experiencing things as they come, to acts of cognition and aesthetic pleasures — consuming them and living ourselves out in them —, we *effect* a certain withdrawal from our absorption, consuming, etc., and completely "adhere" to ourselves in these functions. We withdraw the total concentration of our attention given to them, and the intensity of experience that flows upon us freely in their exercise is weakened. In the twilight of our natural functions so obtained a new concentration point is proposed for our attention: for the net of relations is directed automatically toward a multitude of objects and aims; one single direction is singled out which, matched by a new network emerging as the substitute of the "natural" one, concentrates all relations "inward" by bringing all dispersed relational diversities to one single point of focus where all of them meet.

Entering a creative process means, in fact, for the creative agent to withdraw from all fronts of activities hitherto practiced, from all the world's well-travelled highways, into a "tunnel" which the human being then patiently drills for his life's specific concerns and their realization in a subterranean itinerary.

Indeed, the trajectory of the creative process is comparable to work in a tunnel which is drilled under the surface of the lived-world and covers a long distance: drilling it, the subject establishes another "world" as his very own milieu, which emerges according to its own rules. At the end of the itinerary we join again the full light of the life-world's easy, self-dispersed existence, *but the "place" in which we re-emerge is not the one from which we started*. The distance covered counts. While the creative process is working out its winding road, the lived world also continues *its* progress. We never enter the same stream twice; the created object, by means of which we re-emerge, has to face a different world than the one in which it was initiated.

What is this world which persists while the creative élan is fugacious? How is the creative agent, the human being, man, related to the life-world? What role does the relation of the creative agent to the life-world impart to the creative process?

(c) *The creative agent as a part of the constituted world*

Whatever may be the ultimate significance of the last cornerstones of physical reality, it remains without a direct impact upon the creative process. As we have already shown, the problem of creation appears only at a certain level of human concerns, the level which can emerge in life once the basic vital problems of natural subsistence have been dismissed from sight as satisfactorily solved. The lived world, which is the natural milieu of the creative man, emerges when the human being has freed his intelligence from a direct enslavement to the vital functions which made him an integral and inseparable factor of the meaningful system of nature. *The human animal needed to free himself from his ties, from the strict adherence to the vital significance of his circumambient condition as well as from his own life course, and leaving this one-sided track behind him — and still following the aim of perpetuating life — to throw himself into the adventure of inventing and projecting his own avenues of existence.*

Not only does the course of human life begin with his entrance as an individual into the world, but man is "born to the world" and his circumambient environment, as much as the world, is "born to him" as the response to his infinite intents to project himself ahead, to project himself into the "exterior" sphere of his narrow autonomous frame. Man's basic concerns, like those of the animal, to secure for himself conditions for his survival, already outline a circuit of *vital significance* as "exterior" to him. This narrow sphere extends further into the flexible dimensions of a life-world with its full circuit of *life-significance*. This full circuit encompasses not only the mere area of survival. When intelligence enters into activity, extrapolating man's specific tendencies into further circuits of significance of life elements, there is an expansion into a dimension of personal feeling, prompting the *aesthetic sense* toward a more intense experience of life, and the *moral sense* toward reflection and principles of evaluation, leaving aside vital utilitarianism; finally, it charges self-criticism to search for the aim and meaning of life itself.

Through this extrapolation of man's concern emerge the spheres of ideas, moral, aesthetic and religious values, and of other human beings: the world in which man's life unfolds in a network of relations which shrink or expand with the shrinking or expansion of his experience, but which, in all its subjective variations, maintains a fundamental scheme. This scheme is shared by mankind. It seems to be repeated from generation to generation and is stylized differently in different periods of the development of mankind, according to the particular forms of experiences that are either brought to perfection or weakened.

As the *creative agent*, man is not only organically immersed within the vital significance of life-nature but, as propounded in the previous section, he is, beyond it, immersed with all his experiencing and reflexive faculties in the life-world, the culture of the period to which he was born, which he inherits and propagates. Indeed, "being born to the world" is not to be born to a primeval condition of humanity emerging from the "enslavement by nature," but it means to extrapolate a world around oneself correcting, bending, shaping one's "natural" inclinations by the responses obtained by one's thrust and in significant conditions established by tradition. The form, style, of the lived-world into which the human individual enters cannot be inherited in a passive way, but through a most concrete re-enacting of its *modi operandi*. This re-enactment is the vehicle of its appropriation of a most individual, personal, subjective life-world.

Thus always in the process of being re-enacted by the new human beings, who bring in corroboration, transformation, etc., which cause the development of humanity to move on, the life-world never stops for an instant in its constant progress. The lived-world acquires circuits of significance, new "dimensions," "forms," accents, evaluating principles, etc. It is the unique personal construct of each individual and, simultaneously, it is the result of a common effort by all. Its progress is never completed; its "form" is never ready nor can it acquire a definite status. Together with the advance of individual experience and with the advance of collective knowledge, the life-world stays in a perpetual process of constitution.

The situation of the human being who, through his creative endeavor, becomes the "creative agent" is peculiar. The creative agent participates vitally, socially, culturally with his "guts" in the lived-world. He himself goes through the mesh of the significant web of its system, as if stabilized within it. The creative agent is, by all his intentions, tendencies, acquired forms of acting, thinking, feeling, etc., expressing this very constituted world in the *present phase* of its development, as its integral factor. He might nevertheless experience himself as being entirely free from its constraints because of his most intimate commitment to the forms which he intends to give to the "future" lived world, and yet he is immersed in its present phase so integrally that he cannot draw easily and knowledgeably a line between his opinions and those which are being predominantly expressed in his period at a given time, between his taste and that which predominates in the cultural phase he participates in. His approach toward other human beings, life, life-transcending nostalgias, his ways of behavior which he has developed in the conduct of life with his contemporaries and those which his social milieu has bestowed and which he has re-enacted on his own account, make him an integral element of the life-world in its actual phase.

The creative agent is, as a human individual, so immersed in the life-world caught in the process of constitution that he seems to be "conditioned" and limited by it in almost every respect. No wonder that art criticism has always insisted upon the social conditioning of the creative activity. And yet his move to "create" means the desire to tear himself from, to go beyond this web and its acquired design; this move alienates him from it by his striving toward future forms, which he himself will project. The urge to go beyond the acquired brings him ultimately into a radical conflict with the life-world in its present phase. He has to "suspend it."

(d) *The created work enters the constituted world as its integral part*

At the opposite end of the spectrum the result of the creative activity of man, the "created work," affirms its entrance into existence by *breaking into the lived-world as its integral part. The created work's act of acquiring an existential status culminates in its appearance among other objects of the life-world as one of them.* Its "appearance" means, on the one hand, to have complied with the conditions which the already constituted world implies. On the other hand, it means that the established frame of the constituted world cracks, becomes enlarged and more flexible in making room for a *new* object. Indeed, the very meaning of "creation," as we will soon clarify, is first to produce objects which have not yet been in existence as part of the constituted world in a certain phase of its progress; and second, *to offer a challenge to the established life-world pattern which, in order to receive it, must break its formal frame, adjust, adapt. The emergence of a work of creation within the constituted world means a transformation of this pattern and of the significant aspect of this world itself in response to the novel, unprecedented significant elements of which this creative object consists.* Indeed, the created object challenges the previously established forms of feeling, thinking, evaluating. It becomes, through its novelty, a focal point, drawing attention and provoking the recipient, spectator, reader, etc. by offering new stimuli for cognition, judgment and evaluation to take a particular attitude toward it.

In response to this stimulus and this challenging nature of this new element of the world, there is a development of new points of view, new ways of feeling, thinking, evaluating. Also, consequent upon the "appearance" of the created object, with its striking, provocative impact, the present constituted world — this world itself — appears too narrow, dull and sclerosed to satisfy our awakened appetites. We shake its apparent stagnation by our response to the new "object." Thus, in short, in order to integrate the created object into the *then present phase of the constituted world, this world reconstitutes itself.*

From the phase of the constituted world in which the creative agent on the point of becoming engaged in the creative process stood, to the phase of the emergence of the *creative product*, as the result of the creative process which unfolded, the constituted world underwent an essential transformation.

The creative process which follows its own rules and its very own subterranean path-world contained in, and yet withdrawn from the world — and participating in it through its agent — *is a transition between these two successive phases.* As such, it performs a *two-fold role.* First, *it is the factor of the renovation and of the constructive advance of the life-world itself.* Second, *it is the existential factor of the passage from one mode of existence to another.* This crucial point will come up later on, in full.

SECTION 2. MAN AS THE CREATIVE AGENT TRANSGRESSES
THE "CONDITIONING" OF THE CONSTITUTED WORLD

(a) *The constituted world becomes problematic*

Creative activity is the expression of man's innermost desire, not only
to transcend himself, but to transcend the constraints of life's network
which he suddenly experiences as a web in which he is caught in a
conflicting position with his own natural tendencies to "follow" passively the code of life's aims. It stirs all the forces confluent in the inner
workings of his existence. Whether he understands creativity as springing from the primeval depth of his being, participating in the cosmic
operations — and believes he can "transcend" his life-world conditions
by digging "below" the area of life always present to his mind — or
whether he seeks it as a participation in a "sphere above" the reach of
his circumambient world, transcending himself "through that above,"
his "creativity" springs from the entire range of the involvement he
entertains in his beingness through his whole functioning. It is the effect
of its exuberance and the overflow of its forces. It means man's aspiration to give existence to a new form of life-significance and to establish
it as an "object," his urge to produce it, his dissatisfaction with the old
system of life's meaningfulness which he projected for himself; it means
the fresh vigorous sap bursting forth within him, making the old forms
explode; it means his essential need to "transgress" their dominion.

This "transgression," however, takes a specific shape and route; it
plays a unique role in the universal constructive life-order. Yet its
possibility remains a puzzling problem.

We have already emphasized the completeness of man's involvement
in the constituted life-world. Being himself the weaver of the net in
which he is caught, how could man possibly extricate himself from it?
May any attempt at moving beyond this frame mean anything other
than just progressing in its further construction?

This total engagement of man in the constitutive activity appears
even more strikingly if we consider that *he is engaged in an intersubjective network*. Furthermore, not only is he caught in, but also conditioned by, forms of meaningfulness that are already established in his
way of experiencing, evaluating and judging, and by the very laws this
constitution follows and by the nature of its operations. Indeed, man's
involvement in the constituted world is the involvement of his nature,

his fundamental ways of functioning, behavior, responsiveness, sensing, feeling, valuating, judging, thinking, etc. It covers the complete range of his constitutive operations.

Thus as long as man only — and so Husserl saw it — performs "passively" the "natural" course of constitutive operations, he remains his own prisoner. His *urge* to break through, to transgress, to reach out in order to have a prospect of success, should correspond to some virtualities which he could conjure from within himself *other than* the constitutive apparatus capable of a system of operations *other than* those leading to the constitution of the lived-world as a recurrent type of life-milieu. It would have to follow laws and rules different from those according to which constitution invariably proceeds. In fact, already on the incipient stage in its claim (which gives it its dynamic force), the *creative urge intends to transgress the boundaries of the reach that the system of operations and laws prescribes for the constitutive activity*. In its final stage, that of the *creative result* of the long itinerary that the *creative process* — the trajectory of the transgressing endeavor — covers, its entering the constituted world means for the *created product* the *explosion of its frames, its revolutionization, and the introduction of a guiding principle for its transformation along a new line*.

The question arises, "What is the relation between the system of constitution as the routine human functioning and that of creativity, which emerges with the creative process?" Had they followed the same rules, movement toward the transgression would be a mere utopia. And, yet, how do we account for the transformation of the constituted world necessary to integrate the creative product? What is the relation of the constituted world in its progress to the creative processes emerging from and carried on on its ground by human beings, who are its bearers?

These questions outline the path of inquiry to be followed in our pursuit of the nature of creative experience.

Undoubtedly, a deal has to be made between man's allegiance to the lived-world and his endeavor to expand his life-avenues beyond its wall, which he undertakes in the creative experience. Ultimately, "man-the-creator" functions as a watershed between the constitutive individu-alization of life, on the one hand, and the creative self-interpretation of life, on the other. He performs them both simultaneously, combining and separating their functions already from the instant in which the creative urge engages him in the creative process. Remaining always vitally engaged in the constitutive system, he transgresses through his functions the rules of constitution to some limited and yet essential extent.

Only in his virtuality of bringing about the orchestration of this new functional system is man the *creative agent*. As a watershed between the constituted and creative, the *created agent* first represents the root which the creative process holds in the lived-world: the pillar of the *creative context, which thus extends over both subject and object without distinction.* Second, it represents the factor of transgressing the recurrent and repetitive course of life toward its, specifically open-ended and human, transformability.

However, with the surging of the creative urge, and the turmoil which it brings by shaking hitherto unquestioned passive commitment to ourselves as we have experienced ourselves within the world, the seemingly so solid lived-world, perduring invariably as the reliable horizon of man's pursuits, is put into doubt. With the ensuing creative process a new system of meaning-bestowing operations comes to challenge "basic" constitution. These partly oppose each other. In the balance between them the seemingly fragile, erratic and precarious creative process emerges as an undefeatable, iron structure, and a challenge to the stability and regulated advance of the constituted world. This challenge appears to menace the very solidity of the constitutive process since, to meet it, an unavoidable transformation — not only of the already established world, but also of the nuanced qualities of the constitutive functioning (feeling, appreciating, judging, etc.) — must be effected.

THE CREATIVE PROCESS AND THE "COPERNICAN REVOLUTION" IN CONCEIVING THE UNITY OF BEINGNESS:

The Creative Process as the Gathering Center and Operational Thread of Continuity among All Modalities of Being in the Constructive Unfolding of Man's Self-Interpretation-in-Existence

SECTION 1. THE DISTINCTION BETWEEN THE CREATIVE PROCESS AND THE CONSTRUCTIVE DELINEATION OF MAN'S SELF-INTERPRETATION-IN-EXISTENCE

As has been hinted at before,[7] the *human self-individualization* that delineates the constructive advance of the life-course is not the mere constructive effort of life in its *vital* significance, but is already the *result of the creative orchestration of the life-functioning* which, beginning with the phase of the source-experience, becomes the forge of guidelines for the specifically human significance of life, original with respect to our merely vital progress. This self-individualization allows the living being to *invent new avenues for his life.* In short, human life progress is the fruit of his creative powers. However, it is within a peculiar configuration of the orchestrative system that the significant guidelines themselves have to emerge. They are not present in the life-system; neither can they be a spontaneous result of life's self-interpretative course, even if they spring forth from the already creatively orchestrated functional system. This latter knits a tightly articulated sequence of self-interpretation of the course of life which the human being delineates through his life-enactment.

The role of the creative factor within the creative orchestration of the individual's functioning is, first, to introduce flexibility and the possibility of choices within the system that interpretatively confronts life conditions. Its role is to make the short and long-range planning of the possible meaningful schemas in which life-conditions might be interpretatively transformed, broadened, and constructed and reconstructed, according to changeable circumstances and to our aspirations and desires for fulfillment as well. Secondly, its role is to prepare batteries of multiple choices and bring these into sets of circumstances in which life-situations are too narrow to offer a satisfactory line of life conduct.

Thus the individual's life-course assumes a transmuted interpretative modality and, subsequently, a *specifically human significance* due to the works of the *creative orchestration* of this interpretative system. On the one side it has to be emphasized that the creative orchestration of human functions with its differentiation into three constructive faculties: *imagination, intellect,* and *will* — as well as with its four sources of meaningfulness: the *vital, poetic, intelligible*/structural, and *moral* senses — is geared in the spontaneous unfolding of its activity to the progress of the specifically human life. It is the vehicle of culture, civilization, and human history.

On the other side, however, the great questions which have emerged concerning the origin of the individualizing process of life itself (and to which I have elsewhere proposed as an answer a multiphase type of unfolding in complexity, following the Initial Spontaneity) re-appear here, in this specifically human sphere of a self-creative, yet ever changeable and progressive, constructive enterprise. The main question is: What accounts for the essential factors of this *human script*? We may answer by saying provisionally that it is the *entire system of individual functioning which in the case of the human being takes the form of creative orchestration.*

The progress of our vital unfolding creates new, larger and richer avenues for life's advance through the construction of more and more complex mechanisms instrumental in initiating more meaningful self-directed transformations of our brute, primitive resources. In the specifically human constructive enterprise the unique and striking feature to be acknowledged is that, unlike in the unilateral progress of our vital course, it is not just complexity (which is *one* way to advance), but the *complete series* or incalculably rich forms that are being invented and created by the human being for establishing life's meaningfulness which are to be experienced, lived, discoursed upon, appreciated, initiated, rejected, etc., that promotes it. The innumerable "languages" which humanity over the course of history invented, as well as the styles of life, art, culture, etc., bear witness to this seemingly unlimited openness to using, transforming, and inventing ever new ways for the expansion of human life.

SECTION 2. HOW THE CREATIVE PROCESS GENERATES
EXEMPLARY WORKS OF INVENTION WHICH FUNCTION AS
THE PROTOTYPES FOR LIFE'S INTERPRETATIVE PROGRESS

A second question of paramount importance emerges then: "Where do these ever-new forms, which enter into the self-interpretative schema of the creative orchestration — otherwise geared to concrete life pursuits — come from? It should be stressed, at the same time, that not only is this self-interpretative creative system in need of "models" to be used in its concrete work, models which culture through education and osmosis provides, but that without being provided with such "proto-typic" models at each turn of its advance, where those already in use are in their variation and multivalent transmutation exhausting their resources, the entire progress of the specifically human life would be so impoverished that it would degenerate and vanish. The end of old cultures has often happened due to the drying up of the sources from which such renovating models come forth.

It is, in fact, the creative activity proper which the human being is capable of engaging in that provides the *prototypes of significance* which then enter, as models, into the universally inter-human process of culture and into individually human self-interpretative progress. These *proto-typic* instances of human creative activity play a crucial role within the human enterprise. The peculiar mode of the creative orchestration of human functioning, with its particularly intense activation of the faculties — wherein the will acquires dominion over our intellectual structuring proficiency which has its own unique orientation toward the accomplishment of an objective aim — accounts for a uniquely concentrated and goal-oriented process, the *creative process*, in the strict sense. This process is set off from the self-interpretative schema of human life-progress and distances itself precisely by tending toward a *particular aim*, which itself does not belong to the established meaningfulness of the individual's life-course, and by unfolding new meanings as if for its own sake and entirely on its own.

It brings this about not by drawing meaning from an element of our life-circumstances or particular life-situations, but, to the contrary, standing aloof from concrete life concerns, it presents a novel, unprecedented, unforeseeable and alien "object" reposing and complete in itself, which enters into the life-world — the world of the cultural understanding of a given period — and has then to find its proper bearings within it. It has to wait until it has become properly "understood," felt, experienced, in its peculiarity and then "interpreted" in relation to the cultural "objects" already present and their meaningful styles. We talk here of the "exemplary works" of art and science which, by their radical novelty, break into the schema of understanding of a given culture and introduce a new TYPE, as I have called it above, of meaningfulness. It is the new type which is *the guidepost of the creative advance of man's self-interpretation-in-existence*. The new type is then mirrored in innumerable variants — imitations — which enter into all human activities. Even the more similarly powerful specimens of this uniquely forceful novel form/feeling complex are merely "repetitions" of *the type which functions as the prototype of meaningfulness*.

In our present investigations we are dealing precisely with *the inner workings of this creative orchestration where all the guideposts and the very possibility of progress are to be found* — namely, with the center of the creative orchestration which, in its unique concentration and direction, we call "creative inwardness" (insofar as its situation in the ensemble goes) or the "creative forge" (insofar as its specific type of activity is concerned). Indeed, in order to approach this great mystery of life which marks specifically human existence, we have to exfoliate first the nature of the *creative process* which aims at and is subordinated to the creation of a specific object which, reposing in itself, is *the bearer of significant messages that then inform our entire interpretative system*.

SECTION 3. THE INFINITELY EXPANSIVE COHERENCE OF
LIFE'S PLURI-MODAL BEINGNESS REVEALED BY THE
CREATIVE PROCESS LEADING TO A RADICAL OVERTURN OF
THE CLASSIC METAPHYSICO-ONTOLOGICAL FORMULATIONS
OF ISSUES

An investigation of the creative process will serve us as our *filum Ariadne*. This approach is strikingly renovative, for it reveals, in its expansion, the proper status of the perennial philosophical questions providing appropriate ground for examining their elements and, thus, allowing for a reformulation.

We confront there, in fact, the main question that underlies the entire philosophical quest of Western culture, a question which has taken many different philosophical formulations and has been framed in many perspectives: ontological, cosmological, epistemological, and lastly, metaphysical — namely, *the issue of the unity of the All*. This is the dilemma of the possibility of envisaging the universe of knowledge under the heading of an all-embracing schema, ultimate principle, etc., squeezing it into a restrictive totality, or renouncing any unifying principle or a priori ordering by rejecting the quest for order altogether. Contemporary thinkers (e.g., Lévinas and Merleau-Ponty), turning against "totalization," propose as an alternative an inarticulate "infinity." We will instead here propose an *infinitely expanded cohesion of life*. The question of order and unity arises out of the antithesis we seem to find in reality between the nature of its multiple elements and their inter-relations (e.g., continuity/discreteness of existents, division/inter-dependence of "realms of being," autonomy/heteronomy of formal structures, concreteness/universality of phenomenal appearance, contingency/absoluteness in the mode of existence, subjectivity/objectivity of appearances, mind/body, and the distinction or division made between various types of existence: real/ideal, fiction/nonfiction, etc.).

It is precisely in the workings of the creative process that we discover that *these modal differentiations of types of existence, as well as their generative unifying schema, originate in the creative orchestration: either in response to its functional aims, or with the introduction of types of meaningful differentiations in the course of carrying on its enterprise, or as a result of its workings*. Indeed, the creative process introduces us to the locus whence all these differentiations proceed and allows us to see them in an authentic perspective. Our approach goes contrary to classic attitudes, which look for the unity of seemingly disparate "realms of being" — which these perspectives made appear to be radically distinct and, if not irreconcilable in their intrinsic natures, then at least strictly separated. These approaches had developed in the footsteps of the discerning and analytic powers of the intellect, whose devices petrify the fluctuating flux of life and aim at presenting things in distinctions and separations. In our "Copernican revolution" of attitude we will contrast these realms of discourse concerning beingness with the modes of existence as they emerge in the genesis of the forms of life in their very origination. It will appear, then, that their seemingly radical intrinsic independence "in the nature of things" is nothing other than an objectified status which is no more radically given or more of an ultimate ontological foundation than objectivity itself. Objectivity has been clearly shown already in Husserlian constitutive analysis to be an edifice projected by the intentional powers of human consciousness, and is by no means the ground, or "reality." Reaching the ultimate springs (since it has no "ground") of objectivity itself, the ultimate springs that are to be found in *the creative orchestration of life's faculties*, we will resist the habit of approaching things directly by prying into their objective nature, which we by this very approach constitute, as being distinctive, independent, separate, autonomous, etc. We will develop the habit of seeing them emerge in their PRIMOGENITAL FUNCTIONAL PROFICIENCY: that is, they will appear to us *as specific factors of the creative functional system in the specific significant role which they play in its architectonic organization.*

The creative process will indeed show, in its three phases, the OPERATIONAL UNITY OF ALL TYPES OF BEINGNESS IN ITS SELF-INTERPRETATIVE DELINEATION of the life-course within the system of life which is itself thereby meaningfully differentiated. In its *incipient phase*, that of the CREATIVE VISION, we will witness the discrete and yet intergenerative unity of the interplay of all the human faculties (e.g., will, imagination, memory, intellect) as well as of passions, emotions, sensations, drives, impulses, strivings, profound stirrings, and yearnings. Thus, the *existential modalities of beingness will be revealed in their ONTO-GENESIS*.

Within the *second phase*, notably that of the construction of the *creative project* in an objective form, the spread of the constructive operations that draw upon the dynamically charged vision shows us, indeed, that there are no sharp distinctions in "nature," but only different operational proficiencies among the above-enumerated factors of experience in the constructive progress.

As we have illustrated in the first panel of this work, all the traditionally claimed (established) frontiers rooted in the supposed differences in nature of the respective "realms of being": body, soul, intellect, spirit, disappear within the perspective of the creative process; the functions which play their different roles within the creative orchestration reveal that it is precisely as *functional complexes with specific constructive proficiencies — specific with respect to other complexes, to each other, etc. — that body, soul, intellect, and spirit are distinguishable within the great primogenital architectonics of beingness.*

Only when focused intellectually upon their objectified manifestation may the intellect give them the shape and form that we falsely attribute to them *per se*.

The third phase of the creative process, that of the TRANSITION, leads us from the projection of an object in our creative inwardness to an objective form with a separated "type of existence," even an otherwise heterogeneous one. This is the constructive/creative phase of the *passage of the creative object being progressively constructed*, namely, the constructive advance of an objective form while it is being embodied in a "material" (wood, stone, writing, blueprint of a theory to be put into a linguistic form on paper, etc.). This work proceeds simultaneously in three perspectives. It progresses with reference first to a *vision* which, however, is transformed by consideration of the referent at the other end of the spectrum, the "material form," through which the vision will be embodied in an "object." Each of the so-called "media" — language, sound, canvas, wood, stone, movement — has its own material/formal requirements, as well as limitations with respect to possible forms it might assume or which are out of its range. Lastly, and remaining in the very life of this mutually interrogative deliberation, comes the referent of the "significant form," or, simply, the *"significance" of the creative intent*.

It is, as we will see in what follows, with respect to these three perspectives, each of them entailing its own means, criteria, imaginative possibilities and limitations, that the creative enterprise proceeds. The *creative intent* runs through all of them as it carries the activized "will to create" that promotes the enterprise.

But that intent is also being transformed insofar as the personality of man-the-creator evolves in life's temporal spread. The creative intent is fashioned within the compass of the characteristic bents, tendencies, affective dispositions, etc., which make the personality of the creative agent. These latter change under the impact of the varying richness which the creative imagination constantly, in ever-new configurations, proposes. Each of the elements of the creative material which surges is carrying its own specific significance with respect to the temper of life, vision of nature, *meaning of human existence*, and *the very core of the creator's own destiny*. Each of the perspectives offers stimulants for imaginative alternatives and new configurations of possible constructive devices. Each of these perspectives being provisorily accepted, offers a basis for the transformation of selections within the other two. The creative intent which harnesses all of them directs its vital force toward the crystallization of the objective form. The creative construction aims at a material embodiment and is the means by which the philosophically drawn divisions between mind, spirit and body are abolished, overcome, vanquished. Undoubtedly they remain, to persist as discrete domains of beingness, if envisaged in their *objective manifestations*. Within the creative transition, however, the artist, bent upon entrusting a "spiritual" message, sculpting it into a piece of stone, reaches the common springs of the material and the spiritual. He has to feel, to see, to weigh, to assume the volume of the material thinghood within the experience of his own body and mind, in order to carve approximately its contours. In this he is guided by the spirit. The piece of stone is, for him, no longer a separate "physical" object, alien to his own frame; to the contrary, once it is within the reach of his creative intent and is brought to the transitional process giving form to this otherwise alien material, *it is transformed within the creative progress into an integral element of the constructive process itself.* The ballerina executing with her limbs an airy arabesque is no more subject to her physical body as a material, objectified thing among things. She takes this material body, with its weight, its natural proficiencies of motion, as well as with its natural submission to the laws of gravity, into the creative process. In the execution of such airy arabesques (which embody the creative object of dance) her material body is transformed into the executor of the artistic (creative) intent. From its physical limitations it is lifted to the significant function in the creative message being crystallized. This significant message born within the transition phase of the creative process, crystallizing it into an objective/intersubjective significance, enters into the already-established system of *man's self-interpretative existence* in culture, civilization, style and taste. *It accounts for the continuity of the realms of beingness within the creative process of beingness as such.*

Simultaneously, another artificial division, namely that of subject and object, is dissolved. Inasmuch as each human being in his unique inwardness is the "subject" of his concerns and of the manifestations of "inwardness" which is experienced as the core of "oneself," he carries within it a directedness pointing "outside." This two-directional orientation brings about an "innermost" need to "communicate" with the "outer realm," since the "inward" realm is the retreat where he reposes in himself, withdraws into, gathers into himself, and seeks security. In other words, as Merleau-Ponty rightly saw, our functions are directed and performed, not in a self-centered fashion, but within the radius of the "outer" realm, the "objective" realm. While being centered within the "inner" realm, which contains, as if hidden, *the inner agency of the will, feelings and knowledge*, our functional performances are enmeshed with its "outer" expansion, no matter what distance is maintained with respect to other selves, processes and things, the social and cultural world which is formed, and the schema of Nature which is drawn upon.

The distinction between the "subjective" and the "objective" realms of individual human existence has, in modern philosophy, become almost a radical separation, as if the inward were not in its very nature oriented toward the outward. The multiple attempts in contemporary thought to bring them together lack an adequate point of convergence/divergence. Yet, within the phase-like progress of the creative process, in which all the human faculties are engaged, working with all the data which the objective world and others may offer, such a separation between the object and the subject, given the evidence of their *numerous phased intergenerative intertwining*, vanishes. Lastly, given the astonishing and striking fact that what begins in the most remote twilight of the "subjective core" of the creator takes after a tortuous itinerary an "objective" shape and enters the "inter-subjective" outer world in the full light of objectivity, how manifestly spurious are the divisions which the philosophical tradition makes using with ever greater effort intellectual powers to introduce analytic dissections, formal interpretations, etc., into the pulp of life — creating thereby objective phenomena out of what otherwise, in its primogenital nature, is all flux, operation, fusion, generation, and creative construction.

We had, however, to go with Edmund Husserl to the furthest confines of the objectifying powers of the human intellect in its life practice, as well as in philosophical discursive analysis, to obtain the striking insight that the *axis of the phenomenological vision which he followed has to be reversed: it has to move away from objectifying constitution toward the primogenital beginnings and the virtualities of this constitution itself, that is, toward the creative process of the specific type of living being that is man.*

While the creative process will appear in this gigantic enterprise, which we will merely sketch here as the *creative self-interpretation of life* realized within the human being and as the vehicle for replenishing life's reservoir with novel and original principles to be ever-produced to guarantee the self-interpretative life progress of human life, the creative intent of the human being — the creator's most intimately personal contribution of "genius" to this progress — gives it direction. As the entire apparatus of human operational proficiencies in their specific creative orchestration brings in the emergence of the specifically creative modalities of these proficiencies and their intergenerative and interoperative differentiation, so there sets in a constructive cooperation such that within the creative process a discrete operative coherence of all the elements, segments, significant principles and factors — "real," "ideal," "fictitious," "physical," "spiritual," "concrete," "abstract," "universal," "singular," etc. — comes about. It is in assuming respective roles that they appear together in a mutually differentiating emergence. Only under the gaze of the inquiring and discursive intellect, which fixates them in disparate "modes of being" do they acquire sets of divergent features.

Nevertheless, there emerge two questions of paramount importance: the first one, which we have already hinted at in the opening of our inquiry, concerns the very source of or the prompting of the incipient impulse toward the creative endeavor. That is, *mutatis mutandis*, it concerns the incipient impulse toward *man's self-interpretation-in-existence* or toward the *invention of further life routes which the natural spontaneous unfolding of life's self-individualization does not provide*. It is the question of the "Initial Spontaneity" which, as we will see later on, plays a crucial role, not only in the beginning of life, but within the creative orchestration as well.

The second question (which is so intimately bound with the first within the creative context circumscribed by the radius that the creative orchestration of the meaning-bestowing enterprise marks out on the otherwise unchartered ocean of life, that we may consider it its double) is about the nature of the *filum Ariadne* that the creative process spins as it progresses. In fact, the creative process makes its way through the innumerable differentiations among the interpretative elements which are objectified and so appear to be so alien, so divergent or incongenial or contradictory or opposed to each other that they could not, as they stand, enter into a combination. Indeed, unless there be some subterranean or innermost factor present to all of them — or to their virtual interplay — that accounts for the pervading coherence of the Great Game of Creation, the gist of its workings would remain a complete mystery. The creative orchestration may, as we will show, work *de facto* with all the available sources of significance; it may be assumed to be the forge of all the *multiple rationales* of the human world brought in by vital life course, invented or corroborated by man's creative/inventive powers. Our query would not, however, be complete without asking, How do these signifying factors stand in relation to each other and IN VIRTUE OF WHAT do they interplay with each other so that their specific roles may be differentiated within the creative orchestration of life's inventive work?

Heraclitus said that "logos being common to all men, each believes he has his own thought." *Mutatis mutandis* we may say that there being a discrete continuity of beingness in all the segments and modes of the significant genesis of life, there is an inner core of *"creative reason"* which allows the *"logos of life"* *to be brought together on one line with its antithesis, the "anti-logos" of man's quest for a transnatural destiny.* Furthermore, it is the creative reason which brings into the same juncture the *logos of our immeasurable subliminal pulsations which generate the vital sense of life's progress in the twilight of the constructive schema of life together with their antithetic rigorously intellectual mathematical laws.* These float in the "Platonic sky" and are foreign to all the opaque fluctuations of life. Only "creative reason" then may account for the obvious "factual" intertwinings among such disparate moments as facts, retained and fixed for good in concepts of our memory, and the ever-changeable airy floats of fancy; between the desirable and the hateful, between the rationale of calculable attainable aims and Utopian dreams. All of these modalities of significance are operative in innumerable variety and wealth of nuance in every sector of experience, thought, and imagination, and differentiate further, entering into the creative operations in which novel and original significances for life's progress are forged. What subtends their differentiative-unifying core? What maintains their intergenerative continuity in which they constantly transform each other and themselves? This *dianoia thread* running through all the contraries, opposites, parallels, etc. is the greatest mystery and the greatest issue in our inquiry into the creative transaction.

Our analysis will slowly lead toward its revelation. It will emerge in its full force ultimately from discernment of the roles that all elements and moments of life's functioning assume in life's aesthetic conversions of man's self-interpretative progress.

CHAPTER TWO

THE TRAJECTORY OF THE CREATIVE CIPHERING OF THE ORIGINAL LIFE SIGNIFICANCE:

The Resources and Architectonics of the Creative Process

PART I

THE INCIPIENT PHASE OF THE CREATIVE PROCESS

SECTION 1. THE INCIPIENT PHASE OF THE CREATIVE PROCESS AND ITS DYNAMIC RESOURCES: THE INITIAL SPONTANEITY

The mystery of human creativity has always been centered on the sources of its incipient phase, often identified with a most complex psychic phenomenon called "inspiration." But what is most puzzling in it is really its *prompting spontaneity* and its resources. "Inspiration" involves: (a) a deep stirring of our entire beingness; (b) a detachment from our familiar ground by a swing of imagination carrying us into boundless realms; (c) a nostalgia for something "new"; (d) an innermost propulsion to "make something" new ourselves. Why at a certain instant in time and space does such an imperative "impulse" to create something surge within us? Its resourcefulness seems to come from our "depth," the unfathomable depth of the human being. Being seemingly incalculable, unaccountable, it might easily be attributed to some source external to the human being of which the human agent would merely be a receiver. In contrast, to have pursued the trajectory of the hence ensuing creative process back and forth, we come to identify this decisive factor of human endeavor as the *initial spontaneity* which springs forth at the borderline of the vital forces of life's self-individualization and the setting forth of the Human Condition.

The great problem of the initial spontaneity which divides metaphysical issues from those of the presently expounded phenomenology of life, this problem of the forces and energies which cause the emergence of the creative impulse, and take it up and carry it on through all its dynamic phases toward a satisfactory conclusion, will be approached here to the full extent to which it is phenomenologically accessible.

The initial spontaneity is psychologically embedded and manifests itself prominently within the psychological network of the incipient phase of the creative process. By the same stroke it is a tributary of the psychological energies at work. However, as we have already mentioned, its role within the surging of the *initial* impulse indicates that it

175

is already flowing out from the vital/bodily/sentient system of our experience, within which we identify ourselves as experiencing beings; thus it is out of the total functional system of our experience, in which the natural, vital, bodily forces and resources play a crucial dynamic role, that the psychologically embedded impulse arises.[8]

We will pursue the work of the initial spontaneity through its own impetus as well as through the emerging intergenerative spontaneities of this incipient phase in five different registers. These are (1) the psychological, empirical resources and, (2) the dynamics of our inner life which embody the creative vision and never abandon the creative endeavor until its accomplishment in the creative object. The psychic forces serve as fundamental dynamic antennae, carrying the intrinsic underlying intentional blueprint of a structure in a further constructive phase. This latter brings in its own unique dynamic line. Indeed, creative vision itself is already an intentional dynamo; it contains germinally a qualitative complex which projects ahead the constructive endeavor. At the same time it indicates (3) a system of operations. These are simultaneous events so that if the psychological impetus crystallizes in undertaking the constructive endeavor, the system of intentional operations is right in place in order to bring about the unfolding of the constructive progress.

In the incipient phase we have to distinguish, first, a specific state of entire beingness, which Souriau and others call "cynesthesis."[9] Thence surges the *creative impulse*, which then crystallizes into the *creative vision*. The impulse is already prompting the exercise of *Imaginatio Creatrix* on the one hand, and the structural sets of operations, on the other. In fact, to the three sources of spontaneity mentioned above, activating the virtualities of the Human Condition into one specific type of process — the *creative process* — we should add at its beginning phases one further source of spontaneity, which independently activates it during its entire progress.

(4) *Imaginatio Creatrix* is indeed this motor which, by its inventive promptings stirs the *virtualities* of the individualizing beingness from the very beginning; it is its prompting which brings his/her entire framework into turmoil; it is its explosion as well in a wealth of "images," luring the attention of the *creative impulse*, that leads toward the crystallization of the complex of the creative vision. It provides the creative agent with "images" which are then used freely and constantly in the structuring process.

(5) At last, it is the resistance of the "physical substance" of the "medium" with which we work to our proposed operations that, within the period of transition from the creative idea to a physical object in the world — the *creative result*, activates our operational virtualities, holding them, and carrying them on until the accomplished achievement results. Indeed, here the psychological rule that obstacles activate our energies and direct spontaneously our operations step-by-step applies.

Let us now concentrate upon the nature of the initial stage of creative activity; its above-distinguished resources indicate already its *outward-inward source* and the meaning of its particularly *inward* incipient stage.

SECTION 2. THE TWO MOMENTS OF THE INCIPIENT PHASE OF
THE CREATIVE PROCESS

(a) *The creative stirring*

Whether we feel this disturbing denseness spontaneously, or whether we retrieve it after a dull interval by conscious effort of the will, the creative preliminary state of the creative condition is a turmoil disturbing our inner comfort. Resting otherwise in a passive self-contentment, absorbed by the stereotype of life experience and feeling "full," we are inwardly, all of a sudden, as if stung, shaken by a feeling of missing something crucial within ourselves, by an invading nostalgia prompting us to get out and to seek it, by an overwhelming urge to get it by our own means; to make it, to invent it, to "create" it. Strangely enough, with the surging of these moments within us we are stirred in our entire beingness which comes to the fore with a wealth of experience we have not guessed is there. We feel that not only the answer to our urge, but infinitely more, is within us. Indeed, the impulse to create is at first the desire to grasp this inner state of abundance. We lack ideas, forms of thought, points of approach, etc. to seize this sudden expansion of our entire inner beingness. This expansion breaks down the schema of forms with which we have hitherto interpreted and organized our inner and outer world. At its incipient point the creative moment is the feeling of an overflow of the preestablished framework of our life-world and of ourselves, within it.

This state or condition is, however — contrary to those who attribute to it a "mystic" character or that of the "gratuitously given" — the crucial aspect of creation, not even leading necessarily to the phase of creative effort. On the contrary, it is infinitely more often experienced for its own sake than it is given the concrete impulse for a creative activity. Furthermore, it is a frequent observation that this specific tension which accompanies the experience of the expansion of our beingness or of abundance — and which is the subjective, psychological condition of the creative activity — dissipates as soon as, in an effort to grasp it, we attempt to analyze and explain our inner state and find no satisfactory forms to interpret it with. The mind seems definitely satisfied.

Thus, it would seem that in order that this purely subjective inner state may initiate the creative effort *there must occur a further differentiation of this inner condition before the creative orientation is released. It is this differentiation which, in fact, initiates the creative activity proper.*

Although the initial plenitude of our self-experience, our inner stirring, seems rich in infinite virtualities of feelings, ideas and dreams to be expressed, in no way is there anything distinctive, clear, defined. Furthermore, no principle lies ready to crystallize them. There whirls before our reflective mind an infinite wealth of "possible," hitherto unseen, shapes, fragments of images, colors, fascinations of sounds, aromas, profiles of personalities. The "possible" lures us, suggesting leads toward the new "incarnation" of our inner state; they appear as strikingly appealing as if "new." In fact, all of them draw upon the reservoir of our past experiences, but glorify their fragments by a nebulous halo of what remains "invisible," but is there nonetheless.

It is in this indetermination that lies their force. And yet as suggestive as this whirl of "possibles" may be in comparison with the scant and thin inventively pregnant elements, it is this set of elements with which the creative process will or might set out!

In the simple self-experience of the inventive agent — or in its lived contemplation —, this infinite halo of whirling elements is diffused, unclear; these sounds, colors, forms, seemingly expanding in such a profusion and with such a vivid and imposing forcefulness, escape our grasp when we focus our attention on any one of them; their presence is diffuse and ephemeral. In their "nature" they are nothing concrete. As already hinted at above, and as literary critics always insist, they have their source in the reservoir of the memory; and yet they do not re-surge into the present field of our attention in the mode of mere reminiscences of previous experiential material. This *inner stirring of all the virtualities of our Human Condition, which makes them "re-appear" outside of any context* on the level of experience, throws them forth as if from the central point where all the arteries of the inventive mechanism, which is not yet set in motion, might gather. At the verge of being transformed by a specific conscious function, they appear in the mode of *"aesthetic virtualities."*

The "deep well" of memory is shared equally by humankind; so is this condition of the effervescence of our self-experience. This effervescence of our entire beingness may be considered, as is often done, as a state of "inspiration" (that is, as an incipient phase of the creative process bearing the creative impulse along, ready to unfold its promptings, or as the incipient moment of this process) only when from its luring, fascinating confusion of infinite plenitude — in which the merely indifferentiated totality is immediately given while each of its elements eludes us — there emerges an identifying and determining reflection. Indeed, the pressure of the creative impulse carries within itself in germ the structuring apparatus: *imaginatio creatrix* as the core of the intentional structuring mechanism.

From its workings there arises before us a specific emotive form, scant and meager, but which "like God's children," in Goethe's words, differentiates, selects, provides a framework for and arranges concretely the chaotic confluence of experiential imaginary elements into a *dominant theme*, an "image," a "meaning," a "message" to be conveyed: *the creative vision.* "Inspiration" as a subliminal (that is, pre-thematizing) condition becomes a creative factor only after it has acquired a specific form, a *vision*.

(b) *The creative vision*

The "creative vision" is not a mere presentification of a coherent image — be it of particular intensity and clarity, persuasiveness and enhancing force.[10] It is not like the "beatific vision" of a saint glorifying the Divine, nor a "vision" of a politician or an historian foreseeing the course which humanity might take. It will be "creative" only when it will appear to the person along with the *innermost prompting that it is up to her to accomplish it*. The creative vision, in fact, not only presentifies (like constitutive perception) an imaginary complex, but *compels* us to its realization; it activates the dormant forces, virtualities and resources of

consciousness — of the complete human being — toward an undertaking, a specific type of undertaking. Like Leibnizean "pure possibles,"
the *creative vision carries an intrinsic striving toward an existential
accomplishment*; first and foremost, toward the clarification and crystallization of its "message" into a form of *"unique" significance*; second,
since its imaginative "theme" is the representation/embodiment of
significance (and being merely a mental image it has to strive toward
acquiring a communicative/intersubjective status of being), it carries a
prompting toward its embodiment in an objectified form which would
raise it from subjective inwardness into a universally accessible medium
of communication. Concurrently, the creative vision carries within itself,
in fact, a scheme for its virtual "realization," the intention of its
programmatic scheme. In itself, the creative vision is at first this intuition, but one pregnant with ways and means for its unfolding a most
vertiginous process.

SECTION 3. CREATIVE VOLITION

Were the creative vision merely an "image" or "presentification" of any
sort, it would like most images exist solely for the simple aesthetic
consumption of its host. But it seems to point essentially to the will.
First it initiates activity and, second, it issues indications as to its mode
of operation. As we have already hinted, the creative vision is of such a
nature that it differs essentially from the mere work of imagination
which can propose to our attention as "possible" a certain object, but
which reflects merely the contemplative/passive self-consuming attitude
of consciousness. These pictures function as mere elements in its stream
and disappear together with its advance. The creative vision, in contrast, presents itself as a compact qualitative unit which simultaneously
is a specific *activating source and a principle which implies operational
organization as well as a set of operations for its fulfillment.*

Indeed the qualitative nature of the creative vision is a compact set
of images joined with each other in a most intimate way and merely
indicated without sharp contours, but ready to be unfolded to their full
extent and, in this unfolding, postulating already other images either
merely indicated or already implicitly contained. In their configurations
these "imaginings" are not, however, a simple fruit of the associative
power of imagination; their association, although rooted in one or other
system of possible schemes of the associative mechanism, come about

as the result of something else, namely, the elements making out the experiential system of the individual in terms of which his self-interpretation in existence pursues its course. Only the presentational mode is that of an "image," but the content does not repose in any visual, audible, intellectual image-complex, fixed and self-contained. On the contrary, its qualitative aspects refer to the significances of our bodily functions, the genetic line of the volitional unfolding, modalities of ratiocinating, etc. Its virtual resources, otherwise mute, are now vocal and awake and call for their share in the expression of the unique "message." In short, the entire wealth of man's self-interpretative life-course seems to be involved in proposing the creative vision. Consequently the virtuality of the vision that unfolds contrasts radically with mere stationary imagery or ideal possibility. It appeals to all our vital functions, as well as to all our conscious faculties at play to become active, to be brought into the light of consciousness. The creative vision, even in germ, activates the functions of the experiential system toward its unfolding. This is why artists and scientists often recall having been haunted by a vague "idea" until they went after it; it is in this way that the projection of some type of work compels us to continue it. And in this way the work of creation works "in depth," whereas the work of intentional constitution operates only at the outer edge of self-awareness. In this way also our complete personality is involved as well. Due to the involvement of our entire experiential system, which, being first the ground and springboard of the vision and being, second, activated by fulfillment, we can identify ourselves on the rebound with our works which we "visualize in a visionary way" as virtually "in our power," lying in waiting within us to be wrought out, being "on their way," and, most of all, *conveying a uniquely intimate significance which we want to insert into the intersubjective life-world.* In accomplishing this visionary project, we find a special accomplishment of our own beingness. We feel, on the one side, that we have reached the deepest of all personal gains; on the other side, we experience ourselves as if lifted above the common doom of mankind, having instead reached a uniquely meaningful status. In the progress of working at the crystallization of the creative vision its appeal to our now completely vitalized, experiential system accounts not only for the amplitude of the pluridimensionality of vistas and resources from which it draws, but also for the incomparable *experiential plenitude with which we feel gratified* during its development. We feel that "we live our originating work," that we live *in it* and, what is most peculiar, that this is (in contrast to the surface of existence) our "real," most profound and authentic life in which we are engaged. To conclude: *the basic source of the creative force is the volitional prompting springing forth from out of the interior life to forge within our work this authentic significance of our own unique existence.*

SECTION 4. CREATIVE INTUITION AS THE ANTENNA
BETWEEN THE CREATIVE VISION AND ITS CRYSTALLIZATION
IN THE "IDEA OF THE CREATIVE WORK"

From the creative point of view, intuition reveals itself as already *constituted.* The creative process is initiated when, from the undifferentiated and effervescent matrix, there emerges into the focus of our attention the creative vision — seemingly scant if compared with the infinite, luring richness of the virtualities, but powerful in organizing the complete field of consciousness because of the depth of its origins.

Yet this experiential complex is immersed within the current meaningful system of our everyday life-course, moving automatically onwards. The point from which the meaningfulness of the creative vision is launched out of the self-experience of a vital/emotive stirring of our being — in itself "aesthetic," but devoid of particular meaning — is its very core: the *creative intuition.* The creative process sets out to differentiate itself from the otherwise undefined meaningfulness of this particular experience by its *intuitive core.* It is this intuitive core which indicates the process' implicit structuralization and its virtually contained system of operations, this latter meant for the virtual manifestation of its content in its striving toward existence.

We use here the term "intuition" in a way comparable to that of Bergson. Bergson, who opposes vehemently the assumption of a purely "utilitarian" character of cognition or of the mind, sees intuition (intuitive power) as contained in a supra-intellectual "emotion." Intuition, intuitive power, may become, due to its forcefulness, a generating source of ideas. It is itself by no means prompted by an idea but by an affective *ébranlement.*

The experiential plenitude we are discussing here is shared by the creative process with other modes of self-experience; it is its *vital subjective condition.* Yet its origin is due to a specific turn in our entire fruitioning in which consciousness plays a decisive role. The otherwise undifferentiated and whirling state of consciousness acquires now the synthesizing form of structurally condensed *intuitive insight*, which means already that there is an active mobilization of all the individual virtualities, as well as an outline of operations into which they should be channeled. Already in germ the creative vision is essentially "finalistic."

Within the present analysis creative intuition is, in its origin and nature, neither intellectual nor emotive. In itself it has no form or meaning, but follows the promptings of the Human Condition to give a *sense*, a specifically human sense, to the *primeval logos* of life, promptings which the life-course carries out once the Imaginatio Creatrix is set at work. This prompting, surging from the midst of the *creative orchestration*, and appealing to all our functions, causes the creative intuition to surge and engage deliberately in a radically new type of a meaning-giving process. It means a radical overturn of priorities.

In contrast to the "utilitarian," or as I say "vitally significant," constitutive channel of the process setting life's course, the *Primeval Logos of Life distills from within itself the intuitive instance which takes on the significance of the creative configuration of the creative-vision complex*, as its synthetic dominant significance; this latter significance abandons the concerns of everyday life.

Thus intuition invariably surges already constituted — but within creative experience; however, the vision, idea, process and its significance are not "vital" but, on the contrary are "aesthetic" or, better, "poetic."

Their sudden surging from the *primeval logos* is due to the creative stirrings of man's entire frame.

The analysis of the incipient stage of the creative process shows:

(1) that, contrary to traditional views, there seems to be no mystery involved in the origin of creative experience; "inspiration," intuition might well be unpredictable, unforeseen, incalculable, unforced, etc., yet we may say with Goethe that, as in the old French game of Cadille in which the fall of the dice might be to a large degree decisive and unforeseen, it is left entirely to the skill of the player to meet the situation thus created. To make *specific use* of what may be the outcome is where the creative business begins.

(2) In view of the fact that the incipient phase of human creativity is characterized by a complete system of activation of consciousness, the supposition is at hand that this particular intensity, effervescence and revelation of the virtualized content of consciousness, called "inspiration," or creative impulse, is not in itself the result of a particular

configuration of conscious functions. Thus, although the structurization progress of the creative process may be seen, in what follows, as essentially the work of consciousness, in this analysis consciousness expands further than any conception of an intentional network could reach. Furthermore, the origin and genetic impetus of the creative endeavor appears already to lie beyond any reach of the conscious faculties. On the contrary, our investigation, instead of assuming consciousness, opens all the questions concerning its nature and role. We will discuss the role of the creative vision in the progress of the creative process in our subsequent analysis.

SECTION 5. THE WORK AS THE CREATIVE PRODUCT

It may be unexpected that from the incipient phase of the creative process we would move now directly to its final point; that from the mere hint of a project coupled with the propulsion to undertake its fulfillment we would move directly to the final result, jumping over the extended and complex trajectory to that point. The reason for our *anticipating* before its time, at this point, this final result, is that in spite of the variability of both termini during the fulfilling trajectory, which might result in a complete discrepancy between the varying types of propulsion (vision), its crystallized project (*idea of the creative work*) and its accomplished result (the creative object), these two face each other from the very start as *constructive correlates*. As such they frame the creative process at both of its extremities. To exfoliate their constructive correlation in its changeable nature will introduce us to the heart of the progress of the creative process.

Already in the creative intuition there is, in fact, implied in germ the tentative outline of *the creative system*; there is also an essential orientation of the creative vision in its hazy content, image-complex or scheme, toward a form of "being," an "object," in which this image-complex, etc. would be crystallized. The propulsion which it entails is precisely to promote the creative process which it outlines for the accomplishment of this "objective," crystallized form.

However, it is only an "objective form" which is thus indicated to fulfill the anticipatory nature of the vision. It needs a *complete constructing process*. This constructive process begins its work proper, first, by the formation of the *idea of the creative aim*, the idea of a "virtual object." Second, it stretches into an extended, long-winded phase in which, through the selection of means (e.g., media expression, technique, etc.), a transition can be achieved between the entirely interiorized subjective, intentional idea and its crystallization in an *intersubjectively intentional object*, as a *form of beingness*, that is a constructive creative process. Only in the course of this process, may the created object anticipated, but until then indeterminate, be outlined and determined in its basic features.

The phase of *transition constitutes the core of the creative process*. It is also of crucial significance for the main ontological-anthropological questions. Once the transition is accomplished and the creative result enters and establishes itself among other things within the framework of the objective life-world, the "umbilical cord" between it and the creative agent, its source and bearer, like that between the mother and child, breaks and their, until then united, "bodies" are radically separated; this is the moment of "birth" into intersubjectively significant life. A poem, a painting, a monument, is then at the exact point of its constructed accomplished state, even if in the subjective conception of the painter or poet it still remains unsatisfactory and in need of further elaboration; yet, when as a worldly object it stands "on its own" in front of the spectator, it acquires a relatively independent, existential status, independent of its maker. It is ready to answer for itself.

Furthermore, as has been pointed out above, one of the basic directives of the creative vision is that it evolves not only toward the crystallization of its intuitive significance into a form of being, but that this crystallization itself serves its innermost striving and acquires an appropriate significance: namely, that of *communicative expression.* Some like J. P. Sartre think that the work of art carries essentially a social message. Some think that the artist constructs his work, embodying in it an intersubjective form of meaningfulness, without intending to express anything personal addressed to a given society, group of individuals, or even to any particular individual. And yet even if he creates essentially "for himself," it is in order to clarify for himself, as the "Other" within him who observes and judges, etc. his ideas and emotions, the mysterious stirrings of his being. He attempts to bring these out of the obscure twilight into the light of reflection and, in this clarification, enable them to communicate to himself, as the "Other" who is not merely absorbed in life, but oversees it, its authentic truth, its hidden message. Consequently, the work of art, a scientific theory, etc. essentially "communicate" something, and their very being may be identified with their function of communicating and the unique type of message to be conveyed: *a novel, unprecedented type of message on the significance of life.*

Thus it is upon this message that the accent falls. This message, which at the end of the creative trajectory is severed from the fluctuating and inexorably advancing flux of the subjective/intentional creative process, is fixed in an objective/intentional structure which remains and perdures while the subjective process flows on like a river into which, we can say with Heraclitus, we never enter twice, and maybe not even once, since we are ourselves this river. By fixing its message and perduring, the creative result affirms itself and is received into the intersubjective life-world.

It is no wonder that on the one hand the ties of the created work to the subjective aspect of this message — originating from the human situation, social circumstance and innermost personal experience of its maker — have made the art/literary critic cover this entire range of subjective tendencies as the possible key to the understanding of the work. On the other hand, the phenomenological approach traced by Moritz Geiger has emphasized the self-containment of an accomplished work; hence in the aesthetics of Roman Ingarden, as well as in the approach of the New Critics, the work is interpreted in its intrinsic, universally objective structure alone.

While our analysis precludes from the start understanding of the created work in direct relation to "personal experiences" in the life-course of the poet, writer, artist or scholar, yet having, at last, found the crucial access to the issue of the nature and role of the created work in the course of investigation of its origin and genesis within the entire scheme of *man's self-interpretation in existence*, we see the work's role as one unique in the self-interpretative progress and as consisting *precisely in bringing out absolutely novel elements of life-significance.* In this view the created work itself is a message, although neither a subjective, existential voice of its maker, nor a meaningful system governed by the life-subservient functions of reason/intentionality.

As we will see, its nature resides in neither place. *The unique significance which a created work incorporates is suspended upon its aboriginal interplay with its creative vision.*

The reason for vacillation in approach to the ready-made creative object lies in the fact that the work of creation, once detached from its maker as an "independent" object, is not independent, autonomous, self-contained and existentially self-sufficient, like a rock, a tree, a living being which reposes in itself, being *in itself what it is*. The fact that it is essentially a message that makes the core of a work's beingness does not allow it to close in upon itself, and be self-contained or self-explanatory. Indeed, a naive, uncritical acquaintance with a work of creation reveals its *double polarity: its message or significance is relative to the recipient*. As a communicable message it is appropriately structured in relation to the conditions of communication. To understand the secret, hidden springs of its meaning, we have to follow its intrinsic pointer toward its origin, that is toward the creative process in which it has been conceived and crystallized. The intrinsic analysis of the work alone does not yield the key to its meaningfulness; by its very nature the created work calls for a *creative analysis* which, however, should not be understood in the traditional sense of analysis of the subjective processes and experiences of the maker, but in a specific sense which will come out in our investigations.

We will begin by pointing out the shortcomings of intrinsic analysis of a work of art.

(a) *The intrinsic cognition of the creative work confined to represented objective schemes*

Creation emerges like a problem, or more like an enigma from works of art. It is in effect the work of art which surprises us by the place that it has just filled among other objects. It distinguishes itself by its own unique power to hold our attention in an intense manner, to give us, by the excellence of its form and by the richness of its qualities, a fullness of emotion that it evokes in us. We attempt to comprehend the secret of its power and of its perfection, and it is toward its origin that we naturally turn. A more critical attitude, however, redirects our attention toward the work itself. It would seem that, standing before us in its complete state, we need only concentrate our attention on it; in submitting it to a rigorous phenomenological analysis, one would deprive it of all its mystery. False hope! The work as it presents itself for direct analysis does not at all offer its complete "substance." It hides its profound meaning for it is seen through a series of schema while its inner workings remain hidden. It is like trying to analyze marionettes by their form and dress, while the manipulations which create living characters in the theatre remain unknown. Without its inner workings, the work of art does not even begin to come to life; it remains inert, lifeless.

We approach, in fact, the created object through its own cognitive devices which it extends toward us. This position, however, is in radical contrast to Ingarden's approach in which these cognitive devices come from the intrinsic structure of the work of art alone, and which rejects outright the structural schemata as the decisive device of its cognition. In fact, Ingarden stresses as decisive the role of the particular medium of expression which constitutes its "material substance." Words and sentences, in their concatenations in a literary work, sounds in their rhythmic and harmonic arrangements outlined in a musical score, plastic shapes and colors in painting, and volume in architecture and sculpture are organized into spatio-temporal schemes necessary for entering the spatio-temporal axis of the life-world. But these media do not themselves possess a spatio-temporal nature on their own: they "project" spatio-temporal, structural schemes correlative to the stream of temporal experience and the spatiality of successive stages of the recipient. It is with reference to this stream that emotions, feelings and ideas are supposed to be re-constructed within the recipient's own framework. In short, the work of art or of science does not partake in its essence of the temporality of the world-process. A poem or a novel needs time to be read or heard; the moment takes time to be apprehended and revealed to us from various spatial angles in its totality. A scientific theory also needs time to be studied and understood. This is, however, not the time of the work itself, as a type of object, but that of the recipient, whereas the work "extends temporally" through an aesthetic scheme in its structure in which, as in a literary work, certain aesthetic complexes of experience either succeed each other in a cause and effect relation, are simultaneous, or are separated from each other, resulting in a structural skeleton that is a system of reference for the lived experience of the recipient, guidelines to be filled in by his continuous experiential flux; a musical work, through the specific encroaching of the sonorous elements succeeding each other and thus extends in continuous duration a specific "pseudo-temporal" structure. This structure, while itself atemporal, makes room for itself within worldly time by exploding its intervals and directing the pace, arrangement and intensity of the new temporal succession according to its own devices.

Through its structure and its content the created object offers a series of objective schemes upon the basis of which the percipient — as the American contextualists have rightly observed — amplifies the given in a "fusion" with it into a complete object, which becomes again part of subjective experience. Being partly objectively outlined, but in need of a partly subjective, strictly individual completion, the creative object cannot yield its entire "content" and meaningfulness as it stands before us; it is essentially subject to an unlimited number of different "interpretations." We are always striving to pin down the correct and precise meaning or message that it bears but, due to its schematic, perspectivistic structure, the intrinsic analysis of the creative object falls short of receiving its innermost significance.

A particularly striking case of the insufficiency of intrinsic analysis of the literary work is offered by certain works, such as, for instance, those which are not confined to giving a particular view of reality, or to creating a poetic reality themselves, but attempt to reach "beyond" reality and, like expressionism, or some works of the romantic period, convey an all-encompassing "transcending" message, view, or insight. As we have shown elsewhere,[11] it appears in the analysis of the work itself that the structure is selected to serve this purpose and that all the content of the work stands not for itself, but for what it is ultimately meant to reveal.

(b) *Intrinsic analysis of the work of art and its all-encompassing,*
     transcending perspective; the immanent reality and the
     all-encompassing vision

Within our approach to the creative work, the way in which the role of its intrinsic analysis appears obviously differs from classic phenomenological aesthetics. The immediate aim of the intrinsic analysis of the work of art, or of science, is to arrive, through a differentiation of the various elements of its content, at a discovery of their particular functions within the whole structure, in order to grasp a centered perspective on it, to reach a middle point where the totality of its subordinate elements will appear transparent in their functional interconnections and respective functional roles within an overall meaningfulness. That is the formal requirement of analysis responsible for correctly understanding the "message" which the created work is meant to convey. This message, however, is, as we have already intimated, of utmost intuitive simplicity and consequently is embodied in a complete apparatus in the chosen medium, giving it an appropriate form as a "thing" in order to introduce it into the complex intersubjective realm. Secondly, this message is itself a quintessence of a universal approach to life, or the world, of the meaning of life and of its ultimate sense and, consequently in order to be expressed, the message needs a complete setting for such a world-view. What a creator strives to grasp is that which goes beyond his established life-framework which, itself, is part of the established life-world. Consequently it is necessary, first, to provide a novel setting for this message which reaches beyond the setting that the "old" world-view could provide. In short, a real work of creation founds a new human reality. Whether referring to Kepler's Laws of the solar system, Newton's Laws of gravitation, each single poem of Mallarmé or to Rodin's sculpture "Bourgois de Calais," the striking effect of the work is that it opens for the recipient and introduces him to a hitherto closed dimension of understanding and perception whereby his previous experience of reality, and his perspective upon the human universe, are transformed.

In certain great works of art one has the impression that the central theme is already a novel, original view upon reality. Balzac's *Comédie humaine*, in spite of the particular psychological and sociological interest of the plots and of the personages he so skillfully sketches in their innermost workings, seems nevertheless to obtain its culminating significance by giving a hitherto hidden view of the period, and beyond, revealing a new view of humanity itself. So Zola's fictions, in their "realistic" tendency, do not depict life "as it is," because the same type of events could and have been experienced by other artists in an entirely different vein. They aim at creating a view of life, at establishing an avenue of experience of the "true reality of life," that seems as hopeless as the struggle of the individual, with his natural tendencies on the one hand and social forces on the other, an effort doomed from the beginning. These forces unmercifully seize the individual who, it seems, is unable to marshal the power necessary to throw off the yoke. So Flemish painting and expressionistic drama (not to mention Chagall's and Rouault's canvasses and the whole range of abstract art) aim at revealing a new significance of human reality, of life.

It can be ventured at the outset, what will later on receive justification, that one of the signs of authentic creative work is to have founded a new universe of thought and sensibility centered upon itself, self-sufficient and complete in its sense of life, a new reality.

It is the particular feature of such a "poetic reality," either artistic or the outcome of a scientific theory as well, that it is self-enclosed. If there is a gap in its presentation, if there is an intrinsic split or inconsistency within its functional network of meaningfulness, this reality founders and the work appears transparent, does not stand on its own feet, fails. This reality which the work establishes is not an intrinsic element of its structure or content, but is their result; yet it belongs to its framework, designing its furthest extent and its very "sense."

The crystallization of this meaningful experiential work of creation demonstrates this going beyond any intrinsic content in its "message" and the subordination of the work's structure more strikingly in some works than in others. Let us for instance analyze the case of a Polish romantic dramatic work by Krasiński in comparison with German expressionistic drama.[12]

Through intrinsic analysis of the work of art we can indeed establish the overall structure of the work and determine the particular elements in their functioning and structuring of the "plot of action," or "situation theme," often considered the central element of some types of literary or plastic art. By so doing we may grasp the idea of the work as it is inherent in the work and, finally, its meaning or significance for its cultural period on the one hand, and for its maker on the other, and thus arrive at the differentiation of the specific universe of thought and sensation that the work opens. But with works of art like Zygmunt Krasiński's *The Undivine Comedy*, Kafka's *Castle*, or *Trial*, we, having accomplished this analysis, have still clearly failed to see what its center of significance is. And this center of significance poses another problem, due to (a) a specific incompleteness of understanding or grasp of its ideas, and (b) the lack within its content of the final "key" to its mysterious "intent." Though all the other aspects of the work be seen — its being finished, established in its frame, resolved in its outline, and polished —, if analysis is restricted to their structure, these remain a puzzle or a dark mystery. With the "message" as such being an essential aspect of the created work, with all other aspects oriented toward this function of communication, then, when the quest for an understanding of its "meaning" or "message" remains unresolved the communication fails, the work remains incomprehensible.

In the face of this failure we are naturally brought beyond the immanent content of the work, beyond the objective structure, and are instead directed back toward its originary source. However it is not the psychological, changeable and ephemeral processes in which the process constructing the work was embedded that are singled out by our quest. Nor does this intuitive message to be retrieved, that transcends the objective, limited frame of the creative work, point toward personal experiences of the creator; these inform its progress toward realizing its own impetus by their intensity, variety and richness, and so accompany inspiration and the creative impulse. The personal life — the emotional strains and stresses, encounters with other human beings in their depth, with emotional and passionate intensity — might well be a subjective stratum, as well as one of the prompting forces along which the creative stream curves in its subterranean winding. Yet none of these experiential circuits could account for the "meaning" which the creative work unfolds. In searching for the ultimate "sense," "meaningfulness," "message" of a creative work, we are led to the creative process as a particular and unique itinerary shaping the work which takes place in and along with all life-experiences with their forces as if "through them," and yet delineates its constructive course, first and foremost, as a distinctive, irreducible line of inward activity. Following its trajectory backwards we reach its creative vision, with the creative intuition enlightening the incipient stage which was the "message" the creative agent first conceived, assumed, tentatively grasped and then strove to clarify for himself in a universally communicative form, working at it within his life-conditions, within the stricture of the laws of creative production and the limitations of the media.

Our search for this pristine vision of the work at its source, transcending its objective force, points not toward the haphazard personal experiences of the maker nor toward the course of his life with its events and crises — as relevant to the work as they might appear — but toward a distinctively different subterranean itinerary of his "inner life," one which makes a path for itself within the other events and which, after Coleridge, we might call the "*biographia literaria*," the biography of the artistic, creative process in its enlightenment as seen in the successive creative endeavors of the same creator.[13] There can be no doubt that the single, specific creative effort, oriented toward one distinctive aim, is not a sporadic, accidental and unique event in the "inner life" of the individual. In a way, each separate effort continues the previous ones, and even so anticipates the subsequent ones. Each new created work of the same maker is a stepping stone to the next one; in some cases there may be variations on a "theme" which is being tried in all possible configurations. While considering the totality of a painter's work we often have the impression that a series of his paintings, each of them a distinctive, separate, self-centered object in "reality," is, in fact, a work of repetition, in which an attempt is made at improving certain aspects of workmanship, a vision of expression, in which progressively the greater majority of problems of a certain type are solved — as, for instance in Watteau's landscapes or in Italian theatre paintings — until, at a certain point (as in the *Embarquement for Cithera*), all these dispersed solutions find their synthesis in a masterpiece. This masterpiece appears, then, as the aim toward which all the previous fragmentary efforts converge. This "repetition" phenomenon of the creative progress is even more striking in a scientific or philosophical field. There seems to be, in science and philosophy, an all-encompassing aim of the creative quest for which the particular points of theories created are clearly fragmentary preparations in the one big endeavor, partaking of a complete synthetic view.

Indeed, says Prevost, going through Stendhal's diary, "*La Filosofia Nova*," in which at the age of twenty Stendhal records his decision to impose upon himself a rigorous discipline of effort in order to create a great work, the inward development of the author cannot be dissociated from his technical apprenticeship.[14] The augmentation of the vividness of insight, intensity of expression, sharpness of discrimination and selection, which means real progress of style in any endeavor, is certainly the effect of an inner progress, not in a purely subjective understanding of that, but as an acquisition through repetitious attempts of certain permanent dispositions of the creative spirit at work. Prevost shows that the path of apprenticeship followed by Stendhal, which began with the banality of imitation of the classic theater, of the Italian *Opéra Comique*, and proceeded through the ascetic project of personal discipline which brought about a deepening of knowledge and culture, and continued through a project of thorough study of human types and the Arts, shows a continuous, albeit diffused, creative spirit already at work.

Immanent analysis of the created work, in radical contrast to a "fabricated" one, aims through its all-encompassing transcending message at the "supra-objective"; it reveals the narrow limits of the life-significance which remains circumscribed by a subjective/objective axis. But it does not imply either a "mystical," supra-rational realm or a specific dimension of the spirit "above," accessible only to art or science. It circumscribes the reach of the creative function of the creative, not being enclosed centered, in the narrow frame of the human consciousness-like constitution of the standard life-world by human boundaries. Beyond itself, it indicates something unique to the creative function — in contrast to the intentional: the creative vision. The creative vision predetermines, already at this incipient point, the creative process as something entirely *sui generis*, different from the processes of empirical psychology, as well as from those of Husserlian intentionality. Although imbedded in them, the creative process is led independently by its creative intuition, without any direct causal relation to either process that would motivate psychologically the quality or significance of the creative content which is entirely irreducible. Whatever we might borrow from purely empirical or intentional experience, it becomes transmuted and transformed through the orchestrated workings of the creative function of the creative process which is *causa sui*.

Thus we are brought to the creative process itself.

PART II

THE CREATIVE TRAJECTORY BETWEEN THE TWO PHASES OF THE LIFE-WORLD

SECTION 1. THE THREE—PHASE CREATIVE PROCESS

(a) *The three phases*

The creative process is essentially the trajectory of constructive progress toward the accomplishment of an "object" and its establishment within the life-world. It consists of three major phases. We have already circumscribed their spread by indicating the roots "below" the full light of the conscious life of the creative agent, at the one extreme, and that "above" which tends toward an all-encompassing view of the human universe which goes beyond the logos of life itself at the other. The creative vision marks the incipient phase of the creative endeavor at one extreme and the accomplished creative work with its novel *life-cipher* indicating the final point of the process at the other extreme.

One of them surges from a *phase of the life-world* in which the creative agent is absorbed and from within which he initiates the process of creation, while he suspends the all-absorbing impact of the hitherto prevailing significance of life. The creative process unfolds, indeed, its own "life," subterranean to the life-world current. But, bringing the creative product into the life-world, it returns to it more forcefully than ever. yet it is a *different phase of the life-world which it enters into*. Thus the creative process is essentially *transitional*: a subterranean stream renovating "life" between two sedate and already established phases of the life-world. As such it plays most significant roles with respect to questions concerning the *origin of types, of beings, modes of existence, continuity/discontinuity of beingness*, etc. They will surface as we go along, opening a new perspective in ontological queries.

(b) *The advent of the creative object* (*work*) *and the three phases of its trajectory*

Whether we approach it from the point of view of its incipient moment,

195

or from that of the insufficiency of the intrinsic analysis of the objective structure of the creative result when complete and disengaged from its generic ties, *the creative process appears* essentially as the process of the constructive generation of an independent separable object; it appears as a telic process having a goal not in itself, like the process of our inner growth, but in the existential advent of a novel "object" into the life-world.

As we have already mentioned, the creative vision distinguishes itself from other forms of "vision" by projecting itself toward an objectification. We may argue that a " political vision" also projects itself toward incarnation in a social setting; in this it has a creative aspect. However, the properly creative vision does not imply some form of intersubjective crystallization, as with religious insights, revelatory appeals, etc. It postulates an *embodiment* in an *independent, existentially distinctive, objective form* which is capable of securing for itself and *assuming a significant place among other objects of the life-world* from whence its significance radiates.

The constructive trajectory of the creative object is initiated by the *first phase*, in which (A) the *creative vision* emerges from the passional, pre-experiential, as well as experiential/emotive density as a compact complex which progressively unfolds its programmatic content: (1) operational, (2) qualitative, and (3) objectifying. It loosens its grip when the creative process proper takes over. The creative process is essentially the constructive trajectory of the object. The process itself is a TRANSITIONAL one. The finalistic nature of the creative vision outlines its process-like realization, starting with the purely subjective phase in which (B) the *objective idea* of the object to be created is crystallized and formed. It is with the formation of the objective idea of the work that the constructive trajectory begins. In fact, it is formed by the creative orchestration already at work. Through a selective process in various dimensions, its range of possibilities is already determined by the vision, and then narrowed down through objective limitations of various types, finally, by the appropriateness of the objective form to be chosen and the corresponding media for its realization.

With the objective idea of the work the *second phase* of creative endeavor starts. The second phase, like the first, is not a separate series of events. On the contrary, at this point we have to see as a succession what, in fact, often happens simultaneously and in interaction; and yet, whatever its actual entanglements, it follows a logical line which (in order to understand its manner of progressing) we have to disengage from acts of consciousness swarming in all directions. As the first phase encroaches already upon the second by consulting, in a preliminary perusal, the objective conditions needed to specify the vision itself, so the second phase, that of the formation of an *idea of the work* to be envisaged, encroaches already upon the *third phase* by simultaneously projecting its great lines and consulting its virtualities poised for selection: (C) *the phase of the transition of the objective idea into a medium of expression*, of its crystallization into an objective form.

(c) *The surging of the creative process in the perspective of "subjective" experience — personal growth*

There are different ways in which the creative process as such seems to begin. We have to delineate in the first place what is meant by the creative process as a type of activity in which an individual engages at a certain point of his development and which he pursues throughout a period of time, developing his creative proficiencies, skills and energies, and activity, which is all connected with his inner development and which grows promoting it and partaking of it. This understanding of the "creative process at large" shows that it proceeds through a series of fragmentary activities, each of them separated from all the others through its particular aim in the form of an objective telos. The "creative process at large" does not possess a predetermined aim. Rather, it is a *process-like particular form of the inner development and progress of the individual*; its aim is to increase the creative powers in response to the personal nostalgia of its bearer. When we talk about love, for instance, as "creative," we mean that it promotes the inner growth of the individual and may eventually, if the individual is engaged in a creative process at large, contribute to forwarding his creative proficiencies and capabilities. The creative process at large means for the individual person a striving, an inner struggle with him or herself, in an effort to overcome the natural passive flow of life, its individual limitations — a daring undertaking to measure one's forces with the universally established order in a bold attempt to break from the established, constituted framework. The subjective form of the creative effort will transcend the hitherto valid, conceptual, emotional, spiritual framework, which constitutes the life-world of the daring adventurer. No wonder it takes on the form of an impetus, momentum, "élan," in which we feel transported "beyond ourselves." This leap beyond our own context means also a break with the established net of reference, and with the seemingly inescapable lack of innovation. We subjectively experience this impetus as spreading a "diffused light" within us, indicating something shining through an immeasurable, mysterious darkness, which light we then attempt to interpret using concepts that emphasize its emanation from ordinary, natural experience, appearing "spiritual," "mystical," or like "the light of creation." Out of this invisible beyond we work through the creative process to wrest from it a "glimmer," and to retain a scanty but distinct intuitive segment which takes on the role of indicating an objective telos.

The ways in which each particular, limited, and strictly distinctive creative process starts are multiple. It may be argued that there are essentially two ways in which the creative process in subjective experience begins: either we have an "illuminating notion" of the work to be accomplished before we undertake it, or we have to go through a laborious series of attempts, through laborious research on the subject matter through trial and error — as often seems to be the case in scientific research — before we hit upon an "idea" which, then, illuminates the previous labor by giving to it a reorganized and novel unity.

But we also know cases, not infrequent, in which (as with Poincaré) a complete theory seems to be ready in our mind, waiting for elaboration; and then we know the long, laborious and often tortuous strain on intelligence to crystallize this seemingly "ready" work which, in practice, betrays its unreadiness.[15]

Furthermore, the surrealists, who claim that the creative accomplishment demands the freeing of consciousness from constraints, insisted upon the entirely spontaneous — that is, effortless, and even nonreflexive — nature of the creative procedure: an "automatic" notation of what comes from the depths of consciousness through the pressures dissolved and released from their customary bounds. They claim, thus, that the authentic work of creation is an unreflexive release of depth formations, depth-activity, without any intuitive, intellectual construct directing it.

Whatever may subjectively be the apparent start of the creative process that partakes of the whole complex stream of the individual's cognitive and volitive processes, it seems, however, that the search of a biologist gathering data about a species and making protocol observations somewhat in the dark might then become the preliminary step toward a creative process, though, on the other hand, it might prove to be fruitless or nothing other than a verification or corroboration of already established data. Nor does the fact of a seemingly "ready" appearance of the theorem in reflexive consciousness, nor, finally, the apparently effortless and unreflexive notation of "gratuitously" offered shapes, colors, forms or ideas mean a beginning of the creative process. It would be so, had we reasons to identify the creative process exclusively with a reflexive activity of consciousness of the specific type of which the experiencing subject is constantly aware. Yet there is no reason to assume that (1) reflexive activity necessitates or is accompanied by a second, immanent perception of it, and that consequently we must always be aware of our reflexive processes; or (2) that, even if we had to acknowledge that creative activity is a reflexive activity *par excellence*, the creative process is a game played in the forefront of conscious activity. We would have to admit that even with this evidence, not all segments of the process are performed within the present field of consciousness. All these observations made by the creative agent belong to the subjective experiential aspect of the creative process only insofar as they are psychologically embedded. They do not pertain to its authentic core.

We might have solved our theorems in sleep, and it is often during sleep, that is, the withdrawal of consciousness from operations concerning events inciting it from the outside, that we advance in our creative search after appropriate forms, solutions, etc. This does not mean, however, either that this solution came from some source "outside" of our own functional system or that it came about without a certain specific creative transformation of our entire creative orchestration of functions having been engaged in bringing it about. The creative process comes into its own by differentiating itself from the complex array of subjective/intentional reflexive processes and emerging out of them; in its wake is the creative vision, which proposes itself as the organizing principle of the process' objective, constitutive structuration.

The "creative vision," whether brought subjectively into the full light of awareness or whether remaining in its twilight, is, as its organizing principle, the initiator and promoter of the creative process which might then (1) itself be operating in the twilight of the mind until it breaks out into the actual field of consciousness in a ready-made form; (2) it may also be released progressively from the shadowy region, being enticed by the intensity and concentration of reflection itself, which enters into a distilling and sifting function; or (3) the creative vision may proceed in the full light of consciousness with the vision clearly in front of the reflective and self-aware activity of the creative agent, who sets out on a search after appropriate elements to be incorporated into a scheme of the creative project.

The possibility of at least these three subjective types of experience of the agent in the creative procedure, and moreover our thesis that, as *creative* experiences, they necessarily stem from the creative vision, need to be substantiated in further analysis of the creative mechanisms. At this point it is necessary to mention that the creative vision which is this germinal project of the ultimate objective of the creative process first proposes a *significant moment* that is novel, with respect to the field of consciousness and of meaningfulness, and thus novel with respect to the *meaningful system of being*, hitherto recurrently used in the constitutive schemata of the life-world as its framework of references in its present phase. This significant element proposed by the "creative intuition" may assume its creative function only if, further, it shows an *organizing virtue*, outlining a structural scheme which then divides into (1) the operational, and (2) the structural function.

(d) *An overview of the creative process in itself (in the "objective" perspective)*

The organizing proficiency of this intuitive element of the creative vision appeals, first, to the objective associative "hooks" among virtual and possible qualitative elements themselves available and to appropriate forms toward the objective of crystallization into an "idea of the work." There is a net of associative, possible connections inherent in the qualitatively significant core of the intuition which indicates (e.g., that the color for its existential crystallization needs to be a color of "something," and to be a color of a "surface"), furthermore, that it must be of some intensity, gradation, nuance, shape, etc. Also, that in order to obtain certain color-effects, some colors have to be brought together to the exclusion of others. Secondly, from the point of view of the conscious operations, there is to be distinguished a particular constructive system — to which we will return later, in detail — which, through a series of analyzing, discriminating and selecting procedures, seeks to establish associative links among elements to be selected with reference to a guiding "theme" or "principle," which is nothing other at first than the creative vision itself. These *objective* associative junctures (hooks) among qualitative elements and the subjective organizing system of operations together serve as a basis for all types of fragmentary creative processes which may relate to one, or to the other, or partly to both, and proceed at various levels of reflective activity and with varying degrees of self-reflection. Third, its organizing proficiency resides, in part, in the fact that the creative vision is a qualitatively poignant *universal image*, a *structural quality* indissociable and perfectly simple in its complex and specific nature. Its compelling dynamic is due to the fact that it is of an emotional nature, thus involving volition and making an appeal to imagination! Due to its intrinsic, operational virtualities, to reflect upon it means already an *attempt to transform it into the idea of the creative object.*

PART III

THE PASSAGE FROM THE CREATIVE VISION
TO THE IDEA OF THE CREATIVE WORK

SECTION 1. CREATION VERSUS INVENTION

The specific characteristic of the creative vision is that we cannot adequately grasp it in itself otherwise than in its function with respect to the creative process that it initiates. In other words, when we approach the creative vision in its qualitative content, we attempt to transform it into the *idea of the creative object*.

Already at this point, which signifies the beginning of the creative work-in-progress proper, we must distinguish between "creation," as a *specific and complex process*, and "invention," as a *particular function which, although crucial and indispensable for the work of creation, brings to it its central factor around which all the other functions of the human being converge, and yet remains only one among many of its factors*. Taken in itself, in its specific nature, *invention functions on its very own*, outside the whole complex of the creative workings.

The basic distinction may be seen in the fact that creation aims (1) at an instauration of a novel, original, significant complex as a matrix unifying questions and answers of multiple issues; and (2) at finding an embodiment in an independent object within the formal structure of an object — at a type of independent "beingness" which will then stand on its own among other objects of the world. Invention, in contrast, is (a) in its function more restrictive. Although it is invention which triggers the entire set of functional virtualities as a way to introduce originality and novelty *par excellence*, it aims at resolving *one particular problem*, to accomplish *one specific task or endeavor* which enters into a vast complex of other problems, etc. (b) Its mode of accomplishment stands — as Arthur Koestler has so rightly grasped — as a "radical jump" between two discrete phases of a situation without any apparent continuity; and continuity characterizes the creative endeavor. (3) It does not attempt or accomplish the construction of an *object* in discrete phases of a situation without the apparent continuity which characterizes the creative endeavor through its workings; nor does it purport to instance *a new item* in its particular mode of existence. The products

202

of what we call "technical invention," machines, means of transportation, etc., are only in part invented; the other part is the result of creative work. Invention also means a rupture with our habitual way of solving a problem. It may be presented in the manner of Kessler and Boirel in terms of joining together two different matrices. In agreement with Bernis we may say that it applies to specific substances and problems to be worked upon in relation to the fields where it is applied and in which it operates using specific types of devices.

The creative work aiming at a complex construction is perpetually involved with an infinite number of particular tasks, problems, and selections. This specific grasp and handling of the situation in which a radical step between two seemingly disconnected platforms is required, which grasp invention alone gives, makes it crucial and indispensable — indispensable, yet insufficient. From the point of view of the originality exhibited by the creative work one could say that its specifically "creative" factor is invention; it operates this subterranean "click" that brings the disparate elements to coalesce within the "inventive moment." Yet from the point of view of the *significant role* which is supposed to be accomplished by the inventive moment, namely that of introducing elements of novelty and originality with respect to meaningful avenues of life within the life-world-total which it breaks into and within whose sclerosed system of meanings it has to be explicated, one has to admit that the vast repercussion of the work of creation (which is due to its constructing a new, significant, experiential schema envisaging the universe, for its new vision of human reality and hence a new conceptual framework to be devised) can be effected only (3) by a long-winded process going through *all* the meaning-bestowing phases, beginning from the vital/organic, through the vital/sentient, etc., which mean phases of differentiation of the logos of life up to the spiritual "anti-logos." (4) The work of creativity determines itself as such only when *finally it is embodied in the intentional plenitude of an object, affirming itself through its complete endowment as a pluri-significant part of the world, standing on its own*; that is, when a "place" has been made in praxis, as well as in experience, for networks of the life-world to receive it.

The creative process, in contrast to the work of invention, is an *architectonic progress of significant construction*; it leads to the emotional and intellectual strategies prerequisite for the existential act of creation, in which a synthesis is reached, installing the object within the life-world; its architectonic strategies prepare for the constructed object breaking in and assuming a position. We will follow its intricacies throughout our study in all its stages. So it is appropriate here at their first appearance to clarify succinctly the respective nature and distinctiveness of both creation and invention.

SECTION 2. FROM THE CREATIVE VISION TO THE CREATIVE
IDEA OF THE WORK

As stated before, the content of the creative vision is given intuitively in a pre-reflexive experience in which we identify our present state of mind by experiencing an "opening" upon a "new dimension" of "reality": a color/shape, a deep fascination which draws us entirely into our mind and senses; a cosmic mystery, which transports us beyond the narrow frame of the world we customarily experience. We may well stop at this fascinating experience, in a contemplative, self-consuming absorption; it appears inexhaustible but, as a part of our temporal, inward flux, it wears off and vanishes. However, it carries within an "objective" germ which does not dissolve with our subjective absorption. Furthermore, as already indicated from several angles, this objective germ carries a nucleus of virtual realization, its "substantializations." Lastly, it is not *static*, but bursting with spontaneities toward this substantialization, or "embodiment." When we want to grasp what it is that it reaches for, what it is that cannot be exhausted by our absorbing experience, we have to dissociate ourselves from our experiential identity with the intuitive moment of this visionary content and reflect upon it from a distance — "objectify" it. It is this process of "objectification" which is prompted by the operational aspect of the vision, and through it we initiate the creative process in its full extent, transforming the intuitive content into the objective idea of a future creative work. *This transformation is definitive. When I pass from the stage of contemplation to that of transmuting it, the content is viewed from the point of view of its virtualities and the postulation of expression, stylization, perspective of situation*, etc. Valéry tells us that he sees entirely differently when he contemplates and when he takes his pencil to draw. The creative vision envisaged "objectively" transforms itself into a creative project: *a creative idea*.

What are the basic operations of this transformation? What is the guarantee of the identify of the vision with the creative idea? What are the directive lines of the transformatory progress? What are the reference points of its continuity such that we may, in fact, talk about the correlation of the vision with the idea of a work that will be laboriously construed through three major functional lines — the psychological, the imaginative, and the intentional — and through otherwise disconnected processes? Could the work of creation be the result of chance and accident and not of a tightly organized process?

Finally, we must ask: What are the materials out of which the creative idea of a work is construed in such a way that its construction — as well as its further implications for the creative process — exclude the possibility of total haphazardness?

SECTION 3. IMAGINATION AND MEMORY IN THE "DECIPHERING" AND "CIPHERING" OF THE ORIGINARY SIGNIFICANCE OF THE WORK

When, in order to understand the origin of a certain work, we analyze its intrinsically present elements — in the case of writing, for instance — we either look for reminiscences of material we already know that might have been borrowed from other works, or for episodes from the author's life which, according to his biography, occurred in his travels, occupations, hobbies or associations with acquaintances. We seek what they might have provided the author with (e.g., protagonists, dwellings, events, etc.), particular elements, like descriptions of landscapes, feelings, characterizations of personages described, etc. Approaching the created work we are struck by its strangeness — originality — by which it stands out in radical contrast to all around us. In order to penetrate its meaningfulness we seek to establish a contact between the "strange" new form and some crucial moments of the content. In scientific theories and philosophy we look back toward insights and intuitions framed already in theories arrived at and preceding our work, which could coincide; or we seek after either affirmative or related evidence; or, lastly, we are forced to follow a new path of inquiry leading to a different, more adequate, formulation of progress at stake. These may be "enlightening" in themselves and offer answers to the same difficulties with which we deal. Experiences and observations of the natural and of the social world underlying scientific theories "ring a bell" in our "inner ear." In musical and plastic arts we try to associate given melodies, sonorities and structural effects with those of other

works, past or contemporary, and to compare its "atmosphere" with the
pervading climate and style of the contemporary period, which it either
follows or opposes. In approaching the work in its striking originality
and trying to establish contact with it, we proceed then through
verification and indentification of the already known and familiar; we
look for it assuming, naturally, that the maker might have worked
primarily with familiar material accessible to us and not with some
extraordinary elements extraneous to our experience, which would lead
not to an original outcome in significance but to altogether estranged
and thus insignificant results. They would ultimately be inaccessible and
unacceptable because they could not be elucidated by prior knowledge
and so would have to remain unassimilated by the previously established system of meaning of the intersubjective life-world.

We see, then, that in the "de-ciphering" — as I call it — of the
original/originary significance of the creative work, imagination and
memory are joined together. In their conjunction, into which all the
other functions are drawn, resides as well the decisive, creative/inven-
tive moment of construction, one proper solely to the creative process:
*the ciphering of the novel, unprecedented significance of life to be given
to our primeval material of the creative promptings*. These promptings
exemplified in the creative vision in its subliminal (pre-conscious)
nature acquire a *new cipher* — significance — in the creative idea.

We have accepted as the beginning of the creative process the
emergence of a novel objective, significant structuration in the midst of
an indeterminate, experiential plenitude. Then we want to see how this
intuitively contemplative quality contains within itself the virtual form
of a project which appears in the making, while we pass from the
intuitive, creative vision to its significant cipher, objectivized now in an
"idea." However, this passage of ciphering draws qualitatively upon an
enormous amount of material. Undoubtedly, rich experiential material
gathered from the life of the maker was necessary in order that the
buoyant inner life of a person may reach the initial intensity and
turmoil whence the incipient phase of the creative propulsion obtains
its source. The wealth and intensity of personal experience remains,
however, loose, haphazard and undifferentiated — even in our self-
reflection, which tries to assign it a cause and effect order — until *sua
sponte* the creative vision which transforms it emerges. Literary critics,
however, usually confound the two and, while looking for the material
of the *objective idea of a work*, they simultaneously inquire about the

source and material of the creative vision, *thus overlooking the vision itself*. On the one side, these two sources have to be strictly distinguished. On the other side, the creative vision and the idea of the work have to be distinguished as well. It seems that while, in the case of the "ciphering" of the creative idea, the primordial factor is a selective and *par excellence* reflexive activity at work which can give us a perfectly rational chain of motivations and explain the transformatory route from the received material to the elaborated work, in the case of creative vision, however, whatever may be the preliminary work of consciousness and its resources, there is *no direct motivational link between it and the emergence of the creative quality*. It emerges entirely *sua sponte* and its quality not only cannot be traced to any other material qualities of experience, but even might often appear in spite of them. As such it might play a unique role which we then will interpret in the *ontologico-metaphysical perspective of the "Great Unity of Beingness," transmitting the primogenital logos of life into the subliminal realm of the Human Condition and prompting the creative orchestration of a new cipher.*

In this respect we have to distinguish, first, between "perceptual memory" and the work of imagination in supplying "synthetic images" or "inventive images." Never a better account of the proceedings of this creative encounter between imagination and memory was given than in John Livingston Lowes' analysis of Coleridge's notebooks. Yet, let us emphasize from the very start that Livingston Lowes, in his synthetic conception of inventing images, missed the crucial point of their *significant* conversion in the emergence of a *new cipher*. We may follow there, nevertheless, the preliminary works of the creative spirit to their full extent, the unexpected results and then the deliberate and wilful use of this material.

As a matter of fact, the vital business of a writer is to "*read*" and to observe, of a painter to *look* and to observe. But this reading and observing are already of a specific sort. We might read or see things entirely for their own sake to enjoy them and assimilate what they offer, but we might also, as artists do, read and see them for their own sake in the deeper sense of a search for meaning, not with reference to what the composition and the intent of their maker determined them to stand for, but from the point of view of their innermost virtualities which abide on their own, separable from the given frame. In this sense we may speak of the "raw stuff" of poetry and art in general. But this "raw stuff" comes first from the artist's direct experience in his life-struggle or enjoyment. An "artist's experience" is an adventure going through most disparate, varied, chaotic fragments of life's processes or aesthetic experiences which struck his attention; his memory is a home for waifs and strays of verse, fragments of colors, of sounds, a mirror of fitful and kaleidoscopic moods and a record of germinal ideas. The excerpts of readings he records have been extracted from the whole for the sake of their potential virtualities to engender his imagination or their poetic associative power; the patches of colors, which he records and with which he often starts a composition, are extracted from large visual fields as the falcon's eye catches here and there the intensity of suggestive power. Like Coleridge, recording in his notebooks, the poet looks for striking descriptions of contrast which, like that of the image of the sun in gold and the image of ice that waxed and waned with the moon, stimulate an extraordinarily intense mood.[16] He looks for the generative powers of "elements" and, thus, piercing to the secret objective spring of poetry and art, reaches beneath the crust of fact. We see here, beneath the subliminal field of the twilight of consciousness, the origin of the distinction between the "reality of fact" and "poetic" reality.

There is indeed nothing which is repulsive to the artist — nothing which could not become a factor of beauty. Therefore a poet like Coleridge does not place any limits on his intellectual curiosity. Extracts from the "Letters of the Missionary Jesuits" by Father Bourzes, in which the descriptions of a "great many fishes playing in the sea, which have made a kind of artificial fire in the water that was very pleasant to look on" and of how "the wind carrying the tops of waves made a kind of rain, in which the rays of the sun painted the colors of a rainbow" stir his imagination through their own virtuality to evoke images by the creative power of imagination such as are not present in the reality of nature which the words actually describe. It is, then, not by virtue of this reality described by Bourzes, but because of their *intrinsic virtualities* that use is made of them in "The Rime of the Ancient Mariner." In the "poetic reality" of the poem they are metamorphosed. The fishes described by Captain Cook, which struck Coleridge's fancy, red, blue and green in the "rotting sea," encircled with "silver and velvet black," and the water snakes mentioned in *New Voyages Around the World* by Dampier, do not actually possess any enhancing qualities. And yet all these elements of prosaic reality can be identified in a stanza of the "Rime of the Ancient Mariner." Found separately, they are here coalesced in a metamorphosed image:

> Beyond the shadow of the ship
> I watch'd the water-snakes:
> They moved in tracks of shining white,
> And when they rear'd, the elfish light
> Fell off in hoary flakes.

> Within the shadow of the ship
> I watch'd their rich attire:
> Blue, glossy, green, and velvet black,
> They coil'd and swam; and every track
> Was a flash of golden fire.

This "raw," crass material gathered from the reality of fact, displays first, as Livingston Lowes points out, a virtual associative power, associative points of reference and links: (a) the fishes or sea animals were attractively colored; (b) they appeared in the moonlight near the ship; (c) they had an imaginative spell like an apparition; (d) they were all related to the putrefaction of the sea. Second, although parts of a prosaic, matter of fact context, these elements have in themselves — and especially in relation to their prospective links — an evocative power to stir creative imagination. Moreover, they had the freshness of a simple and accurate description of reality as naively experienced. But, finally, and formally, these descriptions of reality have the appeal of the hitherto *unknown* and the strange aspect of an exterior source of information about something new and revelatory, about the unknown world just discovered.[17]

Stressing right away the distinction between the nature of the "raw source material" of experience and its transformed, "sublimated" or "poetized" or "aestheticized" nature in poetry immediately makes the work of the creative functions stand out by drawing the line between the cognitive/constitutive and the poetic/creative functions. As pointed out above, in this transformation the conjoined work of Imaginatio Creatrix and of memory appears from the first, but they could not have been brought together into cooperation without the reflective mode of consciousness.

SECTION 4. THE ACCUMULATIVE FUNCTION OF MEMORY

There are, in fact, several essential factors at work due to which such a transformation of the experiential data within a novel context becomes possible. Yet, what has to be immediately noted is that there are preliminary operations of the functional apparatus which prepared such a transformatory operation and which are as indispensable in the reflexive elaboration of the creative idea as they are in the spontaneous emergence of the creative vision.

In the first place, the reflective consciousness must have been on alert in order to notice significance in these elements of "raw material." The attentiveness to them in virtue of their evocative potency is the result of an imaginative factor at work. It does not yet mean, however, that any precise objective nor any constructive tendency is present. We might, as has been pointed out, take a special pleasure in evoking and contemplating images of ordinary experience, which stand out because of their striking quality. In the second place, there must have been a specific spontaneous associative pattern in the accumulative function of memory. One would be tempted to assume that experiential factors passing from the present stage of the field of consciousness into the twilight of the past are *spontaneously segregated into two categories*: (1) those which stand out somewhat and can then be retrieved from the repository of the past; and (2) those which become amalgamated with the undifferentiated experiential halo and have lost their particular distinctive vividness. We might argue then that this prominence of some of them is due to their particular vividness in experience, attracting attention, but it seems only reasonable to assume that this vividness itself is due first to their peculiar place within the complete experiential pattern of the field of consciousness, and is then transposed passing into a new pattern of objective connectedness which the workings of structuring intentions establish between the present field of consciousness and the pattern of the past one, projecting in an anticipatory way toward the future.

Thus the "accumulative function" of consciousness — the function of memory — would not be reduced to accumulating an entirely haphazard inventory, but follows a line of "consequence," which would then allow this repository of experience to be retrieved and to reappear in the field of actual consciousness at given moments as either *representational memory of past experience*, or *the same in a selectively transposed form in a new creative synthesis*.

And yet we cannot follow the temptation to assume that memory itself would be operating within a larger imaginary schema, that is, oriented toward a possible creative object. There is too much evidence in the observations of the creative work of artists, scholars, and philosophers that out of the same raw material, and out of the same aestheticized images, different and divergent creative works could have proceeded and most often those created are not those first suggestions prompted, but others — not even related "objectively" to the first ones.

In other words, no matter how suggestive memory in conjunction with Imaginatio Creatrix may be, no *direct* passage can be construed from the revived and metamorphosed reservoir of materials to the creative process oriented toward an object.

The unique inspirational, intuitive element of the creative vision, which may function as such because of its power of associative evocations — qualitative and operational — could not be a matter simply of combination or merely qualitative or imaginative transposition or transformation. It emerges from the undifferentiated precisely through its striking and unique moment of *significant novelty*. Although this undifferentiated plenitude is no longer the raw material of fragments of reality observed at random once some of its elements are united in one intense experience of a particular intensity and unity, an imaginatively potentialized and aestheticized whole, it cannot be shown that its elements are directly transposed into the structural quality of the vision. *This quality transcends them all, and appears indecomposable and is more universal than any of the components of ordinary experience.* It emerges as distinctive, irreducible and autonomous with respect to the preceding stage of experience. It is not the "confluence of the recollections" alone which, as Coleridge said in the *Biographia Literaria*, would be in the "twilight of imagination and memory just a vestibule of consciousness" explaining the nature of "that shadowy half-being, that state of nascent existence," which emerges as the universal image of the vision.

But above all, the originality and unique novelty which strike us in the creative vision reside not in its structural imagery, but in the new significant intuition with which it is permeated and which constitutes its "heartbeat." The fact that this uniquely original, creative intuition emerges *sua sponte* as an unpredictable, significant indication and pointer constitutes the *true mystery of creation. This mystery does not refer, however, to a source beyond the realm of the creative agent in his beingness and that of his extended consciousness, but to the laws and rules of the latter's operations. These entail that, obviously, a most particular configuration of vital/sentient/emotive conscious functions is necessary to prepare the preliminary stage such that, first, the pattern of objective connectedness, on the one hand, and of the individual/personal, experiential scheme, on the other hand, together organize the schema according to which memory revives its past experiential contents.* We may also pursue the workings of memory together with Imaginatio Creatrix leading to such a specific state of functional concentration that the intensity of experience, together with the confluence of vivified experiential elements is brought about. *Yet, the particular emergence of the creative vision in its creative intuition, gathering about it the structural quality and the specific nature of the project in germ, cannot be reduced to any product of the mechanisms of consciousness; it merely uses this mechanism. Its variability is the real undeniable mystery of creation, which prevents it from ever being predictable, planned or directed by any developmental or educational devices or any special "training" in that area.*

SECTION 5. THE "OBJECTIVE RULES" OF "COMPOSSIBILITY" IN THE COMING TOGETHER OF IMAGINATIVE ELEMENTS IN THE CREATIVE IDEA

We have already mentioned that the raw material of recollections possesses "associative hooks" — as Livingston Lowes calls them — yet these do not explain, except in part, the objective "compossibility," to use a favorite expression of Leibnitz, of creative, imaginative elements coming together. Contrary to Livingston Lowes' faith in their power, I do not yet see how they have been picked up and "stored" together, to reappear in Milton's "precincts of light" as material for ulterior, creative operations. I propose that, in order to make the "objective hooks" among imaginary elements relevant to the creative construction, it is, first, necessary to see that they gather together with reference to a *universal and potential frame*; to render the objective hooks relevant for their preliminary function in creative operations, the aesthetic functions (*roles*) which they would have assumed in conjunction within a common framework, over against each other, like the colors in a spectrum, are devised. To begin with, we will refer to Bachelard's insight into the primitive source of spiritual energies which he, following Jung, sees in "primitive images," the existence of which is a prerequisite condition and an expression of mental powers to be exercised in imagination. According to him, these primitive images are related to the four basic substances (fire, water, earth, and air), and are pivotal points of imagination, first, as points of reference for interpreting, organizing, coordinating and distributing raw sensory material and, second, as four points of reference for organizing our emotional and spiritual framework.

Leaving the discussion of this theory aside, it offers a significant observation, namely, that the intrinsic evocative power of images, which varies in degree and intensity, is due to their relevance for coalescing into large images; without being reflexively implicit, the latter appear as organizing frames for the mental operations. Along this line there may be outlined the following *objective* basis for the realization of the preliminary constructive operations, delineating the passage from one qualitative pattern to another:

(1) The suggestive, evocative power of singular images appear with reference to large, universal, but vaguely determined images.

(2) These images are not explicitly "given," presentified," but *indicated* implicitly by the coalescing tendency of the particular images, and they are conversely characterized by their function of offering a framework for this coalescence.

Corresponding to this *objective condition* that lies in the nature of the imaginary "material" itself, we may distinguish standing out a prominent corollary: a subjective, *unifying tendency of the function of consciousness which brings about this coalescence.* As a matter of fact, we cannot explain this coalescence of particular images into one that is more universal, merely on the basis of an objective mechanism intrinsic to the "life"of the imaginary function. No objective mechanism could account for their confluence. If it was simply through a simultaneous presence in the same actual field of consciousness that, due to their objective compossibility, they would be bound together through their intrinsic hooks, like parts of a picture-puzzle, they would appear there in all their particular features. But this is not the case. The possibility of particular images coalescing in one universal image which comes about only in practice lies, first, in the fact that they carry this possibility in their "essence," and in spite of other specific features they might individually display. Second, their coming together on the basis of these and some other virtual movements indicates a specific operation of consciousness: "operational imagination" or "fancy." What we vaguely

call "imagination" seems in its basic form to correspond to two functions at work: the first could be called a "unifying function," which
operates through an analytic procedure of variation of all the possibilities in their entire range (e.g., all the hues of red in all their
intensities). The second function is "discrimination," or the "selection"
of some, leaving aside their particular differences and sharp edges,
while concentrating upon the common, essential element in reference to
the *universal image* as a virtual framework and to other "compossible"
elements capable of being combined. Hence comes the particular
intensity of the specific type of experience with which the creative
vision vibrates in itself and which intensifies in a passage into the idea
of the creative work, in contradistinction to ordinary experience of
reality.

This unifying operation, however, would not suffice to account for
the specific richness and enhancing appeal of the universal image aimed
at in the confluence of particular images. There must be a function
probing deeper into the intergenerative nature of singular imaginary
moments such that the exchangeability of particular elements may be
established, not toward a mere mutual adjustment in the selective
procedure, but toward a *mutual intergeneration*. It must be not only a
function of recognition by comparison and evaluation (as in the constructive selection of the constitutive process), but also a function of a
generative impulse loaded with a striving toward encompassing the
significant meaningfulness of the past experience. *This impulse must
break through the imaginative patterns of the past, as well as current
organizing and reorganizing operations of memory/operational imagination, toward the birth of unprecedented experience. It is on the wings of
the intergeneration of compossible moments that the creative intuition
ciphers the surging significance from the hidden springs of the "raw"
material.*

*Hence the radical difference between the "raw material" of experience
and the intensity of richness and plenitude of the reconstrued experience
ciphered anew and crystallized in features which, in contrast to the
informative experience of reality, we call "aesthetic" or "poetic."*

This enhancement of fragments, one stripped of its color, the other
of its shape, a third of its phosphorescent light, etc., incorporated
together into the new conception of a watersnake in *The Rime of the
Ancient Mariner*, could not be explained otherwise than by assuming a

latent framework to which all of them were referred in this analytic and evaluating process. Thus due to these two factors — the objective associability, the "objective hooks" of the particular experiences, on the one hand, and the "analytic and selective functions" of operative imagination on the other — there arises a most striking experiential completeness at *a single glance*, in which all the particular features which hinder such a completeness of integration in the perception of reality are brought into the background of the actual field of consciousness, withdrawn without, however, being dismissed. From their somewhat retired position, they function as a natural experiential reference. Yet the plenitude and completeness of the emerging novel experience is due to the *novel sense with which the image of the watersnake is ciphered.*

Thus a passage from the vibrating, but objectively undefined intuitive complex of the creative vision, into an objective creative idea, takes place — creatively.

The crystallized idea within the creative work presents in the perspective of imagination/memory a metamorphosed image of reality, transposed from the raw material into an *aesthetic reality*, it having passed through the twilight of consciousness where the "meta-morphosis" through the creative ciphering of the vision occurred. Technically, we see in the *Ancient Mariner* such an imaginative meta-morphosis at work when the activity of the swimming of the watersnake is replaced by "coiled and swam." No mortal eye, comments Lowes, has even seen the watersnake "coil and swim." [18]

The most striking example of such a specific function of imagination with respect to the reservoir of our past experiences, ideas, images, is given by the work of Proust. [19] Whatever more it took to make it a creative work, an "exemplary work" in the words of Kant, a masterpiece, there is one striking thing of which it is composed: *the raw material of the pedestrian life of his epoch.* Reading the fascinating beginning of the *De Coté des Guérmantes*, we are carried away in a stream of experiences in which there is no dull instant, no aimless drift, no pause. Thus the line of development remains compact, intense, and the quality dense, with one element drawing already upon the following one, compelling it to appear in full light; reflecting upon it, we might become aware that this intensity, vividness, fascination, is not due to the nature of the things being narrated, which are far from being especially original, attractive or revelatory in themselves. It is not the general theme nor the plot that captivates out attention. It is the specific assortment of experiential elements brought together into focus, the intrinsic density of the general development, which melts all its contents in the same pot and endows all of them with an experiential thickness, an extra-ordinary evocative power. Reality itself, to which these scraps refer, as experienced by the living individuals described, did not possess this experiential power. Only through a specific co-operation of operative imagination and memory of real life, which the whole of humanity shares, may such a fascinating and captivatingly *poetic* account be given.

Recapitulating, we might say that (1) *although these transformatory functions of memory/imagination may motivate the emergence of the creative vision, yet they alone do not account for its specific quality and nature which are irreducible in their originary condition.* Furthermore, although the same proceeding of imagination/memory/perception might prepare a milieu for the creative process, by operationally carrying out the passage from the vision into the idea of the work, the *correlation of the particular scraps of experience with the universal image* (which seems somewhat to produce a constructive work quasi-mechanically and might well be the preliminary condition used throughout the whole process of creative experience), this initial idea of the work *is merely a preliminary condition of the creative process in its full expanse.* This process surges and unfolds when, from the creative vision which is a universal quality proposed for objective concretization, we are drawn to determine the nature of this quality and its implications for its objective realization, the first step toward which is the creative vision to be explicated in terms of the idea of the creative object: *the project of creation.* Even creative, emotive imagination cannot alone explain the work of creation.

We have, so far, sketched the nature and role of the "objective" elements with which the creative process begins: the so-called "images." However, it became apparent that, whatever an "image" may otherwise represent, the "irrealities" to use Sartre's expression, although in themselves somewhat "static," essentially representational, and inert, within the creative process acquire a *generative and intergenerative proficiency.*

This is to say that these seemingly "objective" principles of the "creative architectonics" contain latent proficiencies for entering into co-operation or are "co-natural" with the operational, "subjective" principles of the creative process which consists of a play of process-like organized forces.

We will now continue to unravel the architectonics of the creative process, from the perspective of the *orchestration of the creative operations: the so-called* "subjective" side of the *creative orchestration* of the functional human self-interpretation in existence.

Again it will appear that, to begin with, we will first rely in our investigation upon the "objective" principles of this "subjective," functional orchestration. Then we will slowly come to reach the functional faculties in their specific distribution of roles.

PART IV

THE OPERATIONAL ARCHITECTONICS OF
THE SURGING CREATIVE FUNCTION IN
THE INITIAL CREATIVE CONSTRUCTIVISM

SECTION 1. THE ORGANIZING PRINCIPLES

The major problems which we face in the attempt to pass from the creative vision to the idea of a work as a project, are first to fixate intuition in its inspiring significance in terms of a qualitative/meaningful complex; second, to simultaneously devise its appropriate form; and, last, to select a possible objective structure for it. It is interesting to note how intimately the "meaning" of a poem, that is its "poetic message" — *its life-significant factor* — is related to its artistic form. We do not seek, in reading a poem, an intellectual argument or statement about what a poem "talks about": love, nature, life. Instead, each time we read it anew we distill from the analysis of its aesthetico-poetic texture a sentient/ emotive/spiritual meaning which brings into our entire experiential schema a novel explosive significance.

The poem's "old" meaningfulness, sclerosed already to a few rational segments, is transfigured and infused with new sap which flows through all our sentient/emotive/spiritual arteries and renews our contact with the All of life. The poet, writer, scholar, *has this unique task of devising such a full-fledged, poetic incarnation of the creative intuition,* in such a way that this *poetic message of the intuition may be explicated from its germinal stage to the fullest extent within its object.* Unlike other constructive processes, it seems that the first step toward realization is *not to proceed by a dissociative analysis of the intuition, but rather to follow the intuitive suggestiveness.* There is, indeed, in the *intuitive experiential quality* of the creative vision a radiating spread of overwhelming suggestiveness. We analytically consult the vision throughout the creative process, yet at the initially crucial stage of determining its range of possible objects we try to grasp it *at one glance* and see what it amounts to or immediately entails. In our self-encompassing glance we look beyond, however, a singular "passive," "constitutive" synthesis. We strain our attention, in the first place, to detect inventively *such a qualitative element that could function as the principle of organization in the laborious construction process which is both prompted and anticipated.* What is indicated at this point in its intuitive outline still to be unfolded has to be, first, intuitively scrutinized in its pluri-perspectival, virtual content as to the eventual significant moment which seeks to be incarnated. Second, this very striving of the virtual significant moments brought forth by the creative intuition, on the one hand, prompts, in a special way, imaginatio creatrix — already awakened — and, on the other hand, activates the entire system of the objectifying constitutive function which is called upon to provide objective forces.

In the middle, "mediating," position the *active role* of memory surges at this point, not only proposing, with the collaboration of the imaginative swing, its radiating "images," whether emotive or representational, that have previously been "inventoried," but also scanning the entire inventory in various perspectives backward and forward. Memory's essential work, however, that of tentatively co-ordinating the *significant,* intuitive moments with possible imaginative objective forms, is not entirely its own. What has to be strongly emphasized is that at this junction of functional impulses, prompted by the creative vision toward constructive realization in an objectified, meaningful form, the above-stressed functional complexes stir the complete *creative architectonics* to emerge. The Human Condition, in this way, releases its entire potential: between creative imagination and active memory the principles of the objectifying constitutive function are allied with the intuitive promptings for the creation of a radically novel, universal meaningfulness of life, resulting in *creative operational architectonics.* Its workings will, then, transmute the old lines into new, well-worn tracks into an adventurous no man's land. Through their workings they will transform the mere forces, prompting energies and spontaneities into *the iron will of creation.*

What are the basic constructive principles instrumental in the construing of the idea of the work which direct the workings of this operational architectonics and sustain it? Anticipating, let us point out that, interestingly enough, they present again a melding of "static" objective and "operational" subjective motives.

The idea of the created work is a controversial subject much discussed. We have already indicated that it constitutes the factor by virtue of which the creator engages himself in the creative enterprise. However, what is here to be investigated first is by virtue of that element — evocation, call, stimulus, transcendent aim, etc. — which is the "machinery" of creation released to bring about the idea of the work; how are the creative architectonics orchestrated for actual launching?

In this question the focus is not the nature of the first instigator which set the underlying germination in operation throughout the confluent elements which were already gathered, virtualized and lying there ready to be put into motion, needing only the last element to explode, so to speak, from the inside. It is, in fact, to be stated now — anticipating our later investigations that will substantiate this thesis — that the "sources of creation" consist precisely in such an *interior mechanism*, released from The Human Condition, which, once projected and established by an appropriate stimulus, needs only to be set in motion. Goethe tells us in his journal (*Dichtung und Wahrheit*) that the potential material for *Die Leiden des Jungen Werthers* had been ready for a long time and, despite an urge to crystallize it into a work, the essential determining and organizing factor was lacking until Goethe heard news of a suicidal death of his friend, Jerusalem. At the striking stimulus of this news "Werther," once a hoary creative vision, appeared spontaneously in its creative idea, in a conception fully crystallized.

What is at stake here is the type of this creative architectonics' operational system and the way of putting it in motion. Taking the source of the creative process back to an underlying germinating stage from which a mechanism surges, we must ask whether this germinal stage contains the *operational articulation of a preliminary orchestration of conscious functions in such a way that it needs only a "last" organizing factor to bring it into motion, or whether it is a spontaneous release of a new architectonic configuration of functions, expected to occur where all the virtual elements are ready,* and/or, lastly, whether this creative architectonic configuration of the human functioning *is progressively established in the genetic progress of a man deploying his proficiencies for "self-interpretation-in-existence,"* and once having *reached the stage of complete orchestration of human functioning in the deployment of the specifically human phase, the germination lies virtual in essence, waiting for crystallization into specific creative endeavors, as analyzed here.*

This last issue is the leitmotif of our inquiry. With this question we enter into the heart of our enterprise. However, at this point of our analysis of the singular creative endeavor some essential contributions toward its treatment come to light. Setting aside for a moment the vast ramifications of the great issue of *homo creator*, we must observe that those who, like the surrealists or the supporters of "automatic writing," claim that the entire creative work is accomplished in the twilight of consciousness, to be released as an automatic process by one moment's breaking out from the hidden inwardness, seem to overlook or to ignore the *crucially significant phase of the passage between the inventive, intuitive inward turmoil,* which remains in the hazy contours of the twilight of consciousness and the *differentiating, re-memorating, scanning, deliberating,* etc., *workings of the partly imaginative, partly reflexive functioning* that operates in the full light of consciousness by selective operations and choice.

In contrast, Romain Rolland, analyzing Beethoven's process of creation, attempts to show that (1) Beethoven, from the very start, visualized the ensemble of the work in a hazy way which did not concretely appear to him otherwise than as (2) a "curve" (this seems to be particularly clear in *Eroica*), the particular elements of which had to be found through patient labor.[20] Romain Rolland's point supports our conception of the work as a passage from the hazy vision to the idea as a project — Beethoven supposedly did not invent these particular elements, but discovered them, thus forging the elements of a foreshadowed ensemble, the material of which he carried within himself. Hence the moment for the formation of the guideline(s) for the creative process does not occur mechanically, but is the outcome of a "free" (because it is inventive) impulse that reaches beyond the given choice.

In the light of our forthcoming analysis, such a determining factor is, then, an indication of the presence of a latent creative apparatus being coordinated. Essentially it is a result of selection and choice, and yet "inventive choice," that is, of an active as well as a reflexive circuit of operations conjoined with circuits of both *subliminal* and *intentional* operations. We may trace them through the circuits of the will as well, whether they fall simultaneously under the attention of immanent perception or not.

From this standpoint of the "inside" perspective of the operational architectonics, the "static" and the "dynamic" mingle.

There are various types of this primordial organizing principle. Some see in the guiding "idea" a certain insight, intuition or thesis about the meaning of "reality"; it may also be a certain "ideological" appeal, a pragmatic principle meant to spur an attitude toward life-conduct, or a purely aesthetic concept. These elements may well lurk already in the fulgurating medley of imaginative moments in the creative vision; or they may be sought only while advancing toward the formation of an objective idea; yet it is through the accomplished "idea of the creative work" that we understand its complete tentative project, which sets the creative process in motion and, in order to see how this project may be organized in its qualitative complexity and structural differentiation, there is need for a principle which in itself is of such a nature that it may accomplish such a structurizing function.

SECTION 2. THE ARCHITECTONIC PROFICIENCIES OF THE THEME/TOPIC/PLOT, ETC.

We will not indulge here in too many concrete analyses of works of art, of which an enormous amount of instructive material is available in literary and scholarly treatises. For our purpose, that of revealing the inner workings of the creative orchestration, it suffices to discuss some relevant instances of the organizing moment. And, in contrast to our previous bringing forth of the theme, we must right away curtail its universality. In spite of the fact that analysis of a great majority of works of art, literature, painting and dance show how the theme/topic, interpreted either as plot or as a course of "action," is the central content of the created work organizing it in fact, the validity of such an assumption, to a greater extent than any other, is not universal. Upon examination of numerous contemporary novels we see that the theme as the plot is diluted and loses its role. We see, in the remarkable novel by Julien Gracque, *Le Rivage des Syrtes*, where, though it moves along a line of consistent activity, we discover that it is not its plot that guides the conception and consequently the organization of the novel. Events which are presented as the arteries along which the substance of the novel flows have no significance in themselves. *Dramatis personae* fade away, likewise, ceding to mysterious points of suspense charged with atmosphere. As Mr. Bardet points out when commenting upon it, these moments of suspense, distributed throughout the work, are of an emotional nature, open perspectives of mystery and cosmic "truth," bearing the *idea* of the work. The role of the idea of the work reaches fulfillment: it is the idea which patterns their constructive disposition in order that the unfolding action and the moments of suspense balance, support, intensify and vitalize each other in the establishment of their contextual reality. The selection of the elements of the work is calculated with respect to both — the intuitive significance, on the one hand, and the idea itself — strategically projected to give them an appropriate compositional order.

In view of this contrary perspective upon the role of the theme/topic it is appropriate to reexamine the conception of the topic as an organizing principle of the work; by so doing we will gain deeper insight into creative architectonics. We have already gained preliminary access to the formation of the creative idea: it is, first, the organizational pattern that incorporates the plot/topic into the creative objective schema. But where, to start, the plot/theme plays a secondary role, it is obvious that it is indispensable to shift the leading organizational role elsewhere, namely, *that a pattern of organization emerge that causes an articulation of the leading creative intuition of the vision in relation to the decisive elements to make the idea precise in its significance and by coordinating them functionally, achieve a crystallization of the main tendency.* Furthermore, it is indispensable to coordinate as well all the other essential and variable elements of the idea of the work, indicating and directing their selection within the creative progress of construction in their qualitative nature, intensity, vividness, nuance, point of view, etc. Lastly, it is essential to single out an appropriate, formal organization with its networks of connectedness to other significant objectivities.

Thus the nature of the idea of a work of creation appears not as a mere "tendency" or "ideal," but as a *rational scheme* of the work, tentatively projecting as well its prospective *final shape* as the *ways and means of its accomplishment.* But as an "idea," it shows a unique nature. In contradistinction to ideas understood in the traditional Platonic realistic sense (still preserved in Ingardenian aesthetics), the nature of the "idea of the creative work" originates within the creative context which must be explicated. That is, first, the creative idea appears *not* as a pre-given, transcendental, *a priori* of the great human enterprise, introducing through constitutive constructivism meaningful avenues of life (e.g., constitution) which, in their perduring — supratemporal — existence, assume a static *regulative* role. The creative idea is not pre-given but *inventively constructed*; not static, but "in process." It originates, first, in the inventive process of its intrinsic composition; second by being adjusted; third, through transformation during the course of the creative process. The creative idea also plays, indeed, a *regulative* role. But the way it regulates is adjusted and re-adjusted, not remaining static, but (a) being galvanized with the "forces" prompting its incarnation into the form of an object, and (b) vibrating with the active imagery of its underlying vision.

With these features, the creative idea of the work incorporates the objective/formal and the subjective/operational threads of creative self-interpretation-in-existence within one, crucial, existential knot.

And yet to understand it better we have to make a closer investigation of the principle of its own creation. We will do that by revising the role of the "topic." We can, indeed, in a certain way, agree with Rudrauf, that *"L'invention géniale ne peut s'exercer utilement que dans le cadre des lois formatrices et regulatrices d'un thème."*[21] It is an observed fact that the compositional potentialities for a work of art or science are not unlimited; furthermore, there exist a *certain* number of laws prescribing the possible variants of a compositional theme, such as, for instance, the theme of "annunciation." It seems also to be an undeniable fact, as Perrugini shows, that the topic exercises a profound influence upon the choice of the work, its pictorial conception, the psychological climate of the work and, consequently, upon the technique as well. For example, Watteau's choice of topic for the painting *"L'amour au théâtre français,"* in relation to the contemporary life of the period and its tradition of Italian *Comedia del Arte* to which Watteau devoted considerable attention, is the deciding factor for the entire structure of the work.

We must examine then what specific, creative role the topic/theme assumes with respect to the creative process. What do we infer from the terms "topic" or "theme?" Is the model taken from real life, drawn from nature, or from imagination? Is it an idea, a problem, or a story (which Perrugini finds so crucial for the ballet)?

With Rudrauf's analysis, in contrast to our foregoing examples from literature, we penetrate into the purely rational aspect of plastic art, which operates with opaque material factors, rather than purely abstract considerations. Having distinguished the rational sub-structure in the material aspect of painting, Rudrauf, starting with the ready-made work of art, reaches into the operational basis of the structuralizing operations. He exposes the correlative rational laws of the creative process, which both the creative agent — and consequently the work to be born — had to obey.

Following Leonardo's conviction that *"La pittura e cosa mentale,"* he distinguishes, in the first place, the "objective conditions" of the medium of expression. According to him, there are two types of pictorial space: "a non-characterized" space, and a "characterized" space. Since space is the basic objective material and frame of the plastic work, this pictorial space should be organized in relation to a figurative topic. Rudrauf, opposing Woelfflin, whose division of the pictorial composition into "open" and "closed" has been, until recently, dominant in art criticism, classifies types of composition from the rhythmic point of view into "diffused" and "scanned." In relation to the topic, the objective laws of composition simultaneously play a "constructive," as well as a "restrictive," role. The diffused composition, according to Rudrauf, does not satisfy the aesthetic exigencies assumed with respect to the work of creation as a finished product; to the scanned composition is attributed the role of organizing the crystallization of the intentional/subjectivized topic into a pictorial form. In the first place, a coordination has to take place between the interpretation of the topic by the artist and the disposition of pictorial space. By "stretching out," according to a special rhythm that is strongly hierarchized — which contains principal and secondary accentuations with a varying but always neatly sensible vigor — the spatial expansion is coordinated with the structural stretch of the topic. There are varying degrees of closeness of this coordination through which the specific spatial compositional shape of the topic is assumed. In fact, according to Rudrauf's rhythmic principle, composition may be (1) centered, (2) focused, or (3) polarized. In other words, the intentional/subjective topic receives its objectivized spatial interpretation. The generic virtuality of the topic lies both in polarizing its basic elements and also in disposing them di-symmetrically. This organizing rhythmic disposition of the topic allows it to exercise a constructive role in devising a compositional organization of the pictorial space and in indicating the most appropriate media for its crystallization.[22]

The topic of "Annunciation" analyzed by Rudrauf is a subject involving two personages, a human being and an angel — different in origin. Implied in this difference is a radical contrast in their characterization. The difference in their physical appearance serves as an appropriate example; it epitomizes the essential features of both polarity and di-symmetry. Di-symmetry lies in the contrast: here a "supernatural" being from a region "beyond," there an earthly human individual with all that that involves.[23] The polarity is present because they are both "out" on the same spatial plane through the contact they are about to establish, as if, to use a thought of T. S. Eliot's, the "nontemporal instant established itself in the midst of the temporal area." They are rhythmically drawn to each other, influencing each other in their respective attitudes, poses, forms, expressions, etc. Their mutual influence occurs according to the contrast to be expected due to their divergent natures, but also according to a concordance, indispensable for the contact to be established, so that the message of the topic may pass through. Accordingly, the space divides naturally into two compartments: the "interior," in which the Virgin, the earthly creature, is contained and the "exterior," from which the angel — the supernatural being from "beyond" — comes. The space of this latter is characterized in such a way that this exterior demonstrates and "signifies" the messenger's provenance in the "beyond."

Yet it is not this compositional division of space which comes first as a necessary prerequisite for the spatial arrangement of the topic. In the work of Roger van der Weyden, where the scene is enclosed within one spatial compartment, the light which serves as a liaison with the "exterior" or "beyond" is placed inversely, at the side of the Virgin and not at that of the Angel. However, the topic is not impaired; the light indicates that the "beyond" is already a "place" of contact for both and that the virgin has already received the message. Thus space is rhythmically divided. There are various compositional devices used by various painters for this division (e.g., like the interior and exterior of the edifice where the Virgin awaits the arrival of the visitor coming from the outside, like as well the light from the side of the door, through which the visitor obviously arrived, if he is already present in the room). But even when there is no apparent spatial division, as in Roger Van der Weyden's "Annunciation," and the light is inverted, placed next to the Virgin rather than to the Angel, the light still indicates the distinction between the two realms present there within a single pictorial space, permitting a kind of organization of the compositional details which follow this distribution of spatial rhythms, and evolve around it, creating other rhythmic centers on their own.

This accent on the organizing faculty of the rhythmic content is by no means new. We had an awareness of it in Greek and Latin poetry, where rhythm carried the basic organizational weight. In modern times we have poets like Goethe, Stendhal and numerous others who are acutely aware of the rhythmic nature of prosody.

SECTION 3. THE INTERPLAY: THE THEME IN ITS
TRANSFORMATIVE CRYSTALLIZATION

In an analogical vein there is also just such a rhythmic principle in scientific research and theory writing where, especially with the concern in mathematics and logic for methodological style, a strong emphasis is put upon "elegant" presentation of theoretical thinking. What is of interest for us here is the incontestable organizational value of the topic for the idea of the work, as well as, consequently, for its embodiment, especially in such a fundamental matter as establishing a level of contact between the abstract, rational structure of the work, barely outlined by the topic and its physical medium, such as space or words and their concatenations.

Virginia Woolf's diary introduces us into the tortuous ways that a creative vision takes shape in a crystallization of the idea/plan of a work.[24] *The Waves* had to follow a long, long itinerary before a clear idea of the novel was worked out. On the Thursday of September 30, 1926, Virginia Woolf makes a metaphysical entry:

I wished to add some remarks on this, on the mystical side of this solicitude; how it is not oneself but something in the universe that one's left with. It is this that is frightening and exciting in the midst of my profound gloom, depression, boredom, whatever it is. One sees a fin passing far out. What image can I reach to convey what I mean? Really there is none, I think . . . I hazard the guess that it may be the impulse behind another book . . .

But there is a specific condition of this state of mind and the experience which Virginia Woolf notices makes it extraordinary; not just any state of depression or boredom:

The interesting thing is that in all my feeling and thinking I have never come up against it before . . .

Here we are at the first glimpse of creative vision, which fascinates by its uniqueness and the intensity of its quality and yet presents no clear image of its existence. The writer notices: "at present my mind is totally blank and virgin of books. I want to watch and see how the idea at first occurs . . ."

On June 18, 1927 she adds a new entry, the fruit of a long germination: a theme to capture this metaphysical, transcending vision is proposing itself, already, outlining some major postulates of the idea of the work and mixed up with it:

... suddenly I rhapsodised ... and told over the story of the moths, which I think I will write very quickly .... Now the Moths will I think fill out the skeleton which I dashed in here; the play-poem idea; the idea of some continuous stream, not solely of human thought, but of the ship, the night, etc., all flowing together: intersected by the arrival of the bright moths. A man and a woman are to be sitting at table talking. Or shall they remain silent? It is to be a love story; she is finally to let the last great moth in. The contrasts might be something of this sort; she might talk, or think, about the age of the earth; the death of the humanity; then the moths keep on coming. Perhaps the man could be left absolutely dim. France: hear the sea; at night; a garden under the window ...

This scheme of a situation: two personages, ships, a short development framed in the rhythmic form of a play-poem, culminating in the coming in of moths, are the theme meant to capture the essence and the message of the metaphysical experience, the vagueness and unavoidable, streamlike monotony of life. In disengaging the strains of the extremely complex web which this theme proposes, the idea of the work is evolving.

The idea of *The Moths* occurs as an "abstract mystical eyeless" book: a "play-poem" and, in working it out, several points of reference to be consulted appear. At first,

... one reviewer says that I have come to a crisis in the matter of style: it is now so fluent and fluid that it runs through the mind like water. That disease began in the *Lighthouse*. The first part came fluid — how I wrote and wrote! Shall I now check and consolidate, more in the *Dalloway* and *Jacob's Room* style? I rather think the upshot will be books that relieve other books: a variety of styles and subjects: for after all that is my temperament, I think, to be very little persuaded of the truth of anything — what I say, what people say — always to follow, blindly, instinctively with a sense of leaping over a precipice — the call of — the call of — now, if I write *The Moths* I must come to terms with these mystical feelings.

— (Entry of November 7, 1928)

And she writes on November 28th:

As for my next book, I am going to hold myself from writing till I have it impending in me: grown heavy in my mind like a ripe pear; pendant, gravid, asking to be cut or it will fall.

That is the best description of what is meant by the "idea of the work" and of what it implies. We have to omit the long process of this idea shaping itself in Virginia Woolf's mind becoming *The Moths*. How, progressively and in succession, various aspects of the theme, the moths, the flower pot in the center, the conception of the woman, "Who is she? I am very anxious that she should have no name. I don't want a Lavinia or a Penelope: I want 'she' . . ." were scrutinized, embodied and disembodied again into literary elements a novel trial meaning "a perpetual crumbling and renewing of the plant" in the center which, together with the flying in of moths, represents thematic, dynamic charges of significance to be transmitted by the message (entry May 28, 1929).

At this point, the need to accommodate the message of the vision with the potential idea in its objective requirements and limitations causes a complete shift toward an entirely different representational situation (entry June 23, 1929):

. . . I now begin to see *The Moths* rather too clearly, or at least strenuously, for my comfort. I think it will begin like this: dawn; the shells on a beach; I don't know — voices of cock and nightingale; and then all the children at a long table — lessons. . . . Well, all sorts of characters are to be there. Then the person who is at the table can call out anyone of them at any moment; and build up by that person the mood, tell a story; for instance about digs and nurses; or some adventure of a child's kind; all to be very Arabian Nights; and so on: this shall be childhood; but it must not be *my* childhood; and boats on the pond; the sense of children; unreality; things oddly proportioned. Then another person or figure must be selected. The unreal world must be round all this — the phantom waves. The Moth must come in; the beautiful single moth. Could one not get waves to be heard all through? Or the farmyard noises? Some odd irrelevant noises. She might have a book — one book to read in — another to write in — old letters. Early morning light — but this need not be insisted on; because there must be great freedom from 'reality.' Yet everything must have relevance.

Well all this is of course the 'real' life; and nothingness only comes in the absence of this . . .

We see how the working out of the idea by scrutinizing the first proposed theme with reference to the creative vision has introduced a substantial shift in the composition of the theme itself. The stream of the "interior time," which at first was incorporated in the flying in of the moths into the closed room, the emotional climate of which was to be derived from the woman talking, or the subject of thought, has been resituated — in correspondence to the extension of the scene — into a larger framework by the noise of the waves. And we will see next that with other constraints which objective conditions exercise upon the selection of elements for the idea, the main symbol of the first theme will be abandoned, and with it the theme itself will be transformed. As a matter of fact, she writes on September 10th:

Moths, I suddenly remember, don't fly by day. And there can't be a lighted candle. Altogether the shape of the book wants considering — and with time I could do it.

So *Moths* have changed in their very theme and become *Waves* and the writing was begun, by fits and starts, and became what it is.

On April 29, 1930 the last sentence of the first draft of *The Waves* was written.

This brief example shows how peripatetic a theme is once the conscious elaboration of the idea of the work begins. And there are several possible starting points for this elaboration in response to the actual central constitutive factor of the theme itself: a story, a pattern of dynamic charges, a purely aesthetic scheme, a set of principles for a theory, the skeleton of a monument or the shape of a volume. The conscious elaboration of the idea, carried on by the functional subjective forces, charged with them, encroaches already upon the last stage of the creative process, that of *the transition* from an intentional, purely rational structure of its plan, which the idea entails, into another mode of existence incarnated into an objective mold among real beings and things.

Through these analyses we already encroach, indeed, upon the phase of the transitional processes of the creative constructivism which are naturally sequential to the preceding ones. From the virtual elements of the incipient phase granted to the creative endeavor by the creative vision as well as warranted by the selection of the possibles, we will pass to the constraints exercised by the objective formal and material situation of its "embodiment" and entrance into the real world as the terminal point of this creative progress. First, we have however to elaborate further the role of the crystallization of the creative idea of the work with respect to the main issues in which the creative process is involved.

SECTION 4. THE TOPIC OR THE GENERAL THEME

Thus the importance of the topic-factor cannot be dismissed in view of the fact that the significant content of the topic, its "message," that will be otherwise delivered by the plot as a sequence of human action, such as in the case of "Annunciation," can pass even without its figurative representation in the form of such a sequence. Contemporary, non-figurative and abstract art has shown that the same message can be conveyed through several types of composition, figurative or abstract. It makes us see that the basic organizing principle of every work of creation is neither the message itself (because it is intuitively compact in its significance and "formless" and cannot, without taking a specific form, suffice to organize the singular outline of a work) nor is it the topic, understood as a plot or a story or as a sequence of action distributing pictorial space. These fall short of covering the whole range of works of creation in which the plot often has either a diminished importance, receding before other factors, or — as in the most recent strictly "pictorial" paintings — where the aesthetic valuation of effects centers upon the color, its intensities skillfully calculating shape arrangements within the given space of the canvas. In such works the creative intuition carries a *purely aesthetic significance* being situated within the network of *purely artistic* rules and these have propensities to stimulate the emotive, aesthetic responses of *aesthetic enjoyment* in moods and emotions. The complex, purely aesthetic significance in thematic pictorial complexes differentiates a painting from others. The same holds true for sculpture and minor genres. This is particularly striking in the music of Stravinsky and Penderecki and those who go beyond them.

It is the *theme* of the work upon which and in reference to which the "idea" of the work, as it is intuitively/aesthetically crystallized, is centered, as the most appropriate topical or non-figurative factors are adjusted by it — plastic rhythms of colors in their intensities, contrasts of shapes in mass/line effects, sound complexes, etc. The theme directs the crystallization which guides the *purely* aesthetic message of the theme, which aiming at a purely aesthetic significance, selects from among an infinity of possible purely artistic categories, types, styles, elements, etc., those relevant to its basic tendency and significance for incarnation in the work.

SECTION 5. THE SPONTANEOUS DIVISION OF
THE ARTS AND GENRES

If in painting and sculpture and architecture, for instance, a *principle of transition* from the purely aesthetic/artistic/intellectual theme to space and volume is required, in a literary work this transition principle is more immediate. As a matter of fact, already in the working out of the idea, say of a poem, we crystallize the image into words and word concatenations; we devise already a certain rhythmic arrangement of the ideas expressed, emotions to be awakened, words to which the objective rhythmic forms of the literary art, as such, offer a mold. Beyond this division of the Arts as such, genres of composition play a primary architectonic role, e.g., the sonnet, blank verse, a short story, a form of scientific theory, a theorem, an axiomatic system, a chronicle, a diary, etc., etc., serve as the first formal principle for the theme. These forms of the genre function already as a formal principle in the construction of the idea of the work. With them, the processes of transition are already essentially initiated and projected in the formation of the idea.

The constructive guidance of the plastic theme becomes, in the case of non-figurative art, which has the *intuitive significance of pure aestheticity* as its creative message, particularly instructive within the framework of our inquiry. In fact, because it is a concrete borderline case, it allows us to penetrate into the difference between the *universal forms of artistry*, on the one hand, and *the preconstitutive "substances" of Nature in their subliminal significance within the human primogenital life-condition*, on the other. Phenomenological investigation of the ways the human transcendental apparatus proceeds in the constitution of the empirical, "real," or "natural" realm has, in the works of Husserl,[25] shown us first that it is our constitutive apparatus which projects the contingent — material — features in which a physical object "appears": its substantiality, its shape-color-smell-touch scheme and the characteristics of its appearance with respect to our constitutive faculty, aim at objectification. The investigations of M. Merleau-Ponty, corroborating Husserl's insights, have stressed the subjective/objective instrumentality of the human primary motor-operations, as well as of secondary kinesthetic — motion — operations in this process.

Our present investigations have revealed the pre-topical/pre-mental access to the creative act in Art — that is, we have shown that the crux of art, namely the *aesthetic moment*, does not *essentially* depend upon the human *transcendental objectification for its initiation*, but may be released as if "directly" — on its own — pointing us in two philosophically important directions.

First, as we will demonstrate further in our analysis of the *transitional phase* of the creative constructivism, our subliminal preconscious and pre-rational functioning, which stretches directly into our functions of sentient, vital, "organic" significance, is already attuned to its turn from *vitally oriented* to *creative orchestration*. We may thus bring together directly the abstract laws of "artistry" with our entire vitally functioning system: "bodily" motility, sentient reaction, etc. That is, the creative swing is not a "*cosa mentale*." It is also the "*cosa vitale*" of our entire beingness. Second, *aesthetic enjoyment carries a "sense"* of its own, independently of intellectual reason, which is the domain of the intentional constitutive function.

SECTION 6. THE CREATIVE IDEA WITH ITS ARCHITECTONIC PLAN CONTAINS THE OUTLINE OF THE ENTIRE CREATIVE PROGRESS

One of the great contributions to our understanding of what Art is about has been made by contemporary art; it has resolutely shifted away from the prerequisite, traditional emphasis on the display of a theme, a plot, a story, as the center of whatever else was to be presented, to "things themselves." The art of Rouault, or Chevalier — who has done the redecorations at Chartres — pushed the presentational aspect to the background, bringing the religious content and message to the fore; instead of fashioning figurative and story-plotting situations, which may well convey this content symbolically but which at the same time distract the viewer from the purely spiritual message because of their real-life form, the contemporary artist attempts to omit the figural level of representation as much as possible, and to reach the spiritual directly through his purely artistic devices. He presents the media of purely pictorial expression. Picasso's "Saltimbalques" still seems topic-bound in the organization of the space and forms of expression; but his more abstract works go straight from the often highly intellectual, spiritual, or even metaphysical message into expressiveness through colors and shapes "in their own right." Chagal uses various representational elements — his brides, horses, bouquets and seemingly contrived topics — to create a mood or metaphysical élan. Of course, it should be added right away that the objectively constituted forms are thereby not totally overcome; there remain always strict objective restrictions referring, albeit vaguely, to formal objective laws of space and its constitutive nature itself, unless compositional art is frankly abandoned for a simply decorative genre.

In the same vein, in fiction (e.g., the French *Nouveau Roman*) and poetry the emphasis has shifted from the plot to complexes of feelings, emotions, etc. Poetry like that of Guillaume Apollinaire (e.g., his famous *La Chanson du Mal-Aimé*), James Joyce (*Collected Poems*), Ezra Pound (*Pisan Cantos*), and following him, the poetry of T. S. Eliot (*The Wasteland*), as well as the greater part of American poetry and its world-wide reverberations make the plot explode into incoherent fragments, as the result of a dynamic charge hidden underneath which carries the sense of the poem.

Innumerable examples could be given to the effect that there is an almost inexaustible number of different factors which can be decisive for the conception of works of art and science to be created which can then be classified into the great categories of ways in which man tries to open new significant avenues within the narrow vital framework of life and the pedestrian concreteness of everyday experience.

And correlatively there are innumerable kinds of elements that have to be crystallized in the complete work, one of them being the "theme."

Although itself changeable in the process of this establishment, the theme still functions as the relatively stable guide postulating other aspects, indicating their dimensions, etc., and generally it may continue to be called the "theme." Once the idea of the work settles upon a theme as its axis, it is "ripe" and prompts as its rationally graspable project an objective of existential crystallization and begins searching for its essential postulates. If a theme is present as the axis of the idea of the work, it is its nature that is being scrutinized concerning its specific "incarnation." On the one hand, if there is a plot that is a course of action which may convey, through its tragic/comic conflict, a metaphysical view of life or a particularly revealing mood, an "ideal" making life worth living, or a thesis about reality, it can be the axis around which the idea of the work will evolve. A fragment of a plot which makes an imprint on our imagination and suggests these deeper dimensions of human life may play, as well, the role of a theme which then we will try to incorporate into a larger and more precise context within the creative idea. On the other hand, with reference to the theme, the creative process proper is simultaneously set in motion. In fact, the theme, which has emerged from the creative vision, carries the suggestive power of the creative vision itself, projected in front of the inward/outward spread, but here mobilized by Imaginatio Creatrix. Thus human functioning, with its powers of body and mind, meets the projected structural form which in its making corresponds to the creative potential of the Human Condition. This structural form is indeed the result of the processes of discrimination, decision, choice, variation, adjustment, etc. Its constructive genesis means (1) the transmutation processes ranging from the vitally significant functions to the *inventive/creative multiplicity of significance*; (2) *the selection of the functional threads for installing a creative orchestration of functions*; and (3) *the emergence of a specific operational system which was called earlier the creative operational architectonics.*

The organization of functions into a pattern leading to the form of an idea of the work is the fundamental condition contributed by consciousness for its creative operations. This is in virtue of the fact that conscious functions may, under certain specific conditions, assume the pattern of orchestration, structuring their operations into a four-polar synthesis in which, projected by Imaginatio Creatrix: (1) an infinitely expanding area of "active images" may be brought into a constructive project together, according to (2) the vital forces of our bodily/psychic schema, and (3) the subliminal virtualities of the human condition, and, lastly, (4) the objective rules of the life-world constitution. *A novel, consistent, articulated creative consciousness that synthesizes all the operations is thus organized and may assume the creative function.*

In trying to incorporate the theme into the objective frame of the idea of the work we have, indeed, started a conscious strategy. This is no longer the "inward creatrix" of the passive imaginative synthesis of dispersed elements into a coalescing unity, but an active mechanism of searching, differentiation, deliberation, variation, and choice. It is upon the material prepared by the "passive imagination" and fancy and which invades chaotically the field of actual consciousness and fills it beyond its borders with material — which is, however, already activated by imaginatio creatrix and is flexible, pliant, plastic — that the selective evaluation and choosing take place. These functions are orchestrated into such a structurally compact and yet active pattern that they acquire the appearance of an "agent." However, in a way comparable to the nature of intelligence as revealed by Piaget — in a challenge to tradition, which saw it as a specific power, agent, or faculty — this orchestration is not a special "agency" but merely *a specific organization of human functions*. Creative operations do not necessitate a specific agent, power, or faculty, but are *a specific orchestration of active and passive conscious functions* of the human individual, *who, in directing this orchestration, is a creative agent.*

Facing the suggestiveness of the theme, the orchestrated functions begin the search for the proper material and forms for the incarnation of the idea of the work, following a hierarchical arrangement. There seems to be a preestablished outline of the project's itinerary; it is suggested by the structure of this project, expressing, on the one hand, the architectonic workings of the creatively orchestrated functions, and, on the other, corresponding to the universal architectonic requirements of the objective structure of the creative result being aimed at. It seems, indeed, that this prospective structure of the object incarnating the creative idea is like a loom upon which a tentative, continually-searching and critical weaving now begins. The reflective activity of consciousness scrutinizes with a falcon's eye the potential material of experience invading the actual field of the consciousness of the artist, scientist, or philosopher, in which, through reflection, recurrent reference to the theme searching for appropriate constructive material opens further and wider perspectives into the reservoir of memory and the force of imagination. More complicated, deeper and vaster dimensions open up in our store of sensations, emotions, ideas and volitions: their infinite vibrating and changing nuances fulgurate in the creator's mind and captivate his feelings. Under each probing glance of reflection, and in response to the indications of the theme, these dimensions are ready to take on different aspects in order to enter into new connections. Evaluated for their proficiency in satisfying the demands of some crucial postulates (first, of the theme, and, second, at the opposite correlative end, those of the objective structure of which these dimensions are to become a part), numerous "objective" points of view are consulted: for instance, the prospective aesthetic function of the work, its social impact, the particular place which the significance of the work may assume within the established life-world through its particular style, etc. Thus, the construction of the project proceeds through evaluation, deliberation, and choice. All these three functions strictly coordinated (but not mechanized, since they correct each other constantly) go forward, and often backward, for mutual verification and coordination toward the final decision making. They perform a selective architectonic role and, in opposition to the passive synthesis of imagination, which proceeds by associations alone, they control the throng of images which are already there or which emerge through the generative melting, mixing and coalescing; and each new juxtaposition of elements means a new imaginative stimulation of the operational network toward further intergenerative fulgurations of new images.

The directing role of the creative intuition, working itself through the idea, passes then and brings together the most abstract mental operations, along with the physical operations dealing with the crude material, to embody the mental "plan" being formulated by the architectonic functioning which reaches into all the others. Operations like plan-laying, cement mixing, choice of a special appropriate sort of canvas, colors, metals, sounds, "ideas," building bricks, stones, woods, etc., which lead to the exercise of the function of "embodiment" in the "right" type of clay, bronze or wood in the "right," particularly appropriate place, do constitute the third and "*transitional phase*" *of the creative process*, but they are already being considered with the elucidation of the creative idea in a general way.

It should again be emphasized that the architectonic scheme of operations that the objective structure amounts to is distinctive of the "plan." It is not a blueprint or a honeycomb waiting there to be filled in. On the contrary, while the "plan" is that, *this structural schema emerges in its* functional exercise together and through the particular architectonic operations; it is "pre-given" only insofar as its rules, outlining in their order the major architectonic operations, belong to the intrinsic rules and regulations of the constructive functioning. Its step-by-step constructive progress, whose order/sequence cannot in any way be reversed (color ground precedes final touches in a painting, for instance), is correlated with the objective structure of the work to emerge. Yet at no point during the creative progress thus outlined may the creative agent lose sight of the guiding intuition imbued with the significant message which he is thus exfoliating and seeks to crystallize.

In this consistent order of activities orchestrated in relation to the architectonic progress of the objective structure, there are several aspects to be considered. Although this order is essentially irreversible, its actual progress is often apparently chaotic. By choosing one particular element we become aware of the inappropriateness of another already chosen. We have then to retreat from the previous decision and try to see whether the new one is appropriate with reference to our regulative guidelines already established. If so, then we replace the nonpertinent element by a novel choice though as we work with it it might again appear, as it often does, that probing deeper into that particular perspective of our selecting process, other elements already chosen will be inappropriate, and so our last step in the decision-making process remains doubtful. In this "self-critical" process we might be brought to abandon the complete, far-advanced architectonic scheme and plan altogether.

We might get, as well, a new, more adequate and deeper insight into the nature of the theme which has so far guided our previous procedure, finding that in our previous interpretation a certain essential element which has now come forcefully into light does not exhibit the necessary intensity; we might be led to reinterpret the theme itself.

Furthermore, it often happens that, in these self-critical processes, the theme might through analytic probing undergo essential transformations in response to the potentialities of the objective structuration, on the one hand, and to the prospective media for the functional expression of its message, on the other. However, as long as the significant message remains *the same*, we are dealing with *the same* creative process.

If, however, in this universal process of self-criticism, we reiterate the validity of the significant message, shifting then onto an entirely different track, the creative process is thus definitely disrupted and abandoned. It may, however, be replaced by a new one, emerging in response to a *new* intuitive message.

It appears, then, that the architectonic activity of the creative process, subsuming all types of operations for its end, is of a specific, non-repeatable nature.

Although the process maintains a strictly rational line of constructive procedure to be followed, yet there is nothing in this line that would strictly preestablish or prescribe its sequence. It proceeds by trial and error, left entirely to its own spontaneities and checking itself in its proceeding only with reference to the above-discussed "relatively stable" guidelines in the self-critical progress of an endless process of self-correction. These guiding points themselves not only do not "prescribe" anything directly, but merely postulate certain answers to problems which they themselves pose: from an entire spectrum of possibles, the most appropriate and acceptable is chosen. Now, often several spectra are equally appropriate and the choice of each particular individual element within one draws in consequence attention upon all the other elements of its range or even all the other spectra consulted previously or still to be consulted. To change the spectrum of, for instance, colors, with respect to one singular patch on the canvas, means often that the artist has to repaint the whole canvas in order to adjust all the other color elements in their peculiar spectra with respect to this particular patch.

Thus the operational *activity* of the creative process seems particularly unpredictable, uncertain and, in opposition to the *passive* operations of imagination, not automatized, but *inventively erratic*.

This specific erratic nature is essentially correlated with a deeper organizational tendency, a constant concern that there be a most concise and strict rational order in the successive selections. This erratic, inventive character of the creative process in its selective architectonic operations, its searching essence, is most vividly shown by the fact that, as pointed out in the famous controversy between Hemingway and Steinbeck, it is controversial *whether progress in the creative process is achieved through failure or through success* in the innumerable attempts undertaken. Concerning scientific creativity, as Popper justly observed, we advance by disproving the validity of our hypothesis rather than by constructing new ones which are seemingly more advanced than the initial ones, while these latter hypotheses themselves are soon disproved. The validity of elements rescued from such a universal shipwreck as the collapse of a theory seems more solid; mistakes revealed point to new perspectives that are more advanced in the line of exploration. In particular, we can witness this process in research in astronomy: how, for instance, Kepler, by realizing the inadequacy of his previous assumptions, advances toward a more adequate, lucid, concept of the solar system.

The opposition between this infinitely complex range of possibilities varying in the very process of choice and resulting in this essentially erratic, because *constantly inventive*, procedure, and its correlated postulate of a most strictly rational although discrete constructive coherence, which alone guarantees faithfulness to the aim set before these operations, makes the creative process a strenuous undertaking, draining the human being of all his resources. Indeed, all the resources of the individual being are involved in it and drawn upon. The human being arrives through the creative process at a most concentrated state of his propensities. Consequently, creation — in its full sense — is a rare activity.

The architectonic constructivism is, as stressed from the outset of our inquiry, characterized by its telic orientation, which is *matched by the creator's concern or particular "responsibility"* with respect to the goal aimed at; it offers a specific "finished off" aspect to the creative result and to its maker a special experience of "accomplishment."

On the other side, the fact that it does not follow an *a priori*, objectively established routine in an automatized way, arranged in schemata (like the constitutive process constructing an object), but within a chaos of dispersed elements out of which it selects inventively the threads and patterns for the weaving of a cloth, having only the theme as a loom and some regulations and laws of the material as objective postulates, requirements and restrictions, gives to the creative process an incomparable *freedom*. For the regulative factors are only relatively stable, and there is a reciprocity between the weaving and the theme, and finally, all the other regulative points of reference conveying the style (according to social and aesthetic, among other actually valid, conventions) might in the process of self-critically-guided weaving be transformed and replaced by others, all of which confers upon this freedom a flexibility which *only the inventive genius of man may bring into the narrow constraints of the vital significance of life.* It is this unique flexibility that gives human creativity a kinship with the human dream of the "absolute" freedom.

Lastly, this purposive orientation of the creative process, its imperative need for selection and decision-making, combined with the feeling of responsibility that is generated, gives to the creative process a particular emotive accompaniment unknown in cognitive functions, that is, *an urge toward accomplishing the aim*, the proposed aim that draws into itself, like a haven in the midst of a stormy sea voyage, a *specific fervor* of concentrated activities and often a feverish strife through which the object to be construed takes complete possession of the maker. One somewhat lives with one's creation, as we can see through Virginia Woolf's diary, in which the inner life and the everyday existence subordinate to it are emptied of any autonomous content that would make us hold on to it, and so lose their own meaning and value and become only necessary conditions for the work of creation as it ploughs its way through to existence. That is, *we see there how the creative activity becomes an all-embracing and transforming factor of life: it enriches and transforms ever anew through its novel life significance and self-interpretation in existence.*

SECTION 7. THE THREE STEPS OF THE PASSAGE — THE ORIGIN OF THE WORK OF ART AND ITS EXISTENTIAL CONTINUITY

(a) *The three steps*

Passing from the stage in which I contemplate the creative vision to that at which the creative idea is crystallized, and thus the creative process initiated, I am seized first by its intrinsic urge to communicate; that is, the contemplative function of the spirit undergoes a transformation in response to the structural aspects of the vision itself — as well as in response to a sustained strong-willed purpose — which prompts a need for *passing* from strictly personal experiencing into an objective formation and itself indicates operations toward this objectification. This drive toward objectification is identical with the idea's acquisition of an intersubjective communicable form. It is a stage at which I ask myself, further, *what* is there to be communicated. Finally, the same propulsion intrinsic to the origin of the creative idea leads me to the stage at which I envisage the *means of this communication*. In this transformative passage from the vision to the idea there are three steps of radical transfiguration of the operational apparatus which enter into play in order to initiate the creative process. And yet these three steps constitute one extensive, discretely continuous, inseparable whole. The intrinsic, qualitatively radiating urge of the creative intuition and its crystallizing effect in the "idea of the work" are already present in germ (in their varying spectra of possible structural outlines of operational procedure as well as in the project of the constructive itinerary that is to be taken by the initial spontaneity prompting it all) within the incipient stage of the creative vision. Whenever there is an occurrence of the creative impulse setting in motion the preliminary and searching operations of the mind, the instant in which the first hint of a constructive, organizing and novel objective surges within the total functional system of human beingness, all our resources are mobilized, indicating that we are entering into the game of the Imaginatio Creatrix, and, thereby, the constructive system is reorganized into the "creative orchestration" toward the fulfillment of this aim.

There is, indeed, in the intrinsic encroachment upon each other of these three steps, such a pervading continuity of purpose — in spite of the simultaneous discreteness of the numerous processes and operations which are set at work to fulfill it — that, in the first place, we

cannot discern when the creative vision is a mere virtuality and when it
becomes actualized into an idea, a project of the work. For its actualization, all these three steps are indispensable.

(b) *The discrete existential continuity of the creative advance*

Furthermore, this first ("subjective") incipient phase of the creative
vision — the "creative inwardness" — encroaches so intimately (through
its crystallization into the objective idea/project of the work) upon the
second phase of the creative process that it cannot be clearly distinguished from it. Indeed, it is the elaboration of this idea in an arduous
constructing progress within the *inward/outward* oriented constructive
process that constitutes the core of creativity: its basic existential
phases. It is crystallized only when it severs its ties with the sets of
constructive processes, when it loses thereby relatedness to the creative
orchestration of its maker in order to be established among other
objects of the world. Yet if the idea/project has not been so crystallized,
it has never been a virtuality, because virtuality implies that the whole
process of creation is, in the incipient stage, so well-established — and
so well-grounded in the functional proficiencies of the maker — that its
realization cannot fail. If such a realization fails, this means either that
the creative vision was not flawless in its constructive virtualities and in
its foundation in the individual spirit and that, consequently, the creative object which it suggested had never been virtual, or that the actual
creative undertaking was hindered by a life process within which its
maker remains. We may make here, due to our conception that all three
phases of the creative process are constructive, activizing, and always
architectonically oriented toward the concrete objective aim (envisaged
as imminently continuing each other in their constructive activity already
outlined in the incipient phase of the creative process) — we may make
here — a sharp distinction between the "mere work of imagination"
which suggests fantastic and fascinating images which surge in order to
be contemplated, but appear as images of a dream, devoid of the vigor
that prompts existential realization. The creator may also be a "dreamer"
engaged in projecting and enjoying the contemplation of dream images,
but a dreamer is not *eo ipso* a creator. Sartre is, then, right in saying
that there are no creative geniuses who fail to create. If they do not
create they do not possess creative genius, since genius does not consist
in contemplating, but in *making*.

Secondly, *the nature of the continuity of the three phases of the creative process allows the abstract and fallacious distinction between supposedly "subjective" and "objective" phases of creation to be overcome. The striking aspect of the creative process is that within the most "subjective" operation (e.g., analyzing the creative vision in order to transform it into the objective idea, that is, into the project of the work to be accomplished), we already take into consideration the media of this accomplishment, that is, the relation of the purely abstract intellectual plan of the work to the "physical material," the mold in which the idea has to be communicatively expressed. As, on the one hand, there can be no sharp line drawn between the conception of the possible creative work and its realization, so, on the other hand, there can be no sharp division drawn between the purely "subjective," that is, the work exclusive of reflection, and the "objective," or the work of our human physical organs. In the phase of transition of the objective idea into a physical medium of expression, not only do we select an appropriate medium for the chosen idea, but the search for the medium and its intrinsic virtualities, its available spectra and its specific properties, makes us revise the idea itself on the rebound in such a way that its plan can adopt the intrinsic prerequisites of this transformation. The relation between the "subjective" operations of the mind with their given constructive material and the "objective" physical conditions of the established world is, throughout the creative process, a two-way street type of correspondence. From the point of view of the essential unity of this process itself, no sharp boundary may be traced between them.* We often see how a painter adjusts the main color scheme of his palette to the specific color spectrum of the landscape and paints accordingly, not following uniquely the inclinations of his "inner eye"; and how, inversely, the sculptor looks for an "idea" for a monument which would just fit the volume, shape and color of a piece of marble or stone he just happens to have, but which already stirs in him some latent intuitive images and, for their sake, he has become fond of that piece of stone which appears to him to already contain that statue.

The passage from the creative vision to the idea of the work is initiated when, from the identification of our visionary experience and its content, we are led by its quality to ask ourselves what it is we are contemplating, what it is that awakens our desire, insists on being communicated. We stumble immediately upon a discrepancy present in this desire: there is, indeed, nothing precise, nothing formally shaped and qualitatively determined in the content of our contemplation. In principle the creative vision permits itself to be realized in a musical, as well as a poetic or plastic, form; that is, it could take equally the form of a musical sequence, of a portrait, a landscape, a pictorial composition or a philosophical essay. It happens, as well, that it can find an outlet in a purely theoretical masterpiece of art criticism, scientific theory, etc.

This shows that the elucidation of the content of the creative vision means a radical step is taken. Radical, in the sense that what is given predetermines, indeed (to some degree only), the outcome and directs the process of the search for its own elucidation. But, simultaneously, this outcome has to be determined according to its universal directedness, or from a vast realm of possibilities among universal types, objective forms, categories, styles, etc. To assert this is to assert that we are facing here the basic decision in the process of selection and evaluation.

This passage is a crucial moment in the creative constructive progress. It can be compared with the "problematic situation" in Dewey's description, in which there is an unusual type of question, a type that does not have — as is the case with "usual" questions — solutions already indicated in terms of a type, category, and even situated in a given spectrum, with indications of restrictions of their use. The question which creates a "problematic situation" like, for instance, a decision concerning morals, "Is it better to betray a friend than to harm a brother?" does not seem to contain any specific prescription as to its solution; it throws open several avenues of consideration: religious, cultural, ethical, aesthetic, personal, and pragmatic, concerning the interests of the protagonist in such a way that the commitments being referred to are put at stake with almost equal, and yet not entirely equal, weights. An answer to such a question may not be immediately evident, involving as it does basic realms of human life: emotional, ethical, religious, practical, intellectual, etc.

In order to be solved, the problematic situation calls, in the first place, for a deep inquiry into many alternative approaches with their possible solutions, all intertwined in some particular way. Second, it demands evaluation and selection of the nearest appropriate alternatives; third, it imposes a choice which, however, is to be qualified also by the impact to be expected from its actualization. An abstractly found solution that often appears theoretically the most appropriate, if considered from the point of view of the effects which follow its application, just does not satisfy some criteria, e.g., of justice. The judgment of Solomon is, in this perspective, not a measure of justice rendered, but an experiment relying upon his profound knowledge of the human soul. From the point of view of final, practical justice, it often may seem better to a judge to save the life of a criminal, even if almost all evidence is against him, than to run the risk of sentencing an innocent man, although from the theoretical point of view, if the balance of evidence is against the dispensation of justice, a death sentence would be demanded.

The "creative situation" — if we may use such an analogy —, like every problematic situation, implies, thus, the appearance of innumerable possibles in terms of evaluation, selection, and decision-making. It is to some extent prescribed and guided in these operations by the formulation of the "question" itself which occurs through the vibrant quality and the intuitive promptings of the creative vision. Comparably, the creative situation has restrictions in (1) the objective possibilities and virtualities of the elements to be selected themselves; (2) the objective postulates of the objective telos pursued; and (3) further postulates and restrictions intrinsic to its existential conditions as the vision aims to become an object, part of the life-world. This process of selection is guided, on the one hand, by the indications of the creative vision; on the other hand, however, it is checked in its evaluation and choice by objective conditions coming from the world in which the project of creation intends to establish the created work.

As a matter of fact it seems that *the formation of the creative idea of a new and original work constitutes the central phase of the creative process, a phase in which all the others are implicitly or marginally contained. This phase directly and indirectly stretches to all the creative procedures of the given creative process.*

PART V

THE ARCHITECTONIC LOGIC IN
THE EXISTENTIAL PASSAGE FROM THE VIRTUAL
TO THE REAL — THE WILL

SECTION 1. THE PHASE OF TRANSITION IN THE CREATIVE
PROCESS FROM SUBJECTIVE INTERIORITY TO THE
LIFE-WORLD: THE SURGING AND THE FORCE OF THE WILL

Inasmuch as the creative process is erratic and proceeds by fits and starts, it proceeds with an iron "logic." It is an "architectonic" logic, *presiding, as we will see, over the logos of beingness-in-the-genetic-process.* We will follow this *architectonic logic* now, in the third, transitional phase, of the creative process.

First of all let us state that "architectonic logic" exhibits a thread of continuity in its sequences, continuity which does not lie in the conclusion being implicitly contained in the steps of the premises. On the contrary, each step means an advance over the preceding one. Instead of static "premises" its "conclusion" draws upon each of the constructive operational segments with their self-enclosed telic principles. Building itself up, this conclusion-in-progress constitutes the thread joining their constructive network, built from the numerous sequences. They themselves join spontaneously realms of objects that ultimately appear to be, of disparate ontological modalities in the perspective of the constituted world: creative imaginings, memorized or sensed moments of life, "real," intellectual elements, passional strivings, etc. Each of them carries its *own mode of significance or rationale. Spreading through this pluri-rational network of the constructive advance, the architectonic logic is itself "constructive."* In joining the multiple rationalities already available it allows in this very *creative act* for their inventive inter-generation. *The creative process is, indeed, the forge of the infinite mode of the significance of life that the human being, man/creator, may devise for his uniquely personal self-interpretation in existence.*

The various operations carrying on the creative endeavor may, in fact, all seem mixed together; they might occur and proceed to be at times apparently inverse to the "iron" consistency of the "logic" of factual progress; they might encroach upon each other; and yet they are not be

246

confused either in their respective, clearly delineated roles, nor in the irreversible order of the architectonic order which they simultaneously project and follow in the line of constructive progress which emerges.

By the *phase of transition in the creative process* we mean the *third and final architectonic segment of constructive operations*, which, continuing — having already been initiated, as well as partly performed in the phase of the construction of the creative idea — aims at the "incarnation" of the idea in an "objective," intersubjectively communicable "medium." *This means that from the forge of creative inwardness we are attempting to transpose the idea into an intersubjective form of the life-world.*

Hardly needing emphasis is the fact that the transitional architectonics of this passage, first, cannot be considered to be independent of antecedent phases: the order outlined in the architectonic plan which the idea entails, and its spontaneous impetus, is the result of the creative spontaneities at work from the outset. Second, it is, however, also obvious that it has a twofold initial point: first, only with the elucidation of the creative idea in which the architectonic plan emerges, can the transitional phase begin; second, its start is marked clearly and unmistakably by a new moment surging within the heretofore vaguely oriented spontaneous vigor of inward promptings. All of a sudden in their midst *a will to accomplish emerges.* We may extrapolate here toward a view that it is *the urge to accomplish that is the origin of a clearly articulated "power of will."*

Let us anticipate here and point out an extremely important distinction which comes to light. Indeed, it is only in the investigation of the architectonics of the creative process in its role of inventing and establishing a new avenue of life through a new life-significant element that we may observe this surging of the act of will in its pristine, essential, nature. In the passage from the creative idea to the realization in a constructive, long-winded, and ramified architectonics of its intrinsic plan, a click occurs. The spontaneities of the vitally significant life progress of the individual being, even when invigorated by the specific passional and intuitive promptings of the creative vision, do not amount to more than life's forceful striving onward. Within their own frame, these spontaneities unfold a "desire" to live, a subsequent "desire" to satisfy life-course requirements, a "desire to survive," and, lastly, a "desire" to expand the narrow, vital meaningfulness of the "natural" life itself toward a "higher" meaningfulness of one's very own, etc. Yet, these vague, vitally significant desires do not suffice to carry on the ever-renewing, repeated effort, step-by-step, segment-by-segment of a self-devised constructive process which is the active mobilization of our entire functioning at its peak; desire is a mere striving for a repeatable, but instantaneous, line that is not predetermined, and is measured step by step; it is a passive response to actual inner promptings carried by the vitally significant operational system. To pass from such a diffuse bundle of desires and the passional nostalgia of the creative vision to the undertaking of a constructive plan of action in the tightly articulated architectonic logic, an entirely different motor is indispensable. *In fact, it is what we call the "will" that surges, or fails to surge in some individual instances in which the creative idea finds no follow-up in an immeasurable instant to fulfill the expectations of the virtualities, to respond to the promptings and to undertake the accomplishment of the telos which they are aiming at. With this unique type of click, there occurs the conversion of the vague and diffused spontaneities of our desires into a concise aim, whereupon all is directed toward and concentrated on its fulfillment through forceful drive and determination.*

Its articulations occur as the synthesis of the vigorous but architectonically tightly delineated operations to be actualized in order that the constructive progress is carried on. It is the anticipation/fulfillment structure of the architectonic plan demonstrated by the virtualities of the creative idea that carries the repetitive recurrence of willful effort along in the entire progress of the creative construction. The "will to accomplish" is then continually stirred and prompted anew by each new effort. It is invigorated by the progress toward the fulfillment of the aim as well as by the obstacles which it finds on its way. It is also stirred and intensified as much by the necessity to struggle or to seek the solutions or ways that are missing as by the encouragement which satisfaction with prompt success offers.

Far from being a special faculty distributing some functions into special constructive configurations, the will — so long a mystery for philosophers — reveals itself in the creative context as the *inventively oriented force articulated toward the accomplishment of some aim.*

(This insight into the specific origin, source and nature of the will coincides with the view of the existential thinkers who, like Ortega y Gasset and, later, Sartre, see the nature of man in his devising a project of self-realization in life; that is, in our perspective, in his being prompted, by the will to accomplish a life project.)

Coming back to the creative project let us focus again on its phase of transition. This means the beginning of strenuous work: from being the subjectively interiorized intentionality of the project, the creative work has to assume a different objectivized existential status. Strikingly, there is no radical passage between the two existential stages because the mode of the successive existential status has already been delineated in the initial phase of the idea; even more, its structural groundwork has been preestablished at that stage. The transitional phase has to follow up by trying to apply to its aim the indicated media to the full extent they are capable of incarnating and crystallizing the intentional idea in an objective, existentially self-enclosed and distinctive form. Nevertheless, there is a basic distinction between the two phases of operations and the transitional progress itself. Whereas the two previous phases are experienced by the creative agent as the exercise of his creative freedom in the exuberant play of spontaneous fulgurations, there begins with the endeavor to accomplish the embodiment of the creative project the concentrated effort to harness the free play of intuitive imagination and to work out in a concentrated synthetic "creative craftsmanship" all the steps of its concrete objective construction in a chosen material. In contrast to the seemingly infinite expansion of our imaginative powers which we experience in the idea-forming phase (in which we may even go on to transform the very theme of the work and all the other points of reference in their first, intuitively preestablished nature, which extends our actual field of consciousness toward the reservoir of experience, of memory, as well as of the potentialities of the future), in the phase of transition in which we measure our actual possession of the constructive material with the exigencies of the task, we confront with surprise the realization that our "supplies," which appeared inexhaustible, were in reality scant and in need of enrichment in order to carry on the process of transition.

In this confrontation between our assumed "unlimited" faculties, our potential, our seemingly unrestricted powers for work and its accompanying feeling of enthusiasm, exuberance, on the one side, (What else is enthusiasm than feeling the unlimited extent of our being? What else is exuberance than the feeling that our faculties are not limited in their exercise?) — and, on the other side, the limited choice involved in working with the restrictive postulates of the means required for the transitional constructivism come to the fore. In this confrontation surges the *will to accomplish*; it receives the shock of obstacles to be overcome which belongs to the challenge to our invigorating mechanism and, in reaction, it triggers the progress of transition. This shock is what we call a "confrontation between two existential modes": *the illusion of the imaginative swing versus the "reality of facts," or potentiality versus the conditions of its actualization.* Indeed, with the onset of the transitional deliberations and recognition of our *actual* proficiencies, talent and capacities, as we consider the demand to give our intuition a concrete existential foothold and the means at our disposal necessary for the accomplishment of this aim, we come to reappraise our endowment. From elated enthusiasms, we are brought down to ask: how much are we as maker endowed with factors allowing us to master this transition?

The creative vision appears to us gratuitously given. By its very nature it appears *sua sponte* and takes possession of us; this incipient phase of creation does not lead to a confrontation with ourselves for the sake of confrontation; it does not imply any necessary prerequisites concerning education, training, development of the human individual, or skills to be able to enact it. Although we might infer from its procedure that the elaboration of the creative idea assumes many prerequisites for its proper accomplishment (such as possession of highly developed speculative power and imagination, proficiency at assimilation of previously created and established works as source material, knowledge of forms as well as of procedures and styles and ways to construct them), yet it is assumed *tacite* that these proficiencies are naturally there, that to possess them "naturally" is what makes the creator a creator. All these things are somewhat lying in waiting, prior to the emergence of the creative undertaking which we are describing, needing only development, and they might be somewhat presumed as a prerequisite of the individual for the emergence of the creative idea, *but they do not enter into the nature of the creative phenomenon with which we are singularly concerned at this point.*

SECTION 2. THE TRANSITION PHASE AS
THE CREATIVE ACTIVITY PROPER:
ITS VERY OWN INTRINSIC LAWS; DIFFERENTIATION OF
THE TYPES OF CREATIVITY IN ART, SCIENCE, ETC.

An altogether different situation arises with the conditions of the transition process. *Here the prospective creative agent is confronted with himself.* The transition process itself implies certain specific skills which are to be used in its course, and which themselves are in the process of transformation, adaptation and development, in order to acquire an appropriate fitness to each particular constructive function which the plan of the idea of the work postulates. The specificity of these functions and their strict connection with the postulates concerning the nature of the work to be accomplished, on the one side, and the specific functional demands outlined in the idea and leading toward specific intended results (e.g., a crystallization of such a theme within a particular climate exclusive of others, resulting in a unique creative message, etc.) on the other side, call for appropriate skills. By following the guidelines of these proposed tasks in the transitional phase, the emphasis falls upon forming specific proficiencies for "making" (working with the chosen material, e.g., stone, bronze, language, scientific research, musical sonority, dance skills, etc.), on the one hand, and for sharpening inquisitive imagination, observation and sensibilities in order to devise the appropriate adjustment of the media (e.g., colors of the palette) with the concrete sharpening of the idea of the work, on the other hand, out of all those general skills acquired by the maker in times prior to this particular performance. Thus the phase of transition consists in the "mediating" and the working out of its instruments. The specific adaptation, crystallization, consolidation, transformation and specification of the skills necessary for the transition that mediates constructivism to a chain activity with a trajectory between the creative idea and its message expanding in suggestive rays and the restrictive postulates of the material medium in which it finds its mode of expression, need to be coordinated. This is the creative activity proper: a chain of acts, processes, operations and segments of action which involves all the philosophically distinguished realms of ontological modalities (intentional, "ideal," "real," empirical, etc.). *The "phenomenon of creation" resides indeed in a special way in the process of transition. It constitutes the heart of beingness, within which all ordering — forming — structural principles in germinal proficiencies come together and whence the ontological modalities differentiate with respect to the constructive roles these proficiencies assume.*

The phase of transition is, as shown above, no longer that of infinite expansion and freedom but, on the contrary, that of gradual shrinking and constraint which is imposed by "materiality," "reality," the "life-world," laws of objectivity and the "artistry" intrinsic to man's transcendental nature.

Aristotle's conception of art as "imitation," conceiving of art as necessarily either "below" or "above" nature loses its significance altogether if we consider that the effort of transition is to find such media that the purely intentional project will actually compete with products of the constituted life-world.

The creative process in its transitional phase has as a rival, in fact, the processes of nature in devising such procedures that, starting from different premises than those of the natural genetic life-process, start within its unfolding vital significance, and aim nevertheless at also constructing an objective and existing entity with a complete spread of modes: aesthetic, theoretical, and technical from the point of view of the life-forms it brings into the life-world. Within our perspective which grasps human "art," we could not talk about art as an "imitation" of nature. To assume that art reproduces a "model," to be copied in the artistically created object, is to trivialize art and to miss totally its role in the Human Condition, as well as in the advance of life. It is through the factor of inventiveness latent in the Human Condition and released in the creative process that it purports to rival nature. In the creative process *inventiveness is not an instantaneous occurrence; it is a constant element of the architectonics of the transition from plan to crystallized entity.* Even in works of art like the sagas of a nation or family, and certain types of figurative painting which put an overemphasis upon "fidelity to nature," this stress itself, this fidelity, assumes that the work will be one which is meant to accomplish a form of "reconstruction" — either of the constituted structures in our experience, or of the workings of nature itself (e.g., the architecture of Buckminster Fuller). Yet this re-construction cannot proceed except according to architectonic rules and regulations which have to be invented for this purpose.

Thus the masterpieces of imitation "copy" a flower, piece of fruit, or a vase which one has in front of oneself, either reproducing its appearance directly in a *trompe-l'oeil*, or consulting it in order to find out "how it was done" by nature or man. There is an "imitating" nature, too, in a still-life invented by a great master that is later reproduced by his disciples. The inventive function of consciousness is at work to devise a *new* and, for the given object and its medium, a particular appropriate mode differing from those used by nature to produce an apple, pear, or fish. A carpenter may even make a table so as to obtain an effect similar to that made upon us by nature.

It has again to be emphasized that this is also a different approach than simply discovering the rules and structural devices of the constitutive processes, by which objectivity — or nature *as objectified* — is constructed. Undoubtedly, as the impressionists have shown us, the painter seeking for *his* secret scrutinizes the ways and approaches of the constitutive "appearances" of reality. The "realist style" attempts to transpose the "appearances" of thing-hood onto the canvas. And yet, except for photography, no great realistic painter has presented us with "crude" "images" as they appear in everyday experience (Böcklin, Wölfflin, Géricault, Matejko, etc.); each gives to the "realistic" images his unique "style" of *seeing*, viewing, and thereby endowing the "facts" of the object and beings with a unique significance — heroic, tragic, pathetic — perspectives which open up scenes of human life to be pondered.

To accomplish this task of endowing nature with a special significance, that is to re-create the response which we may have toward it in an "artificial" object of re-construction which does not belong to nature, there are different laws for the creative perception of it (which we spoke of at the outset of this investigation and which we now return to) in order that the objective embodiment be invented. It will be different from that of the constitutive objectification.

In the true masterpieces of painting (the Dutch landscapes of Ruisdael, the "*scènes champêtres*" of the great Italian masters, the Madonnas in fields and gardens, etc.) there is such a *striking qualitative synthesis*, such an intensity of colors and, in a comparatively minute space, such a concentration of shapes "represented," that no landscape of nature could even contain even the tiniest portion of all that is synthesized in the work of art. The constitutive structuration of real objects, conversely, makes space expand *ad infinitum*. Whatever the laws followed by the constitution of reality as it gives significance to facts and events with respect to the arrangement of figurative elements, it is certain that even those works of art said to be of "natural stature" occupy in their compositional arrangement an incomparably smaller, more "compact" space, a sort of "space apart" in a "perspectivistic" way than real beings which "have a place in space" following the laws of volume. As we know, there is a vast science of "perspective" representation, as well as of the opposite "flat" rendition of pictorial space in the presentation of objects or their elements (Cézanne, Picasso) or of just purely aesthetic "meanings."

Each type of creative activity has taken a long time, involving much practice, to discover and invent its own basic rules which in creativity substitute and compete with those used by nature: rules that bring in a specifically human way of viewing, feeling, sensing and understanding everything which otherwise merely offers support for the satisfaction of our vital life progress.

In painting the laws of perspective, or basic relations of colors, etc., are just such elementary laws with which the transitional devices and operations have to contend; so in music the laws of harmony, dissonance, rhythm/anti-rhythm, etc., must be followed; so in poetry there are the rules of rhyming, of rhythmical arrangements with reference to words and sounds, balances of intensities of emotions, of association of images, etc.; so in mathematics there are the logical laws of theoretical proof and disproof in the establishing of a theorem, as well as rules of the axiomatic arrangement of the elements in a theory particular to its specific type. *Indeed it is in the architectonics of the phase of transition that a spontaneous differentiation of creative types according to the different constructive guidelines is governed by a divergent medium of final objectifying embodiment.* It is obvious that, on the one hand, an entirely different set of architectonic laws and rules is followed in music's "imitating" nature (e.g., Rameau's bird chants versus birds' actual singing). Similarly, a radically different intrinsic organization system proper to its own type is present in applied mathematical theory and in any natural sequence of phenomena to which it is applied. The most complex of arts — dance — which in its crystallization incarnates itself in several dimensions of reality which are kept apart by other creative genres, bringing movement, sight, hearing and design together, had to invent the most complex set of laws in order to establish its rivalry with nature. Manipulating by its own devices and developed skills the natural resources of the human being at the heart of the most fundamental laws which nature itself has to obey, it challenges nature. Indeed, great dancers, like Serge Lifar, Margot Fontaine, or Nureyev and Baryshnikov, challenge nature in its fundamental laws of gravitation when, for an instant, they remain immobile in the air, or seem, through an unbelievably poised leap of prolonged duration, to float in the air, to have overcome the laws of natural motion.

SECTION 3. THE OPERATIONAL SYNTHESIS OF
THE CREATIVE ARCHITECTONICS: EXECUTION SKILL AND
TECHNIQUE IN THE TRANSITIONAL CONSTRUCTIVE ADVANCE

The essential role of the creative transition is, then, to devise in a ramified, many-sided and "plurivocal" process that advances by tentatively
placed steps, one by one, a complete constructive system, a system that
is complete because it takes into account both the initial impulse with
its intuitive promptings, at the one extreme, and the final aim of these
promptings with its own postulates, at the other extreme. In this process
the entire network of the architectonics of the creative function is on
trial, since it involves a total *conversion of functions* — a total overturn
of functional orientation occurs from the passive life-decoding of the
constitution of life-routes to the active inventing of new avenues of life.
Subsequently, the second role of this phase is to respond to the intrinsic
postulates of the rational plan of the creative work — those most
appropriate for incarnating and conveying its message —, while conforming to the pattern of laws of the possible "objective structuration"
which expresses basic relatedness to the laws of the natural world.

These seemingly factual, concrete problems to be solved in the
transitional phase do not change anything in its creative being *par
excellence* like the other two preceding phases which have delineated
and projected it.

Indeed, problems concerning the technique to be applied, the style to
be devised, the material to be used, etc., are not matters of "mechanical
practice" or automatized "skills". Skills are nevertheless by their nature
involved with the issues concerning the plan of the work, that is, with its
architectonic references in the proficiencies involved in the inner workings of the execution of the creative project as a network of specially
articulated movements (molding bronze, carving stone, steel, placing
patches of color on the canvas; touching the keyboard of a pianoforte,
etc.) and motivate each other reciprocally.

Technique and the whole complex of skills as instruments for executing the plan are thus to be constantly referred to inventive adjustments
and searches for new approaches. To convert our subjective/imagina-
tive ideas, emotions, and feelings into an objective form, we inventively
seek out the most appropriate means. We have to test these before we
know whether they fit. Each attempt, if it fails, stirs our inventive
imagination to seek other solutions. In fact, invention does not surge

and operate other than in the search for a technique, the skill required to forge a "material substance" into an intended form that interprets it. It operates especially in response to the difficulties of the "matter" and to the postulates of the intuition involved in the creation of "style." As Stendhal expressed it, in *Filosofia Nova*,[27] "*En fait de style . . . la forme fait partie de la chose; une transposition de mots, montre l'object d'un autre coté . . .*"

The method of approaching a canvas, of giving it a layer of colorful paint, the technique in laying down the first draft of a design, the eye to find the appropriate color and its nuance, the mixing of the standard oils or watercolors in order to transpose the vision into the visualized, into a glimpse evoking an appropriate response within a correspondingly selected pattern of colors, putting it upon a canvas or paper, these transpose inventively the creative interconnected elements of the inner workings of the idea and its plan. The architectonic plan, vibrating with operational suggestiveness through the workings of the inventive imagination, plays the function of indicator of the spectra of elements of which some may fulfill the requirements of the transposition. These requirements have to satisfy numerous postulates. In the main, they have to carry the metamorphosis that is the "embodiment" along the lines of sensibility, feeling, emotions, and passional drives, in a threefold differentiation that addresses (a) the specific — yet only universally presented — bend indicated in the idea/plan of the work; (b) the expression of the peculiar — and yet operatively dominant — tendency/ intent that synthesizes *the unique personal self-interpretative system into what we call the "personality" of the creative agent*; and (c) the line along which the transposing indications for selection but even more for the *forging, molding, and shaping of novel "experiential substances," as these crystallize within the pluri-significant system of an embodiment* (the adoptive postulate of its material proficiencies) take place. The "hand" has to practice in order to obtain a kinesthetic orchestration such that a particularly smooth swing of a line or curve may be drawn; this special "smoothness" of its movement on a board, paper, or canvas, however — creating a style — is the plastic insinuation/suggestion/ expression of a sensing which is chosen as that most appropriate. The aesthetic quality carries an element of the significance, through which the creative intuition that prompts the breakthrough into the inter-subjective world is metamorphosed. (*Morphe*, here, means "form" as much as "substance." Neither of these two expressions has any correlate in experience alone.)

The "touch" of the pianist, so incomparably unique in the case of great masters, is similarly the result of a kinesthetic orchestration forging or molding the means of transposing the creative idea. Both examples show how the skills and technique(s) of the transitional phase are suspended upon the complete architectonics of the creative orchestration. Yet, they required the architectonics of their aim. The "technique" develops with respect to all three lines, yet the intuitive message is what it aims at. Thus the same technique of a creator of a school, or of anyone who adheres to it, is responsible for many consecutive works, but only insofar as it is relevant to the carrying out of the creative project. That is, the creative plan/project evolves both according to its progress toward realization, and according to the *iron logic* of its leading intuition, and outlines *schemes of execution* which function as an intermediary link, belonging to the plan/project itself and extending its postulating promptings into a virtual, plurivocal order of operations between the idea of the work and the concrete techniques and media that incarnate it.

SECTION 4. SEQUENCES OF OPERATIONAL INVENTIVENESS:
THE ARCHITECTONIC LOGIC OF BEINGNESS IN
THE GENERATIVE PROCESS

It may be said that each choice of a type of constructive element for a creative work implies the choice of an entire system of *consequential*, objective order.

We may, in fact, distinguish three types of *"objective" sequences of operational inventiveness* according to (1) the basic series of creative construction that concerns material corresponding to the unique and objective ontological laws of the intentional object — the object of creation; and (2) the series of *consequential* order inherent in the objective nature and objective connectedness of (a) the construction material, and (b) the spatio-temporality of creation versus reality. Yet these operational inventions, as we saw, convert to or assume the role of "executing" the indications of the creative project. Thus its sequences are to be seen also as *sequences of inventive execution*.

The sequences of inventive execution appear thus as consisting of several objective, serially arranged orders or "consequences" which create networks of encounter between "art" (the artistic, scientific, technological, etc.) which is human endeavor itself, the natural life progress. This essential "art" core of creation accounts for the fact that — in radical opposition to Bergson's view — whatever the result of human creation may be, it is always an "artifax" in contrast to things and beings in "nature" which acquire their composition and form from the whims of vital cosmic energies and forces.

These objective consequences give, also, expression to the reconciliatory device between the subjective/operational and objective/structural conditions of "creativity" in its imaginative core wherein are joined seemingly limitless freedom and the specific "technique" of craftsmanship.

Indeed, the light chosen for painting a scene, a still life, or anything at all, implies a series of "consequences" between shades and lights strictly interconnected; colors appear "dark" or "light," with corresponding variations in intensities. The same "light" conditions have to be maintained by the artist throughout the entire duration of the painting procedures. If we paint the "same" landscape at different times of the day, under different light, a chaos full of internal contradictions would follow. The same holds for the strictly determined conditions of scientific laboratory and field work in chemistry, biology, etc., and all other types of scientific research involving observation and analysis. If the same conditions are not kept, or, if in changing them special appropriate provisions are not made, if instead of observing the development of a seed within *one set* of conditions we switch to a different set without making an allowance for this, the sequence of observations is disturbed — since a consecutive order of observation is assumed to be related to a particular set and not to another set of conditions and, so, the continuity of the order of observation is disrupted. Whereas the continuity of the constitutive process (e.g., perception) is guaranteed by the same point of reference for all singular acts identifying the "object," whose structure is the guide (*leitmotif*) of the process, in contrast, the creative inventive process establishes the "identity" of its procedures through constructive devices which are their "core" and "aim." In it continuity is as much a matter of the creative inventive intuition, at the one extreme, as it is of the continuation of the process with the same objective conditions and core-technique, at the other.

The change of this set of conditions implies a corresponding change of the consecutive order of analysis and observation.

The same "consequential order" of conditions is operative in literary creativity. It is revealing to learn how the long hesitations of Tolstoi in choosing and "identifying" inventively the physical and psychological type of Maria, the heroine of *Resurrection*,[28] could cause the whole outline to vacillate, as well as the "content" of the idea and plan of the work, along with the plot and type of tragic *dénouement*.

Changing a particular detail in making a poem provokes, in consequence, a complete remapping of its outline. Adding a patch of color to a landscape, somehow stirring our imagination, may bring about, in a series of consequential order, its complete "repainting" in a different color tonality. Furthermore, in response to the change of color tonality — and consequently to the change of emotional climate (e.g., blue and green "creating" a reposeful, peaceful and passive mood with, in contrast, gold and purple-red evoking emotionally stirring, disquieting, dynamic feelings) —, the compositional arrangement and the design may of necessity have to be changed, take a different contour line, and become differently accentuated, and acquire thereby a different shape and form.

The schemes of execution take into consideration and indicate the particular *structural* conditions for the emergence of the structure of thing-hood, differentiated respectively in various types of objects within the life-world. The artist or scientist aims at the closest determination of his work in terms of the most minute specific details, yet the constructive process as well as the pattern of interconnectedness of the elements of this determination follow schemas entirely different from those of the processes of transcendental constitution, on the one hand, and of the analogous "real object" in its ontic substructure, on the other hand. The painting presents everything seemingly only in one dimension; yet the back of the head and the right side, if the left is in focus, are not lacking, although they remain visually absent. They are "hidden" in the way in which, analogously, the back of a head is hidden if we look at a person's face. Within the system of objective regulations of the constitution of the real object in perception, this back of the real person is strictly determined in all its universal and concrete features within the same schema as the front, wherein nothing is lacking; we cannot see it due to the laws of space and of sense perception itself, but it belongs of necessity to the objective structure indicated by the front. And yet there are various surprises which could occur as a result of judging all sides of a real, empirical, physical being merely on the basis of the perception of one side: the left side of a face might hide a scar, the back of the head might, upon check, surprise us with a wound or deformation which, in reality, would be strictly determined. In plastic art (e.g., in a portrait) the back of the head is not painted, but presumed; it is not concretely determined, but co-determined, not only according to objective laws for such types of real being, but foremost by what the network of creative consequences to which the visible front belongs implies for it.

We cannot, indeed, expect a silver gray hair on the back of a young and blond lady, or the inverse. No such surprise in a portrait, since the unseen is there not determined directly, but can only be presumed on the grounds of what is present as co-present.

This presumptiveness is based, thus, on an "iron logic": the universal laws of objective structuration as the *Leitfaden* of perception, to use Husserl's term, are filled with the *representational concreteness of plastic elements*. Although the coordination between the two is as strict as it is in the use of constitutive perception, yet it is of an entirely different type. First, the universal laws of objectivity may be loosened or twisted in innumerable ways and, yet, keeping to a "minimal" objective structuration, the universal co-ordination with reality is maintained enough to be able to co-ordinate the "objective logic" of constitutive forms with the "plurivocal logic" of the "creative architectonics." Second, the filling-in of the universal objective pattern with presentational, plastic (audible, etc.) pseudo-concreteness is something radically different in the schema of creative execution than it is in the constitutive process. In the latter process the filling material is *empirically intentional*; that is, its possible selection is, through the intentional set of conscious processes, strictly coordinated with objective guidelines (*Leitfaden*) — the structure of "Thinghood" or "individuality" —, whereas the *creative architectonics are in their selection of presentation material entirely "open-ended."* This selection follows, on the one hand, the universal indication laid down in its path by the architectonic selection, not in a strictly prescribed objective co-ordination, *but in an inventively/imaginatively variating fashion.* Not only may the front of a head stretch, as in El Greco's paintings, in a way incommensurate with "natural" proportion, but its color scheme and its scheme of expressiveness may, as in contemporary abstract art, go in all directions. And yet, in an *exemplary work*, this execution of the filling-in scheme establishes its own color/shape/expression system in which each pictorial element plays a strictly attributed role with respect to the whole (e.g., the portraits by Rembrandt), so that changing any of them would change the entire representational unity.

It has to be immediately emphasized that this very *filling-in material* is of an entirely different sort than the empirical/intentional elements of the constitutive process of real objects. It is not re-presentational in the sense that it "stands for" an object (a part of the system of "reality"). It is *presentational*, meaning it *stands for itself*; it does not follow a *prescribed signifying* system. On the contrary, it is being devised in its already present objectively significant skeleton in such a way as to allow *such a configuration of a new material/aesthetic objectivity — a new type of aesthetic objectivity — that the old significance of reality to which it is correlated may be "upturned," "con-verted" and "trans-muted."*

Interestingly enough, when art goes beyond the line of a certain "minimum" *presentational co-ordination with* objective reality (or leaves the established system of meaningfulness altogether), its presentation has a merely *fragmentary significance*, for example, the novel insight into the aesthetic feelings of depth of color, configurations of form in so-called "flat paintings," where only extraordinary color schemes (e.g., the canvasses of Gyorgi Kepes) are exposed, or abstract shapes (e.g., the graphics of Fischer). What these offer is of merely artistic and aesthetic significance. This is coordinated with insight into the "reality of colors and of shapes" in themselves; this is an "upending" or "overturn" of the usual way in which we experience colors and shapes as making elements of constituted reality. Yet this does not bring new life-significance to it; it reveals the dimension of artistry with surface colors, shapes and volumes as they may surge in an artist's direct contact with the *elementary workings of Nature*.

Ingarden talks about a series of empty spaces in the structure of the work of art as such. In his view, they are ontological conditions of the work of art seen as an intentional object; both on the side of the work's structure, as well as that of its cognition. He misses, however, the crucial, that is, existential, role played in the originary making of schemes by the execution which determines the selection that establishes perspectives of presentation while projecting the schemes of factual artistic work. The *leitmotif* is here the given "theme." Among the objectively oriented schemes of execution are, as discussed above, those which (a) coordinate structuration and presentation with the special laws of objectivity, but also (b) those which devise a schema of execution which emphasizes in particular either temporal, or intellectual, presentation. We witness in the literary work of art, especially in fiction, that in contra-distinction to the perfectly continuous unfolding of events in "reality" which make the stream of duration "full" and "complete," a novel, or even a so-called chronicle or autobiography referring directly to events which took place in reality, is merely a sequence of specially chosen events, selected with a creative intent in mind, to the disregard of others; *their selection is calculated inventively in order to construct the significance of the story.*

It seems, at first glance, that the temporal and spatial schemes of execution would apply in full merely to works in which there are so-called "represented objects." Yet this is not so. On the contrary, much more demanding and vigorous insight and calculation are required for the inventive outlining and many-sided coordination of the spatio/temporally oriented progress of the creative work. In non-figurative art there are also schemes of execution present. These do not directly refer to the choice of elements with regard to so-called surface objectivity — to reality — but rather to the basic laws of space and temporality as such. They coordinate the basic laws of the painting, as workmanship, with the essential laws of spatiality and temporality as they are found, on the one hand, in human experience, and, on the other, in the handling of the "material." Here the schemes will have to solve problems concerning the choice of shapes, colors, and sonorities in relation to the experiential system of a human being to realize the effect desired: the conveying of an original message.

The revolution worked by modern art, in nonfigurative painting as well as in dodecaphonic music, consists precisely in the abandonment of the traditionally used systems of schemes of execution and replacing them with different types of schemes. The artist, prompted by the urge of his creative intuition to present a novel vision of life, seeks new schemes and is always in the process of experimenting: with the potentialities of the media, with the perspectives of invention, with his own vision sifted through the sieve of his personality, etc. This offers new solutions to technical problems and reveals the hitherto unknown objective conditions of creation in a given field.

When we talk about "execution" in music we usually have in mind virtuosity of performance. However, although the "reproduction" in the performance of a musical composition is certainly "creative," the actual creative *origin* of music lies in the composition of the work itself. There the schema of execution within the creative process and the essential, but very experiential, "substance" takes on a different modality.

Gisèle Brélet shows that the relation of music to its medium is most direct. According to her, musical creation proceeds through work that has temporality as its material. In fact, when we envisage the composition of the musical work, the creative activity in music, we might have the impression that in the passage from the vision to the idea of the work, prior to the grasp of a "form," it is, in a secondary way, a melody, a chord, a significant sonorous sequence before we "hear" these elements "within," calling to be recreated, reconstructed, etc. We have duration in our experiential field as a present, temporal "substance." Its origin is out of nowhere and spreads out in front of us, uncoiling itself within us and expanding ourselves with it. In some ways, we do not hear the musical intuition as something coming "to us" from the "outside"; it sings in us, causing our entire being to reverberate; it is our chanting soul. In this temporal substance, the melody seems to unfold in cadences, in bounces and falls, and seems to be ready to be incarnated in concrete sonority.

It would seem, then, that, due to this experiential identification of the one stream of creative impulses in their specific nature with what is simultaneously the "objective" material of its inter-subjective crystallization, creativity in music works upon a special type of "material," and that, consequently, for the transition from the interiority of the creative idea to production in the inter-subjective life-world, not only might a different kind of scheme of execution be postulated, but perhaps a scheme could be considered unnecessary. This is far-fetched; the musical work of art is not the "music of our soul." We have to distinguish the experiential time of the naturally unfolding course of our life's progress/stream of consciousness, which has its own cadences and intervals, and "musical time" which, in order to be intersubjectively acceptable, must place itself beyond the vagaries and vicissitudes of individual, experiential time, whether that of empirical life-experience, or that of transcendental constitution. Music must invent its own rules, which project their own logic of creative constructivism and that are somewhat "absolute" with respect to the individual flux of experience as well as with respect to the personal experiential molds and tendencies of the instant (moods, caprices, sudden reactions to events, etc.).

Irreducible to the rule of empirical/transcendental temporality, of "objectivity," or to the "objective time" of the world, measured by the clock, it has to keep a coordinating link with them.

Side by side with the rules of harmony, which orient the creative transition for classical music in the construction of its genres, symphony, sonata, concerts, variations on a theme, etc., we have recently seen exploration of long-range sonorous sequences, seemingly without regular, repetitive or melodic architectonics and, in fact, without strictly articulative structure. The sonorous material subsists in (a) sonorous qualities, intensities, "colors" (e.g., screeching or shrill vibrating sounds), etc.; (b) dispositions of sonorous stretches in the line of temporal continuities toward the construction of successive sonorous segments, new "harmonies" with their own climatic moments, etc. (e.g., Penderecki's *Utrenia*, etc.); and (c) associative disharmonies and mood-evocative sonorities, etc.

The new sonorous qualities "discovered," the pre-objective sound dimension and its laws, the new distributive rules for articulating the sonorous sequences in the construction of new rhythmic cadences, these mean an exploration *of the borderline virtualities* of the "elementary sound" within the three dimensions of temporality (that of empirical life-experience, that of transcendental constitution, and the objective clock-measured time of the world, e.g., the time of a sonata performance). *All these three lines enter the schema of the musical transitional phase of composition.*

Musical composition, whatever style it be, does not consist of an arbitrary flow of sonorities comparable to the spontaneous flow of our individual experience, but rather of a scheme that is composed of selected elements, one that readjusts in order to determine the modalities of sounds — the intervals of silence etc., to be chosen appropriately, as well as the lengths and abbreviations of sonorous durations. All of these are subordinated to a certain melodic, or purely sonorous, or rhythmic effect that the composer seeks.

In music, as in any other art, the composer must unfold, sharpen, and continuously rework his skills and his technique, and progress toward a renovation of his proficiencies in handling the creative architectonics.

The problems of schemes of execution are most clearly differentiated, discussed and defined in scientific activity. Methodology in a science is a special science; it has as its objective the determination of the transitional phase in all its steps. In empirical science this begins already at the stage of observations and their circumstances, in discriminating which are those preferable to others. Criteria are established for the *evaluation and selection of their significant elements.* It seems that, as scientists, we may accept these "objective" rules without being guided by any creative urge, intuition or vision. Furthermore, scientific methodology, beginning with Francis Bacon, claims to offer the principles for the appropriate interpretation of these significant elements in order to obtain *significant results*; lastly, it indicates how these results could be *generalized and incorporated into a theme.* Its coordinative links with the operations of Nature would be "verified," and thereby validated once the entire complex is finally incorporated into a "scientific theory."

In such a way it would seem that scientific methodology offers a clear-cut — if in detail much discussed and variously interpreted — method, a way to proceed in scientific "discovery," which encompasses all the main stages of the creative process which we have outlined so far. It would then seem that the incipient phase may be entirely "de-interiorized" and reduced to a series of factual, mental operations. Furthermore, it would seem that there is no need for a singular scientist to be a "creator" in the strong sense of *being able to initiate from within himself as from an absolute and unique source the inventive constructivism.* Lastly, it would seem that the crucially delicate, personal, imagination/memory/will/effort of orchestrating all of the human functional system toward creative architectonics is not at work. In fact, it is not without reason that we consider science to be an effort at "discovery" and not of "creation." Furthermore, we consider the coordination with objectivity to be its crucial point, and not imaginative originality that leads to a break with the laws of objectivity for the creation of new types.

Lastly, we assume that intelligence, a sense of observation, and an inquisitive mind are enough to pursue scientific "research." Should scientific "discovery" be accountable for its *exemplary* instances, such as the discovery of the laws, which like those of gravity, of natural selection, etc., broke with the previously established view of nature and have been revolutionary in their significance for the human condition, opening new avenues of life and breaking with a universalized, almost automatized pattern of constructive progress, then we could consider discovery to be a scientific form of creativity. However, this is far from being the case; we know that even scientific research, though directed according to a pre-set *method*, is by no means synonymous with mere "discovery."

Discovery, in its *exemplary* sense, calls for a creative moment. In its *repetitiveness* it draws upon previously established instances of genuine discovering; it always refers to an already established theory. And yet when we consider the process of discovery, whether it be in the natural sciences, the social sciences, or in abstract, mathematical science, "discovery," which indicates by its very connotation a break with the established view and understanding of some state of affairs, is by no means graspable through any pattern of method; on the contrary, it is just as interiorized (even in its incipient phase) and has as much creative architectonics in its further phases as does the process of creation *per se* that we are describing. *The steps which methodologies of scientific research deal with and attempt to delineate express partly, first, the rules of a universalized repetition of progress already accomplished* (like copying a painting instead of venturing into the labyrinth of its origination and new type), *or, secondly, the marginal work of application.*

We have mentioned still a third perspective within which the referential, as well as the guiding, factor of a particular origin have an equally determining impact upon the inventive forces that exercise their generative proficiencies in the projection of the sequences which operate the creative transition from the mental to the bodily, from the intentional to the physical realms of significance. This is the most complex perspective of the so-called "personality" of the creative agent which, in a uniquely specific way, shapes the bents, tendencies, and approaches of his attitude toward his work.

His "universally human" tentacles within the life-system, the "universally human" types of functional significance that the individual sharing of the life-world consists in, acquires with the unfolding of the creative function further developed functional complexes. These mold trends, lines and circuits of new factors that are original in their nuances and intensity with respect to the universal individual orientation, and which are instrumental in endowing with life-significance our otherwise neutral, merely life-promoting junctions. These particular traits of character (e.g., indulgence, revengefulness, obstinacy, justice, etc.), the "types of temperament" (cf. Kretschmer's typology of temperaments) and "personal dispositions" (e.g., toward cheerfulness or gloom), not only mold qualitatively the passional, manifold streaming forth of the stirrings of imagination, but they also exercise a dominant influence (a) *in the constructive operations of the creative architectonics with respect to the "emotional modes of signification"* (e.g., the "passionate," "colorful," "melancholic," "cheerful," "ironic," "pathetic" types of qualitative significance), and (b) *in the molding of the symbolic representation of plurivocal experiential material*: "uplifting" or "debasing," symbolic modalities (e.g., the modalities of the sacred or profane, of heroic virtue or deplorable weakness, nobility or baseness, righteousness or treachery, etc.), modalities of symbolic representation which emphasize beauty or ugliness, wisdom or folly, etc.[29] The symbolic forms of Antiquity offer striking examples of the directness in which a form taken from life may represent through an inventive transformation a variety of concrete experiences (e.g., the satyrs, the naiads, the sirens in the legend of Ulysses as symbols of treachery, Penelope as a symbol of faithfulness, Croesus of wealth, etc.). In the medieval "bestiaries" various types of animals acquired universalized symbolic qualities, the virtues or the vices of human beings (e.g., the eagle symbolized nobility; the hare, cowardice; the bull, strength, etc.)

(c) The "dispositions" of personality also exercise a crucial influence upon creative activity in the inclination of the selection of symbolic modalities in the operations leading to the significant transforming crystallization of the creative intuition into the idea of the work. The forming of symbolic qualities also benefits from or is even strongly influenced by the above-mentioned intimately personal traits.

SECTION 5. THE PERSONALITY OF THE CREATIVE AGENT IN
THE ARCHITECTONIC PHASE OF THE CREATIVE PROCESS
AND IN ITS RELATEDNESS TO THE LIFE-WORLD AND
THE HUMAN CONDITION

However, the most striking expression of the specific personal complex of talents, dispositions, traits of character and emotive tendencies manifests itself in the *transitional phase of the creative embodiment of the intuitive significance.* Indeed, *there it is that the personal traits of the creative agent seen as a living individual within the life-world in their self-interpretative function have to take a uniquely individual "position"*

*or "attitude" toward the life-world in the phase from which the creative
impulse surged in revolt against it and against the life-world, to which
the work to be accomplished is meant to bring a new, renovating
meaningfulness, thus transforming the life-world in a new phase.*

It is in this architectonic phase that the intimate constants of a life-
attitude have to measure themselves over against the deepest tendencies
of the person toward possibilities which the Human Condition as it is
intimately "pre-experienced" or, to put it better, poignantly "present,"
may offer.

Here, however, we are taking a deep plunge into the *specifically
"individualized" transcendental pre-determination of the living being.*
Situated within the ties of the life-networks endowed with individualized
natural resourcefulness, and thereby taking part in a vitally significant
interplay with cosmic forces, the human being draws his "pre-deter-
mining life situation" by balancing out their impacts. Lastly, releasing
and unfolding his own vitally significant life-arteries at the cross-section
of their forces, the human being draws special primogenital pre-
dispositions of a transcendental-universal *and yet uniquely singular
situation* within this plan.

As has been brought to the fore by psychologists (e.g., Karl Jung)
and later corroborated in various ways by others (e.g., Gaston Bachelard), there are types of transcendentally universal impacts of this play
of forces upon the human situation from within, which the living being
summons and delineates as *his own self-interpretative life-system.* It
seems that these pre-dispositions act upon the creative imagination in
its workings. Whether we assume "archetypes" of dreams (Jung) or an
archetypical coordination of imagination by life-substances working
within us (the "elements" of Bachelard), *or whether we distinguish a
type of trancendental "axis" which distributes proto-typic categories of
imagination, such as basic divisions in nature like that between night
and day, and which determines the entire set-up of the personality
and works itself through the creative interpretation of life/the Human
Condition in crystallization of visionary intuition, the fact remains that
the personality of the human being cannot be traced uniquely to the
life-world situation; on the contrary, in its formation with reference to
the game of life/life-world constitution, it already carries propensities and
virtual dispositions that at proper junctures come to exercise their power
or even take over.*

With this succinct account of the main factors that play a part in our creative architectonics, we have at many points come to touch upon the main functional center, from which flow and in which in return gather, all the functional arteries which take part in the creative orchestration. That is, we have touched upon the intimate person of the creative agent who is the existential bearer and the foundation of this orchestration within the life-system. We will in the next section expound upon the nature of the person with its faculties and in relation to the Human Condition as our creative analysis reveals it.

To recapitulate: the phase of transition of the creative process is an intrinsic continuation of the creative constructiveness already outlined by the creative project in its course. This phase as a system of operations, that have the particular objective of incarnating the creative idea into an objective medium, works through plurivocal sequences of operative inventiveness which are partly predetermined by the progress of a particular kind of creativity, but are partly invented in the attainment of the specific creative result intended, with its significance. In the case where this aim is related to a radical change of style, or to a complete "Copernican overturn" in the view of man's place in the cosmos, in nature, that is, in life-meaningfulness within either art or science (e.g., in contemporary plastic art, music and dance — *roman fleuve*, automatic writing, etc. — or the architecture of Buckminster Fuller and technological science which enter into the operations of nature), *these sequences have to be entirely reinvented, together with the "disclosure" of the new virtualities as well as restrictions discovered in the objective medium in the course of the attempt to capture the creative message in it.* Finally, with reference to the plurivocal sequences of operative inventiveness in the execution of the transitional trajectory, problems of a "technical" nature (e.g., the choice of the most appropriate technique for the adaptation of the plan and idea of the work) emerge and are treated and solved within the creative process itself.

SECTION 6. THE PLURIVOCAL LOGIC ORIGINATING
IN ORDER TO SUBTEND THE ARTERIES OF
THE CREATIVE ORCHESTRATION: THE THREE
FUNCTIONAL/PRESENTATIONAL MODES OF NEW
SIGNIFICANCE; THE "CIPHER," THE SYMBOL, THE METAPHOR

(a) The sequences of the constructivism that carry on the processes of the transcendental constitution single out the constructively signifying material by sifting its multiplicity, or as Kant used to say the "manifold" of experiences, through especially constructed "organs" or "senses" (e.g., the empirical perception which operates to strictly discriminate whether the signifying material is a "visual," "audible," "tactile," "sensation of temperature," etc., experience), in order to operate with one type of vitally significant material. In radical contrast, the sequences of operational inventiveness take in, as we have seen, the entire variety of experiential, and pre-experiential, material.

(b) The architectonics of the transitional phase from interiority to physical embodiment, from the imaginative/virtual intuition to the crystallized significance reverberating in a plurivocal evocativeness within the human experiential system involve the entire system of the creative orchestration. Unlike the "passive system" of the constitutive function that takes from the actual field of consciousness the material sifted into singularized constructive avenues of significance, the creative orchestration which has the Imaginatio Creatix as *the center which sets all in motion* reverberates with the suggestive springing forth of the subliminal-pre-conscious and conscious functioning in all functional directions, and penetrates all the functional/operational segments within the human frame, invigorating and expanding the operational complexes in an intergenerative vibration which imparts suggestive inklings. This central role of the Imaginatio Creatrix allows the creative constructivism to avoid an automatized synthesis. The creative process *accomplishes its unity instead within a creative configuration* which, in radical contrast to the objectifying synthesis of the constitutive constructivism, does not present just one significant "form" under which all its elements are to be subsumed. On the contrary, by "configuration" is meant an irreducible, *sui generis*, type of unity of *heterogeneous elements belonging independently to (and sidewise signifying them in) the whole of a plurality of "forms." Thus, each of the elements "resounds" within this unity with its own signifying "voice," intergenerating, intermingling, and competing for priority in being "heard" with the others. The creative configuration is thus "plurivocal" and pluri-significant, with one dominant significant complex: the original, new, life-significance it brings about.*

(c) The unity of the creative configuration — the elements of which extend, as emphasized in various contexts in this study, through the entire spread of our life-tentacles — is, as we have indicated above, operated by means of *innumerable circuits*. By a "circuit," in contrast to a linear process, is to be understood a *centrifugal operational scheme* that bears upon a variety of processes and operational complexes, and consists in their being selected and then falling in line around a dominant significant movement. In this dominant significance consists the virtuality prompting its origin, its nature and its specific role, which comes now to the fore in our investigation. We must, first, differentiate between *the "creative dominant," that is, the original creative intuition crystallized in the passage from the creative vision to the creative idea, a new unprecedented significant "cipher,"* and the "significant dominants" which emerge in each of the operational circuits. We have already been touching upon the crucial role of the creative ciphering that endows experiential complexes with new sense and creates bodily/sensing/ conscious significance (cf. *supra*, pp. 204—205, 267—269).

(d) Now it is time to describe the mediating steps and means of the significant circuits which are composed to (i) especially carry on the constructive sequences of operational inventiveness, and (ii) fulfill within the circuits special architectonic roles.

Studies of the symbol, symbolic form, metaphor, etc. abound. These are in the main undertaken with some bias or other, especially in the perspective of intrinsic structure or cognition studies, the so-called "interpretation of the text" (Paul Ricoeur, J. Derrida), or in that of structuralist anthropology (Lévi-Straus, Mircea Eliade, etc.). At last we may "discover" them in their *proper* place and role.

Leaving aside otherwise confusing, rather than instructive, minutiae for another occasion, it is enough to state that at the junction of various subliminal and experiential moments which come together at the prompting of their constructive virtualities which the Imaginatio Creatrix has stirred out of a latent state, we encounter *qualitative/formal complexes which the inventive click of the imagination makes surge* in order to mediate between the disarray of plurivocal/plurisignificant virtualities and their unity which the creative orchestration as one architectonic factor promotes. First, at the level of the radical existential transmutation of sense, that is, in the passage from the "vitally" to the specifically "humanly" significant moments, the subliminal factors of the Human Condition — that is, the entire creative orchestration — having been activated, a radical transmutation of significance occurs: a new, original *cipher* emerges which expresses this transmuted sense.

The cipher plays a primordial role within the creative endeavor of the living being. It is the light of the creative vision. Yet, it appears at that point merely in an intuitive glimmering. Incomparable in its quality, irreducible and irreplaceable in its experiential forceful suggestiveness, it lacks — as we have seen — clear significance; it remains *plurivocal, by its very nature.*

In order to grasp the creative vision in its core-significance, it has to be exfoliated within an entire creative/experiential apparatus and be brought into a clarified subjective "idea." It is in this process of inventive clarification that the appropriate associative/suggestive exper-iential elements that flow together, organize themselves into coherence spontaneously under the guidelines of the operational architectonics. The inventive imagination, then, triggers off its unifying moment in the shape of a universalized intentional/imaginary form *that combines them all in a transmuted fashion into a "symbol."* Represented by a symbol, they have lost their singular "voices"; none retains its operational vigor; no direct link lies between the concrete prompting to go ahead with suggestive experiential material and the "mental" imaginative, in itself, inert, form of the symbol. The eagle as a country's symbol does not relate in any direct way to any concrete element of what it stands for. Yet, in its universal form, it retains a global representational force bearing an immeasurable wealth of experiential significance itself having already been imbued with symbolic formation.

Through the symbolic form, the experiential confluence of elements acquires a constructive unity. Through the dominant significant moment around which its representational essence is formed, it exercises a further constructive role within, first, the *crystallization of the primo-genital cipher in the creative idea,* and second, *within every operational circuit which serves as a stepping stone along the constructive advance of creation.* The symbolic form is as important in the selection of the processes that organize under its banner numerous plurivocal and heterogeneous experiential elements as it is in the construction and formation of the molds for the sequences of operational inventiveness.

It is the symbolic form in its *role of proposing originally significant moments under which a rich variety of plurivocal elements may find directly a commonly shared significance, that makes the symbolic com-plex of experience a uniquely important creative mediator between the spontaneous flux of life's recurrent and all-absorbing anonymity and the specifically human effort to grasp its course and governing principles as a whole,* as if from a distance, and to wrest from Nature's province the power to divert its seemingly inexorable currents, thereby, like Icarus, fashioning wings to transcend its laws, or like Prometheus stealing the secret of the gods, and inventing his own means for securing meaningfulness for his own existence.

(e) Lastly, we cannot forget the operational value of the metaphor. What is in scholarly studies called currently a "metaphor" is, in our perspective, *a significant unit which, being of an intellectual/imaginative nature, does not repose meaningfully in itself as does a feeling, an idea, or an image; its significance resides, rather, in its role of "standing for something else other than itself."* We may say that already the symbol does not repose in itself because it represents complex material of which it is the "bearer." However, this material is in an essential way "implied" in it. In contrast, *the metaphor is a configuration of co-significant elements unified by a dominant significant moment which stands for their concrete relation to it.* This relation consists in a *specific type of pattern in which the relationship between the configuration of elements in the metaphoric unit is a trans-figuration.*

The configuration of the elements in the metaphoric unit corresponds to the main significant tendency — or symbolic mode — of the experiential complex already objectified in the form of either an idea or a conceptual/intentional structure. *Within the metaphoric configuration we find, indeed, a trans-figuration of the content for which it stands.* This trans-figuration, which itself occurs according to the principles of the inventive/imaginative architectonic orchestration, reorganizes the significant elements which are intellectual/imaginative correlates of those of another significant complex and may shift the correlative significance from one to another dominant element. Maintaining, however, an appropriate balance, this trans-figuration proposes *a variety of significant complexes capable of standing for the same objectified experience in one way or another.*

Thus the metaphor plays a most important mediating function in the constructive advance of the creative process, first by offering variety in the presentation of material to be considered in a synthesizing form, and second, by introducing thereby great flexibility in its associative and suggestive variations for the use of the selective processes by the architectonics of the creative process in all its phases.

In short, *ciphering, symbolic representing and metaphoric "standing for" are the three essential functional modes which are instrumental in the creative constructivism.* They function as a "transformation" of its significant virtualities — energies, forces, promptings, with their own significant properties, and constructive proficiencies — at the crucially important junctures; not only do they mediate, but they also *allow for the constructive advance by promulgating simultaneously an inventive, innovative synthesis, which simplifies the clarifying and fixating processes of objectifying,* on the one hand, as well as *introducing flexibility for the discriminating and selective processes through which the creative process continues its entire course,* on the other.

Through the constant tying and untying of the constructive elements, the course of creation advances. This polyphony of plurivocal elements, which is played at every step of its progress, under the regulative schema of the creative orchestration of human function, on the one hand, and, following the guidelines of the creative architectonic advance, is, on the other, subtended by the *iron logic of the creative constructivism,* a logic which cannot be identified with any one type of rational connectedness, *but is proper alone to the creative forging of the plurivocal significance of life: of all its multiple rationalities.*

PART VI

THE INTERGENERATIVE EXISTENTIAL INTERPLAY IN THE TRANSITION PHASE OF CREATIVITY

SECTION 1. THE DEFINITIVE REALIZATION OF THE WORK OF CREATION ACQUIRING EXISTENTIAL STATUS

When we consider the decisive steps by which the work of creation is slowly led from the intentional construct of the creative mind into the real world, where it has to announce its significant message and so occupy a "place" as a definitive form of an independent object — independent from the individual/subjective acts in which it has been conceived — we must consider various differences among types of created objects.

A scientific creation which presents itself in the form of a theory — a theory to be "verified" — takes its foothold in the real world, like the literary work of art, through the "text" of a script written down and thus made available in the intersubjective sphere in its infinite number of "realizations" by whomever will get acquainted with it through reading, hearing it being read, or just hearing about it. The same may hold for the musical score which is the basis for individual concretizations in musical performance. But already, here, there is a difference. "Reading" the score, an expert musician is already familiar with it; and yet, as a work of art, this score has not acquired its definitive objective status — it still needs a "performance" to make it a *complete musical work*. The special mode of *material realization of an abstract structure* involves a considerable amount of variation, depending upon the skills, style, talent, understanding, and the co-creative spirit of respective performers, who also bring to it a specific mood, atmosphere, etc. of their own. The *"performance phase" still belongs to the creative phase of embodiment*. In contrast to the "realization processes" occurring in the recipient of the work of art in literature (the reader), it is embodiment itself of the work which prompts a reaching beyond its ideal/intentional structure into empirical reality. Only then does it appear as the full-fledged, although intentional, object, when "performed" in front of the audience, which in turn captures it and receives and fulfills its virtual features in an infinitely varied range of subjective, individual "actualities."[30]

275

By giving the final creative touches the *performance* transposes the structural indication from a strictly rational form of notation to the realm of experience — whereas the *reception* by the audience just fills in a considerable amount of empty space in the "experiential/intellectual skeleton" open to the perceiver and waiting to be filled in through his imagination, animating feelings, associations, etc. The technical achievement of the transitional construction has to prove itself efficient; its efficiency resides in its assuming a "solid" standing on its own, a strikingly convincing position in the real world. Its positive impact — that is, its positive reception — is like the launching of a most admirable, precisely-built rocket; yet this rocket, if not made operational, not actually "performed," not launched as intended, would be like a dead body, wreckage, not even an object, and certainly not an object that is an integral part of the real world. Thus, the realization of its intended workability, efficiency in a "real world enactment," is essential; that is, an object integrating itself in the life-world has to be able to fulfill certain conditions, and be an instrument of operations suited to already existing worldly objects. Its "taking part" in this world means that it is a springboard or a point of reference for an active, operational contribution to current life. "Entrance into the life-world," so understood, *depends ultimately on its reception.*

The particularly selective role to be fulfilled, in turn, by the real world, constitutes the final step of the creative function and demands consideration of its possible variations in the process of creation. This means the particular dependence of the score or text upon the selection of directors, actors, set, scenery in its individual features, and of its general overall style as well. It is significant that this final step, the "incarnation phase," demands persons other than the writer to accomplish it in an "enactment." The stage director, musical director, costume designer, cast, etc., are so many individual human personalities through whose mutual understanding the director (of the play, opera, vaudeville, etc.) has to reach to the final decision, the particular concrete elements of real life that will fill in these empty intentional spaces, each selection, each time, drawing on a great many possibilities within the same range. Each new realization of the same play introduces changes in this selection.

These possible variations, as well as their best selection, have to be always present (as we will discuss later on) in the eye of the writer or composer who indicates the most important constants, such as stage directions, etc. Often the playwright has even a very specific, "ideal" performing style and even a specific cast in mind (e.g., Claudel saw Edvige Feuillère as the ideal exponent of his plays). It is well known what power a stage director has or can have in this final incarnation of the drama. (Robert Kemp, the French drama critic, has brought this out in a poignant way, in describing Louis Jouvet's staging of the classic play by Corneille, *Illusion Comique*.)

This spurs us to investigate in more detail the metaphysico-existential significance of the real world's role in the creative process at the point of the *enactment in its phase of transition*.

From among creative endeavors we have to distinguish (1) those which aim at the creation of objects whose significance remains within themselves, like works of plastic art, literature and scientific theory; (2) those which, like the dramatic arts, aim at active, operational participation in the world and which enrich this world by representing in themselves something specific — although reposing in themselves they are meant to enter into relation with the rest of the world *through what they are*; and (3) those, which like technical discoveries do not enter the world *for their own sake*, but are devised for the sake of something else, for the sake of the world's needs, involving an activity to be performed for its furtherance.

Furthermore, within the second type, there are to be distinguished three phases in works of the performing arts, those which (like ballet, opera, all forms of drama, comedy, etc.) are not meant to be completed just in their notation, libretto or score, but whose completion has to occur in their being performed. Their entrance into the real world, their actualization within individual perception, cannot be accomplished otherwise than through the medium of human activity and as a fragment of real life. Indeed, a musical score, an opera libretto, a drama, extends in its complete existential-ontic nature along an existentially continuing line to the human-being in action as the final transitory segment of its passage into the real world. This extension marks the terminus of the creative process.

This reference to real beings, not as mere "perceivers" offering the concretization of the work but as the media of its final transition, is essential for the creative process. Only through the incarnation of the *score or libretto in a series of human actions*, involving a complete set-up of real life (including the "decor" — the background of this real life necessary for the situation in which the action has to take place as the action of real people) is the objectification of the creative project completed. All these elements of real life necessary for the definitive incarnation of the text fill in the *essential* — not total — pattern of the intentional structures operating the last selection of the creative process; the filling out of the calculated empty spaces of this structure is reserved, otherwise, for the perceiver.

SECTION 2. FROM OBJECTIVE DIRECTIVES TO THE "REAL LIFE" ENACTMENT

(a) *The laws of the "workings of Nature" as the ultimate point of reference for creative architectonics*

As we did in exploring the incipient phase of the creative endeavor, we have been attempting to show how the creative act takes its source from within the life-world through roots that drill into the experiential system of the maker, thus drawing upon his energies while expanding within a seemingly limitless horizon; even so, its decisive phase, that of the crystallization of a merely subjective/intentional idea into an intra-wordly object, introduces the realm of consciousness into the *real world in all its "dimensions,"* or, to in our perspective put it better, *its significant circuits.* Still, on the one hand, we must not forget that this realm of consciousness — the creative inwardness — is itself a network of functions which, even if we have to attribute to it a predominantly "conscious" character, stands out on its own above the stereotypic functional patterns of the vitally conditioned intentionality as an entirely original and irreducible, imaginatively open, inventive scheme. On the other hand, we must constantly keep in mind that this unique functional system is, in itself, not floating in the air. On the contrary, and most importantly, it is borne along by bringing together the preconscious, vitally and organically significant circuits of "brute" forces — strivings, passions, impulses, feelings — in a transmutting, subliminal matrix. Thus, the creative process makes the life-world expand.

To accomplish this re-entry into the life-world, the creative process is guided by its laws and objective regulations; regulations of forms and substances as well as of operations and values; thus, for entrance into the world, the price of some freedom is paid. The creative process is comparable to an incubation period. In order to structure a new being, although all the forces and energies of the world-process may be involved in its workings, the work of generation has to be accomplished in a sort of seclusion from the world at large, in a sort of withdrawal from it. Having initially drawn upon its wealth, emerging from within it, and then having left its validity and impact "suspended," the creative process has, in a cyclic turn, to take the world into account, going back to it. In every type of the creative endeavor that takes into account nature and the laws of the world, the creative process becomes a locus of the scrutiny and elucidation of innumerable elements from all realms of the living present. The phase of transition is precisely the trajectory of these encounters with all modes of the real. Even if the "material substruct" of the creative product is as esoteric as human thought (e.g., thought, which in its own rational ways establishes a scientific theory), yet this thought, as a theory, suspended exclusively upon the transcendental laws of thinking, on the one hand, and creative inventiveness on the other, *first has to take into account the* status quo *in the "objective" world of the elements about which it theorizes and, second, has to consider the preexisting theories concerning the same data, new research available, new instruments, etc.,* as well; and third, thought has to assess social attitudes toward its elements, that is, the receptivity conditions. (For instance, in music there would be not only the laws of harmony to be consulted, among other strictly technical ones, but also those of man's auditory capacities, rhythmical responses, the taste of the period, etc.).

In the inventive processes contributing to the passage from the eminently concrete *emotional/passional vision* to the *subjective/emotional intentionality of the abstract idea,* we witness the first steps of the *existentio-ontic transmutation,* and of the forging of links of discrete continuity. These steps of unification take place, first, between the vital significance of forces with their passional urgings, and nostalgias which break with the vital limitations — having imagination as their wings; then, this latter projects links which bring them together with the intuitional rationality which emerges as the instrument of the radical constructive step of this passage. Lastly, they are linked together with the "ideal" *eidoi* or "transcendentally regulative" forces.

Here in the period of transition from the *felt* intentionality of the idea to its crystallization in the *rational* construct of a worldly object where we follow step-by-step the passage from consciousness to its furthest expansion in its correlate in the life-world, we pass from the by-then-accomplished highest forms of intentional consciousness,

through objective constructive regulations, to enactment in real, physical acts. Indeed, it has to be emphasized again that the creative process
at this end turns into a real-life event: *the real-life creative enactment.*
This passage from constructive regulations to a real, factual series of acts
shows the two-sided aspect of the same inventive existential circuit.
Indeed, when we see how the selective search for and adjustment of (a)
an imaginative idea, (b) objective aims, and (c) inventive productive
operations as means for the actualization of the merely virtual are
essentially linked to — anchored in — physical operations that are
otherwise existentially heterogeneous (e.g., the cutting of stone, the
carving of wood, twisting the body in movements of the dance, etc.), we
must observe that the *inventiveness of bringing together these three*
above-mentioned — and otherwise disparate — factors that still remain
in a net of mutual reference, without which they would have no sense,
is of crucial existential significance. It is through the *inventive inter-*
functioning of their respective virtualities, which now form an intergen-
erative coherence, that the respective existential mode either generates
(e.g., the intentional life-world object) *or joins with another mode*
(conscious-physical). However, in this "enactment" within the life-world
in the execution phase of the constructiveness of the creative process,
the regulative "objective" principles coming from the life-world and its
actual phase of culture merit more attention.

Indeed, the most striking and the most complex example of the role
played in the creative process by the real-life enactment is to be found
in the case of theatrical creation. Seemingly, it is the "text" of the play
which is the creative product comparable to that of a novel or of a
poem and, yet, as I have analyzed it in my *Poetica Nova*, dramatic art
consists in enactment.[31] As. E. Souriau so justly says, the text of a play,
in opposition to "*cette immatérialité de l'oeuvre écrite . . . ne commence*
qu'au fait concret de la réprésentation."[32]

For theatrical art consists, as a matter of fact, not only in a pluri-
significant structure like that of other types of art but, on the one hand,
in the created work, the written play, with all its own literary pluri-
significant circuits — in the creative idea in which reference must be
made to its essentially worldly status (e.g., concerning the plot: human
psychology; concerning the situation represented: sociological laws and
cultural period; concerning the human condition: its life prospects;
concerning materiality: rhythm and sonority, etc.). On the other hand
real theatrical art is the only art which consists essentially in *enactment*

itself. All the types of theatrical production from "realistic" drama to ballet and mime may well, in their constructive ideas and creative plans, be fixed in a "script," but they do not "dwell" in it, as a literary work dwells in the written word, or a sculpture in a block of stone or bronze. From the intentional/objectified structure of meaningfulness fixed in the script, the emphasis is shifted to the situation within the life-world. This shift is one away from the drama's *merely* outlined plot of action, in which life-world perspectives are merely indicated in abstract schemas, to its actual embodiment in a full "real-life" presentation with people "acting it out" with their concrete and complete sets of human powers. The staging situates the plot in a "real-life simile," on the one hand. There it is that the theatrical art resides and lives. On the other hand, it is again the essence of the theatrical art that this activity, of which the written script is just — as it is called in ballet — a "notation," instead of being a private event, has to pass, take the form of a "performance," has to be acted out in front of an "audience," which also consists of a number of real human beings.

(b) *The sequence of inventive operations in the existential transition and the "performer" as the architectonic artery into the real world*

The dramatic work of art does not present itself within the life-world with the words of a "text," lines and colors upon a canvas, or shapes in stone. In agreement with Henri Gouhier, we find it within the transitional phase, coming into being through the existence of *the actor*. It is through the actor that the written play, otherwise no more than an intentional skeleton, is to be born into the real world in its existential fullness. It is from the *existential reality of the actor that it has to draw its own real life.* And yet, this existential mediation by the actor as a living, real, complete human being poses innumerable problems for the creative architectonics of the theatrical work of art. In fact, performed art demonstrates to the fullest extent *the phase of transition as a real-life event.* First, it calls for a special *theatrical sequence* of inventive operations within the creative process in which the transitional phase, in its existential passage, is particularly elaborate. The "life of the theater," which consists of deliberating and solving these problems each time with each performance anew, is the personification of this real-life event. Second, drama puts emphasis on the actor as a real life-world person and the "proper" actualization of the work. Third, in this perspective, drama makes the actor not only a co-creator of the work, but simultaneously one who is "co-created" by it for this specific purpose. Yet, most importantly, the role of the actor is correlated with a *receptive* public. It is this network of real-life co-creative relations which emerges and, hence, carries that real-life event of the creative transition.

SECTION 3. THE PERSONALITY OF THE ACTOR VS. THAT OF THE PERSONIFICATION IN THE ACTING

In the first place, the play can be performed in a spectrum of ways, with none of them, however, ever crystallizing it properly. An anonymous poet of 1745 described, in fact, the contrasting errors into which an actor may fall:

> Some who would Gaiety and Passion show,
> With smart, lisp'd catch make half formed word to flow;
> Swift Roll of jargon sound, a rapid flood,
> With not one word distinctly understood:
> Others to seem articulate and clear,
> With dull, loud, slow, plain Sound fatigue the ear;
> All words, all lines, the same grave Cadence deep,
> And drowsily lull audience to sleep.

Of course this is the matter of the "trade" of acting, of "performance technique." Yet the technique is involved in conflicts over approach which stem from the personal inclinations of the actor: a living, changeable, sensitive individual with a specific personality, individuality, with specific bents of temperament, moods, and expressiveness. These predispose him to be an especially good exponent of one protagonist in a spectacle, rather than of another.

Secondly, the full concrete reality of the actor, with his particular life, destiny, emotionality and personality is necessary in order to incarnate a personage in a play; by the same stroke, however, abstraction has to be made from the "personal biography" of the actor as a human being: from his way of life, his taste and preferences, his personal reaction in front of concrete life, a situation comparable to that of the play into which he is to enter, etc. This poses a curious dilemma; the same dispositions of the performer which have to dynamically carry the passions of a particular role, have to be depersonified and suppressed in order to meet the specific demands of the role. The same personality of the actress that enables her to skillfully play the role of Phaedra and not of Hermione, has to be suspended and neutralized in order that it be Phaedra or Hermione that come to life and not an exhibition of the actress' own fits and emotions.

The actor is the artistic "creator" of *his role* in his/her identification with the role — while styling him/herself to it and lending to it, in turn, his own spontaneity and passion; and it is there that is contained, it seems, the final creative element of the drama. But this does not arise by itself. It is directed by the "other." Although, unlike as in poetry or painting, the actor's performance is a fluid and floating process that leaves no lasting record, and no artistic, created object, since the performance lives and dies each night, yet in the good actor there is a process of creating correlative to that of the playwright, which serves to complement it as the final concretization evolves; "creative," in the sense of giving *such* and *no other* body to the work, of giving it one de- finite form, strictly precise in all the details in which it differs from the further "co-creativity" of the spectator. Although there is much more in the network of creative interplay between the actor and the spectator than just a "consent" or a "perceptive interpretation," nevertheless the acts of the spectator do not create any essential feature of the drama: they only wrestle over that which is proposed before them. We will come to this later on.

The actor co-creates with the playwright. There are many opinions about the attitude to be taken by the actor in order to accomplish his role. The prevailing emotionalistic approach, letting the actor release his natural passions and emotions and put them into his role as a natural outlet, was challenged already by Shakespeare, who advised the actor: "In the very torrent, tempest, and I may say, whirlwind of your passions, you must acquire and beget a temperance, that may give it smoothness." By "smoothness" is meant, indeed, the unity of action in the play. The plot or "action" outlined in "one stroke," and the psychological atmos- phere concentrated on the plot have to merge into a homogeneous "microcosmos." The momentous feelings, passions and modes of in- dividuality of the living actor have to be forgotten, and if it is from his individual passions that the emotional line of the play takes its force and dynamic, these passions still have to be devoid of the momentous emotional ups and downs of the living man; these have to be transmuted and subdued to serve the line of the drama alone without breaks and side issues, or extraneous feelings, etc. Every emotional element has to appear exclusively in the function of promoting the development of the drama proper. The actor has to identify himself so deeply with the drama as to forget himself as an independent individual. Diderot, in his famous views on acting, presents the theory that, in order to move the audience, the actor has to remain unmoved.[33] He has to develop a discipline, a technique of emotional experience. It is to this technique that the writer makes an appeal through his stage directions.

In his *Method*, Stanislawski more recently also takes up this point of the actor's working upon himself. He must train himself to become master of his own emotions, valuable as they may be as a means of understanding the hero he has to portray, and of his reaction, too — of his spontaneous inclinations.[34] Thus the actor's technique *presupposes his work upon himself*. This complete effacement of the individual personality of the actor in that of the personage he portrays is seen already in the Greek theater. Using masks, actors become anonymous individuals. Indeed, the actor is the only artist whose "raw material," whose "instruments" are those of his self, his intelligence, his sensibility, his muscles, voice, eyes, etc. — his specific personality predisposing him to certain performances and at the same time needing curbing, molding, transforming, and distancing. It is this finalizing of the crystallization of the idea of the work by the actor that the playwright takes into account. The playwright must "see" a specific type of performance before his inner eye while he composes his play. To this effect he gives stage directions which indicate also the style of the performance as a whole. The work of the actor is not, unless in the monologue, strictly individualized, but is coordinated with that of a group. This coordination has to be especially orchestrated so that the sequence of inventive operations are tuned to the same pitch and tone, and it is not an uncoordinated chaos that appears, but an amorphous unity, without cleavages and inconsistencies; a microcosm which radiates its own atmosphere and mood.

The performance's orchestration of the group-personages is left by the writer to the stage director who, through a concordance of the individual interpretations chosen by him, gives to this performance novel and significant directions — "style." There is a profound flexibility in ways of conveying the emotional message which a "great" drama ultimately aims at bringing forth. Chekov's dramas (e.g., *The Cherry Orchard*), staged in a "realistic" style, set in a real house with all the pettiness of small items and with a realistic style of performance, can hardly fail to exude a pessimistic aura of individual doom and decay which predominates in a stylized "romantic" staging. The same play, however, in an impressionistic setting, emphasizing in contrast the main feelings and the meaningfulness of the dialogues will, going to the end of the line, create a melancholy realization of the universal destiny of people caught in the evolution of history.

This plurality of "actors" who embody and enact the multiple personalities which they incarnate are functionally essential to the nature of the theater. The playwright is, thus, as was pointed out above, confronted with another set of special types of laws and devices which refer to the nature of the enactment of art. It is not only that for a drama, comedy, or ballet, etc., as an "intentional work," pluridimensional references to the laws of the real world are constructive in its becoming a real-life event, but a special, second set of references is also required: one for the "performers," with their individual endowments, talents, and personalities; this set of references is essential.

The perspective of "performance" in real-life enactment in a way transforms in several respects the significance of the "text," on the one hand, and its embodiment as "real event," on the other. The text, as an intentional object, may be read just like a novel or a poem, but doubling it in a larger extension and with the feature of finality. A play changes also its effect and significance in the passage from being read to being performed. Thus, however constructively important are the purely "literary" laws of the genre — drama, comedy, vaudeville, opera, monologue, etc. — the special set of architectonic "rules" concerning "theatricality" proper are of equal importance. This accounts for the creative constructive sequences of the genre to be performed. The basic rules of "theatricality" demand a "notation" with a sharply outlined conflict of personages and ideas. And these conflicts appear in specific situations. Yet, as we often observe, although in a novel and written play the presentation of situations involves selections by the author in accordance with specific points, the same novel, when arranged for a performance undergoes a second type of selection with the skipping or dropping of some segments. New situations, which were not elaborated in the original, are developed to replace these in order that the conflict and its solutions can be taken from a more reflective, meditative presentation and brought into prominence by the poignancy of the "real event" of the enactment. What in a written, intentionally present dramatic work might have its strongest effect "between scenes" in meditation and reflection — even just a hint to reflect on — is now meant to be performed. To come into its own, this moment has to become poignant by other means. The reflective moment need not be overlooked and lost among the visual, auditory, mimical, etc. tensions of the psychological effect and atmosphere. The poignancy of the situation has to be measured in terms of this expression which is lent to situations and ideas, moods and feelings noted in the script by the performance of living persons as they in their real life motility create the intentional schema by incarnating it in a *simile of real situations.* Often such a poignant effect is, indeed, obtained by a word, a sentence or a gesture, which must have been weighed very carefully upon the scales of all theatrically constructive perspectives, rules and established elements, and calculated with respect to them.

The theatricality of the performed spectacle imposing a special network of rules upon the creative choice centers upon the phase of transition, here so crucial. There are, in fact, performance rules pertaining to the modes: *how* the significant message of plots, conflicts, their development and solution, is going to crystallize when incarnated in the behavior of living individuals and its temporal unfolding. An experienced playwright already "sees" his work in the creative plan as being performed and visualizes not only the actualization of the plot through human beings, but "sees" his protagonists in their poetically stylized movement, moods, characters, atmosphere, timbre of voice, gestures, mimicry, temperaments, etc. recreated by actors with the particular personalities most appropriate for bringing out his "point."

It would seem that an opera, being more complex than a play (since it contains an additional musical dimension), would have even more complex constructive rules and regulations coming from the life-world to consider. However, here musical excellency and perfection are the essential and principle factor, and others are subservient to it. The plot of the tragedy or comedy distributes the order of the basic musical line: the principle events, the arias, duets, choruses and dances. Yet, at the same time, the plot is put in second place after the demands of musical excellency. Often, otherwise quite ridiculous recitativos are sung because of the beauty of the musical line they posses; theatrically weak, or even bad, situations do not hamper the musical unity and the total effect. Beethoven's *Fidelio* could hardly stand the theatrical test with its long and dull recitativos, and artificially conceived plot, and yet, its rare musical qualities make it one of the most beautiful operas of its period. Haydn's oratorio, *The Seasons*, written for an awkward poetic libretto by James Thompson, was, according to Haydn's biographer G. A. Griesinger (1810), an ordeal for the composer, who complained of the unpoetic text and how hard it was for him to "wax enthusiastic music over such things as 'Heysasa, Hopsasa', etc.". Yet it is a marvelous work due to its music. This hegemony of music in opera allows for the fact that most often the work does not emerge within the unity of one creative process, but the composer collaborates with a poet and takes his literary work as a pretext for composing music, music becoming, then, the major factor. Rarely is the cooperation between the poet and the composer rooted in such a community of minds as that that existed between Mozart and Schickaneder, as they created together *The Enchanted Flute*. No wonder it incarnates an unusual perfection of harmony between the elevated spirit of the partitum, its appropriately constructed plot, and the music by which it is infused and molded!

Theatricality may, in its significant core (which implies the conflict of personages and ideas) become a tribune for ideas, as has been so rightly pointed out by M. Souriau. Thesis and antithesis may face each other in action clad with characteristic traits of personality sketched with their universal but, also, most personally rooted motivations. These separate personages to be crystallized in flesh and blood on the stage represent forces independent from each other, each of which has its own ground and reasons. Each actor performing the actions brings to his or her "role" with his/her flesh and blood, the most specific foundation of his own peculiar personality for these particular forces. At the same time, since the "performers" together have to converge in an architectonic unity, the interior psychological motivations which animate social revolutions and emotions, and personal revolts, exaltations, enthusiasms and despair as well, and which confront each other on the basis of their real-life personalities, constitute a "human microcosmos" different in each conception of the performance. The performers have, furthermore, come together in the conception of the unity of such a one, specific human microcosm. To obtain this effect, a unifying view and a single guideline of theatrical sequence of inventive operations integrating the acting individuals and their prerogatives in the adaptation of this view is postulated. To decipher the elements postulated and to give them coordinating shapes is the "real-life role" of the stage director.

We see that there is a possible gap between the significance of the *idea of the work* and its *real-life realization*: an intermediary step between the conception of the whole formed by the playwright in the idea of the work and the whole which emerges in the final realization of its architectonics in the life-world transition. The various possibilities of "interpreting" the "microcosmic" unity of the play implies a possible variety of specific "stylizations" of real life in the enactment. Theatricality, through its sequences of inventive operations, ultimately brings about *the definitive re-creative transformation of the real through the style of the performance. The creative process penetrates with the style of performance most intimately into the life-world's meaning-bestowing channels, bringing about the direct transformation of its life-significance.*

SECTION 4. THE EXISTENTIAL TRANSITION OF
THE SIGNIFICANT MESSAGE INTO THE MEANINGFULNESS OF
THE LIFE-WORLD: THE "RECEPTIVE INTERPRETATION" AND
THE STATUS OF THE CREATIVE WORK WITHIN
THE "REAL WORLD"

(a) *The real life enactment and the "judgment of existence"*

With this, we enter into the very heart of art's creative existential role. As already pointed out, art has to be "received"; its significant message has to be interpreted within the experiential system of those receiving it. This point is demonstrated most acutely by dramatic art in its entire spread, as discussed above. We have already pointed out the particular real-life enactment relativity of spectacle with respect to the performer and the spectator. As emphasized before, the dramatic work as such does not fully "exist" in the script. Limited to the script, to the text, it is nothing more than an incomplete skeleton of a literary work. It acquires its specific nature and is crystallized in its *own* form, as we have shown above, in the real world; but, as Henri Gouhier emphasized, its essential completion is something more than the "incarnation" of the notation of the script in real-life individuals; it is necessary for a spectator to perform the final "judgment of existence." A novel, poem, etc. are all present in the intentional structure of the script, "waiting" for the receiver/reader who has to endow it with the concretization of his/her lived experience, lending it the life that the intentional form, all articulated and outlined, needs.

Music and ballet, in order to become alive, also need to be concretized in a performance. But we do not need an *audience* to give a full concretization to a sonata we play, or to a dance, if we perform them "for ourselves." Of course, as in every art, the public, the critic and the other are always a point of reference. A painting and a monument would still exist without them. The scenic stage has this peculiarity, that it does not exist for the sake of the performer himself. *It is oriented, on the contrary, in its very nature to being received by the Other.* The very essence of dramatic art, beginning with Greek theater and medieval court jesters, is in its amusing, moving and releasing tensions in the Other. Unlike rituals, which stress the identification of the individual with the rite, the theater is in all its forms exhibitionist: to put forth, to show, to display. Only by being displayed is the dramatic function performed.

Going to the extreme in this direction, Allardyce Nicoll says: "All dramatic art depends ultimately for its form and content on the audience." He contends that the spectators of 1590 gave birth to *As You Like It*; the spectators of 1600, to *Hamlet*.[35] Nicoll reveals the very intimate interaction between the audience and the drama of the period of the Restoration. The audience of this period, although shown to be thoughtless and depraved, nevertheless, through its reactions, its applause and scorn, seems to have imposed upon writers and players demands which complied with tastes brought into the playhouse-culture: grace, wit, and an aristocratic elegance which was quite new. Although the plays which the audience of the Restoration inspired into existence competed in licentiousness, they also stimulated love and refinement of dialogue to which this same audience was not accustomed in real life (e.g., the characters of the comedies of Dryden and Shadwell, of Etherege and Congreve, were tutored in an ease of manner and behavior as well as in a delicacy of language if not of thought which their forefathers could never have known).[36]

This very close architectonic interplay between the performance and the audience in the spectacle is thus a two-way traffic. The audience has its say but, in turn, it is deeply influenced and molded in its ways of feeling, seeing life, and judging (probably more directly than by any other art). Consequently, the drama might well be less ahead of its time than other forms of creative activity which, instead of growing with the real world, break into it. Since it takes its life from the cultural dispositions of the actors and from the receptivity of the public, it does not crystallize properly in the receptivity of the audience if its significant modes of feeling and sentiment are too remote from current trends; it does not burst aflame and come alive properly; it fails and disappears from the repertory.

However, in spite of some essential truth in Nicoll's view that "the drama's laws the drama's patrons give," we cannot agree with his belief that "fundamentally independent genius counts far less in the world of the theatre than does the general atmosphere of the time." At the same time that the audience approaches the spectacle (drama) with the anticipation of an opportunity to relate to it through familiar features, it expects also something "new" that will "move" them. If it is in fact to significantly strike a chord in our own life, that chord has to be a "hidden chord," one spared from current culturally motivated emotions and one different from current stimuli, motivations, etc.[37]

The presence of something so novel and original, with respect to the present phase of the life-world's potential is what makes the difference between the spectacle as a work of art and theater productions comparable to those of the Roman circuses which are commissioned to offer to the public *panem et circenses*.

This "in mid-air" existential position of the creative process in the drama, which consists in a real-life creative exchange (communication) between the performance and the public, exhibits most strikingly the existential status of the creative process in the phase of transition in a real-life event.

(b) *The creative transition and the theatrical instinct*

In conjunction with the particularly extensive architectonics of the phase of transition, dramatic art calls in addition for a specific principle of inventive synthesis: the "theatrical instinct," which plays a crucial role in the creative orchestration of the faculties. This art, tying all the constructive strings of literary creativity and those of plastic and auditory representations of reality together within a real-life enactment, calls for and reveals a specific *dramatic life "instinct."* We would be tempted to see its presence already in the game of a child who plays "dramas" and "comedies" for himself but in which he brings together the creative imagination of the author and that of an illusionary spectator. Yet the child's playing is not a full creative performance. In the complex process of the transitional orchestration of a drama, the significant circuits of several "worlds" have to be orchestrated into one significant pattern. Their interplay has to be "dramatized," that means, caught at its "highest" points of relevance to the significant message it is meant to bring about and convey.[38] The presence of such a dramatic instinct in drama is precisely what makes the difference between dramas, like those of Claudel, which attain their proper measure of grandeur on the stage, and others, like those of Peguy, which are better merely read.

A playwright has to live creatively in *all* the "worlds." He has to combine in his creative process, within one idea and architectonic plan, more than the elements of the play as a literary intentional object, that is, the vision, the idea, the structure and the development of the plot, as fixed in the "text." For this text amounts to more than just a notation of "moves," because beyond the objective rules of the ideal "literary" structure with its own conventions and languages, it has to be confronted with the real-life conventions of the cultural period — the language actually spoken, the taste, etc., on the one side, and real living individuals, passions, actions, and dialogues, such as could actually be exchanged between them, on the other. The whole range of variation in violence, mood, or expressiveness in complex contexts, sketched as "ideally" possible and left to the imagination of the reader, have instead to be considered as they will *actually be enacted* with the full effect and significance of a *real act*.[38a] Thus it seems that with this interplay of various "realities," the idea of the spectacle is not present in the phase of transition and in the theatrical life-context only; for it is not "ideally" imagined but has to be, so to speak, "sensed" by the author, vibrating in his eye and ear in all its virtualities and its possible variations from the second phase of the creative process on. The interplay dictates the *crucially significant knots of the theatrical sequences of inventive operations.*

SECTION 5. THE QUESTION OF THE PROTOTYPE OF THE "MOTOR MODES" BY WHICH THE SPECIFICALLY HUMAN INDIVIDUAL ENACTS HIS SIGNIFICANT LIFE-COURSE

We have mentioned in the study introductory to this work the various types of operations through which the living being differentiates his own life-course from within the natural play of forces and the life system. We have differentiated them according to types of *life-significance, with which they establish the life-world situation of the individual.* I have also indicated — a point to which we will return — that, with the advent of the source-experience in which the creative

orchestration of the functions occurs with respect to the virtualities of
the Human Condition, there emerge three specifically human meaning-
bestowing factors: *aesthetic enjoyment, the moral sense, and intellectual
reason.*

Now it is time to consider the *types of operations which make up the
major significant "motor-modes of the life-enactment."* Let us recall
again that the living individual delineates his self-individualizing, self-
interpretative life-course, first by organic operational sequences as well
as by the vitally significant processes, segments subservient to a larger
project, each of which is constructively oriented; yet these motor modes
of life's progress do not in themselves fulfill a significant role or a more
complex vitally significant "activity" of animal telic orientation beyond
the at hand needs of life-preservation.

The organic/vital/psychic operations and processes are those
through which the living individual keeps himself alive and growing.
This modality operates through the circuits of our complex organs and
limbs. These latter are specialized for the performance of kinesthetic
movements to make innumerable responses to life urgencies and to
carry out an infinite variety of vitally significant tasks. They are automatized in segments serving special purposes (e.g., movements of the
hands, grasping a moving object, holding, stretching, lifting, etc. —
movements of the legs, bending knees, walking, climbing, kicking,
pressing a spade or a brake, etc.). These motor complexes are to be
distinguished from tightly articulated motile sequences composed of
innumerable "mute" sequences of motor operations which together
enter into a *constructive project which contains a limited task as an
aim in itself*. We call these "acts" or "actions." With them we cross in
our constructive orientation over the threshold of animal motility and
its purposively organized and vitally subservient telic orientation to
specifically human life enactment.

Action has recently become a popular and much discussed topic.
Within our perspective, *which establishes the origin of meaning at its
very seminal roots in the virtualities of the Human Condition and which
is itself suspended on the workings of the life-system, our conception of
action, being geared to such a constructive project, presumes first a
specifically human constructively "projecting" apparatus: observation,
discrimination, deliberation, selection and decision — that is, a human
consciousness. Second, this action presumes the interlinkings of this
human apparatus with the life-world system.*

As a real event within the life-world, however, action, or an act (if it is a project actualized in a synthetic form) lies beyond the *elementary vital significance of life*. It carries necessarily within its "telic principle" the mark of, at least, *one of the three sense-giving faculties: moral, aesthetic, and intellectual*. In other words, *action, as such, is already an outgrowth of man's creative orchestration of his functions*. It is also an *event within the life-world system*. Consequently it is *essentially characterized by some specific forms of the life-world within which it takes place* (e.g., it is characterized by the universal cultural forms of a nation, social group, etc. and of its socio-cultural period). In fact, an action is always an exponent of a culture and bears the stamp of its "style." (It is interesting to note how, on the one hand, historical research advances by interpreting actions of the past according to the standards of the present, and, on the other hand, how differently the same action appears from different cultural perspectives.) In short, action or an act is always qualified; it is a result of immeasurable historico-cultural sedimentations. Particularly culturally determined is the so-called "ethical action" (e.g., how inaccessible to an average contemporary reader or spectator is the understanding of the actions in Sophocles' *Oedipus Rex* or *Electra*, Corneille's *Cid*, and Racine's *Andromaque*).

When we ask ourselves how an act expresses the human individual, the person, we certainly look for how all the features of the person are involved and quintessentially present in their action — personal disposition (e.g., courage or cowardice, prudence or lightheartedness, cheerfulness or gloominess, etc.), specific traits of character (responsibility or unreliability, honesty of deceitfulness, etc.), knowledgeability about actual situation in the life-world at large, etc. Beyond that, an action may express also ambitions, sympathies, talents, etc. *But all these traits simultaneously express the style of the culture to which the person belongs and its current predominant views, biases, tendencies, etc.*

In short, *no type of action itself may reveal the universal nature of the human being in its inner workings as such*. For this we have to turn to a primordial type of "action": *the creative process in its phase of real life-event, or in its enactment.*

In fact, the creative process offers us the prototype of human action. To begin with, let us review the nature of action and the crucial issues which it involves.

SECTION 6. THE CREATED OBJECT OVERFLOWS WITH ITS
FLUCTUATING VIRTUALLY POTENT CORE OF "MEANING"
INTO THE CONSTITUTED WORLD THAT IT ENTERS

(a) *Latent virtualities and their structural vehicle throughout time*

The essential feature of the created work, its objective, universal structure, is, in contradistinction to naturally generated beings which contain
within themselves their entire enfoldment, and, in contrast as well to
manufactured things, which have significance strictly confined to their
use, *essentially an architectonic skeleton upon which the specific architectonic construction is suspended.*

This structural skeleton, on the one side, determines the types of the
objective form of the creative work (e.g., a novel, a symphony, a
theorem, etc.); on the other side, it is the setting of the specific objective
form, which the creative plan prescribes for the architectonic construction. It occupies a crucial position in the objectifying establishment of
the creative work. Yet, the significance of the creative work lies elsewhere; *the intrinsic structure is just the objective vehicle for its entrance
and participation in the intersubjective human world. In contrast, it is
the vision of the work as it has crystallized its intuitive/inventive message;
its idea, which shines through, animates and nourishes the "life" of the
creative work within the life-world. It does this by containing a reservoir
of spontaneous, intuitive, latent virtualities that lie "dormant," waiting to
be awakened by any one of several appropriate imaginative impulses.*

To recognize the primary role of the creative vision that encompasses the objective intentional structure of the work of creation means
to be capable, at last, of understanding, *first, that it is its role to radically
renew the life-world when it breaks into it; second, that it serves as a
recurrent guidepost in the progress of culture; and last, that it is its
function to provide a juncture at the breaking points in the continuing
progress of man in his historicity.*

The particularly distinctive feature of the created work is that
ultimately its objective structure is to be left behind on its way to being
received and diffused within the meaningful schema of human intersubjective life. Once embodied, that is, on its having "broken into" the
world in its thing-hood, it is first a pretext for its rational configuration
that, upon being projected, becomes integrated within an overall meaningful system. Secondly, this *meaningful configuration itself does not*

exist for its own sake; it is a vehicle of a logos in a new modality. This "rational" quintessence of the vision remains in radical opposition to the meaningful nature of manufactured utilitarian objects, whose rationality is reduced to their usefulness for man — to "made" objects, which have a significance relative to either the use to be made of them or to their relevance for the progress of the lived world.

Among all intraworldly things, the created object is the only one which, without being autonomous in its intentional nature, (remaining relative then in its existence to man's consciousness), is, in its rational construct, *self-contained and self-centered: a meaningful microcosmos in itself.*

Indeed, the particularly relevant feature of the created object, which whether it be in the realm of the fine arts, science, literature, or technology is endowed with a unique position among the objects of the lived world, is that it is *irreducible to any utilitarian or pragmatic approach; it is an aim in itself.* Although it remains existentially precarious as an intentional object, yet *in itself it is a closed system, containing its own principles of significance and implying its furthest reaching conclusions.* What is within a strictly objectified perspective seen as a "constant" intrinsic structure of the created work, is, in fact, a creatively invented and projected structural pattern of the specific work. It is placed by the creative constructivism in an intermediary, but existentially constant, position between the structural architectonics presiding over the invention of types and the relative stability of the structural system of objective reality. In a symphony, all that belongs to its unfolding — the rules of its temporal sequence or development — begins with a musically significant segment and is continued by a series of such segments reaching a point of maximum "amplitude" from which it "descends" and completes its various ramifications until it closes with the last sounds that die away.

In a novel which develops one or several sequences of a story, the successive phases of the story are contained in the antecedent ones by indicated assumptions. If the end of the story does not lie within the range of developments implied as possible even most remotely in expectation — possibility implied in the text and thus completing the outline of the development being presented and, thus, creating the aesthetic effect of a total surprise —, the entire rationale of the unfolding lacks plausibility. In the same way, a scientific theory contains all of its assumptions which are either directly indicated or implied. Such "plausibility" has various modes. It contributes to a special *internal logic* of the work of creation. In contrast to the rationales of all types of the life-world, in either its empirical or ideal dimensions, it introduces the surprise, the "unpredictable" "turn of events," the outcome — unpredictable, because it follows *the lead of an intergenerative consequential connectedness* other than those which function in the already established meaningful system of the life-world.

The creative constructivism is inventive precisely in this, that it projects an unprecedented *scheme* of "things," "ideas," "development," that is, of "intuitive sequences," *in order to form an original cipher with a new significance of life.* Once being received and established within a meaningful system of the life-world, and having renewed it, this cipher is absorbed into its objectified network, ready to be surpassed by the novelty of the next creative event. There was no key in readiness available for its "de-ciphering." We had then to look to the intergenerative connectedness of the various constructive circuits which establish, first, the *schema*, second, the *intuitive sequences*, and third, the cipher which bears this key within itself. Once discovered, it served to reinterpret the human life-experience in all fields: scientific, aesthetic, practical, etc. Yet this key is useless for deciphering the next creative work which invents again its own "logic" to fit its own new life-significant factor.

Thus we cannot aim at grasping a "matrix of truth" of the creative logic. It is "inventive/creative" precisely in this, that each time it invents a new (its own) type of significance, it also invents its own appropriate logical system to match. This intrinsic "consistency" of the creative work makes it a sort of microcosm. But it is a microcosm of a unique sort. It is entirely misleading to attempt to extrapolate its meaning in an analogy to the real world and to speak about the "world" of a novel, drama, painting, etc.

In the creative analysis situated at the cross section of all the main arteries of the Human Condition, the work of creation appears *suspended upon the creative intent while incorporating its innovative intuition upon which the emphasis falls.* The structure of the work recedes to a merely intermediary position; *the significant vision of the work comes first.* However, it has to be granted that it is its structural skeleton, once established, that allows it to accomplish the transmission of its significant messages and to maintain its position within the life-world in spite of the life-world's fluctuations with the passage of time. Due to its invariable skeleton for an ideal/intentional structure, the creative work carries a coherent form of universally objectified meaning, and yet, simultaneously, through its essential and intended incompleteness, it opens fields of a variety of receptive experiences and interpretations. This accounts for its specific "life" in being enjoyed by the recipient and its perdurance in time. But it also allows it to "grow" and "outgrow" the world it enters.

Through its constant core of structural architectonics the creative work stands out in the established world it enters as the bearer of an absolutely novel and original significance in relation to the established cultural monuments, predominant ways of feeling, evaluative approaches, styles of expression and currents of ideas; it challenges them to react. It makes the preestablished scheme of experiential functions which orchestrate them explode and stimulates the emergence of new ones capable of meeting its own distinctive demands. Concurrently, however, through creatively calculated schemes of incompleteness within the structural architectonics which allow for an imaginative play of concrete experience at the receiving end, they have, in fact, to be explicitly or implicitly filled out in their reception. This makes for a specific overflow and fluctuation within the meaningful reverberation of the constant structural skeleton. There is, in fact, a large margin left in the strategy of the architectonic formation for such indetermination, providing for the subjective, individual differences among the recipients in their enjoyment of the work. These concern patterns of associations aroused in response to the stimuli of the skeleton of the work, subjective differences in sensibility, worldview, moods, as well as reference to momentous personal situations.

Thus the vehicle of intersubjectivity that is the work of art, while it becomes integrated into the present life-world through its enjoyment, causes the work enjoyed to outgrow the life-world through the infinite richness of possible fluctuations in experiential meaning.

Let us emphasize again the fact that, in the process of being received — enjoyed — and thereby of becoming an integral part of the lived world that is transformed in the process of adjusting to its novel and original nature, the work in its overflow of fluctuating meaning is a vehicle of transtemporal continuity. It is not confined within the period, style, or phase of the lived-world, which it has imbued with its significance; although belonging to one, it will be received and reinterpreted in another cultural period, and reintegrated again into the new phase of the constituted world.

In spite of the fact that the work of art is original in the strong sense as the innovator of its meaningfulness only *once*, in relation to the particular phase of the world in which it has emerged into existence, and although this is the only phase which has been reconstituted in response to its revolutionizing influence, yet by its virtual meaningfulness, it overflows its meaningful frame. At a certain point, when its experiential virtualities with respect to the essential meaningful system of its cultural period have been fully exploited in all the spheres of influence within its reach, it appears empty, used, "old hat." And yet the work contains virtualities for significant enjoyment in response to the emergence of other new stimuli. It transgresses into this period, too, into which it is as essentially integrated as it is into any other phase of the constituted world through its unlimited richness of fluctuating overflow of experiential meaning.

SECTION 7. THE CREATIVE WORK AS THE BRIDGE OVER THE DISCONTINUITY OF THE HISTORICAL ADVANCE AND THE FACTOR OF ITS PROGRESS

We see that great works of fine art, great literary achievements, do not merely "survive" the cultural crises and bends of humanity, but act as bridges between times. Also, the great ideas and theories of appreciation of art, nature, history, as well as of philosophy, are after a time of neglect brought back into focus and offer supple material for reinterpretation in the light of present intellectual strivings and attitudes. Even theories about the world like Copernicus' theory of the solar system, or Newton's Laws, etc., which have long since been corroborated, transformed, and improved, are studied again and again in the search for some "new" insights which may have been hidden at times, but are there latent, offering new grains of truth for a new approach.

We have the best exemplification of this in the progress of philosophical thought. The history of philosophy is a continual return to the old "sources"; Plato's dialogues, Aristotle's metaphysics and ethics, Spinoza's theory of substance and Leibniz's monadology are throughout the centuries constantly brought under new scrutiny to reveal some new aspects and engender new thought.

The most striking example of this inexhaustible richness latent in the well-known and seemingly sclerosed forms of great works of philosophy, is pre-Socratic philosophy; sometimes undervalued as "primitive," it has been revived in contemporary philosophical thought, revealing a fecundity of ideas that have radically influenced the thought of Heidegger and his followers.

We witness the same return to the "source" seeking inspiration for a cultural renewal in all realms of the arts: sculpture, drama, poetry, etc. In Western tradition they have always remained "fresh," as sources of new inspiration and as examples of the perfection of accomplishment. We see the best example of this in the recurring fascination with Ancient Greece. The classic period (e.g., the drama of Shakespeare, Goethe, Hebbel and Schiller among others) dipped deeply into the hidden springs of Greek art and created an entirely novel and original style. We remember only too well that the Renaissance's humanistic aspiration was inspired by the Greek ideal, out of which came an original type, the "Renaissance man." Singular great works of art seem also to serve as "models," always to be challenged in their virtual significance by each new style or approach. Each style, approach, and period, if not each great artist, has attempted to "re-create" them with a new view of life, a new technique, transforming their message. Which great playwright has not created his Electra, Don Juan, Antigone, or Helen of Troy, to mention only the most striking examples? What a vast itinerary of transformations in ways of feeling and thinking and in style of writing and means of communicating is covered in the history of drama from Sophocles' *Antigone* to the plays of Jean Anouilh!

Another striking example of the inexhaustible latent virtualities of a work, ciphered in a new literary theme and set in modern times, is that of the renewed re-enactment of Otway's *Venice Preserved*.

A classical drama in the style of *The Merchant of Venice,* this play which is full of activity revolving around an agitated and romantic plot, reveals a particular richness of feeling and subtlety of emotional significance in the interpretation of its "intrigue" given to it by Hugo von Hoffmansthal in a changed perspective. Following his own inclinations and style, von Hoffmansthal places the accent not on the political intrigue, dominant in Otway's conception, but on an intimate personal conflict within a subtly rarefied climate. The theme of *Venice Preserved* yields, in this contemporary perspective, an occasion for a masterpiece of human depth, noble attitudes and inner struggle; the experiential significance of love, devotion, and self-sacrifice flow from the highly aestheticized vision lying behind the theme of *Venice Preserved* and retrieved by von Hoffmansthal.

The same theme, focusing however upon a different aspect of the structural architectonics and striking an entirely different chord, is taken up again by Simone Weil, revealing other dimensions of its richness. An unoccupied, idle group of discharged mercenary soldiers staying aimlessly in the prosperous, leisurely and happy town of Venice, but excluded from its life, forges a plot against the town's government. They aim at making a place for themselves within the established structure. Simone Weil, strikes a deep sensitive chord in the theme of *Venice Preserved* in the light of her own inspiration, and transforms the plot into a symbolic tragedy of the uprooted human minority that belongs nowhere. In response to the tendency of our times, the theme reveals a latent universal meaning concerning the human condition. The original intuition of its vision encounters Simone Weil's original message: there is tragedy in man's being uprooted from happy familiarity with nature and his human community.

SECTION 8. INDETERMINATENESS VS. THE IMMUTABLE CORE OF PERSISTENCE IN INTERPRETATION

The significance of situations, utterances, and attitudes presented in any medium (in figurative art, music, linguistics, etc.) offers a halo of indeterminateness through an intrinsically fixated potential for "reinterpretation." This accounts for controversies among critics on the appearance of a new work, each of them seeing in it different things according to his own attitude, attributing to it a variety of meanings; but these belong to the *"subjective"* variations of the work, whereas we are concerned here with how the work perdures historical vicissitudes instead of being absorbed by the life-world, and how, submitted to revisions, it may reveal latent possibilities for new aspects through insights gained in response to new points of view.

In fact, one would naively assume that the translations of great classic works (e.g., the *Iliad* and the *Odyssey*) into a modern language of a later period would remain "valid" throughout time, if "faithful" to the original. Yet we see that the progress of culture outgrows great translations; that each great period of culture finds the translation accomplished in the previous one unsatisfactory, not only from the point of view of the change in the language into which the classic work has been translated, but also with respect to the advance in scholarship which calls for a more accurate and precise rendering of the text in accordance with the cultural life to which it refers. Lastly, new re-thinking in the translation of a classical text is necessary in view of the fact that, together with the progress made by the language of transla-tion, the patterns of its particular culture (human behavior, feeling, appreciation, etc.) have evolved; indeed, the language of present-day communication, understanding and appreciation (its core-meanings, associations, connotations, etc.) undergoes an essential transformation in response to the cultural pattern and its climate. Consequently, the language of the previous period, with all its cultural connotations that no longer have their force, these having since been replaced by others, obscures the translated text instead of achieving a "pure" rendering that can be properly received.

That such a basic revision of a great classical text, through a newly acquired cultural accuracy, may give astonishing results, such that the personages, situations, and the significance of their conflicts "come alive" and are renewed, can be seen in *The Argonauts* by Apollonius of Rhodes (*Argonautica*), in its two different translations, the one dating from 1854 by R. Merkle, and the other, most recent one, by Herman H. Frankle from 1961. The amazingly-significant fact is that *The Argonauts*, rethought linguistically into our cultural pattern, reveals the notoriously evil personality of Medea in a light entirely different from that in the nineteenth-century version. Instead of a familiar, vicious and shrewd woman, bent on mischief, we have before us a lovely young girl possessed by an overwhelming passion for the beautiful Jason, the victim of her innate magic powers. Instead of being horrified by her misdeeds, we sympathize with her tragic conflict as she is torn between her family and her lover, and we pity her in advance of her final betrayal and abandonment. We are inclined to pity her rather than condemn her for all her cruelties and to consider them as *fatum*, as the result of her tragic and most cruel destiny.

This transformation of the personality of Medea within a novel translation that followed the cultural progress of a language, is a striking example of the virtual richness deposited in the source of the creative vision of the work and transmittable through its structure, braving changes of culture and its crises.

SECTION 9. THE ENTRANCE OF THE CREATIVE WORK
THROUGH THE RECEIVING PROCESS THAT IS SUSPENDED
UPON ITS VISIONARY VIRTUALITIES

However, another aspect of this perdurance in the advance of human progress cannot be forgotten.

We are talking about how the work of creation enters the constituted world by making it react, and break with its sclerosed forms, and become absorbed in new ones, and then readjust itself with respect to the creative intruder's original import. This "entrance" proceeds, then, by a receptive process on the part of the lived world. Yet it is a well-known fact that even great works have not been recognized "at first." Furthermore, not all created works enter the constituted world in the full-fledged sense, that is, by properly attracting the attention of critics and the vast public of consumers who, through their reaction, backed by authorities in the field, make an appropriate appraisal of it, bringing forth into the limelight its most significant factors for general attention. The time necessary for this course of events, which allows the created work to "enter" the life world in the strong, complete sense, varies for different works, and may never come about.

CONCLUSIVE INSIGHTS INTO THE QUESTION OF "REALITY" AS THE OUTCOME OF OUR FOREGOING INVESTIGATIONS

SECTION 1. INDIVIDUALIZING LIFE ASSESSED AS THE SOURCE OF ONTOLOGICO-METAPHYSICAL MEANINGFULNESS

(a) *The reality of life*

As we began our explorations of the ways along which human reality has been established by raising the question of reality *per se*, so our quest at its end leads us back to that question. Indeed, within the creative context we have at last gained the proper perspective on this great metaphysico-ontological issue, which emerged from a one-sided assumption that "givenness" is the first and last ground for investigating "reality." Once it has been shown how the otherwise "blind," "mute," and self-enclosing sphere of beingness of individualizing life explodes from within, under the promptings of the Human Condition, which bring about an ever-inventively-expanding plurivocal and pluridimensional universe of the human spirit, the issue of reality shifts definitely from the flat bias of "givenness" to that of the *spontaneous workings and creative inventiveness* of individualizing beingness. From the epistemological level it shifts to the metaphysics of life and its proto-ontology. That is, after we have covered the tortuous paths of the architectonic works of the primogenital factors of life, the issue of reality emerges in its germinal significance as that of the "reality of life." It is there that it is to be explored and formulated before we draw from it speculative formulations.

The question of reality, which in itself is not inspired by vital concerns in the current of life's urgencies, yet is urgent for life's transaction, emerges by degrees with the progrees of the philosophical streak of the human mind in our establishment of the significant life-course. Each of these degrees punctuates a step in the further spinning of the *significant life-thread* which, in its advance, unfolds progressively, first conscious and then intellectual complexes, weaving them into the entire life fabric. At certain stages of this progress of our *life-script*, which is intertwined in a co-significant way with those of all other beings, a half- or fully-aware global pattern is projected according to the life-significant *radius* of our existential involvement and reach. This radius unifying vaguely, but with an implicit cogency, all the fragments of the significant life-course into a continuous representational design makes our philosophical wonder the *vortex* of the individualizing self-orientation, of the in- and/or out-directedness of the significant impulse/reaction instances in which it can work, and work out, its own way with co-existential links with other individuals. It is always attentive to striking the right balance between its *own* life schema and the *rest*. It is this balance — *equipoise* — that is, in turn, the life-world order. We are so absorbed by the "reality" in which we dwell that to understand its significance we spontaneously put it into doubt and, through this doubt and questioning of its possibility, we give it full-fledged significance.

The design or image of the global totality of our life expanse in question is not a representation of the intellectual "face" of the global unity of the circumambient world. The human being is present in the "image" he himself constructs; he is present within it at its center. He is also present in it through *his experienced self-absorption in it.* Lastly, this image is a synthesis of his self and of the life that is uniquely his own, in which he finds himself, and by recognizing his place in it within all the ties he entertains (with life's elements, processes, tasks to be accomplished), he recognizes his *concrete tasks of vital significance and their concatenation.* In this recognition — instead of following intuitively the vital impulses, to counteract obstacles to his survival and to propose appropriate reactions —, he may reflect upon complexes of "situations"; he may ponder the intertwinings of their segments of casual connectedness, priorities to be given in action, the best means to fulfill needs, etc. In short, he may move from instinctive functioning to plotting, appreciating, discriminating, and planning this so very complex "design" or image, this "lived view" we call "reality" ever-progressing in awareness of the circumambient conditions — and so move above them, achieving a global view of his human possibilities and our living condition in general.

The issue of reality surges, however, only with our reflection upon the stability/contingency of the web of which the image/design of the global totality consists and within which we are woven ourselves. It surges with respect to various modes of its significance: possibility/actuality, real/illusory, certain/unpredictable, necessary/arbitrary, etc. It is of crucial, vital importance for the reflecting mind to clarify its status with respect to them: its existential significance. Is it not grasped by us within our life-script in the vital experience in which we dwell and function, devising our life-course?

This texture/image of reality comprises in a pluridimensional way all the types of our existentially significant threads as they are spun by our existential functions from those that are the most primordial biological/ vital through the operations that support the body's motility, its organic units in their co-cooperative schemas, and our half-aware behavioral patterns of reaction/response and our wilful deliberating action/ under- taking schemas as well. Always interwoven with all these, and expanding their frame, is the entire deliberating/appreciative scale of intellectual apparatus that patterns in a flexible way the conscious dimension of our life-script in all its perspectives. Furthermore, as it appears from the above, this image, far from being a "mirroring," static and repetitious one is, on the contrary, in an ever-changing, reconstructing flux. Yet its vortex within the groundwork of the human condition remains permanent. This image, as "reality," is already created.

(b) *Life's "reality" in its epistemological modality of presentation as opposed to illusion, imagination, hallucination, and fiction*

What we call "reality" is characterized in itself in the first place by being there for us in an apparently *stable* fashion — serving reliably as the background of the present state of affairs: in its *continuation* is grounded the forseeable development of these affairs in the future, a development that is predictable as to its consequences. Since it is woven into our experience as the "real" world of beings, processes, things, events and with ourselves interwoven into its progress, captivated by it and absorbed by its texture, we have no reason to question its "being there." Nor do we have sufficient distance from it to have any doubts concerning that which is naturally experienced by us and further pre- sents itself to us together with our own existence. This is the experience which Claudel and Merleau Ponty, after him, have called *co-naissance* (to be born together with). To "be born together with" means the experience of "reality," of our own being, as in the act of existing together with other beings, things, processes and everything which constitutes the entirety of our existential spread within an infinite realm of "all that is alive." We ask about the nature of this experience only when we are presented with aspects of things, and with our own or other people's feelings, happenings, etc. which either do not fall into the global experiential pattern of what we call with Husserl our "life-world" — a pattern that we embrace vaguely in its totality on the basis of the core of experiences that are ours and by which we stretch dynamically into its network — or contradict the natural expectations which we form on the basis of this experiential life-world pattern. In such occurrences, which astonish us when we check carefully on the ways in which these strange types of experiences are cognitively shaped, we distinguish the modes of *their appearance* from that of our reliable, sound, and stable *ground of expectations*; they obviously should not exist in the pattern of the workings of reality; we discover then that its apparent claim to "reality" to be the ground for the course of our vital enactment is just a *pretense* and, in contrast, merits the significance of "illusory" reality only, because this pattern reveals itself merely in its life-proficiencies instead of in the force that actualizes those proficiencies. First, it appears to not correspond to the actualizing conditions in its spatio-temporal grounding, which grounding the relatively stable and reliable order of the outward and inward workings of existence within our life-world postulates. Second, confronted with certain experiences when we fall back upon life's reality to check their validity — experiences, in which things and beings appear adumbrated and clad in nuanced features —, we find that they belong to a *different order than that of concrete vital existence*. Lastly, we see their insignificance when we reach above the actually given facts toward other future and still unknown developments within the life-world. Indeed, checking the "possibility" of these facts over against the actual stage of life, we find that they cannot be considered natural consequences of the present state of affairs, and that they are not what can be expected to happen according to the "logic of real facts" enmeshed within a real network, but are "imaginary."

At the same time we may disregard the "logic of real facts," with their seemingly inescapable consequences, classing them with imaginary aspects — not necessarily falling out of the real-life pattern, but adumbrated, varied, and differently disposed and interconnected — and thus project a *real-life simile* in an imaginary network of events, developments, etc. That is, we may invent a counterpart to the groundwork of our existence, which is reality, not an "absurd" one (contradicting it) but such a one that instead of being immersed in its existential pattern and flux — grounded in it — it is floating by its *own* rules. There it is that when confronting these imaginary experiences with "reality" we reassure ourselves that, as similar as this fictitious universe may be to real life, yet it is not "real." It belongs to a separate "world of fiction."

(c) Reality as the objectivity of the life-world

With these few succinct differentiations, we may already state that what we mean by "reality" is not only the relatively stable texture of our own absorption within the existential networks of life, but also a *specific mode of presentation of this existence*. We above called it provisionally "image" or "pattern." (There is no appropriate single concept under which it could be subsumed.) It is a pattern/image not of ourselves alone, but (if we experience ourselves at all) of ourselves *together with all the other components of the spread of our existing life-world*. Furthermore, this presentation of the texture of existence is not uniquely our own, as is the case with a real-life simile, in any form (e.g., hallucination or illusion); *rather, to be our own, it has to be shareable* with all other beings. Experiencing it, we interact within a network of the life-world in which we are intertwined *with all the other living creatures* and — albeit in various differentiations and degrees — experience the *existential reality of this network in its concatenations.* These concatenations spread into circuits of life's operations further and further away from our direct interaction, and yet we may, in reflection, see their compass upon the furthest horizon.

   This unique mode of presentation of existence — reality — is governed by the above-mentioned "logic of real facts." Its stability in the ever-recurring cycles of life, as well as in the seemingly foreseeable future progress within each cycle and above it, is naturally assumed by us to be *grounded in unchangeable rules and laws of our existence within the world of beings and things.* As pointed out above, it is the human being who is the central factor of this pattern, and its constitutive laws and regulations are those of the Human Condition coordinated so that we exist together with other living beings: brought to its presence in the "open field of consciousness," we call the metaphysical status of the so described reality of life "objectivity."

(d) Reality as a specific existential modality of life

Edmund Husserl has, in a most penetrating way, shown us the constitution of objectivity in the intersubjectively valid constitutive operations of human consciousness. Although Husserl has stressed the dynamic perspective of the constitutive operations in which the pattern of the intersubjective reality emerges from the universal type of singular human consciousnesses, his contribution to our knowledge of reality consists mainly in his emphasis upon the *structural organization of the life-world which is projected and crystallized in these operations.* It is, in fact, the pattern of the life-world that consists of the intertwining cognitive-constitutive operations of pure, transcendental consciousness (of concrete human beings) that becomes prominent in the Husserlian approach to reality.

Improving upon Husserl, Maurice Merleau-Ponty has brought to the fore the operational perspective in the origin as well as the mode of existence of reality. He has sought the origin of structures and mean- ingfulness according to which the life-world and simultaneously the concrete human being is constituted in the types of *bodily-psychic operations* by the performance of which the human being unfolds his existence. In approaching, then, the nature of the objectivity of the life- world, not through the structurizing functions of transcendental mind, but through the motility of the body that originates them, Merleau- Ponty has moved from an eminently intellectual, image-like conception of reality into its functional origin. "Reality" becomes a universal order of sequences of operations and functions. It resides in what we call the "order of the life-world."

Both of these perspectives — albeit from different sides — stress the ontological basis of similar instances as sources of the origination of order. Yet they forget the *universal flux into which it flows,* or *from which it springs and which carries it onward.* In order to recognize the full significance of the notion of "reality" there remains one more step to be made. Undoubtedly we mean by "reality" an intellectually projected world of life. This world of life, however, should not itself be understood to be identical with the life-world conception of Husserl and Merleau- Ponty, who saw in it a fictitious ideal of a primogenital constitutive struc- ture of subjective-objective life operations representing the originary milieu of man. In the descent they make following its genesis alongside and in human constitutive operations, they overlooked the *evolutive* nature of the constitutive forms alongside and in the evolution of life itself. I have already, from the outset of these inquiries, challenged the validity of the Husserlian life-world conception by introducing the crucial factor in the evolution of its forms: the *self-individualization-in-existence of the living being of which the creative act is the vortex.*

Along with a global, intellectual projection of it as a pluri-dimensional "image," in which we find ourselves immersed, we cannot fail to recognize that reality is grounded in the very unfolding of the *individual existential course*; it is the modality of the beingness which "comes to be" and "passes away," to use Aristotle's terms, in its course. It is projected and established through its progress, which stems from and is operated by our significant operations.

In its unforeseeable circumstances — through entanglements, interplays and combats — the human being is absorbed by the life-struggle of this progress and this struggle carries his existence as much as he forges from within it his capabilities for handling them.

Taking into account the foregoing conclusions, it is never enough to stress the constitutive preeminence of the motility of the body and its interchangeability with the constitution of the universal pattern of the life-world as such. In the two contrary (the Husserlian and the Merleau-Pontean) approaches, we either remain captives of the singularized, individualized patterns, which one of them (Husserl) wants to tie together by way of the kinesthetic tentacles, or we face an ultimately haphazard coalescing, or lastly, an altogether diffused universe, and so the other (Merleau-Ponty) attempts to dissolve all the ordering patterns in a new notion of a "medium" between conscious and bodily experience which he calls the "flesh." Yet no single pattern of Husserl's interconnectedness or of Merleau-Ponty's articulations (e.g., convex and concave) even touches upon this interplay of forces of living beings among themselves in the life and social world. It is the progress of all the concatenations of life which ultimately *regulates all the projection of static patterns meant merely to punctuate the stages or relative stability of individual beingness.* The thrust onward of the functional development of the individual being which carries the constructive progress of the life-world never stops, never crystallizes into an abstract pattern or schema: it keeps the living being perpetually breathless and the life-world an ungraspable play of forces. This is the existential mode of "reality" which characterizes its type of beingness. In short, *the key to full-fledged understanding of "reality," in which all its previously distinguished perspectives and aspects meet, is human life itself in its constructive dynamic with and within the life-world.*

To bring the experiential evidence of the reality of life into a sharper focus we will appropriately contrast it with its "mimesis" in art. Although we find a presentification (as discussed above) of the real in the plastic arts, as well as in music, dance, etc., and it appears that arts like sculpture and architecture belong to reality in singular ways, yet the confrontation between reality, understood in its full sense, and its presentification in literary art offers a most complete gamut of points of comparison. The question of "mimesis" in literature is always the focus of attention in literary studies.

We will limit ourselves to formulating the issue in terms of the above-stated purpose.

SECTION 2. THE MIMESIS OF REALITY

(a) *The "Objectivity" of life versus "life simile"*

In the literary work reality is undoubtedly presentified, yet not in objective primordial experience. It is present in the modality of a "life-simile." It is contained in the literary work in various ways. (1) The work may, in fact, present segments of the life-continuum through the presentation of images constructed upon the model of the life-world with plots, conflicts and experiences similar to those taking place in real life (especially in a novel or drama). (2) It may make reality present by *evoking* real-life experiences of love and hate, fear and anguish, wonder and doubt (especially in poetry, novels and drama). (3) It may *contain ideas and reflections* about life, death, society and human nature, etc., which would "correspond" to those we conceive in our real-life progress. (4) Literary drama brings, through the dramatization of life-simile-segments, enactment itself to reality in its performance onstage, "as if" the life-sequence-image broke into the pulsating life of reality.

Yet the way in which reality is present in the work of literary fiction is stripped of its essential features. In the last of the enumerated fashions, the sequence of events and development seemingly brought into the stream of everydayness is neither absorbed by it, nor do its tendencies and *dénouement* command the natural consequences which events in the life-world unavoidably entail.

Lastly, the opinions, thoughts and ideas experienced by heroes of dramas and novels, as well as by the author in the background, do not possess "practical" authority; neither do they imply responsibility in our responses.

Experience, feelings and emotions that the literary work may evoke, with such force that the reader and spectator may forget life and himself altogether while immersing himself in it, play only on the chords of his sensibility and, once the vibrations and waves they put into motion fulfill their cycle, they pass without leaving a tangible trace. This does not mean that they cannot affect us deeply and have *indirect* influence upon us, which might in turn play a role in our real life. Yet, directly, they never touch it, never partake of its workings. On the top of that, and this is the point which in a conclusive way brings sharpness to my argument, the segments of life-simile which might reflect real life reflect it in a "broken mirror," and life appears — in a mirror — as in merely instantaneous glimpses, with its essentialities dismembered, its crucial continuity disrupted, its groundwork validity suspended.

This occurs in several ways. Stating, then briefly the question — What form does the mimesis of life-reality take in the literary work that stands in contrast to life itself? — we may distinguish the following differentiations.

(i) A segment of a life simile in fiction (e.g., in *Catcher in the Rye* by Salinger) is present, first, distilled in a selective way from the pulp of life: personal, social and physical; whereas the life-reality from which it is distilled is, in contrast, full, pulsating and open to an infinite number of perspectives for selection. One or another gives through the prism of its *specific point of view* an "interpretation" of the real-life-span, establishing new interconnections, causal relations, etc., with the necessity of the haphazardness of their outcome, and fills in the disrupted continuity of the life-span from which it is taken by providing an *imaginary explanatory system*. Even if a "realist" style, like that of Zola's, may claim to present "brute facts," supposedly without any "interpretation," it amounts to a fictitious presumption because we never know the "brute facts"; we may merely live them. Taking the facts as such out of their infinite vital concatenations we arbitrarily cut in a brutal way through innumerable capillaries of the vital networks sustaining them, draining them of their vital spontaneities and forces, and thus annihilating their specific life-significance. In order to grasp them within the intentional system of a literary work we have to supply their elements, abstract and inert, with new significant networks to frame and specify their meaningfulness.

(ii) Not only is the segment of life simile presented in fiction as an interpretative intellectual pattern foreign to the real pulp of life on account of its distortion and restructuration of it, but, moreover, it is a simile of *objectified* life and not of life *itself*. This is the case even with literary styles (literary expressionism, *nouveau roman*) which aim at bringing forth not the constituted life-world structures and patterns as they are already presentified in objectivity, but the conjunctions of operations which account for its origin. The intellectualized patterns of operations do not come in any way close to reality.

They consist of a mere selection of some operative links taken out of the tightly bound concatenation of life itself, whereas this concatenation has its own functional role within the wider spread of the progress of life and in its own function is a thread within the fabric of life's dynamic progress; all such threads are necessary in order that each can itself be *actualized*.

It also represents a certain segment of the life-world's "efficiency-order," interwoven into an infinitely expanding system of causal-con-structive efficiency lines, along which the individual's life within the life-world rushes ahead. This operational-efficiency-order needs life's relentlessly advancing stream which, pulsating with ever-new occurring accomplishments being *actualized*, makes the new development that is still to occur *possible*.

In contrast, the segments in fiction depicting life, in whatever form, offer as the action proceeds merely *abstract images of the existential progress in artificially dismembered chains*. These images themselves do not present life's advance in its "open field." On the contrary, each fictional life-segment is *fixed* once and for all in its viewpoint on life as such, in its perspectives on the span of life, and is selective in its intellectual interpretation of the causal chain of facts underlying it. As such, it presents a desiccated pattern, drained of all the spontaneities and juices which could make it "alive."

Undoubtedly the life segment in fiction entertains a "similitude" to the reality of life. But even the pattern of reality which it proposes for our attention is in no sense a direct image of life, because living reality offers infinite possibilities of interpretation, and this "life-segment" is only one of them; nor is it an antithesis to our life-spread (or our life-world) by presenting seemingly "the same events" in a different course of action than that of our life, but which our life could have taken or may still take in the future.

Thus there is a radical difference in existential modality between the reality of life and its representation in art and literary work. A life segment appearing in a literary work is not "real" *in any sense*; it is neither "actual" nor "possible." *Only the real can be possible* in the existential sense. That is, only what is grounded in the life-world progress and in the continuing stream of life is, or may be, "possible." But not being an actual segment of that stream, the presented patterning of objectivity in its cross-section of operations may appear to be "possible" in the sense of a model which reality could have followed; it might be "conjecturally possible." Yet conjectures do not correspond directly to living, concrete reality. They present either universal principles or elements separated from the whole — detached from the vital links by which they are intertwined with other elements in one fabric, elements that mutually motivate their dynamic progress and shape the sense of its stages. These are arbitrarily brought into a sort of coherence by the shortcut interconnections assumed by "probability." Their links with the continuous forward moving stream severed, they have lost their foothold in life and their hold upon its rules of progression. Consequently, being abstract segments of a life image, they cannot fit into any concrete flux of significant *self-interpretation in existence by an individual.* They must float "above" life, on their own. They cannot be a "model" for any individualizing segment of the real, ever-changing stream of life. In this stream no single concrete link can be missed. Each may be decisive for the actual turn of events. None can be singled out over against others as the actual cause of a significant step in the progression; it could have been different. Thus the real-life simile present in literature, or any genre of art, in any form, does not offer a "possible life," a "possible development" life could experience; it offers only a *"conjectural possibility"* of the interpretation of life. In itself it is a *fictitious reality.*

The strong impact which the fictitious reality of the life-simile exercises upon the reader or spectator who, struck by the concatenation of events, causes, reasons, etc., begins to ponder the situations presented in their universally human significance, may suggest that this abstract pattern offers us "ideal possibilities": possible situations, essential developments, actions and events which do occur, have occurred, or could occur, or that they offer us networks of a "possible world" in its ideal — that is, essential — form, but one which, in the stream of life, is capable of being realized in concrete. To assume this position would be to forget, first, that "ideal possibility" is either a feature of objects of reason (e.g., mathematical objects, etc.) which present all the conditions of ideal objects (ideas, pure qualities), fixated once and for ever in their formal and material structure — objects which do not partake of the stream of change — or whose essential features, as in the case of ideas, are isomorphic to those of really existing beings, things, processes and events and are extracted intuitively from the direct empirical givenness of these latter. Consequently, a sketchy selection of an imaginative assortment of links among them that is projected in a fictional reality in order to bind them together, does not and cannot function as an *ideal* possibility of the concrete. It is a "possibility" relative to the mode of cognition; in this case it is dependent upon imagination to establish and maintain its fictional *status quo*, but ultimately it dissipates when confronted with the verifying standards of empirical conditions, the groundwork of reality.

To sum up we will contrast the concrete reality of life with the literary life-simile in the following way:

(1)   Concrete reality flows onward, carried by its intrinsic forces as the "whole of life";

(1a)   The life-simile in literature is a sequence of life-events abstracted from the pulp of life and fixed once for ever;

(2)   The concrete life-stream is continuous and expands into the unforeseen and unforeseeable open field of the future;

(2a)   The literary life-simile is a discrete chain of causes and effects or of operations seemingly discontinued, so that it is in itself complete, accomplished;

(3)   The reality of life is fluid;

(3a)   The reality of a life-simile, if it is a work of art, is rooted in a determined pattern;

(4)   The real life-stream is a thrust ahead into incalculable circumstances;

(4a)   The literary life-simile is grounded in a calculated schema;

(4b)   Real life is the cradle of infinitely expanding possible developments;

(4c)   The life-simile is fictitious, closed upon itself, bereft of dynamic sources for becoming, and empty of the conditions for real possibilities.

(b) *The creative act and mimesis*

We have been following from the outset and throughout our investigations of the creative process the meaning-forging probings of the creative act — taken as a synthetic specimen of the creative process — in its origin and unfolding within the context circumscribed by the interaction between the reality of the creative agent, the life-world within which he dwells, and the stream of life which carries him even as he works at capturing and transforming its modalities.

What comes now into the focus of interest is how the creative act itself stands with respect to lived reality understood either as *objectivity* or as the *life stream*. That is, we have to ask, how does the mimetic — imitating — aspect of the creative process, in its position between concrete reality, on the one hand, and life-simile, on the other, take shape? Of what does it consist so that it may account for the above-described circumstance that reality can both be lived and be present in the literary work? To bring forth descriptively some aspects of the creative act will emphasize the above-established view of life and allow us to draw conclusions about the creative force as the source of human reality.

In the first place, we must remember that just as the constitution of reality proceeds according to a set of conditions, so does the creative act proceed with respect to the fictitious life-simile. But the sets of conditions differ drastically one from the other. The "mimetic threat" of the creative act does not "imitate" or "reconstruct" reality the way the arts constitutive of reality would. *It constructs the life-simile by its own laws, according to its own rules and by its own means.* Let us just point out the main steps of this constructive thread.

Although we establish the relation between the "external" reality of life and the "internal" reality of the writer's creative process in terms of (1) the transposition of significant moments to a different scheme; (2) the transition from one significant level to another; and (3) the transformation of a type of experience into another tonality, each of these globally so-called sets of operations would indicate seemingly a passage of the elements of real life into those of the life-simile, and yet, if we may figuratively talk this way, this very "passage" has to be operated by a *complete transfusion of the objective sense of these elements into the subjective experience of the writer.*

The creative act begins (as has been repeatedly emphasized above): first, precisely with a preliminary stage of total disintegration of all the constitutive links, structural patterns and media, and with the suspension of all the constructive constitutive objective/subjective rules which governed them. Second, the creative act consists of a transfusion such that the *elements of objectivity scattered in recollection become, within a new selective process, absorbed by the constructive, creative flux and transmuted in their significance* with respect to the creative intent and vision of the *writer/artist.* Third, it consists, as we have been showing above, in a successive series of constructive interrogations by means of which this scattered material, now vivified by new experience, the lived substance of imaginary elements, may be organized into the *life-significant* presentation of a life-simile.

It is then, at this point of re-constructing, within one objective mold, that the creative process makes appeal to the laws, structures, models, regulations, and procedures of transcendental constitution. But as we have seen in our foregoing analysis it is, on the contrary, the creative orchestration, with its own type of constructivism, which takes over; it uses the constitutive system, transforming it in the essence of its significant core, but having recourse to its objective formal devices to a degree which befits its creative intent. Where, in the continuing flux of life, all works encroach upon each other, in art the creator is the only master who may dissolve and bring together, transform, reject or accept on other terms, etc. And this he does by calculating each constructive step freely within existing constraints and with a *self-generating profusion of creative possibles.*

Undoubtedly the construction of the life-simile oscillates between the already-known objective shape of the life-world from which it draws elements, and the new, projected forms of sense which must maintain a relation to objectivity. Yet the calculation of the constructive process proceeds free of the basic law of life, that is, of the continuity peculiar to the life-process which is grounded in the spatio-temporal causal chain, the all-encompassing schema of efficaciousness.

The freedom of the creator in art/literature differentiates the construction of a life-simile from the progress of life. Nothing is aimed at ever becoming actual or possible: "*omnes posset esse aliter.*"

This confrontation of the reality of life with the reality present within the created work has revealed to us the source of *all significance.* It is *in the creative forge of the Human Condition which is installed by the evolution of significant forms of life itself at the junction where the living individual, attaining a peak level of vital complexity, makes from his merely vitally significant self-interpretation-in-existence, an inventive* "*jump.*" His creative virtualities of the Human Condition being released, all the meaning-projecting functions come together. The Imaginatio

Creatrix taking over, the pulsating life opens toward a specifically human endeavor: that of creating new cornerstones of meaning, "exemplary works," novel life-avenues.

To recapitulate: life's projection of the significant threads of vital progress intermingles with the creative-inventive endeavor of man. The creative endeavor is one of life's main endeavors. Yet, on the one hand, life not only has to open up for it, it also submits to its effects. On the other hand there would be *no human life unless the types of significance were not in its progress recurrently renewed from within by original and unprecedented types of life-significant forms.* The common source from which all life-significance — that is, all types of rationales relevant to human existence — springs, manifests itself from the metaphysical point of view, in this decisive fashion: *the creative forge reveals itself to be the inventive transformation of the modalities of existence as well as the factor of their discrete passage from one to another* — from concrete to abstract, from real to ideal, or intentional, etc. Thus it is the factor in the unity of that which in Pope's and Kant's conceptions has been called "the Great Chain of Being." In our perspective, however, which shows that life in its unfolding is the generative ground of all ontologico-metaphysical links, the "order of the All" manifests itself as the UNITY OF EVERYTHING THERE IS ALIVE.

CHAPTER THREE

THE CREATIVE ORCHESTRATION OF
HUMAN FUNCTIONING:

Constructive Faculties and Driving Forces

THE SURGING OF THE CREATIVE ORCHESTRATION WITHIN MAN'S SELF-INTERPRETATION-IN-EXISTENCE: PASSIVITY VS. ACTIVITY

The Spontaneous Differentiation of Constructive Faculties and Forces

FOREGROUND: THE SPECIFICALLY HUMAN MEANINGFULNESS OF LIFE

The specifically human meaningfulness of life, which I propose to present here in its full extent brings a crucial new note to classical attempts to delineate the distinctiveness of the particular type of beingness which we call the "human being." Indeed, we avoid isolating the concept of the human being in its particular type of structure, form, or "nature," etc., for each such isolation assumes at the start a bias as to how the human being will be grasped as "human." Instead of seeking what makes him different, distinctive or specifically "human," this is already assumed. That is we forego metaphysico-ontological as well as anthropological approaches. Any such possible preconception is avoided by approaching the human being in his *evolving genesis within the constructive meaning-projecting progress of life.* Instead of setting him apart from the originary stream of life from which he emerges as a type of beingness and which provides the means by which he carries on his own progress within the stream, it is proposed at the outset of our inquiry that is is precisely the *evolutive genesis of this type of being-in-progress that is the key to unlocking and exfoliating the nature of this type of beingness so that we may situate it in its proper place, role, and function in the entire scheme of life.* (Cf. the Spanish existentialists.) *It is the meaning-bestowing function of this constructive progress in the living being whom we call "man" or "woman" which is the vehicle of beingness.*

The self-individualizing process of life which carries on every type of living beingness progresses through several phases of increasing structural complexity; at a certain phase of life's advance a new type of functional cooperation among the innumerable operational complexes occurs; new functional modalities emerge; new "proficiencies" are actualized from virtual forces; new "powers" are released for new life functions. These do not appear at random or in isolation. To the contrary, they do not surge separately, one by one, and they do not possess an "independent" functional proficiency or capacity to perform a specific operational task. Each power acquires this in cooperative affinity with all the others. They define themselves according to their mutually prescribed functional roles. In short they appear in such or other proficiency *only insofar as they emerge within a novel "orchestration of functions."*

Nevertheless, let us recall that there is a determining factor in this new orchestration which radically transforms the self-individualizing constructive effort of life: IMAGINATIO CREATRIX. New orchestrations of human faculties, each of which gives rise to a novel life-significance which the self-interpretative progress of life's constructive effort from then on acquires and unfolds are indeed determined by the surging of this radically new factor. *Imaginatio Creatrix is precisely the factor determining the new orchestration of a system that aims at a new kind of constructive advance.*

It is with the advent of Imaginatio Creatrix that the new "creative orchestration" of life's faculties establishes a specific significance of life. [To the genesis of the specifically human significance of life another of my works is being devoted. Here we raise some fundamental issues concerning its very *possibility* and the *basic conditions* of its progress.]

We propose, now in the first place, to investigate directly the nature of the workings of the creative imagination within the creative orchestration of the human faculties which come to be differentiated within the new orchestration. Second, in order to fully circumscribe the role of the creative imagination, we have to gain insight into the nature of *man's self-interpretation-in-existence* as a *process intrinsic to the process of life itself.* Third, we have to look into the nature of its progress: at the intrinsic mechanisms which underlie this meaning-bestowing constructive effort, and the conditions of its very advance, as well as its guidelines. In brief, we will investigate of what the fundamental meaning-bestowing factors consist, and how they originate, as well as what accounts for the constructive progress; that is, for novelty and renovative advance.

In other terms, we are in the present work concerned with the nature of what I have called the "creative forge" of life and with the origin of the "significant guidelines" for the specifically human significance-of-life-in-progress.

As Emmanuel Kant has set forth, originality and novelty within human constitutive functions — here meaning-bestowing functions — is found in "exemplary works of art." Within the present perspective in which creative self-interpretation supersedes the Kantian cognitive structuration, it is *the creative origin of "types" of significance which is brought into light*. In the present work we will concentrate precisely upon the nature and origin of the fundamental factor which lays the cornerstones for specifically human self-interpretation-in-existence.

These cornerstones in their irreducible originality and novelty are the significant guideposts without which no constructive progress of life would be possible. We will center upon the juncture that is the core of the creative process, namely upon the creative orchestration as it actuates the origination of new types of significance.

It is such new types of significance that are man's creative works in fine arts, science, technology, etc.: "exemplary works."

SECTION 1. THE SYNERGETIC COHESION OF THE OPERATIONAL FACULTIES IN THE CREATIVE ORCHESTRATION

(a) *The distinction between the functional constructive roles of "operations," "functional organs," and "faculties"*

Let us first establish some basic distinctions between the operational mechanisms of life's functional systems. We begin with *definitions of "operation," "organ," "faculty."*

By "operations" we mean the simple and simplest dynamic means of articulating either by confluence, complementary composition, generative impulse or intergenerative coming together, or lastly, by coalescence into a single functional unit the innumerable elements that enter into the significant articulations of life's genesis. These are characterized by an *intrinsic virtuality for releasing a functional proficiency while entering into the composition of one of the above modalities with an appropriate other element*. They may be seen as "primitive" instances of the driving propulsion toward the individualization of life.

But they may release this functional proficiency only within a functional segment, which is not a mere articulation of elements haphazardly coming together, but is "functional" *insofar as it performs a constructive role.* That is to say, not only does this segment form the pattern, which is its constructive context and which outlines a project to be carried out by its elements' operational cooperation, but this segment could not come to actualization had it not been for *its sharing in the functional organization of an overall constructive system.* Even in the case of the amoeba's generation by "simple" cell, division, it is from a "center" that the functional operations proceed and are directed. At a more complex level of life's constructive advance, such an "agency" directs the operational segments by means of mechanisms subservient to and limited to one constructive task, a limited peculiar task, within the linear, although chained, segmental progress. They are brought together into *operational knots* in which their one-line operational activities are centralized. These are what are usually called "organs."

(b)   *The differentiation of faculties: Imagination, will, intellect, memory*

Within and above these innumerable functional schemas, systems, and segments geared to constructive progress in the individualizing of life, the *"central agency"* of each individualizing enterprise elaborates in its *evolution a specialization of functional proficiencies for a higher degree of functioning.* In this specialization this agency reaches beyond the mechanical performance of the singular organs. In fact, it does not specialize in the complexities of a singular performance, but, to the contrary, in developing *specific capacities in certain types of performance networks.* Drawing upon the living being's performance proficiencies (of e.g., impulsive promptings, appetites, strivings, urgent subliminal stirrings, the directional tendencies of desire and the objective orientations of cognitive deliberation), the spontaneous tendency of the creative orchestration heightens the chief thrust/propulsion of each and all. In an intensified form they are, on the one hand, summoned up to be nourished by the spontaneities of the performance networks; on the other hand, they enter into the constructive projects of the individualizing process in conjunction with its constructive orientations and active forces. As a result, a *specific system emerges within the creative orchestration of the constructive individualizing progress of life, which drawing upon life's subterranean energies and drawn into constructive schemas follows its own synergetic individual line of develop-*

ment. As mentioned above, the constructive advance works always from the *inside* of the primitive life-forces and assumes a leading role over and above them within the overall constructive system of the creative orchestration.

In the above cited variety of foundational natural/subliminal stirrings, it is (1) the *faculty of the will* that finds its resort. The natural stirrings, propulsions, pulsations do provide an operational impetus. However, they are "blind" and "one-directional," promoting some or other tendency. *The will emerges from the creative orchestration as an "enlightened," forceful prompting which gathers all the forces and promptings into a channel through which the unity of the human being finds its expression.* Working itself through the constructive systems or "organs," of the creative orchestration of all the types of human functioning, it becomes specialized in its manifest nature and gathers momentum to become *the driving force of the entire orchestration.* When it is in power and strong, it invigorates the orchestration's entire workings. When it weakens, and its synthesizing energies dissolve, the entire orchestration process loses impetus and functional consistency; its constructive direction falters, losing its power to stir.

(2) *Imaginatio Creatrix* as another specific faculty of the creative orchestration has been visible throughout the course of our investigation. We will turn to it again soon. It will just be mentioned here, that although it has its natural/subliminal ground in animal phantasma (and of course not in the images of remembrance), it surges within the orchestration of the source experience, as a unique novum, which plays, in fact, a decisive role in the emergence of the creative orchestration as such.

Nevertheless, this orchestration would not surge forth, and the creative imagination would not acquire its synergetic nature and its leading function within the creative constructive enterprise — which would not at all exist without it — were it not for the simultaneous surging of the faculty of the will together with (3) that of the *structurizing intellect.*

As a matter of fact, it is by working itself into the schemas of this latter that Imaginatio Creatrix synergizes all the functional proficiencies of vital/sentient/affective significance into a fountain, the stream from which passes through the filters of the structurizing models, formal elements, etc. of the vital significance of life's onward course. Thus Imaginatio Creatrix brings forth an infinite variety of elements for

designs that are novel with respect to life, and original with respect to
the "images" dominating life's established route, designs that offer
possible formal elements for the invention of ever new combinations
and permutations of thought and action, and most of all, for the
creation of new meaningfullness of life.

Here we have indeed, defined the line of differentiation between
the creative orchestration of the objectifying, life-serving constitutive
system on the one hand, and of the specifically creative orchestration
of the creation of the novel types of meaningfulness which elevate the
first.

With an acuity and comprehensiveness unprecedented in history
Edmund Husserl has shown us the workings of the structurizing intellect through the constitutive system of human consciousness. The
theory of transcendental consciousness with its ego-pole, stream of acts
and its correlate in the horizon of objective structures to be actualized
offers precisely the pre-determined objective schema for the free play of
what we have called here the "creative orchestration" of life's self-
individualization-in-existence. Since the constitutive system is in its
being geared to the repetitiveness of linear progress, and the permuta-
tion and combination of thoughts and acts is assumed to take place
within an objective horizon of possible permutations, it is natural that in
stressing the objective route — and in being concerned with objectifying
progress — Husserl has ignored the *underlying crucial specificity of the
creative factor*. Naturally imagination has been assigned a secondary
role within his objectifying constructive enterprise, that of a subservient
function accounting for variation in typical models and thus introducing
flexibility into the process of identification which is the engine of the
constructive advance.

For the same reason, the great principle which he sees as being the
entire groundwork of the constitutive constructive effort, namely the
"passive synthesis," is itself in charge — in a "spontaneously passive"
fashion — of intergenerative "creativity." Yet as has been pointed out in
the previous discussion of the Imaginatio Creatrix, neither fancy nor
imagination — as functions within the works of Husserl's "passive
synthesis" — could account for the origin of types, that is for the very
origin of the constructive specifically human life significance and its
cornerstones. But we should not be surprised that Husserl did not
reach the sources of the constitution of objectivity, for he took the
human significance of life for granted. Having begun with the investiga-

tion of transcendental consciousness at its very peak of constructive complexity — the peak, in which he himself saw the fulfillment of the telos of the human historical genesis — he could *not have seen the amazing uniqueness of its emergence as such.* He had no reason to marvel at how different such an inventive transcendental world is from the life-world of the less-developed vital faculties that have a limited range of vital significance with which to endow our being.

We will not repeat here the Husserlian theory of the "constitutive orchestration," as I would call it in our present perspective. It is enough to sketch in a few paragraphs how the "manifestation" of the specifically human significance of life can acquire an objectified form.

We have seen how the three faculties discussed above emerge within the creative orchestration of life embodied in the human being by assuming their respective roles.

These three faculties, however, require for the performance of their respective roles one overall pattern of *basic* functioning so that the constituted life-world of man may be diversified, particularized, and yet maintained in recurring fashion. It is this universal blueprint matched by a corresponding universal and automatized mechanism that guarantees, first, the recurrent and recognizable identity of beings and things, and secondly, continuity in the progressive phases of life's advance.

Indeed, taking an overview from our perspective of the complete functional system that carries on individualizing life, we see a distinctive central faculty which stands out as the skeleton upon which all of the functional systems are suspended, as well as the central mechanism which conducts the recurrent types of basic performance. This central faculty which outlines the universal ways and means of structuring for all faculties, which ways and means constitute a universal system of reference, is the factor which projects, constructs, and establishes experientially individually "neutral," that is, strictly "rational," forms. Following the traditional usage which attributes formal rationality to man's intellectual power, we shall call it the "faculty of intellect."

The conception of the faculty of intellect that emerges from our investigations corresponds indeed to the core function which Husserl always emphasizes in his analysis of transcendental consciousness, namely, the function of ordering performed by the intentional system of the forms and structures that pervades the conscious activities of man. Husserl devoted the most extensive and minute attention to the workings of intentional consciousness. Most of his analysis cannot but be borne out within our framework of the creative orchestration. Yet our task now is to isolate from the wealth of his considerations this main stream of the intentional — that is, intellectual — activity proper, differentiating it from other functions which as we have already indicated belong to other faculties. In this way, a proper role being acknowledged each, we may avoid Husserl's unduly assumed sovereignty of reason and rectify the distorted view which kept phenomenology from breaking through the vicious circle which intentionality involves.

To begin with let us succinctly outline the function of the intellect which appears as it differentiates itself within the complete system of consciousness. We begin by disentangling from the Husserlian theory of consciousness that which belongs properly to the intellectual faculty. Distinguished from other factors in the basic Husserlian pattern of consciousness, the intellect comprises the flux of intentional acts, the ego-pole, and individual acts. Although the spontaneous surging of the stream of intentional acts which has the ego as its pole is to be considered in its own right, the structure of intentional agency, that is, the organizational features of the flux and its interconnectednessess with the succession of acts, is the function of the intellect. Furthermore, although the ego as the pole of the stream of acts has also to be considered in its own right, that is, in relation to the self-individualizing individual, the making of its interconnectednesses with the stream of acts in their structuring is also the task of the intellect. The ego is, in fact, the center of the intellectual agency which brings all of the intentional work together besides bringing it forth.

This tripolar structure of the flux of acts, the ego-pole, and individual acts forms the spinal column of transcendental consciousness. It extends over a network of formal "possibles" which comprise the temporal as well as formal "horizons" which function as the universal reference system that indicates the outlines of the recurrent core of objectivity as well as the range of its variations. It plays the role of the formal indicator as well as that of the basic formal skeleton of the entire schema of man's self-interpretative life course within his life-world.

In this role the tripolar structure goes even deeper extending to the roots of the establishment of life. As a matter of fact, it is the intellectual agency which projects the two basic conditions of the human phase of life: the individualization of beingness, on the one hand, and, correlative to it, the circumambient life-world, on the other.

Let us now survey succinctly these primogenital life-conditions which the intellect lays down (projects) for the surging forth of both the living being and his life-world.

As I have set forth earlier, "life" as such means primordially differentiation and constructiveness. It means individualization from within a circumambient realm, an individualization which simultaneously transforms that realm into one's own milieu. To individualize implies a differentiation between an "inner" core of self-directing forces and the "outer" field in which they play. This central feature of life indicates the basic condition for its origination as well as for its advance: an individual agency promoting growth, on the one hand, and the circumambient world in which life expands, on the other. At the level of complexity of life attained by the human being, we call this distinction, following Husserl's usage, "transcendental consciousness," on the one hand, and the "life-world," on the other.

Yet the primogenital differentiation belongs to the order-introducing workings of the intellectual powers even at their primitive stages. In fact, life at all its phases also means "experiencing" understood in the largest sense. It is for this reason that Leibniz, who obviously had insight into the inner/outer orientation of growth as such, insisted that the living individual substance of even the simplest form is composed of experiential elements which he called "petites perceptions." Of course, it is only at the human level of life's unfolding that the fullness of what we call "experience" is achieved. Nevertheless, the elementary experiencing (operational stimulus/response, acting/reacting, striving, prompting, pulsating, sensing, feeling, etc.) in which this basic differentiation of inner and outer direction takes place determines life as such. Basically this differentiation paves the way for expanding growth while concurrent expansion means transformation of the circumambient milieu.

In fact, the constructive progress involves selection of appropriate means in order to deal with operational problems and the delineation of ways of advance. That is to say at each phase of life's complexity more complicated methods of selection are adopted and used. The basic distinction which we have indicated above accounts for the three main lines along which the progress of life's constructivism is secured.

First of all, as I described in my work "The Moral Sense in the Foundations of the Social World," from the level of "blind" selection at which the matching of needs and their corresponding means proceeds almost "automatically," we move to deliberate and discriminating choice. This choice, which at the highest level attained within the creative orchestration of life's forces culminates in the judgment of value, is made possible by the activity of the intellect as it is progressively unfolded in the evolution of individual beings. It is within the inner core of the living individual that the intellect develops its strictly rational — that is ordering — mechanisms for: dissociation/association, discrimination/deliberation, analysis/synthesis, evaluation/judgment, and selection/choice. As an active agent the intellect maintains the emotionally neutral, universally valid skeleton of conscious life involvements, which are then infinitely particularized into concrete instances by the entire network of collaborating faculties.

In the same action by which this selective process postulates appropriate means for life's unfolding, the circumambient milieu is being transformed into the life-world of individual existence.

Second, a crucial point is to be made. At its experiential basis life differentiates not only the means for its progress but also constructs in the same operation their appropriate forms. It is again the intellect which through experience differentiates the "inner" and "outer" forms; it does so by transforming this seemingly objective/subjective cleavage into a common median sphere. The life-world, that is, the elementary conditions which are transformed into the milieu of an individual life, is in fact the projection of the individual's postulates for continuing on his course. Here again it is the intellect that like an architect proposes the universal principle for or key to the entire enterprise. It is the complex "presentational/presentifying" function of experiencing which accounts for the emergence and expansion of this common sphere, of this common universe, between the seemingly split individual core of the living beingness and its existential realm, between what ultimately rises to the form of human transcendental consciousness and the life-world. We have, indeed, to pinpoint here the primordial role of the intellect in the affairs of life, in laying down the strategic framework for, and performing then, the *basic function of presentifying-positing-objectifying the individual's life concerns*. This threefold function which synergizes three different, partly overlapping and partly complementary devices for life's workings is of unique significance: it establishes "objectivity" and dimensionality with its basic spatio-temporal axis.

Upon this axis intentional consciousness establishes the basic universal directions of the subjective/objective life progress to be embodied in the infinity of variations which the creative orchestration with the three other faculties then brings about. At this point we have to introduce the crucial factor of the mechanisms which are at work within the active/ passive synthesis accomplished by the functional apparatus of the creative orchestration: notably the role of *memory*.

(4) *Memory* was considered by Henri Bergson to be the specificum of the human being. Within the Husserlian framework, memory assumes a role more specifically in the workings of inner time consciousness, which itself sustains the entire genesis of constitutive progress. Here we are not concerned with the role of memory in the genesis of the temporality of the vital/significant process as would be stressed in Bergson, or with the origin of the temporal sequence that is simultaneous with the origination of the primordial forms of transcendental consciousness that would be the focus for Husserl.

Be that as it may, it is nevertheless a fact that without considering the mechanisms of what we call "memory," which is truly a primogenital function of life — one that comes into its own in the creative orchestration — this very orchestration would not be workable. Self-individualization-in-existence in its specifically human inventive/creative form advances in a temporal succession, and memory plays a specific role in its unfolding. What I mean is, not only does it play its role in the inner-time consciousness that bears it along, but it plays a crucial role in the *inventive/creative line of self-interpretation which is its essence*. Furthermore, the creative process of novel types is a "temporal" process of a specific nature; the temporality of its successive steps in the constructive progress is, as a matter of fact, not at all coordinated with the order of the temporal phases upon and within which it draws. Memory appears here to be of decisive importance. It in fact performs a most complex function. It works in various directions. Not only does it basically relate instances of past experience to those of the present and to projections of the future in the actual field of consciousness of *man-the-creator*, but it acts as the "overseer" of the entire range of experiences ever available to the creator in any form: real, imaginary, fanciful, illusory, intellectual, spiritual, etc., regardless of the temporal phases or contiguities/discrepancies in their temporal succession.

In fact, we might in this respect speak of a *"Creative Memory" working in tandem both with the Imaginatio Creatrix as it proposes ever further horizons to be explored beyond those just now under scrutiny, and with the searching "inner eye" of the creative quest*. In this schema, memory assumes among others, not only the role of gathering and conserving "an inventory of experienced possibles," but, first of all, *the*

role of synchronizing the dispersed thoughts, experiences, given data, etc.
otherwise lost in the independent storerooms of the inventory of memory
that serve the constitutive process. This synchronizing perpetual "over-
view" drawing on the insight of the searching inner eye is precisely that
which sustains the far-reaching continuity of the inventive/creative pro-
gress.

For the creative function of memory, the synchronizer, nothing is too
far back; nothing is lost in the inventory it has stored; nothing is without
some possible connectedness, associative relatedness, linkage, etc.; all is
in flux and ready to be brought to life by the searching eye of our
deliberating mechanisms.

SECTION 2. MEMORY — IMAGINATION — WILL:
THREE CONSTRUCTIVE FACULTIES WHICH INDIVIDUALIZE
LIFE ALONG WITH THE INTELLECT, THE ARCHITECT

(a) *Memory as a vital force of life*

Bergson considers memory to be the factor that determines the passage
from organic to psychic life. In fact, when we consider the constitutive
system of the human being, of which the center is the full-fledgedly developed intentional consciousness, we will give assent to Bergson's attributing such an essential role to memory, albeit for different reasons.

Memory appears within our constitutive/intentional functioning as
the crucial factor of *lived* constitution in contrast to its objectifying/
structurizing system of operations, on the one hand, and its structural
interconnectedness on the other.

The role of memory and its nature appears most clearly precisely
when intentional consciousness is "de-structurized" — that is, when the
human being finds himself on the "brink of existence." In fact, in
pathological cases of mental illness in which the entire system — as a
function of which the life-world of the person and the inter-relation-
ships of the person with other human beings are established — completely disintegrates, memory appears with striking clarity to be a
VITAL FORCE with a double proficiency: first, *projectional* and
concatenating; second, *retrospective* and *retrieving*.

We may say that every intentional act of consciousness, through its
noematic content, projects hooks toward other noematic structures,

that emerge within the same intentional field of consciousness. Yet it does not "project" them "dynamically"; it merely extends its objective structures until they are "hooked" by others that appear; in the same way they are hooked to those which were already enacted and established in the field. We may say, thus, that every noematic content establishes a fragment of structural concatenation within the stream of consciousness. Yet not all the hooks may find a loop in the incoming acts. We may also say that every noesis of acts enters into a concatenation of the intentional processes of the stream of consciousness just by emerging at a certain temporal instant in its sequence. These automatic concatenations would not, however, account for that specific type of continuity that marks the intentional constructive enterprise. They can only explain the "passive synthesis" of the constitutive system and, as Husserl himself discovered, the system's *onward flow* needs a different type of explanation. He had to assume an absolute metaphysical status of time in order to account for it. The situation is quite reversed if we approach the intentional constructive effort not from the pole of conscious effort, but from its opposite side: from the *constructive effort of life*. When consciousness is destructurized, the life milieu and its intentionally established forms disintegrate. It appears, then, that the noematic structural hooks do not possess the power to hold segments of experience together; the human being passes from one experience to the most structurally distant ones. After each experience, the nexus to its experiential context is disrupted. The hooks extended from one experience to others do not serve connectedness. The same is to be observed in the operational connectedness of the noetic continuity. In pathological destructurization, the stream of consciousness may be completely disconnected; its usual experiential order is disintegrated. No way remains of binding one experience to its natural sequence along the operational line.

Neither objective structurizing, nor the subjective operational objectifying line, establishes connectedness or allows for the retrieval of it from the past.

In contrast, it appears that *there is, nevertheless, a strong vital force* active *within the structurally distorted conscious system which seeks connections*. It seeks to find them both in the present and in the past. The more the distorted attempts at structuring fall apart, the more its driving vital force, while left at a loss, seeks other channels. Here it is that we see that the structurizing schema which proceed along with the intentional constitutive line (operational noetic/and patterning/noematic) belong to a *driving force prompted by the initial spontaneity of life* which carries it and which possesses in itself the *virtuality of projecting a constructively advancing "vital dynamic" of connectedness.* This is one of the life-promoting functions which accounts for the operational continuity of otherwise discontinuous structurizing patterns. More precisely, *this vital force seems to be one of the main constructive agencies of the entelechial principle of life's self-individualizing beingness.*

In point of fact, when we observe in the human being a regression in the ability to make structural ties within the life-world, in the extreme stages of the disintegration of his constitutive functions, that is when he becomes entirely apathetic, having retained only some vital reflexes for keeping his organism and himself alive, the absence of an active striving toward regaining interconnectedness of experience indicates in the first place the disintegration of the usual forms of experience; and, in the second place, it may be seen as a weakening leading to the extinction of the vital spontaneities. The organic life operates, then, only as an autonomous mechanism and on its own. The self-individualizing process is at the same time almost extinct. But if such a total dissolution of the self-individualizing progress is not reached, than at any other phase of the destructurizing process there is visible a strong striving toward tying together all the possible links of experience into the "same" life-world again. We encounter in such situations the lack of the proper principles for maintaining such an interconnectedness. The patient's experiences are either aborted or distorted and do not come together within the usual constitutive flux; the very principle of the intrawordly interconnectedness which otherwise subjacently guides the constitutive processes is lost or completely distorted. The human being, in his often frantic effort to relate to others, ties experiential elements together in such a topsy-turvy way that he cannot "make sense" in the context of "normal," that is, universal life-world meaningfulness. Or, in his effort to reintegrate his experiences into the common schema of life's current, the human being connects them completely at random, choosing quite discordant elements.

This effort to reintegrate, to relate, to retrieve the common significance of one's existence, which consists in making the appropriate hook-ups among experiential elements and fragments, refers necessarily as much to a need present to communicate/share one's meaningful existence as to the ability to relate the present element of experience through which we want to accomplish that to fragments of experiences past (without forgetting the horizon of the future toward which this striving tends). Here it is that the nature and function of memory comes to light with greatest force and clarity. The *vital entelechial drive* remains blind without the proper collaboration of structurizing intentionality; when experiences are aborted or distorted, or extinct, or when the structurizing guidelines have deviated or are distorted, no reconstructive ties can be projected toward a reestablishment of communal life. We see in the slow progress in which these ties are retrieved that some significant spectra or realms of experience have to be retrieved or established from scratch. And yet the vital striving to establish interconnectedness works in all directions: it brings into focus the experiences of the present field of consciousness and centers attention on them; it prompts attention backwards into the "reservoir of images from the past," even if it retrieves them in an uncoordinated fashion; and it projects attention toward future experiences. This frantic prompting, working within fixational fragments and attempting to "review" their lived significance, manifests a striving to interconnect experiential elements for the sake of retracing anew the main avenues of life.

(b) *The role of memory in experiencing the three types of destructuring of the person/life-world patterns*

Let us begin by proposing that, it is at the advanced representational level (that is, the level of the complete closure of objective structures by constitutive consciousness — structures which abstractly represent complexes of vital concern to the living being brought to the level of their classification in the schema of a world/life order) that we observe the role of memory at the peak of its work. We take it into consideration namely, when it functions through the constitutive structurizing system. Yet memory's vital function of prompting constructive interconnectedness between life's segments, and of prompting the constructive continuity of the operations through which individualized life becomes established in its beingness, is, on the one hand, at work from the incipient moment of life. However, the entelechial principle guiding the vitally significant process through which self-individualization advances cannot put these operations into play. Thus, on the other hand, the initial spontaneity which prompts and carries life's process at large has to have the means necessary for performing this role. *It carries memory as the vital force which connects the driving forces of initial spontaneity, on the one side, and the entelechial principle, which indicates the line of constructive progress, on the other side.* I want to say that the vitally significant operations emerge within a continuous — although from the patterning, noetic/noematic point of view, discrete — line, within which a flexibility of choice and correction is available, precisely because there is present within the spontaneous drive this vital force of memory which animates and energizes the structurizing system for interconnecting and filling in the gaps between discrete experiences.

The flow of initial spontaneity is not mute and blind: it spreads functional tentacles toward the construction of vitally productive mechanisms for the use of an entelechially oriented beingness.

Memory in this role is functioning at all phases of life's self-individualizing progress. Yet — and here we are coming to a crucial point of interest for our present investigations — while it serves the entelechial principle of constructive advance at the phase of the vital significance of life, it changes gradually its guiding direction in order to follow the advancing complexity of individualizing forms.

In fact, with the onset of *the source-experience* which, under the influence of the just-emerging Imaginatio Creatrix, breaks with the rigid — although progressively loosening — meaning-bestowing/structurizing rules of vital significance, a simultaneous reorientation of life's avenues occurs. Their expansion, under the promptings of the inventive strivings, into novel structurizing forms no longer follows the lines predelineated by life's purposes, but projects new ones invented by the human agency. With this new turn the memory's connectedness-prompting enters into a different structurizing system. Its meaning-bestowing proficiency is no longer restricted to the vital significance of experience; in fact, *only now with the surging of a full-fledged conscious system is the hitherto vaguely conceived order of functional life-significance expanded and radically transformed into a representational objective life-world. This latter not only maintains the vital significance of life, but acquires a novel, creative, "specifically human significance of life."* Thus the service of a restrictive vital order is not to be the purpose of the vital force of memory; to the contrary, it has to adjust with unlimited flexibility to *transformable experiences* in order to accommodate the *tendencies and strivings of inventive and creative patterning which aims at ever-new systems of significance for life's elements.*

Numberless studies have been devoted by literary theoreticians and writers as well as artists themselves to describing the way in which memory works within the creative process or within the cognition of the work of art. We have also shown here some of the striking moments of its work. We will focus on its basic life-promoting role.

(c) *"Creative memory" in the reconstructive "deconstruction" of the person/life-world pattern*

This succinct presentation of the destructurization of the constitutive system of the person shows that its dynamism is in some ways analogous to that of the previously discussed initiation of the creative process and proceeds in a similar manner. Namely, we begin to be stirred by profound dissatisfaction with the world within which we live and by a simultaneous yearning to give it new meaning that would redeem its sclerosed finitude; yet, *in contrast* to the pathological scenario, we are already *moved here by a renovating hint.* Under its unclearly formulated and yet overwhelming pressure, the life world, and our own objectified image within it, begin to reel. With the onset of the creative vision and of our work on its objectification into a model to be followed in our "revolutionary" action, we progressively detach from our experience the hitherto valid and stabilized forms, molds, and significant complexes, within which our experiential life-universe has been shaped; we do not do this haphazardly or unwittingly. In contrast to pathological destructurization of the constitutive system, as such, our *creative destructurization* is, first of all, the effect of our critical approach to our present forms of experience and our *deliberative* dismembering of their shapes and interconnections. Further, and secondly, this dismembering does not — again in contrast to the pathological process — go forward under pressure from vital/social occurrences which could not have been avoided, planned, or directed, but proceeds by taking as a reference *new constructive principles which lie in waiting to direct the reconstruction of the scene.* Third, this destructurization is neither a mere falling apart of interconnected forms in which types of experience just vanish, leaving empty spaces, nor is it the deformation or truncation of the forms of structural combinations. That which in the pathological deconstruction of constituted ego-life-world patterns signifies the defective functioning of the constitutive system itself, in its (as Husserl emphasized so much) "passive" unfolding, is, *in the creative deconstruction of ego-life-world patterns, the prompting force for the renovation of the constitutive system.*

In other terms, the falling apart of already stabilized and installed forms is here not negative but positive, and is not passive, but actively calculated. The role of memory activated by creative imagination is here of paramount importance. Although there might develop a leit-motif which will lead to pathological deformation and a destructive process, it does not aim at impoverishing, diminishing, or negative effects which might occur quasi-automatically. On the contrary, the *calculation of creative destructurization is a constructive device par excellence which puts the destructurization process at the service of an ultimately restructurizing leitmotif*: its seeming "passivity" is the result of its great intensity as the performance of an *active agent.*

We also designate as "creative destructurization" a type of inter-pretation of a work of art in its creative architectonics. Here, still a different lead for dismembering the established form systems is fol-lowed. As I have shown in my "creative destructurization" of the *Undivine Comedy* of Krasiński and of the German Expressionist Drama, *this destructurization to be meaningful has to follow the architectonics of the creative process present within the work of art* under discussion.[39]

There is still a third type of radical destructurization of the life-world-ego pattern which, this time, is neither negatively deconstructive (that is, leading on to a vitally significant dissolution of forms as well as of their meaningful interconnectedness), nor a creative reconstruction of the life-script of the person within an innovated pattern of life-significance. In point of fact, although the creative effort is, with respect to its agent's "life-script," a "revolutionary" effort, a truly radical destructurization of the life significant patterns is only that which the *quest for transnatural destiny* brings about as a prerequisite for its uniquely peculiar itinerary.

It is uniquely peculiar because, as has been indicated in our discus-sion of the soul, and as we will see in the last part of our investigations, this quest scrutinizes all the significant complexes of life in which the person is embedded, accomplishing this with a most radical inquisi-tiveness — analyzing with a highly acute, active concentration of all personal faculties, all possible aspects of the significance of each experiential segment, and this in all possible perspectives. At the same time, although this "radical questioning" is guided by an aim — namely to discover/invent the "ultimate significance of life as such" — this aim is not in itself reconstructive, restructuring, or renovative. This inter-rogation distorts nothing, and leaves intact all the natural biases and significant aspects and perspectives of the established experiential complexes. It just makes them, under its questioning penetration, fall apart along their natural seams, hooks, and intertwinings. They become detached from the valid pattern falling like dried leaves off a tree when the sap of living spontaneity which nourished them has dried up. However, although nothing will be reconstructed (since the intent of this radical scrutiny is precisely to lay bare the radical limitation of all life-constructive rationalities), this scrutiny neither causes natural experiences to atrophy (as in the case of pathological destructurization), nor does it cause the existential striving of the quest to fall short of its aim. It is our *transnatural destiny* which makes itself a stream bed into which the very pulp of the soul's innermost strivings then flows, and which conducts the progress of the entire game of life's constructive embodiment, and which reveals the rationalities subservient to that embodiment to have been all along its own fruits which lose their flavor and value as the quest advances. Is the destiny which brings all this about invented or discovered?

This is the great question that will emerge at every step of our inquiry in the third and last panel of our inquiry. Let us here indicate what prompts the question.

Although the person is engaged in scrutinizing its established forms of thought by means of guidelines to life's meaningfulness that are already present, this uniquely radical task could never be pursued without memory itself being enhanced by the spell of creative imagina-tion. We may say that the creative imagination is at its peak here when it inspires memory to retrieve, at every instant, significant experiential elements for exposure to innumerable rays of possible significance. The creative imagination extends the scope of memory, scanning past experiences by providing an infinitely inventive spectrum of associa-tions with present concerns. It is as if the entire universe of man, as such, is scrutinized and disentangled. And yet the constructive functions of the creative orchestration are only indirectly animated and involved. Their constructive strivings coincide with the striving of the quest for a transnatural destiny only insofar as it adds its prompting to the positive task being pursued; the architectonic constructive effort of the full creative orchestration is held in abeyance.

There is often an effort made to endow the steps of the transnatural itinerary with objective forms which would make it comprehensible to others. There exists an abundant literature of descriptions, "confessions," and "teachings" of "spirituality" in which objectively significant patterns have been invented to convey the experience. This objectification of the fulfillment of our transnatural destiny betrays, however, its very essence, which is both unobjectified and unobjectifiable.

(d) *Memory as the key to sustained creative effort withstanding the adverse play of vital forces within the functional equipoise of Man's self-interpretation-in-existence*

 (i) *In the midst of the play of vital forces, memory as the mediator of the equipoise in man's self-interpretative continuity*

One more crucial contribution of memory to the progress of the individualizing constructive enterprise of life is the mediation which it performs between significant/sentient fragments of experiences belonging to the same experiential sequence, as well as between different experiential sequences.

When we consider the play of forces within the vital field of the existential constructive effort, we see that innumerable sequences of undertakings are necessary in order to fulfill the basic functional requirements of the life-progress at every step. The success of these undertakings is met with a special sentient response which we call "satisfaction"; its absence causes another type of sentient response which we call "disappointment" or "frustration." The one stimulates further such undertakings by strengthening the will; the other weakens the drive to achieve.

We witness the amazing forcefulness of life's elementary drives to propagate, to construct, to advance. The brute forces of life are never "discouraged" by a failure to establish themselves in circumambient situations; neither do they need any "encouragement" to advance. But the sentient functioning of our more complex individualized life, together with the selection and choice which make for the individual undertaking — their sensitivity to propitious circumstances for such an undertaking — simultaneously have a further individualizing effect. Within the play of life's forces this sentient functioning comprises the protective instinct, and is attuned to the "proper timing" for its exercise. Memory plays here, first, the role of making associative links among instances of success or failure and their circumstances at the various stages of the constructive sequence; that is, in the phases of its progress. Second, it is the mediating role of memory which brings together different types of experiential sequences in which either satisfaction or failure has occurred within the complete network of our ongoing experiential functioning. It brings them together as sentient instances precisely at the level of the sentient effects which they produce. Thus the discouraging effects of what, in one field of experience, could have been a discouraging failure, may be "balanced out" by an instance of satisfaction so that a kind of "equipoise" is maintained — equipoise in the person's experience of self with respect to fulfillment in forging one's individuality.

Although this *crucial maintenance of equipoise is already present in various degrees and fashions at all the phases of the sentient — that is, the self-interpretative phases of life's progress — it becomes progressively more significant as we advance in the complexities of the self-interpretation in existence proper to the human being.* It takes its *culminating form in the vital/social equipoise of the human being engaged in creative activity proper.*

The creative agent, as we have shown him, is entirely immersed in the play of the vital/social forces of life. Yet, he sets out about transforming the life-world within which this play goes on while remaining in it himself. Thus the creative effort, which has to be sustained through a long stretch of the life-course without being a homogeneous streak through it, at each and every point faces dangers of being aborted, submerged, or absorbed by the vital/social processes. In its very nature the creative effort is the result of discontinuous strivings. Each of them has to synthesize the entire functioning of the creative agent in order to bring all of our *virtualities* and *proficiencies* into focus. It is our vastly enlarged associative function of memory which plays the crucial role in maintaining this sustained effort by mediating between inspirations, intuitions, acquired proficiencies and conceived aims, and by throwing associative hooks between all kinds of experiential fragments and moments. In this, of course, memory is inspired by the Imaginatio Creatrix.

Memory brings forth experiential material lost from the sight of our present consciousness; it throws associative hooks into fields of experience which otherwise would remain alien to each other; it mediates between one experiential complex of the creative effort being performed and the preceding ones and projects those into the ones being anticipated. (Livingston Lowes' *The Road to Xanadu*, discussed above, offers a superb illustration of the work of memory being vertiginously expanded by creative imagination.) In short, the sustained discrete continuity of the creative process would be unthinkable without the crucial mediating role of memory.

(ii)   *The balance of powers: The master-builder and the architect*

However, there is still another process that is simultaneous with the first action of memory in creative activity, but it only indirectly concerns the creative process. It is directly concerned with the person of the human being engaged in this process insofar as it *permits a sustained effort with the adverse play of vital/social forces.* How can the person, in the first place, make a pact with them? How can one's commitments be distributed among life's concerns, both those which are indispensable for vital existence, and those addressed by the creative effort which challenge life's meaningfulness? How can such a balance be struck between and among innumerable experiential complexes?

We may well be more committed at times to the one side than to the other but, without keeping an equilibrium, neither of the two can move ahead. For, is not the strongest driving force of the creative effort nourished by the sap of life's elementary resources? Is not at every instant the creative effort embedded in the grain of the entire vitally significant experiential complex from which it pours the riches of sentient qualities into creative molds? Lastly, does not the creative accomplishment bring back to the life-course of the creative agent the significance for his/her existential script, a significance upon which the very meaning of this life-course as a "human existence" depends?

It is, in fact, the role of memory to mediate among the multifarious commitments of the person who carries on the creative endeavor in such a way that a balance is struck. By its portioning our involvements among the multiple significant concerns of vital/social existence, a sort of transmutation of energies occurs: what, on the vital/organic side, would appear to be the loss of its specific energies means on the intellectual/constructive side a "relaxation" of intensities which are weakened by long periods of sustained attention, as well as a stimulation of the Imaginatio Creatrix by the influx of pristine vitally significant sensations. A multiple complementary exchange of vital energies and resources takes place which can occur only if associative and inter-connecting hooks are being thrown between a *multifarious wealth of otherwise dispersed experiential elements in the entire register of human functioning.*

Most interesting is the balance between those two premier organizers: *vital/intellectual rationality,* on the one hand, which holds the post of master builder of life, and the *imaginative/intellectual reason* of the creative mind, on the other hand, which assumes the role of architect as the highest meaning-bestowing agency in the specifically human inter-pretation of life.

In this distribution of roles the two agencies partly overlap in their work. But while the intellectual agency acts as the master builder, the creative mind, its close collaborator, is the architect which draws up all the blueprints and gives indications for their implementation. What a marvelous interchange between the talents and forces of life which carry out vitally meaningful designs, and the creative spirit which seeks to enable the human being to go on fashioning the edifice of his own life in his own way. What is accomplished by one provides resources and backing for the other. When there are shortcomings on the intellectual side, the creative side strives to make up for them through inventive means.

What is accomplished by our inventive and creative efforts touches the deepest strivings at the heart of every living individual. It conveys an experience of one's self holding the means of one's destiny *within* one's self. The creative effort/creative mind, in conducting the work throughout all the vicissitudes of our vital strivings, draws major support from this self-experience. No matter what may befall us, we have the experience of plotting by oneself the steps of our itinerary, following a self-interpretative script without which life would not be our own life at all.

As a consequence, the creative effort sustains not only the accom-plishment of a work, but, simultaneously, it is the *strongest factor which invigorates and stimulates the vital/social forces and energies of personal life.*

This brings us to the great force of the Imaginatio Creatrix whose visions have been lying in wait all the while.

PART II

IMAGINATIO CREATRIX

The "Creative" versus the "Constitutive" Function of Man, and the
"Possible Worlds"

INTRODUCTION: THE BASIC PHILOSOPHICAL ISSUES WHICH MEET IN THE QUESTION OF THE ROLE OF CREATIVE IMAGINATION

Every serious philosophical quest reaches sooner or later the fundamental question of *the origin of the human world and man's role in it.* Philosophy since Descartes has adopted a framework of inquiry in which the factors and sources of the world's origin are sought chiefly in the nature and role of human consciousness; recognition of the nature and role of consciousness seems to be the major accomplishment of modern philosophy. Two major and lasting contributions to this accomplishment, as well as two major treatments of the problem of the origin of the world, have been offered — by Kant in earlier times and by Husserl in our day. And yet both of them, in spite of the wealth of detailed analysis which they have left as a lasting heritage for philosophical scholarship, seem to have failed in the adequate formulation and treatment of this problem. I see the reason for their failure in their main assumptions, which seem to consist, firstly, in a tacit acceptance of the Cartesian conviction of the *absolute sovereignty of logical reason* over other dimensions of human functioning, which ranges in gradations of intelligibility from blind organic operations, impulses on the affective and sensory levels and the whole dynamic dimension of the "passions," to the highest rational operations and the transcending élan of the spirit. Secondly, *both Kant and Husserl have downgraded the structurizing role of the passions by relegating them to the "empirical soul," to the brute functioning of organism.* Therefore when at the culminating point of their quest they were led to search for the crucial clues to the sources and factors of the origin of the human world in the empirical realm of man's functioning, Husserl, in spite of his ever renewed efforts in his last works, never broke through the screen of reason he had established at the start, whereas Kant broke through by recourse to the

342

Einbildungskraft and the role it plays in Genius, but could not handle it satisfactorily since his exit too was already blocked by the constitutive apparatus he had laid down. They were, albeit in different ways, caught by (a) insistence on absolute correlativity between rational consciousness and the human world, and (b) the necessity of equating the actual existing world with the potentialities of constitutive consciousness. Thus coerced into the position of transcendental idealism, which understands the human world as it is, to be absolutely dependent in its existence upon rational consciousness, no other world than this one is possible. (Husserl insisted that the idea of a world different than the actual is absurd.)

My own work, in its slow progress which has been punctuated by various critical treatments of Husserl's transcendentalism, especially of the "absolute status" that transcendental consciousness as an agency of intentionality assumed in classic phenomenology as the sole agency, leads me now to *radically challenge* this classic and current assumption of the sovereignty of reason in the functions which lead to the origin of the human world.

But in order to inquire into the factors and sources of the origin of the human world, should we not in the first place start with fundamental statements *about the nature of both of them*? In fact, in an unprejudiced analysis — one not restricted arbitrarily to the prism of conscious operations — the world appears as a system of things, beings, and events intimately interwoven through the processes they generate, a *relatively stable system* caught in a dynamic structural unfolding. The cornerstone of this progress appears to be irruptions of *original and unpredictably novel entities*, fruits of man's inventive genius. Human beings appear to be the major dynamic factor within this system, not only with respect to progress, but also in the introduction of essential and basic *meaning* through the structurizing work of consciousness. In order to account for the origin of the human world we have to account for both progress and meaning.

In fact, it seems to have been an oversight at the start of this double perspective on the human world that explains why the otherwise incontestable contributions of genius toward the elucidation of the issues concerning the origin of the *life-world* have been vitiated in their scope. Indeed, neither Husserl nor Kant raised the question while marveling at the nature of human reality, or while considering the interplay of the two factors of conservation and renovation; both of them came to it indirectly while seeking the foundation of the validity of science (identifying science with a higher level of the constitutive function). The basic meaning-giving and structurizing agency of man is what has been called "phenomenological or transcendental constitution." However, can the transcendental constitution, as it appears in pheno-menological analysis both Husserlian and post-Husserlian, account for *original, radically novel* meaningful structures introduced into the human world as the fruit of man's inventive genius? Is, as phenomenol-ogy claims, the whole of man's structurizing virtualities to be identified with the constitutive system of consciousness? Classic and current phenomenology answers these questions in the affirmative. To the contrary, in what follows, I propose to deny to constitutive conscious-ness these universally accepted prerogatives by distinguishing within the complete *human functioning system* another structurizing and produc-tive function of man, one conjoined with the constitutive function and yet autonomous from it: *the creative function*.

Unraveling the ways in which it works, its progress and its sources, we propose, that:

(1) the constitutive activity of consciousness is not the one and only system of man's functioning, but merely one among other possible conscious functions;

(2) *the creative function* being another, I submit that analysis of its workings reaches deeper into the nature of man's complete functioning by: (a) bringing to light various hidden factors of human functioning instrumental in the origin of the human world, dispelling the traditional division into "faculties," (b) revindicating the basic role of the impulsive, emotive, and affective dimension of the passions, and (c) showing the specific type of *orchestration* of human virtualities in the *creative function* and establishing: (i) the *creative imagination* as the agency of the *a priori* in "creative freedom" as well as (ii) the *plurifunctionality of human consciousness as the source of possible worlds*.

Thus an opening appears toward the *phenomenological realism of possible worlds*. It is obvious that by "realism" we do not mean any of its traditional conceptions but an entirely new conception which is suspended upon the recognition of man's creative powers.

SECTION 1. THE DIFFERENTIATION OF THE TWO FUNCTIONS,
THE CREATIVE AND THE CONSTITUTIVE, WITH REFERENCE
TO THE MODAL OPPOSITES: "ACTIVITY AND PASSIVITY IN
HUMAN FUNCTIONING"

As we have already pointed out, no serious philosophical quest can
bypass concern with the origin of human reality. In both of philosophy's
classic phases, the ontological and the transcendental, this concern is
the focal point of interest. A wealth of analysis has thrown light upon
many puzzling questions concerning the sources, principles, and vehicles
of the establishment of order upon which human reality and life itself
depends.

In our proposed attempt to diversify our approach to human functioning by finding how both the perdurance and novelty — routine and
invention — present in the human world may be accounted for, we will
encounter invariably some classic pairs of principles that stand in
opposition, which classify the ways of proceeding proper to types of
functioning along their opposed respective lines. It appears that, first of
all, the question about the conditions of unprecedented and novel
instances emerging in the midst of the world is routine: e.g., works of
great art and invention which we find while disentangling the array of
problems which are thereby thrown open to treatment are naturally
divided into problems of the *passivity/activity* of human functioning. In
the classic approach to our issue we find this demarcation principle
applied already at the incipient stage of cognition, that is, perception.

Indeed, phenomenology shares the Lockean-Kantian conviction that
it is transcendent perception, or sensory experience, that is the original,
primeval source from which surge the germinal elements of human
reality, and from which take off, as Locke so firmly states, all of man's
cognitive faculties in their respective modes.

This crucial role attributed to perception stems in the Lockean
tradition from emphasizing in sensory perception the particular vividness of the presence of the cognitive object within the cognitive act,
which Husserl calls "bodily self-hood," and assuming it to be the
strongest mode of evidence. Since upon this analysis only perception
— transcendent as well as immanent — seems, of all the cognitive
instances, to be endowed with the "self-given" presence of its object,
perception is accepted as the basic mode of cognition ("original" in
Husserl's terms) that lays the foundation and outlines the construction

of the edifice of human reality for all the others. In both the Lockean-Kantian and the phenomenological convictions — although in the latter for more nuanced reasons — the cognitive-constitutive flow of experience, which intermingles present sensation with remembrance, imagination, and expectation, the flow through which — as it seems — we *nolens volens* exist as it perdures from instant to instant without our being in a position to choose it, decide upon it, or, as is so, without even being surprised by it, is understood as our "submission" to it. Kant, laying stress upon the singular sense perception as an occurrence with a quality and content of its own, calls this special state of our being "receptivity." Husserl, approaching experience from the processional nature of perception and the "involuntary" and yet "indispensable" nature of its flow, calls it "passive genesis." Indeed, we never stop to sense, feel, remember, be aware of something, etc., unless we leave the "normal" state of mind.

For Kant, although these foundations laid by experience for the origin of the world are "received" by the cognizing subject at the first level, that is at the level of the "manifold of experience," without his willing or selecting their form and order in the *a priori* forms of space and time with reference to the categorical schemata — which corresponds to the Husserlian process of "passive genesis" — without which they would be neither cognitive nor constructive of our reality, an "activity" of the subject is already involved. In the Husserlian conception of the original experience of perception, or as Husserl calls it the "*Urstiftung der Realität*," the manifold, despite a shift in emphasis from Kantian instaneity in the structuration of the manifold (all happening at once), to a processional unfolding of the perceptual process consisting of *a series of perceptual glimpses* put into motion and oriented by the perceptual development, "receptivity" takes a strictly "passive" turn.

Furthermore, the "passive genesis," being the complete set up of all the perceptual forms, operates by a "spontaneous" — here, "involuntary" — unfolding of a perceptual *series of individual glimpses*, carried along by their anticipatory fulfillment structure.[40] The content and the, so to speak, grappling hooks of this progression, as well as these glimpses' point of reference, being preestablished, guarantee, on the one hand, the continuity of the structurizing constitution of the object and on the other hand the statement and correction of possible errors. Evidently human reality emerges from what, after Husserl, we call appropriately "passive genesis" or "synthesis," from this basic flow of experience which carries us willy nilly onwards. The so-called "passiv-ity," that is, the pre-installed inevitability of its progress, is, in fact, the expression of its way of organization. Its "spontaneous" unrolling, far from being a blind outburst, is to the contrary preestablished by rules, principles, and blueprints which prepare progressively appropriate means as the vehicles of its accomplishment. Due to the preestablished principles and norms for its universal progress and to the fact that this progress established laboriously, as Bergson has shown, in the backyard of nature becomes thoroughly *automatized* in the forefront of its operations, which is intentional consciousness, we accomplish the most complex and intricate operations of a cognitive-constitutive nature effortlessly and involuntarily. To this mechanized apparatus, which carries along the established universal function of man, we owe an enormously complex and rich intersubjective world. From this anony-mous and universally shared ground of primordial experience we ascend to deliberation and selection only at the level of theoretical thinking, reflection and judgment; there it is that, according to Husserl, consciousness becomes "active."

However, does this mean that at the level of "active consciousness" we are freed from the preestablished pattern of the structurization laid down by original perception? Would there be a disruption in the continuity of our constitutive system with the basic functions following a set of directives, and the others oriented by individual whim? If that were the case, how then could the world, at the more advanced level of construction for which the higher intellectual activities of man are essential, achieve its unity and homogeneous nature, and not fall apart into chaos?

In fact, as we have already pointed out elsewhere,[41] the originary experience being the motor for the emergence of all conscious function-ing and the lawgiver schematizing its activity according to its own preestablished regulations and structurizing principles, the constitutive system holds together at all its levels following *the same trend and subservient to the same telos*. This trend is clear. Although recognition of intentionality as the essential nature of consciousness seems to introduce a "neutral" medium, that is, one unprejudiced with respect to stands taken upon the great metaphysical questions concerning the nature and origin of the world, e.g., the idealism/realism issue, with all the detailed work made in the field, it becomes obvious that inten-tionality as understood by Husserl and classical phenomenology is the vehicle for a specifically and rigorously rational structurizing level of the constitution of the world. In fact, Husserl himself admits the basic point in his interpretation of both originary experience and the further constitutive levels of intentionality, writing:

Die Wahrnemung und ihre parallelen Bewusstseinsweisen der Anschauung sind aber die ersten Grundgestalten des Bewusstseins, die für den Aufbau des spezifisch logischen Bewusstseins in Frage kommen, sie sind erste Grundlagen im logischen Bau, die gelegt und verstanden werden müssen. Wir schweifen also nicht etwa ab, sondern wir sind dabei schon Logiker, ohne es zu wissen.[42]

Clearly, intentionality is interpreted by classical phenomenology as the vehicle of exclusively *logically rational structurization*, its operations following the outline, preestablished regulations and principles of the "passive," that is, effortless and involuntary, unfolding of the originary experience.[43] Its regulative principles, and its aim, will be treated later on. The question arises: "How could the constitutive genetic system, as understood by classical phenomenology, account for the origin of entities, obvious fruits of man's conscious efforts, which are *original* and *unprecedented* in the established world? That is, how could the constitutive trend of our functioning account for the origin of novel structures that break into the frame of the constituted world, transforming it *down to its sources*: the very quality of the originary experience? In other words, we submit that the constitutive routine cannot account for works of *human creativity*.

It is in the contrast with the creative activity of man that the preceding denunciation of the hidden presuppositions of constitution comes to light. In fact, as I have shown elsewhere, it is the creative structurizing activity, where it is open to phenomenological inspection, that is also triggered by perception.[44] Even more the *creative impulse* which triggers the spontaneity of the creative process takes off on the foundation of the *already constituted world*. However, it starts with a dual attitude toward it: first, it assumes synthetically the existence of the constituted world and its present state; secondly, *it revolts against it*. The creative activity emerges *denying validity to the constituted world*, in its given present state, as an adequate interpreter of human reality. It is a revolt against the routine, the automatism, and the inertly accepted rules of the constitutive system we passively flow with, and the involuntary submission which they call for; these are the target of the revolt of the *creative impulse* which aims to *transcend* this imposed, involuntary, anonymous trend of nature. To do this the creative impulse must break the routine first; then, after having within a self-devised entity put together a novel interpretation of reality, it must disrupt the regular channels of the constitutive world-process by making it intrude upon the constituted world and take foothold within it. Thus, the *creative process* maintains a twofold relationship with the constitutive one: it situates itself *between two different temporal phases of the constituted world by stemming from it and then breaking off from it, and then, breaking back into it in order to transform it.*

Indeed, *creative perception*, the decisive incipient point of the *creative process* reposes, *first*, upon the already present constituted *life-world of the creative agent*. Preceded by unaccountable *subjective dealings* of the creator-to-be with constituted reality, it actually triggers the creative activity by opening a new line of sight within the fixated reality. Whether it is in an immanent perceptual vision as in the case of poetry, science, and fiction, or in the transcendent perception of the plastic arts, the inherited and passively constructed forms and affective contents of experience are repudiated. All our operational virtualities, as their chains in the constitutive system slacken, become galvanized and take off in an effort to reconstruct the Real.

However, to show just how the "passivity" of constitutive automatization is limited in its role and how the creative activity establishes itself in a contrasting *voluntary* and *free* agent, we must reach back to their common ground, to the creative activity's genesis as a specific function *orchestrating anew all the productive operative virtualities of man into the framework of the creative context* and revindicating the neglected role of the impulsive and affective realm of the passions. (We speak here about "creativity" in the precise and restrictive sense in which the "creative process" terminates in an aimed at, concrete and intersubjectively accessible "product.")

SECTION 2. THE GENESIS OF THE CREATIVE FUNCTION:
THE CREATIVE CONTEXT, ITS FRAMEWORK

(a) *The differentiation of the two functions with respect to the axiological opposites: voluntary/involuntary*

In the foregoing analysis of poetic creativity I have shown how the *creative impulse* that surges from the rationally unattainable realm of man's dealings with his natural strivings, and yearnings, drives and confronts a limited and imposed framework of reality; its tendency then is to break through toward a more adequate version of reality, to loosen all old ties and open the way for a new structurizing system to take over.

The question arises, however, what would be the means by which the *creative impulse* could stimulate and bring about a new functional system? Furthermore, what would be the specific, radically different mode of this new functional agency, such that it could break away from the routine *life-world* constitution, free itself from the preestablished models, and invent new patterns and types? Finally we must wonder whether phenomenological analysis can uncover these hidden springs of our virtualities and establish rationally those distinctive features of their dynamic flux which elude the structures of reason.

In fact, in order to answer this last but crucial question in the affirmative we propose to outline the analytically established notion of the "creative context." In sketching its role, origin, and ways of operation, we hope to outline the answer to the other questions as well. It will appear that further distinction between the constitutive and creative functions lies in their radical divergence in modalities — the *creative* "voluntary" mode of operations, and its opposite, the constitutive "involuntary" mode of operations.

(b) *The outline of the creative process as the fundamental dynamism of the creative context*

Let us now succinctly review the main points of our discussions concerning the creative process. The yet undetermined *creative impulse*, on finding the appropriate reponse in our functional virtualities, establishes itself searchingly in its own mode of operation; simultaneously it calls into active commitment a network of particular functional operations. As they bring together the major operational arteries of man, these subsets of functional dynamics, in their consistent and purposeful orientation, constitute the framework of creative operations: *the creative context*. The creative context plays a role comparable to that of a weaving loom, upon which novel reality is going to be woven.

We start, as I have already indicated, at the level of what is called "originary experience," that is at the level of perception, namely, *"creative perception."* It is there that the primordial ties between the affective qualities and forms, their productive agencies having been separated from their constitutive pattern, coalesce into a new pattern, a new operating scheme. The *creative context* taking it from there binds together, firstly, the constitutive operations of man, but then going underneath the lineaments of logical structurization, it binds together the elemental factors of the passions, impulsive, emotive, nostalgic strivings, and the sensory and imaginative operational elements — together with their dynamic reservoirs — and the engendering forces which are otherwise instrumental in the constitutive operations as well. The emerging creative agency determines itself in its distinctive grasp of theme elements at the crucial point of the very germinal origin of the *life-world*, where the form and lived quality of human reality is decided, after having cut their ties with the constitutive system of structurization to which they have been blindly committed, and having bound them into a new orchestration. As the constitutive genesis aims at the structurization of an intentional — and, through the anticipation-fulfill-ment structure of its acts, already proven — object, so this new *orchestration* of man's functioning — through the creative act's tentative projection of its delineation and simultaneous determination of its new framework as well as its mode of operation — is oriented toward a novel aim of its *very own*. But in opposition to the *constitution* of an intentional object, which is in advance pretraced within the mode of the constitutive process itself, this aim of the *creative* process, e.g., the work of art, of poetry, a scientific theory, etc., is not pre-traced by the intrinsic nature of acts but is the *object of a quest*. It is the entire creative process that is engaged in this quest, simultaneously matching up the revolutionary renewing tendency of the *creative impulse* and the human world which it is meant to transform. Concretely, it aims to discover its "final form" and to incorporate it in an intersubjectively valid entity. To introduce it into the *life-world* means to break with its acquired sclerosed forms for the sake of a novel interpretation of the Real. This is the task of the unfolding, ever searching, and questioning, creative process. The *creative process* initiated in the process of *creative perception* comprises the following stages:

Beginning with the "creative vision" which marks the representational aspect of the *creative impulse*, it advances through several stages of searching after the most appropriate way of translating this *vision* into a newly devised "original intentional object" and terminates in the "phase of transition" that is the building stage in which this "merely intentional" object is concretized into an intersubjective entity that enters the already constituted human reality. Throughout its complete progress, the creative process — in radical contradistinction to the preestablished passive flow of constitutive genesis — is a questioning, a search, a trying of untrod paths; it is deliberation and choice from among myriads of ever expanding possibilities; it is a search, not only for its construction and building elements but also for criteria for their choice and the choice of its own operating regulations.

This novel *orchestration* of human functions, which in its dynamism, progresses in a flexible state ready to be unbound and bound anew by different ties, operates in a two-way traffic with the *creative project*, now indicating its transformations, now being transformed by its intrinsic demands to keep all the structurizing operations on constant alert.

Thus, this *creative system of functions* ranging from the *creative impulse* and the *creative orchestration* of man's operative virtualities and forces to the *creative context*, consolidates itself in its progress into a complete, self-oriented, self-propelling, distinctive, autonomous, but above all *self-regulating* agency (although one dependent upon the constitutive function and the established world). An agency which, in contradistinction to the *involuntary* progress of constitutive genesis is an agency of *will par excellence*, this agency, which is neither a mystical nor a mysterious entity within man, will emerge as none other than consciousness in a new structurizing function: *the creative function*.

Consciousness in the *creative function* is no longer a submissive engineer executing routine work in an unquestioning way; nor is it an administrator of the given; it is as if a man "awakened from a dogmatic slumber" discovers himself to be an inventor, or a *demiurgos* projecting the world he constructs. What are the final regulative principles of its orchestration which it follows in its projecting? Are they predetermined or "freely chosen?" What would be the meaning of "free choice," as distinct from selection and deliberation, which is followed by the constitutive genesis that accounts for error and correction and which, according to Husserl, is guaranteed by the "free play of imagination"? "What is the nature and source of these principles, such that ever new material for selection is present as well as appropriate new criteria for their choice?"

With these questions we anticipate two crucial points of every argument underlying the attempt at a philosophical account of the human world in terms of the human role in its origin; first, the question of the *a priori*, second, the question of the contribution of the different human faculties, especially *the role of imagination*. But before we enter into this philosophical controversy we must indicate the functional extent of the *creative context* within which alone, we submit, the "creative imagination" can emerge, so that we prepare our own ground for its treatment.

(c) *The revindication of the passions and of the elemental nature of Man within the creative context*

Indeed, in its progress the *creative function* is a mechanism of discrimination, deliberation, and selection. But so is passive genesis. However, in opposition to this latter which works with the material of rational elements of structurization and their selective principles, the mechanism of choice of the *creative function* is constantly oriented and reoriented in its modalities by fluctuating inclinations, tendencies, expectations, aspirations, hidden longings, aversions, and sympathies; all of these, whether they are dispositional or acquired within the world (being matters of feelings, taste, belief), seem to escape the authority of our rational powers. The selective mechanism of the constitutive function works chiefly at the level of rational structural elements, whereas *creative deliberation* seems to plunge its probes into the deep well of the *passions*. These affect the deliberating function by their being at work within all our *elemental* forces and operational virtualities and at all stages of our functioning. At the crucial creative stage, namely, that at which our incipient impulsive affectivity and sensibility enter into play with the universe of ideas, this interplay stimulates and galvanizes the *creative orchestration* into which it spreads; in return, by entering into the generating scheme of the orchestration's vast and unlimited range of optional associations, this interplay becomes the ground of the *creative renewal*.

It appears that the mute upsurges of passion, of disquiet, pain, fear, anguish, excitement and of the dumb impulses of irritation, anger, elation, the impulse to hit, to run, to embrace — which are hardly experiences, and in which nothing is revealed, nothing given and brought to light — are at the extreme edge of our psyche, registering mechanically the processes of nature; at this level, the creative function sinks its roots.

In the *constitutive process*, the mute operations of our functional endowment appear to have already reached the full extent of its structurizing and presentational proficiency in producing a perfectly intelligible perceptual object. As Plato saw, an interval separates the one from the other; during this interval the instantaneous and dumb reaction travels the long road of the sensory-motor operations and of the proto-constitution of the primitive forms of spatiality and corporeality projected in the perspectives of the past and the horizon of possible futures — and all this with reference to the already established system of the constituted world. There is a necessary and spontaneous assimilation of each experience to this established whole. The lived quality of constituted experience goes thereby through the filter of structurizing processes and is molded by them in such a way that, as Leibniz has so well expressed it, "each of them mirrors the whole world."

The *creative impulse*, however, rejects the preestablished pattern and cuts the ties among the functional agencies — the rules and points of reference of organizing sovereign reason. Here, it is upon the inarticulate movements of passions, impulses, moods and strivings that emphasis falls. The *creative function* elicits their dynamism by projecting a double quest: *first*, it seeks interpretative points of reference for this natural striving that operates within us, mute and yet most *significant* for the human being; *second*, it attempts to discover or invent the significance which this dynamic upsurge of *elemental* passions may have for the reinterpretation of reality that it originally asks for.

In the first movement, *Elemental Nature* lends itself to meaning-giving reason and is assessed in order that it might be raised from its anonymous impersonal status and become "interiorized" in reflection; in the second, inverse movement, interrogating intellectual intuition goes into Nature's present and is reshaped in man, in the whole range of its operations, down to the most elementary.

It is in response to this double quest that a new *orchestration* arises: the operational virtualities of consciousness and of all our functions freed to the full extent from preestablished ties, enter new ones establishing a new organizational pattern. Within its flexible frame, which we have previously called "the creative context," a new alliance is struck between the opaque, mute, "bodily" functions — of which otherwise we receive only faint echoes through our impulses and glimpses into our feelings — and the highest agencies of man's tendency to organize his world: intellectual intuitions, ideas, reasoning, and speculative powers; a new alliance then in the infinite modalities of the transparent *Logos*.

The *creative context* rests upon the new alliance of all the diverse functional dimensions of man.

SECTION 3. IMAGINATIO CREATRIX IN THE CONTROVERSY CONCERNING THE ROLE OF THE FACULTIES — A CRITIQUE OF HUSSERL AND KANT. THE DIFFERENTIATION OF THE TWO FUNCTIONS WITH RESPECT TO THE REGULATIVE PRINCIPLES: THE TRANSCENDENTAL "A PRIORI" AND "CREATIVE FREEDOM"

In our analytic investigations Imaginatio Creatrix has revealed itself to be "omni-present" in man's ciphering the sense of his life. We will now attempt to approach it directly in its role within the complex of human functioning. We will discuss it in the setting of *the conception of the human "functional system" proposed as the answer to the difficulties present in the classic controversy about the distribution of roles among human "faculties" in the origin of the human world.* Let us uncover the foundational line of issues by discussing *the Controversy Concerning the Role of Faculties with a focus upon Imagination in Husserl and Kant.*

As we have already indicated at the outset, it seems that if both Husserl and Kant failed to give an adequate philosophical account of man's role in the origin of the human world it is chiefly because they did not take as their point of departure a view of the world to be accounted for in its nature, but narrowed their approach to one single issue, namely that of the origin of science. Consequently, establishing the system of consciousness from the bias of what made scientific knowledge possible, they overlooked the specific distinctiveness of the creative activities of man. Husserl, as we will attempt to sketch briefly, does not seem to reach this issue. Kant, who takes it up in the *Critique of Judgment* after having in the main already established the world constitution in the first *Critique*, tries to fit it in and falls short of accounting for the originality and novelty of artistic creation.

To bring to light the intricacies in their treatment of the matter, and to trace from their initial assumptions the reasons for their inadequacies, is to lay down a basic network of problems involved in the issue of *creative originality* — into which we will then fit our own proposed solution.

The situation is indeed complex. If we undertake analysis of the *creative process* we see a striking resemblance between the *creative process* in art and the discovery process in science: they both share the essential element of "invention." Furthermore, the creative process in a work of art and the process in which a scientific theory is formed exhibit almost identical mechanisms. However, Kant has already rightly raised the question of their distinctiveness insofar as the *essence* of their products is concerned. He saw the *essence* of the work of art as residing solely in the work of the human *subject*, whereas the *essence* of scientific discovery reflects the data of *nature*. Scientific discovery is taken by both Kant and Husserl to belong to the higher operations of the constitution of the world, but Kant raises the issue of the distinction of faculties upon which we would have to call to explain the radical differences between *scientific discovery* and *artistic creativity*.

In order to explain how the *subjective* talent alone establishes laws for the *essence* of Art, whereas science aims at the discovery and explanation of the laws of nature within the framework of the constitutive scheme established by pure reason, Kant calls upon the specific role of imagination (*Einbildungskraft*). Therefore, with the question of the origin of the world and the role of human creativity in it, we enter into a controversy about the distinctiveness of various human faculties and their specific roles in the world.

In fact, although it for the most part only lurks in the shadows, imagination is at the center of the problem of cognition. We find it, for instance, in Descartes' analysis of the piece of wax, for in seeking to discover the reasons of its independent identity which persists through the changing aspects of cognition, he has recourse to imagination. Indeed, he observes an infinity of possible ways in which the piece of wax may vary in perception.

Only after deciding that imagination could not, on its own as a faculty, bring to the mind this infinite series of possible variations of the wax in perception, and that, consequently, the conception of the identical piece of wax cannot proceed from the workings of imagination, does Descartes feel compelled to acknowledge the reality of extension, or of contingency.[45] We find here imagination brought into the case of sense perception and its "reality"; indeed, by and large, the conception of imagination appears to be bound up with that of perceptual experience and the question of empirical reality.

In Husserl this issue receives a particularly well-developed treatment. However, while he introduces the notion of imagination at the same point as Descartes, namely at the point of the *necessary conditions of the relay of the perceptual process* in its *flexibility as well as in its various modes of presentification, remembrance*, etc., he sees its role in a way completely opposite to Descartes'. In fact, imagination, which in its several forms is assumed in Husserl's complete intentional apparatus to represent the essential network of the complete functioning of man, is attributed an important role. Although in principle the concept that man's operations can be grasped within one network of conscious acts dismisses the classic distinction of faculties — the specific operational organization of fundamental intentionality seems to take care of all the aspects of constitution by its own mechanisms — still, within this unified system, the role of imagination as the factor of modal modification of constitutive operations is quite distinctive.

In fact, in the transcendental analysis of classic phenomenology, imagination is a modality of the intentional acts which, having only a seemingly subsidiary role of complementing *positional* consciousness, is in fact indispensable to its operations. Its features, role, scope and prerogatives are seen within the complete analytic framework as participating integrally in the way in which the constitutive system is grasped and its problems formulated, and can be understood only from within the complete system, down to its basic assumptions.

We may mainly distinguish two roles of imagination, of "fantasy," operating within the Husserlian constitutive system. First, fantasy functions as a "neutralization" of the positional acts, and belongs "ideally" to every modus of *actual* consciousness, e.g., perception, belief, will, etc., as its *possible* counterpart; it corresponds to each exactly by its objective content, but modally presents to each its "neutrality modification" that is void of any reference to an existential status or any claim to a distinctive *objective* position: the objective content which the images exhibit, refers in its essence, according to Husserl's observation, to the content of some act of *actual* consciousness.[46]

Secondly, fantasy as the reservoir of possibles corresponding to each content of experience actually being posited allows for the "free variation " that operates within the process of every experience, starting with — as we have seen in Descartes — the positional act of perception allowing for the flexibility necessary for change, modification and correction of course without loss of continuity in the general constitutive progress of consciousness.[47]

In its first role, imagination — in the strong sense of "pure fantasy" — is seen as performing the role of expanding the horizon of reality by introducing the richness of the infinite variety of the "possible" to the otherwise automatically restrictive constitutive genesis of the "real." Does this mean that it could, and is meant to, account also for originality and novelty breaking into the constitutive scheme? If Husserl himself does not assign this role to imagination, what are his reasons? The question confronting the prerogatives and capacities of imagination can be formulated: "What is the distribution of roles among functions in Husserl's analysis, such that imagination is apparently deprived of positional prerogative?" "Can imagination be the factor of originality and novelty once deprived of the power to posit its objects?"; and finally: "What conditions should imagination fulfill to be able to generate self-given data?" These questions bring us to the scrutiny of its source.

Concerning the second role attributed by Husserl to imagination, namely that of guaranteeing flexibility of deliberation and an expansive variety of progress in the constitutive processes, meaning "freedom" from rigid determination, we must ask questions about the nature of this "freedom" and whether it would suffice to guarantee not only individual variation within prescribed types, but also original data for the radical *renovation of types*. With the issue of freedom, we pass to Kant's cognitive network, the role he attributes to imagination, and the crucial metaphysical question of the *a priori*.

Ultimately we will attempt to show how the question of the self-givenness of the data of imagination is answered by a new analysis of its functional role, aims, and conditions.

In Husserlian analysis of consciousness, perception is, as in Locke, recognized as the basis and starting point of all cognition. With reference to the perceptual temporal field within which the object of perception is the identical pole toward which all acts converge, Husserl distinguishes three essential modes of perceptual consciousness: (1) sensation (*Empfindung*) as the means of the direct presentification (*Gegenwärtigung*) of the object in self-givenness with retention following it immediately, (2) positional representation in remembrance (*Erinnerung*), and (3) representation in reproduction in imagination or "pure fancy." In fact, as we all remember, the notion of imagination or fantasy in general occurs in the Husserlian transcendental analysis within the framework of the analysis of the perceptual field in the stream of constitutive genesis; and specifically it is considered in relation to the modifications of the modes of presentification of the cognitive object through the different phases of the temporal run off that make up the cycle of the perceptual genesis. Let us recall that, in principle, the object of perception in the Husserlian analysis of the constructive system of the *life-world* — the operations of the structurizing organization, and source of which phenomenology proposes to have distinguished within the dynamic process of conscious constitution — is seen as a profile within a continuous time-conditioned series of acts that spring forth in the mode of the originary givenness of perception as its incipient moment, and that with the perceived, as its initiating datum, passes into *reproductive* stages which terminate the modifications of *pure fantasy.* Within this cycle of the perceptual spread, a radical distinction is drawn between the positional modality of the self-givenness of the object *in perception*, which then appears as the only source of self-givenness and thereby of the "original experience," on the one extreme, and the non-positional modality of imagination or "pure fancy," on the other. The modes of givenness of the perceptual object are, within the whole genetic cycle of its constitution, or as Husserl otherwise calls it, within the complete "temporal field" which it covers, differentiated first between those of direct presentification (*Gegenwärtigung*) of the object and those of its representation (*Vergegenwärtigung*).[48] While only the "impressional consciousness" in the actual perceptual progress — which is continued in retention or "primary remembrance," its "comet's tail" — brings the temporal object in its actual presence directly as self-given into the actual field of consciousness, the appearance of the object in consciousness does not terminate there. Were this the case, there would be no continuous world structure, but only a discrete one; further, we might then be deprived of the whole horizon of the intellect and be restricted to a purely animal vegetation. The appearance of the object in consciousness, however, continues in manifold reverberations — no longer in the mode of actual presence, but merely in various modalities of indirect representation and reproduction of the object originally given in perception. There is also a radical distinction between retention (primary remembrance), which actually continues the perceptual givenness, and representation in the "secondary remembrance" (*Wiedererinnerung*). "The last one," writes Husserl, "is the contrary of the originary giving act, no kind of object may emerge from it."[49] The reason for this distinction is that perception and the retention, which continues it, are built upon sensation (*Empfindung*), whereas, to indicate the specific *hyletic* nature of *reproductive acts*, Husserl introduces the notion of "phantasma." Secondly, although situated within the modes of representation (*Vergegenwärtigung*), imagi-

nation in the strong sense, that is "pure fancy," is still radically differentiated from remembrance in its three forms (*Erinnerung, Mitvergegen-
wärtigung,* and *Erwartung*). All these *modi* are reproduced within the
form of fancy, "pure fancy" such as presents a specific, basically
*different modus of consciousness, which stands out as a complementary
counterpart to the originary actual mode of consciousness at large.* It is
"complementary" in the sense that, because of its basically different
status, it is in Husserl's analysis attributed a degree of *freedom* from the
iron chains of the spontaneous unfolding of the originary temporal
progress: thereby it is seen as guaranteeing for this progress, first, a
spectrum of objective choice in structural selection, and second, a
flexibility in structural operations.

Does this mean, however, that "pure fancy" enjoys an independent
status with respect to the constitutive spontaneity regulated by ideas?
Before this critical question can be treated, the status of imagination
within the complete constitutive scheme has to be clarified.

In point of fact, as was already mentioned, imagination is not
"productive" of its objective content but "reproductive" with reference
to the perceptual process, which *alone* is productive. Fancy is, as
Husserl insists, incapable of endowing to givenness an object or any of
its features. "The essence of fantasy," writes Husserl, "is precisely not to
give its object in its selfhood."[50] The other above-mentioned modes of
representation also do not present their object in its selfhood. *Nevertheless* — and here the radical demarcation between the two, in this
respect, basic modes of consciousness is to be drawn — they perform
what Husserl calls "positional representation" (*setzende Vergegenwärtigung*) insofar as they reproduce the content of actual experience and
posit it as an integral part of the actual stream of consciousness at the
place which is reserved for it within the complete specific temporal
field, the field within which the whole cycle of the concrete perceptual
genesis of the object unfolds. To the contrary, pure fantasy reproduces
the content of the actual originary act but does not posit it in *any way*
within *any* temporal field of the actual stream of consciousness; the
reproduction of the object remains outside of the temporal actuality of
the advancing originary genesis — which is not only the source of the
life-world but its groundwork and foothold; it has no hold on this solid
ground, it "floats" (*es schwebt*).

If we consider that both the "selfhood" of the presentification within
the field of consciousness on the *noematic* side and the "positional"

mode of operations on the *noetic* side in their alliance in the perceptual givenness (and for Husserl these are the criteria for the radical distinction between producing and reproducing consciousness) stem from the fascination which he seems to share with Locke in the overwhelming vividness of the immediate givenness in sensory, as well as immanent, perception — using the Lockean language of simple ideas —, then the division of conscious operations into "productive" and "reproductive" and the judgment that imagination "reproduces" reality appears to be a downgrading of imagination and a mere predetermination of the issue of our concern. In point of fact, in order to bring to light the uniqueness of this type of experience, Locke distinguishes between sensory givenness in general and imagination, and emphasizes that the type of experience which brings the simple ideas of sense about may result exclusively from sensory perception; imagination is not in a position to provide such basic building blocks of cognition. Thereby, on the one hand, imagination is denied the capacity of contributing any *new* material to the hence unfolding constitutive process. On the other hand, the role of originating the whole cognitive-constitutive system, which is attributed by Locke to sensory perception — as distinguished from all the conscious operations that follow it — is substantiated, first, by his statement that ultimately the simple ideas of reflection (in Husserl's rendering "immanent perception") derive from the observation of the cognitive operations of sensory perception and, secondly, by Locke's blank statement that simple ideas can neither be destroyed nor produced by any means. In a direct parallel, Husserl, although with considerably more nuance in analysis, also restricts constitution to one source only: *impressional consciousness* at the incipient stage of perception.

Husserl's analysis of the work of art falls perfectly in line with this general tendency in his analysis. In *Ideas I* the figures of the devil, knight, etc. represented in an etching by Dürer, are given as an example of the "reproduction" of the actually given in perception.[51] That is, the objective content of the work of art is in general seen by Husserl not as a "presentification" but a "representation," a "reproduction" referring to the object of actual perception for its original model. As a work of "pure fancy" it dwells in a different mode of consciousness than does the object to which it refers; unlike as in positional consciousness — with either its presentation of the object in its bodily selfhood, as in actual perception, or its modified representation of the object posited by secondary remembrance — it has no positional status with respect to its existence. The figures represented in the etching, works of pure fancy, are neither "being" nor "non-being." As works of fancy they lie outside of the modality of being; they are what Husserl calls "neutralized modifications" of the actually given objects of experience. Pure fancy is seen as the modification of the given, neutralizing its positional representation, that is a remembrance in the largest thinkable sense."[52] The works of fancy (neither "being" nor "non-being") "float," and yet they maintain themselves as conscious operations and products; they lack, in sensation (*Empfindung*) — the very stuff of the temporal stream of consciousness —, the hyletic support of actual consciousness, but they have support in "phantasma." The grounding in phantasma instead of sensation allows imagination its relative independence from the actual stream of genesis and frees its workings from the iron network of spontaneous unfolding. We will investigate now whether imagination can open the way for originality and novelty within the constitutive constructive enterprise, and what is the meaning of its "freedom."

Indeed, seen upon this analysis as a neutralizing modification of positional consciousness, the work of fancy encompasses the whole realm of conscious operations in their dual aspect: to each instance of experience, as well as to every originally given individual, is attached a series of ideally possible modifications in remembrance and of parallel neutralizing modifications in fancy. Therefore, Husserl may attribute to fancy a "universal significance"; as an ideal horizon of possible variations attached to each actual originary givenness it is entrusted with an important role in the workings of positional consciousness; it introduces "freedom."

This "freedom" is not limited to its role of allowing flexibility in the selection of particulars within a given ideal type. Being outside of the spontaneous field of actual experience, fancy in its modification of the given does not suffer the coercion of all the components of the given temporal field. No actual act is in its essence individual, all of them being in their unfolding intertwined within a given temporal complex. "Free" from the network of the actual field, fancy has room to diverge from the given while transforming it in its reproductions. Furthermore, the relay of its productive process outside of the main stream, means not to be restrained by it; the process of reproduction may have different speeds, scanning selections, repetitions, different intensities of representation, of clarity, emphasis upon the different elements. . . .

This "free" run-off allows for incalculable variations from the originary data it imitates.

In this understanding a considerable margin of qualitative transformability is possible, and Husserl might well believe that he has in this way taken care of artistic creativity, especially since artistic activity remains in his analysis minunderstood. However, it is obvious that such a role for imagination is relevant only to the problem of imitation and the issue of the relation between reality and art in *representational* art. The whole complex of questions concerning the *nature of art* is left out of Husserl's analysis. Does the possibility, which the relative "freedom" of fancy guarantees, of a "relative" margin of individual variation within the same type account for the *radical originality of types* which we see particularly strongly exhibited in *abstract art*?

Indeed, the whole spectrum of modification, with all its possible incalculable nuances, that fancy may display in its transformations of the given object remains within the framework of standard constitution as the imitation of the originally given; it plays within the framework of its structure-type which, as we have established elsewhere, is in the constitutive process accomplished with reference to the regulative role of ideas. *Ideas prescribe the reach of individual variations within the distinctiveness of a type.* (Of course, there is also the possibility of marginal modification in the content of a given idea, yet to assume the essential transformability of ideas, and thus a continuous passing from one pattern of order to another, would ultimately imply universal chaos, which is contrary to the experience we have of the world and man.) It might well be Husserl's fascination — so like Locke's — with the enhancing quality of sensory perception, experience *par excellence*, that made him identify self-givenness as a criterion of productive and experiential validity and to restrict its spread to the self-givenness of constitutive perception (transcendent and immanent) alone. But, as we have shown elsewhere,[53] there might well be another typical instance of self-givenness which is, in fact, an indispensable condition for the emergence of novel and original elements within the *life-world* — in another type of perception than that accomplished in passive genesis. Oriented in his investigations of consciousness by his blind tracking of the genetic unfolding of the passive genesis, Husserl is bound to overlook this possibility. The question "Is there only one source of self-givenness?" emerges at this point and dominates the further course of our investigation.

In his pursuit of the source and nature of *origins* Husserl himself is well aware of the limits of the repetitive constitutive system of consciousness. He sees the "productive borderline" of consciousness in the "originary impression" which occurs as a component of "impressional consciousness," the basis of self-givenness in actual experience. Whereas the productive unfolding of spontaneous consciousness goes beyond the impression to its serial modifications, the instances of impression already belonging to the productive system are themselves grounded in the "originary impression" (*Urimpression*) that itself remains foreign to constitutive consciousness; it is not produced but found there, alien to it, "radically new," "the original product"; as such it is the ultimate originary source of its conscious productivity, but it also sets its radical limit.[54] Only the data of the "originary impression" are radically "new." The "*Urimpression*" is then seen as the radical beginning which predelineates the total scope of the constitutive unfolding. Constitutive spontaneity may add to it nothing new.[55]

Having thus scanned with Husserl the major linkage points of the constitutive system, we may state not only that, on this analysis, imagination being bound to the scheme of the passive genesis and subject to its regulations cannot account for the novelty and originality which erupt into the *life-world*, but that the constitutive system itself, understood to be rigidly predelineated by its incipient stage and repetitious, offers no other instance explaining it.

Husserl's recognition of the radical borderline between what the operational system of transcendental consciousness receives, as radically alien to it and new, and what it itself produces — between "impressional consciousness" with its notion of "originary impression" and the productive flow of the passive genesis which goes on from there — is not without an analogy in Kant's distinction between the "manifold of experience" that expresses the state of consciousness being impressed upon (*affiziert*) by what it is not, and by what it receives from without, and the complete aesthetic system of operations that works upon it, forms it, but does not bring to it anything novel.

And yet Kant has gone deeper into the nature of the issue. He made a clear distinction between "originality" and "novelty" in what man "receives" and with which he initiates his basic routine constitutive operations and "originality" and "novelty" which *breaks into* the routine functioning of man and which is man's very own doing. As we have pointed out earlier in this argument, he has distinguished between the specific origins of *nature* and those of *Art*. Having thus diversified the issue, it is again in imagination that he sees the factor of "freedom" from predelineated routine functioning. Within Kant's scheme, imagination is attributed, in fact, the role of an originary and decisive faculty within the scheme of human functioning, and fulfills the conditions indispensable for playing the role of promoting within the workings of this system, radical originality and novelty.

We submit that imagination (*Einbildungskraft*) is, in the Kantian account, truly the source, the *dynamis*, and the engine of the origin of the human world. In point of fact, imagination performs in Kant's complete account both of the crucial roles. In cognition imagination is "reproductive" and "mediating" — although at a pre-perceptual level and not at the post-perceptual level as in Husserl — thus enabling the constitutive process and the routine world construction as its turning point in man's creative endeavor; but as a factor of the *elemental nature* of man imagination is the factor of "radical freedom," freedom from all constraint.

Kant precedes Husserl not only in holding the notion of "impressional consciousness" seen as the incipient stage of all cognition, but also, as we know, in seeing the rigid automatism and repetitiveness of the transcendental system of cognition (it is obvious that in Kant's approach "cognition" is as much "constitutive" of the *life-world* — although not of the subject — as in Husserl's); moreover, it should be brought out that both of them are at first overwhelmed by the translucent rationality of the intellect and so leave the opaque empeiria in the shadows. Then, having surveyed the empire of reason, they are prompted to retrieve it and to revindicate its full rights. As an illustration of this radical turn-about, we may consider the fact that in Kant's scheme imagination enjoys in the realm of cognition even less "freedom" than in Husserl's, but as *Einbildungskraft* in the realm of artistic creativity it is said to have the "radical" freedom of *elemental Nature* as a "blind force of the soul." Indeed, in order to account for the uniqueness and exemplariness of the work of art, imagination is seen as an otherwise unbound power working through an agency not only distinct but separated from the cognitive faculties and referring to them only to check on its work. Can imagination as an independent faculty and agent perform this role? Could the opaque realm of feeling and emotion evoked by the soul, and represented by the undifferentiated agent of imagination, account for the uniqueness of a *novel* construct which, in order to be novel, has to depart from the incalculable variety of *differentiated forms of constitution already present?* To investigate the situation, inquiry into the role of imagination in cognition must come first.

In fact, when Kant summarizes his cognitive system in the introduction in the famous opening to the transcendental logic:

Unsere Erkenntnis entspringt aus zwei Grundquellen des Gemüts, deren die erste ist, die Vorstellungen zu empfangen / die Rezeptivität der Eindrücke, / die zweite das Vermögen, durch diese Vorstellungen einen Gegenstand zu erkennen (Spontaneität der Begriffe); durch die erste wird uns ein Gegenstand gegeben, durch die zweite wird dieser im Verhältnis auf jene Vorstellungen (als blosse Bestimmung des Gemüts) gedacht,[56]

we are still missing the crucial link between imagination and *Einbildungskraft*. Let us recall that the givenness of an object in Kantian constitution is chiefly dependent upon the synthetic organization of the various "representations" (*Vorstellungen*) which are to be brought into the unity of *one* consciousness. Whereas this synthetic unity expressed in concepts is the function of reason (*Verstand*), yet the possibility of the synthesis as such (*Synthesis uberhaupt*) is attributed to a special "blind," although indispensable, function of the soul, without which we would have no cognition whatsoever,[57] in spite of the fact that we are only seldom aware of it. Thus a special, although apparently subsidiary, source or faculty is introduced between sensibility with its pure forms of spatial and temporal extension and reason with its system of intelligible connections and categories. It is understood to be a spontaneously acting agency upon which the operation of the complete cognitive-constitutive organism relies. Within the organizational network of this organism, emphasis is distributed between imagination and the identity of the abstract I that is present in all operations and brings the dispersed and originally chaotic manifold into the synthesis of the *unity of apperception*. Indeed, in Kant's conception both levels of constitutive operations, the givenness and the intelligible synthesis, refer foremost and directly to this necessary point — necessary yet insufficient, since another type of synthesis is indispensable. Kant is at every stage of his reconstruction of the cognitive system perfectly aware that he distills only a rational skeleton of the complete operational system which has too thick a psychologico-empirical dimension; and he gives the clear priority to the rational network, explaining that the empirical dimension alone would not adequately explain the givenness of objects of cognition, the order of the world, and intelligibility as such. However, although in this exposition imagination shares this background position within the cognitive realm, will it remain in this neglect in the elucidation of *real constructive significance*?

Although, as Kant indicates, "objects" could be given without being thought, yet at the empirical level alone we would then hardly have cognition, for which Kant assumes the necessity of an intelligible form. Identifying the type of connections which enter into the intrinsic structure of the constituted objects of cognition with those of logical judgment, he, following Aristotle, deduces from the logical function a series of universal concepts, "categories," which preside over the synthesizing activity of the intellect in the final organization of the manifold of sensibility. Kant concedes that the categories as "pure forms of thought" (*blosse Gedankenformen*) cannot in their universality apply directly to the sensuous manifold (*Gegenstände der Sinne*).[58] The "figurative synthesis" (*Synthesis speziosa, figürlich*), which organizes according to his view the unity of apperception, needs a faculty to mediate between sensuality and intellect. But this is more than a bridge between transcendental aesthetics and transcendental analytics: its role is not to be a structural link but an *operational function* allowing for continuity in the structurizing progress. That is, the role of imagination extends from the "impressional" level of the receiving manifold of the senses due to its capacity for being affected, through the "positing" of the received in forms of time and space (sensuous forms), toward their establishment in the final objective forms of givenness with reference to the categories.

This dynamic role of imagination beneath the network of the structurizing activity of sensibility and intellect — which conducts their operations — is found already in the most concrete empirical dimension and runs through the transcendental one. To be precise: the first datum that is *empirically* given, as Kant sees it, is "appearance" (*Erscheinung*), which if "conscious" is called "perception" (*Wahrnehmung*). But "appearance" is a compound of a manifold of elements and the "content" of "perception" is chaotic and disconnected. (What Kant, viewing the perceptual process "all at once" considers the "manifold of elements," corresponds to what Husserl, viewing perception as the genetic temporal spread, sees as "individual glimpses" (*Abschattungen*), each of them contributing to the constitution of the object of perception, but none containing it on its own.) Left at this empirical level, experience would not amount to the constitution of an organized *life-world*. To have the possible organization of the manifold in one and the same appearance and then the interconnection of disconnected empirical perceptual glimpses, which otherwise cannot coalesce in a full-fledged perception "positing" an object, we need a synthesizing organization of this manifold. This is the first function attributed to imagination; it is meant to bring the manifold of perceptual glimpses into one "picture" (*Bild*). But since the individual elements of the manifold appear without an evident coalescing principle — being a haphazard and heterogeneous variety — a basis for their synthesis has to be established. That is, imagination has, first of all, to bring about such a common denominator in order that her own activity, that of establishing the unity of a "picture," may be accomplished. According to Kant, this happens in a twofold way. First, imagination "reproduces" for her own purpose each of the heteroclitic elements so that all of them together are reflected in one modality, namely that of "apprehension"; second, by "association" it effects the organization of these empirical representations.[59]

And yet, associative synthesis of the empirical alone is not enough for the structural construction of the perceptual object; it introduces merely random, accidental connections, whereas a universally valid combination of elements is required, such that the universal objectivity of the consistent world-order can come about. At this point the "unity of apperception" of all possible acts within the ego-pole provide Kant with the ground necessary for a most universal "homogeneity" (*Affinität*) of all the disparate empirical elements: they are brought to a common denominator as acts of the same I and can be discriminated among themselves. Without the reference of all acts to the "pure I" as a qualitatively undifferentiated, empty, and abstract pole of reference in apperception, one ever-perduring within the stream of appearances, no unity of consciousness as such would be possible. These two principles of unity, the *ego*-pole and imagination conjoined, form the axis of the conscious apparatus: the one bringing about the unity of consciousness in all its heteroclitic operations and acts, the other — being already the concrete vehicle of constitution — establishing the compossibility of the basic constitutive material and the synthesis of the singular fragments as input into the structure of the complete objective unit.

Yet the question arises, by which principles can imagination, which in itself is "blind," *that is, deprived of a discriminatory apparatus*, be a factor of associative discrimination? With respect to what principles are the dissociative features left out and the associative links brought together? If the *dynamis* of imagination were a totally "free" flux — that is, unrestricted by directions, prototypes, a regulative framework of reference —, even the empirical synthesis would be nothing but a product of chance and maybe we would have to remain at the level of Bergson's view of the spontaneous, that it is a whimsical unfolding of Nature's creative *élan*. Yet Bergson, in addressing the human world, introduces into this boundless whimsical flux the differentiating activity of the human intellect. And so Kant cannot remain at the level of appearances and assume that without an *a priori* of reason the cognitive-constitutive process could stop at the level of appearances — which in reality is nothing but an abstracted phase of a cognitive cycle incapable of standing on its own. In order that appearances be brought up to the level of being posited as constitutive of an object — that is tantamount, in Kant's terminology, to the level of "cognition" — they have to be made "intelligible."

Their structural differentiation and composition already being prepared at the level of the synthetic unity of apprehensions is again effected by imagination, not as a "free" agent, but with reference to the categories. That is, the constitution of a unified object of perception out of the fragmentary, chaotic, and diverging instances of the appearances, is accomplished in the work of imagination by "reproducing" them in the homogeneous shape of "apprehensions," and then, by discriminating among them and synthesizing them according to the *a priori* principles and structural regulations of the categories. How does imagination apply universal categories to singular apprehensions of appearances? Or, in other terms, how does the singular element enter into a composition, the pattern of which Kant — unlike Husserl who sees therein an autonomous "essence" — seems to identify with the concept. Moreover, on this analysis there is a need to orient the selective process of the constitution of the object appropriately in order that the *a priori* rules of the intellect (*Verstand*) become applicable. Let us recall that Kant makes appeal to a special faculty, transcendental "*Urteilskraft*" in order to "distinguish whether something falls under a given rule (*casus datae legis*) or not."[60] The power of judgment (*Urteilskraft*) is meant to make the rules of categories applicable (*subsumieren*) to the concrete. To this effect, Kant sees the necessity of a qualitative identity of the content in the objective "representation" of the concept, since the concepts vary considerably from the empirical (sensuous in general) apprehensions of appearances. The *tertium quid* that is, on the one side, homogeneous (*gleichartig*) with the categories and, on the other side, with the appearance — this "representation" (*Vorstellung*) which is purified of the empirical and is yet, both intellectual and sensuous (*sinnlich*), and is called "the transcendental *schema*"[61] — is the product of imagination. As, at the empirical level, imagination performs the role of producing out of the synthesis of the "impressional" manifold a unified "picture," so the *schemata* of the sensuous (*sinnlich*) concepts — being pure synthesis according to the unity rules of concepts in general, which are set by the category and allow the possibility of constituting objects at all — are the work of imagination at the *transcendental level.*[62] The role of imagination in supplying the *schemata* for the work of the intellect is not only the primordial condition for the whole cognitive-constitutive system as Kant sees it, but Kant himself is compelled, first, to introduce the notion of the soul so far left in the background, and second, to refer to the reality of "Nature" which lies below the level of the cognitive-constitutive correlate: "the island" of the transcendental apparatus of cognition, "the uncharted sea" of things in themselves below the transcendental system. He states that imagination is an art hidden in the depths of the human soul and that its real workings would ever remain difficult for us to wring from nature.

Recapitulating our critical inquiry: imagination in Kant's perspective is "productive" at the cognitive-constitutive level, but in a restrictive sense. It "produces" the intermediary link for the structural operations; however, it does not introduce anything *new* to the given. Although imagination is the primary agent of the givenness, its role consists merely in allowing what is received to become formed according to the *a priori* regulations of the mind. Like Kant, Husserl uses imagination to solve the problem of perception. This is, in his view, the primary role of imagination, *to provide the genetic passage from dispersed, concrete, singular "impressions" on the level of the manifold of "apprehensions" to the establishment of their coalescence in a coherent series under the auspices of a universal pattern in which they form together one identical objective structure.* It has in essence a larger role to play, but in the Husserlian scheme of analysis it has no productive "freedom" other than the "free play" of variation. Its origin, "freedom" as an undetermined and undifferentiated "blind force," is caught in its productive operations between the received nature of the "appearances" and the categories.

Nevertheless, and it is noteworthy and should be kept in mind that, first, this operating *dynamis* crucial to the work of the transcendental apparatus might well be harnessed and led by it, but it stems from and dwells in otherwise neglected dimensions of the soul, in both the well of empeiria and its dynamic condition. Secondly, it is the notion of imagination that compels Kant to break through the "secondary" concept of "nature," as constituted within the transcendental system, to the notion of "Nature" as the primeval ground *which seems to be represented in man, as the dimension of the elemental empeiria of the soul.*[63]

It is to imagination as this *elemental* power of *Nature* in the human soul that Kant returns to again to account for novelty and originality in works of art, which he acknowledges in their full significance to be unique and the integral elements of the human world. However, in Kant's approach, acknowledgement of the extraordinary status of the work of art within the *life-world* precludes the possibility that the cognitive-constitutive apparatus could bring it about; inversely, according to Kant, artistic achievement does not yield cognition. Consequently, accounting for artistic creation calls for a further division of the faculties of man's functioning as its specific agency.

In fact, Kant strives to find such a specific way that could account for creativity, one divorced from the routine constitution of the standard world. Having already sketched the issues involved within the general outline of his constitutive system, this background will serve to recall to us the main features of his views on creativity. In fact, in opposition to the object-positing function of cognition, Kant differentiates among all the virtualities of the soul (*Seele, Gemüt*): *the capacity of desire* (*Begehrungsvermögen*) motivating the will and, finally, the *feeling of pleasure and displeasure* (*Lust* and *Unlust*) — *this last positing no object*, but expressing the subjective condition of man. While the capacity for cognition is served by the faculty of intellect and that of desire by will, the feeling of pleasure and displeasure is served by judgment.[64] In point of fact, while intellect and reason apply their representations to objects, the faculty of judgment does not bring about concepts of objects but is oriented solely toward the *subject himself*. Furthermore, while intellect and reason contain an *objective* relation between representations and corresponding objects, the feelings of pleasure and displeasure merely receive the state of determination of the subject.[65] The specific domain of the faculty of judgment lies in its strictly purposeful and subjective orientation which neither constitutes nor reflects an object, but indicates — as does the *aesthetic reflective* judgment — the relation of a representation to the feeling of pleasure or displeasure.[66] With this, a foundation for approaching the creative activity is laid down.

Firstly, for Kant, as we know, human creativity is purposefully oriented by its reference to the faculty of judgment, and that of a particular kind, the judgment of taste; that is, in order to break with the routine and iron logic of transcendental constitution, we have to refer to a set-up of faculties that is extraneous to it, "extra-routine," extraordinary. In its orientation as well as in its source, artistic creativity is brought back to the specifically *subjective resources of the human individual.* The universal "schematism" of the cognitive apparatus is superseded by the uniqueness of the endowment of an exceptional individual: the *Genius.* Considering exclusively the works of great art as works of creativity in explaining their *uniqueness, originality, exemplariness,* Kant refers *directly* to the role of imagination. Of course, he establishes several points of rapport between the judgment of taste and the cognitive faculty, in order to account for the *objective* side of the work of art as part of the *intersubjective* world. The main ones of these seem to be: first, the reference of the judgment of taste, which is the criterion of appreciation and discrimination within the process of art, to concepts of objects, but exclusively with respect to the feeling of pleasure and displeasure. Second, in spite of the uniqueness and unrepeatability of both the work of creativity and that of the creating subject, there is granted by Kant a universality of *subjective conditions* of judgment — which accounts for the universal validity of the pleasure and displeasure we take in the representations of an object. Both of these points mean that there are sets of universal *objective* directions for discrimination within the creative progress with respect to the balance between the subjective and objective conditions a work of art has to fulfill in order to be "original" in the world but not altogether strange to it. Third, Kant attributes to the judgment of taste *a priori* roots in consciousness of the formal purposefulness present in the play of the cognitive powers.[67] Most interesting of all, he even considers the possibility of purely subjective judgments of objects at the pre-constitutive level — at which the cognitive faculties are not yet orchestrated into the transcendental apparatus but remain in "free play" — which appear not as cognition, but which relate to representations without concepts and which are the point of connection between the respective working systems of cognition and creativity.[68] This seemingly extensive relation to the cognitive system may lure us into believing that, for Kant, the cognitive apparatus is concretely involved in the process of creation. Indeed, we may at first, following Gadamer, assume that, although "free from the constraints" of the cognitive *schematism*, creativity has, even at the pre-constitutive level, all the powers of man available to work with.[69] However, then the crucial question occurs: "Where does it get its rules and regulation from?"

The conception of the Genius is meant by Kant to be the answer to this question. Indeed, each constructive act presupposes rules which would guarantee the possibility of its product. The very conception that the Fine Arts are dependent upon judgment might well lead toward its freedom from the automatism of *cognitive routine*. But did Kant's subjective approach lead in the direction of discovering for creativity a different operational system by which to establish itself?

In this respect there is an ambiguity in Kant's conception of genius as the answer to both the question of the source of originality and that of the rules followed in creation. Kant tells us that "Genius" means a "taste." Ultimately, what does the talent of the Genius consist in if not of a special "creative" role of imagination? Imagination is the factor of originality on its own; instead of entering into the *schematism* of pure reason, it surges within the subject "free" of the constraints of the constitutive system and its mechanisms, as the powerful stream of *Elemental Nature* having the intellect (*Verstand*) as its sole partner and as its sole regulative instance for bringing the forces of the soul into effervescence; wakening them to a new life and releasing their spontaneities, imagination becomes "*belebendes Prinzip im Gemüt*."[70] Thus the making of the genius consists of these two forces which supposedly do not restrict each other, but are in "free concordance":

in der freien Übereinstimmung der Einbildungskraft zur Gesetzlichkeit des Verstandes eine solche Proposition und Stimmung dieser Vermögen voraussetze, als keine Befolgung von Regeln, es sei der Wissenschaft oder mechanischen Nachahmung, bewirken, sondern bloss die Natur des Subjeckts hervorbringen kann.[71]

We may then, first, with Gadamer, see the creative role of imagination that at last comes into its own, in its power to awake in all the potentialities of the creating subject — which is certainly the case and a prerequisite of the creative process.[72] Nevertheless, the extremely intricate deliberation and discriminating progress which is necessary in the creative endeavor to establish the criteria for novelty with respect to the already given, remains unexplained by imagination so understood. Both imagination and taste, as the sole promoters of the creative work, cannot, being strictly subjectively oriented — that is, divorced from the inner workings of the cognitive-constitutive structuration — account for the necessary constructive mechanisms. The "radical" freedom of imagination from its origin and the lack or relative constraint on the part of the cognitive apparatus means also a *privation of means for exercising the function of deliberation and selection.* A set of functions performing these operations is indispensable for establishing a balance between the old and the new, the unprecedented and the altogether strange. It seems that in "creative" freedom there is a certain framework within which these opposites take their meaning and that "radical" freedom is inoperative, irrelevant. Moreover, with Kant's emphasis upon the exemplariness and novelty of the work of human creation, we have a strongest possible affirmation of the *positional* status of its content, without which art as the product of imagination would remain, as in Husserl, a mere reflection of cognition. Within the framework of our own analysis the creative work, in order to challenge the constitutive set-up by its *positional* originality, has to be established in the *mode of self-givenness.* How could imagination as a constructively undifferentiated agency operate the self-given positionality of its product? To be "free" already means reference to a "what" and it seems, as we have already attempted to show in our own analysis, that in reality the *creative process works within the framework of the constituted and it is with respect to this world that the balance between the old and the new may be estimated anew in each work of creation.* Thus, could imagination as an objectively independent faculty effect this without availing itself of the mechanisms of the constitutive function? It seems that it could emerge, operative, in "creative freedom" only from a *special integration of all the functions, that she would galvanize in order to draw from the operations of their novel configuration an original invention.* Finally, Kant claims that originality and novelty stem from Nature "itself," of which imagination and taste are only the promulgating agents, each appearing so "free from any constraint as if it were the product of Nature alone." How could, however, *elemental Nature,* with its merely incalculable virtualities and dynamic powers, account for originality, which as we have tried to specify is the outcome of differentiation?

Although given their rightful place, both the elemental realm of the soul and the freedom of imagination, as understood by Kant, seem to lack the capacity for fulfilling the task he attributes to them.

SECTION 4. "IMAGINATIO CREATRIX" AND THE FUNCTIONAL ORCHESTRATION WITHIN THE CREATIVE CONTEXT: THE REGULATIVE CHOICE IN THE "CREATIVE" VERSUS THE "A PRIORI" OF IDEAS IN THE "CONSTITUTIVE" FUNCTION

As we have attempted to show, Kant's conception of imagination as an independent faculty could not fulfill the role which Kant has recognized as imagination's own, that is, it cannot account for the work of human creativity's break with the standard progress of the constituted world. Meanwhile, Husserl does not seem to have even risen to the occasion. Nevertheless, we believe we have, with the help of their succinct appreciation and criticism, sketched the network of the issues with reference to which we might now outline our proposed new approach which already has been prepared by the conception of the *creative orchestration of human functions within the creative context.*

Thus, unlike Husserl's "free play of imagination," which is subservient to the constitutive system and follows its structurizing principle of *a priori* ideas, or Sartre's conception of imagination as a completely independent specific faculty following its own whims, neither definable nor explained, we find *imaginatio creatrix* to be the decisive factor within the *creative context.* If it is in a position to assure novelty in the creative process, it is not as a participant in the system of passive genesis, or even in transcendental constitution in its full extent, but as an agent which emerges with a *specific orchestration of functions* which brings together the mechanisms and forces of the constitutive apparatus with those of the complex realm of the passions. Husserl and Kant cast this latter into the background as belonging to the realm of the soul, as irrational, inaccessible to sovereign reason, and once they rejected it, they could not reintegrate it and give it its proper role.

There, at the point of interplay between ideas and feeling, intellectual intuitions and affective responses, from their point of fusion along unforeseeable lines emerge new, barely outlined or alluded to, qualities of feeling and profiles of forms which, in turn, by intermingling in a vast range of ever-varying elements in the process of deliberation that goes on and on without ceasing, generate in profusion ever-new and ephemeral qualities of feelings and emotions in the whole range of their modalities and fragments, profiles of forms, shapes and interrelations which do not vanish without having generated others still. Both quality and form are so intimately fused into an experiential unit that a distinction is hardly possible. Several observations can be made. First, their *generative* power which goes in all directions through associative references to the already established — although sclerosed and emptied of the fresh pulp of reality — becomes the reservoir upon which the creative function in its quest and deliberation draws. Second, they do not appear in the usual mode of constitutive experience, with *factual* givenness corralled rationally into a definite objective *datum*, but are chaotic and incomplete, elusive and fluctuating as they surge with *suggestive* power and propose themselves straight to such or other structurizing problem. Third, their appearance may be barely suggestive but is *effusive* and *dynamic*, that is, it awakens the exploratory urge to venture into indefinite novel channels to seek even more than they may concretely offer. Thereby this dynamic game between the realm of impulse, and that of the rational and affective intuition *distills a force* which both poses problems to our quest and invigorates the will to seek an answer. A novel alliance with new intertwinings emerges in the form of a new relational pattern among the types of operations, opening a new dimension of qualitative molds for sensations, emotions, feelings ... an infinitely advancing self-generating system ... with a new suggestive, allusive, evocative *force* ... an *invigorating will*, a prompting spirit ... *Imaginatio Creatrix*.

Imagination appears to mediate between two producing levels, that of the generative forces of passions and that of the scrutinizing and selecting power of reason. It may thus seem that our analysis gives support to Kant's view of the mediating role of imagination. However, he saw it residing in cognition, especially perception, whereas we find it in a strikingly different function: *the creative function*. The role which Kant attributes to imagination in artistic creation is, as we have shown, one different from the role it plays in our view. To perform the role we have just described, it must participate in the operations of both the passions and reason. Its very own, distinctively unique mode of operation consists in the *suggestive, evocative* and *invigorating mode of presenting to the deliberating agency of the creative function* previously distinguished elements, thus lifting them out of the flow of experience — in which they would otherwise vanish with the passing stream — to the level of self-presentation. These acts of selection *generate new allusive qualities and forms*. Furthermore, being brought into the spectrum of the already present reservoir of the possible, they inter-generate, and with each incoming series, the range of diversified possibilities of choice expands, ever-renewing itself.

Thus imagination can emerge in this distinctive creative way only with the *creative context* on the basis of its complete set-up. It operates within the *creative orchestration* as the chief mediator which at all levels bridges and brings into cooperation the virtualities of reason and those of the passions. It advances without deciding anything — it merely serves the deliberating agency of the *creative function*. However, in its mediating role, imagination draws conclusions from the progress of the creative process, prompting it incessantly with new suggestions which this progress itself indicates. It is neither a routine agency of constitution as in Husserl, nor an elemental faculty, *Einbildungskraft*, through which Nature prescribes laws to inert genius, as in Kant; nor is it an independent transcendental faculty aloof from reality and from the constitutive genesis, as in Sartre; it is a result and integral factor of *a novel orchestration of man's functioning*.

Indeed, if the *creative function* can perform its role of introducing novelty and originality into the constituted world — which would otherwise go on its routine way toward its prompt extinction since, after having reached all the permutations and combinations the unfolding of its first outlined types would allow, it could not renew them and thus would be condemned to use up all its resources and come to an end — it is due, *first*, to its giving absolute preeminence to *will* and choice, and *second*, to the role of imagination in freeing it from the preestablished, constitutive *a priori* structure of regulations.

We thus reach a question of *capital metaphysical scope*: "What are the ultimate structurizing principles which the *creative function* follows in its operations in selecting the elements of construction and the molding for the concretization of an object?"

As we have shown in our previous work, the constitutive genesis in its process refers for its continuity as well as for a point of reference for identifying and structurizing its intentional object, to ideas. We have also argued that ideas are not an integral part of the constitutive system, but must be *transcendent* to it as *a priori* principles: a framework of reference for the structurizing function of constitution.[73] Could we, in fact, without having such unchangeable, unavoidable, universal regulative principles for the establishment of the life-promoting organization maintain the continuity of life and the homogeneous universe?

However, by the same stroke, this introduction of the automatized routine of generating forms would preclude any *deviation from the type* that each idea prescribes as the range for structurizing diversification and individualization.

How unlike, this is, as we have seen, the *creative function* which remedies and complements and is not an agent of passive and inborn routine but of will and deliberation *par excellence*. Its aim is not to serve the purposes of life; to the contrary, it emerges as an act of defiance against all that acts unquestioningly and automatically. We have attempted to show how the new orchestration of the creative function mobilizes, as Kant already saw, all the modes of operations and faculties at all functional levels and frees them from preestablished routine as well as from its regulations. Furthermore, we have seen how from the new scheme of interplay between elemental functions and reason novel unforeseeable and unpredictable structurizing elements spontaneously generate in profusion, and further, how the *creative imagination* in mediating between the self-germinating qualities and forms and the selective agency of the creative function, proposes ever new structural elements, suggesting their possible ramifications, sequences, and associations. In this way the *creative imagination* accomplishes an additional task still: within the set-up of searching and selective deliberation it proposes novel avenues and, adjusting to decisions already made, indicates their far-reaching consequences, offering simultaneously alternate solutions. In this way the structurizing agency in its decisions is neither bound by any preestablished *a priori* delineating structural regulations or principles, nor is it left to the whims of the deliberating agent. The decision of the agent is, in fact, itself an outcome of a long and impenetrably complex process involving the whole progress of invention, molding and structuration; it is guided by the possibilities generated from the interplay of passions and reason as well as by its own progress. Ultimately it refers to the abysmal wealth of the *Logos* and the *Eros* of life which, as we know, cannot accept any constraint on their freedom and whose choices cannot be rationally accounted for.

To conclude let us suggest that the great question of Leibniz as to *whether our world is the only one possible*, which is in classic and current phenomenology answered emphatically in the affirmative, might be reopened now that we have demonstrated that man is *plurifunctional — the constitutive function being just one of our configurations and the creative function being another*, and, being re-opened, it may receive a new answer.

CHAPTER FOUR

THE HUMAN PERSON AS THE ALL-EMBRACING
FUNCTIONAL COMPLEX

AND

THE TRANSMUTATION CENTER OF THE LOGOS
OF LIFE

THE NOTION OF THE "HUMAN PERSON" AT THE CROSSROADS OF THE UNDERSTANDING OF MAN WITHIN THE LIFE-WORLD PROCESS

INTRODUCTION: THE NOTION OF "PERSON" AS THE POINT OF REFERENCE FOR THE UNDERSTANDING OF MAN WITHIN HIS LIFE-CONDITIONS

In contemporary thought the notion of the "human person" plays the role of a point of reference for understanding the human being. The human being is in our times viewed in concrete terms, that is, not as an abstract model of an entity, but as a living individual struggling for survival with organic life-conditions on the one hand, and world-conditions on the other. Concreteness and flexibility in the notion of the "human person" appear to be most appropriate for the accounting of various features of the human individual, which are approached from different perspectives. Fundamentally, this means: first, to grasp and indicate the distinctiveness of the human being with respect to other living individuals and things, and the modalities of organic and social life; second, to appreciate man's conduct, aims, and rights with respect to the perspectives of his innermost nature. I would venture to say that, in general, too much stress is placed upon the unique accomplishments of the human being and not enough upon his role among other living beings, which this uniqueness compels him to play. That is, in articulating the notion of the "person," we seek to establish a new *meaningfulness* (understanding) *of the specificity of the human being with respect to his organic conditions as well as to conditions which the world within which be delineates his life-course sets for that course.* In our times, in which little is taken for granted, we seek for an ever more adequate understanding of the world and of our place in it. Significantly, we have come to discover that not only the "brute" organic/cosmic/vital facts have no "meaning" unless we ourselves as sentient beings turn them into the conditions of our existence, but also that we might even transform these conditions by our own inventiveness. Therein lies the greatness and the peril of our age.

To establish the significance of the human being within his *vital* conditions, within nature and his lived world, the notion of person is instrumental from various perspectives. First, it appears at the center of the investigations conducted by human science (psychiatry, psychology, social science, etc.).[74] Second, it serves as a center of gravitation in the public debates on cultural, social, and political matters. Third, it remains a crucial notion in personal and religious practices. Although it is conceived in a great number of ways, and in terms of various approaches, in all of them one of the following three functions is attributed to it.

First, the person always appears as a system of organization (or articulation) of the functioning of the living individual within his life-conditions. Second, it is taken as a pattern centralizing the fundamental faculties and virtualities operative in the individual's life-progress. Third, the notion of the "person" expresses through its structure and virtualities a specific phase of the individual's developmental achievement. The epitome of this third model, which includes the other two, is, or culminates in, man's self-conscious functioning. It pinpoints the specifically socio-political significance of life.[75]

(a) *The first two basic models for the conception of the person*

We can say that the *first function* which the notion of the person serves is basic to psychiatry. Introduced into psychiatry by Freud and Jung, the person plays an increasingly central role in diagnosis and therapy.[76] It is intuited as a specific functional pattern by means of which the human being organizes his vital operations at the level of the life-world. Starting with organic processes, the individual unfolds a network of processes relating him to his circumambient world, by means of which, beyond strictly organic growth and subsistence, he projects around him a spatio-temporal dimension. Within this network he himself acquires a meaning as a living being and his circumambient conditions acquire the meaning of a "life-world." This projection by the living individual of intraworldly relations with other living beings, things, events, and processes, endows them with a significance that reaches beyond that of the brute organic survival that is attributed to a *specific functional system*: the "person" (Binswanger).[77] Through his interrelations with other living beings, persons, events, and processes, the individual and his life-world are simultaneously sustained in existence, grow, and expand. Mental illness is here viewed as the dissipation of this functional system: the person — the central functional pattern of intraworldly relations — is disturbed; its functional ties disintegrate (Henri Ey).[78] With any degree of disintegration of the person some corresponding dimension of the life-world loses its significance. The mentally ill person becomes "confused" or "disturbed" but does not leave this world; the physical and social world "is there" for the others as it was before. Yet for the mentally ill it is reduced to its bare physicality. The significance of intraworldly relationships, which previously sustained the person within this world, now vanishes.

The specific role of the person in giving meaning to the world within which the human individual pursues his existence is equally obvious in the *second type* of role attributed to the person. Indeed, from a socio-cultural perspective we attribute to the person a set of faculties, which accounts not only for the organic existence of the human individual but also for his socio-cultural forms. These are organized in a coherent pattern comprising constant, as well as variable, features. Intelligence, imagination, will, are the faculties which all human individuals are assumed to possess. They are the constants, yet the industry with which individuals use them and their capacity to apply them to different circumstances, their adaptability to life-conditions, etc., seems to account for the vast variety of cultural and social differentiations which distinguish humanity as such. Moreover, the various "gifts," "talents," "virtual propensities," etc., which belong to this pattern, are distributed unequally, and in their respective development they account for the uniquely different "personalities" of individual human beings. The meaningfulness of life which, as a result of human creativity, inventiveness, etc., takes different cultural forms — as well as different forms of interpersonal and social relations — is the result of the person so understood.

We see, then, that process-like views of the world (and of the step-wise unfolding of life) attribute to the notion of the person those functions that allow the individual to establish and pursue a coherent, meaningful existence within the flux of changing conditions.

(b) *The third model of the person as a subject/agent within the social world*

The radical shift from the assumption of man's stable situation in the cosmos maintained in antiquity and the Middle Ages, to the fluctuations in his role which he today develops for himself within the social world (an approach that began with modern philosophy and finds its culmination in present-day thought), motivates the third model of the conception of person. In fact, when it comes to the issue of public life we find that philosophy, social science, political thinking, etc., almost unanimously refer to the person as a *relatively stable system of self-conscious manifestation*: an "agent" from whom initiatives and their realization within the social world stem; as the "subject," who is the direct or indirect recipient, victim, beneficiary, etc., of these actions. Seen simultaneously as agent and subject, the person is the cornerstone of public life: the bearer of responsibility toward others as well as of individual rights. Whether it be responsibility or rights in the private, legislative, judicial, political, or religious sectors, in all of them it is assumed that these are responsibilities or rights of the human person.

Both as the agent and as the subject, the person is assumed to be a concrete, fully developed, and self-conscious being.[79] "Self-consciousness" means, in the first place, *the capacity to relate the significance of circumambient conditions to one's own vital needs*. Second, it means to endow one's vital course with the specific meaningfulness of existence. Third and foremost, it means *the capacity to rise above the concrete acts of achieving one's vital development toward the principles, evaluation, and planning of those acts, and to invent new means and ways to advance that development*. In this sense we speak of the person's "transcending" man's biological, social, and political conditions: as a self-conscious agent the person may encompass their singular, concrete significance, and accept or reject it — or, invent and propose a new one. It is the conception of the person as the actor within the social world that gives rise to the enigmatic question: To what degree does man share his life-course and his life-world, and to what degree is he shaped by them? The stand on this matter inspires different formulations of the notion of the "person."[80]

The three abstract models of the person distinguished above are operative in the conception of the person as an agent/subject. We cannot fail to see that the realities all three of them embody fulfill this special task in man's functioning as a living being. Contemporary philosophy unanimously agrees that the specifically human feature is to be able to establish the web of meaningfulness accounting for the self-conscious entity of man, as well as for the meaningfulness of others and of the common life-world. However, in the appreciation of the faculties of man which enter into his meaning-bestowing, priority has so far been given to the intellect. To the work of the intellect alone is attributed not only the orchestration of all other faculties and the establishment through an intentional network of consciousness of the objectivity of life and world existence (Husserl, Max Scheler), but to intellect is also attributed the highest adjudicating role.

It needed a radical turn of direction in phenomenology — from intentional consciousness to the *creative orchestration of human functioning* — in order that the complete meaning-bestowing apparatus of the human being could come to light. It is the human person that is simultaneously the effect and the agent, the embodiment, of this apparatus. In point of fact, all the previously differentiated functional complexes as well as faculties of the creative orchestration and, lastly, their resources, etc., are brought together and bound within the system of the person. However, approached not as it is in the traditional and still current usage through some or other perspective but through the very center whence its functional proficiencies intergenerate and, being bound in their unique ways, radiate from the *synergetic* core of the creative orchestration, we may at last reach the full view of the Human Person. This is not one that is severed from its primogenital ties with the arteries of all life, as the usual focus upon its autonomy has makes us believing. To the contrary, this full view is revealed by making an analogy to the organism, through which all of life's virtual substances pass being processed in specific ways for the sake of the "composition" of a higher "style" of significance of life's constructive advance, for the human person is the "processor" of all the modes of life's forces, forms, energetic complexes, etc. which in a constant influx come with their synergetic virtualities and pass through its intergenerative schemas acquiring in them a frame of new meaningfulness. This latter surges amid and from the all-embracing human significance of life, and yet it expresses all of the forces and predispositions of nature by which it is informed. Thus the human person is at the heart of the meaningfulness of life at large. This needed to be brought to light.

Although it is also universally accepted among contemporary philosophers of various persuasions that it is the *ethical significance* of actions and reactions, feelings and reactions, feelings and decisions, which marks the unique threshold between the vital meaningfulness of life and the specifically human, cultural significance of life, yet this ethical turn in man's self-interpretation is also attributed, in the final analysis, to his rational faculties.[81] The role of the aesthetic factor in life is equally hailed, and yet it is in general only superficially or secondarily treated when the nature of the person is considered: its essentially constitutive role is ignored. In the introductory remarks I have denounced the abuses of reason; this denunciation makes the understanding of the human being an open question.

In light of the foregoing analysis of the notion of the person in use in contemporary thought, the question about the specifically human feature of the living individual boils down to this: What is the origin of the significance which marks a turning point in human development? This passage is indicated by the passage from the *vital meaningfulness* of circumambient conditions to the *socio-cultural* one. But what the specific sense-factor that brings it about is, has to be clarified. We have also to ask how does this "sense" originate?[82] Within our perspective, in which the creative orchestration of human functioning is the framework, this question addresses the specific way or ways in which this factor of sense, virtual in the human condition, becomes operative in man's self-interpretation-in-existence. In my attempt to answer this question I will challenge the sovereignty of reason in three respects. First, I will propose that the decisive factor in the specifically human significance of life is not the intellect, but the primogenital *Aesthetic* and *Moral Senses*. Second, while the vital, social and cultural world draws essentially upon the moral sense, the essential feature of the human individual — his *humanness* — does not reside in his highest rational self-consciousness, but in his *conscious sharing in the universal life-conditions*. This sharing, in fact, is the very *life of consciousness; as a mode of life, it takes its multiple relevance* from the *poetic sense*. Third, this being discovered, man's role and his individual rights have to be balanced against the multiple vital interests of *all other living beings*. The human person *indeed* crystallizes the works of both the poetic and the moral sense and thereby becomes the *fulcrum* of life.

These three factors of sense which the human condition virtually contains are actualized within the creative orchestration of the individual's functioning. It is the creative orchestration which brings about the person.

SECTION 1. THE HUMAN PERSON IN HIS/HER ESSENTIAL MANIFESTATION

In the preceding discussion I have emphasized, first, the crucial role attributed in contemporary thought to the notion of the "person" and clarified the reason for this; second, I have emphasized that this role culminates in its "meaning-establishing" function; and third, I have proposed that it is the "moral meaningfulness," which the human person alone unfolds, that leads a living being to become truly human. In brief, to be "human" is to see life in moral terms.

Last, I have claimed that this moral significance stems from a unique factor. That factor — the moral sense — is, in my view, a "virtual factor" of the "Human Condition" which is decisive for human "nature." It is not a ready-made code of moral conduct to be applied in action. On the contrary, it unfolds together with the vital, psychological, intellectual, and spiritual development of the individual: an unfolding which culminates in the emergence of the person. It is within the person that the moral sense functions. It imbues the actions of the person with its quality. Through the person it spreads into the social world and life. It is my claim that the life of the spirit, which lifts the human being above our strictly human confines and nature, surges and develops as an inner stream of the moral life. Lastly, I submit that it is by means of the moral exercise that the soul spins the thread for the "radical leap," to use Kierkegaard's expression, toward the encounter with the Divine.

It is now time to give a succinct phenomenological view of the person who "embodies" the complete functional complex of the creatively orchestrated current of life, sustaining its forces, as it invents the social world and, turning its back upon Nature, weaves the thread of the "transnatural destiny of Man," aspiring thereby to enter directly into the great game of creation and redemption. That is, it is within the complex of the person that the life-differentiation of the *universal logos* into infinite modalities, as well as its divestment of them, takes place.

(a) *The phenomenology of the human person in a fourfold perspective*

When we want to give a succinct phenomenological account of the human person we have to distinguish three main perspectives. In the first place, the human being appears in its concrete "manifestation," first as an organized, stable core, marking by its substantial persistence a "place" in space and time as a *sense-giver* and a *moral agent*. It is manifested, first, in the "substantial persistence" of its "presence" within the world of life and human interaction: as the "body."[83] Second, the person manifests within the life-world the human being in his "self-identity." This self-identity is partly manifested in the role which the person assumes, namely, in maintaining an identical center from within which man's interaction with other living beings in the external life-world is consistently organized and from within which it springs forth. The person as the identical center reveals itself also through the "forces," "powers," and strivings which lurk behind this interaction and signal the existence of an invisible realm of the person which reposes in itself. Indeed, although caught in the incessant turmoil of *actio et passio* within the circumambient world, on the one hand, and within the irreversible course of an inner transformability of its own capacities, on the other, the person still remains the "same." This self-identity reveals itself indirectly through a persisting pattern of sameness in external interactions within the world of life. Through these, however, appears an equally "substantial persistence" of the person's "invisible," "inner" life of passions, emotions, feelings, drives, nostalgias, etc. In this perspective, the person appears as the *psyche*/the *soul*.

The third perspective upon man opens when, focusing upon this identical pattern of the person ascertaining itself most powerfully, although in an indirectly "visible" way, through life-participation, we witness it in its role as an "ordering factor." The human being through his cognitive and inventive powers assumes in fact the role of architect of the life-world and of the social world. Through cognitive means he projects a system of articulations into the otherwise indissociable, opaque maze of forces. He discerns and measures their intergenerative powers and calculates their effects; he plans and projects. He basically projects the meaningfulness of life.

In fact, in this perspective the person is conceived as a cognitive and inventive apparatus: mind or reason. With the faculty of the intellect at its center, a vertiginous living system of rational ordering, applied to man's individual life-course as well as to that of his circumambient milieu, springs forth. This meaningful system reposes in the scheme of consciousness which spreads over the person's entire realm and penetrates all through the rational articulations of intentional interconnectedness. Thus the person "embodies" the system of the conscious mechanism which generates the *rational meaningfulness of the life-subservient sense.*

But the question arises: Is the person a "sense-giver" of only one — the rational — sense? We have already answered this in the negative. It remains now to present the alternative.

From the above-described self-identical center of the human being made visible through the substantial persistence within the dynamics of life through which the body and the soul are present within the world, there opens up the fourth perspective in which the person — or his humanness — asserts himself within the interactions of the life-world. Indeed, the person asserts himself by the self-enactment of his life-course. Not only are all the vital operations, by means of which his physical, organic, and psychic faculties are unveiled, the very expression of the person, but their modalities, directions and aims are the person's "choice." The person acts: the person is an *agent*. Although most of the vital choices are situated within the play of conditioning forces, yet in the midst of this conditioning the *personal agent* not only deciphers the possible choices from life-situations, but he also introduces *his own distinctive sense into the evaluation of alternatives*: the *moral sense*. It is as the *moral agent* that the person stands out as being "human" within the business of life.

Let us now envisage how the body, the soul, the conscious mechanism and the moral agent manifest together the nature of the human person.

SECTION 2. THE MANIFEST PERSON

(a) *The body complex*

In approaching the human being from the standpoint of his process-like nature we may appear to go against common sense. Do we not experience the human being, whether as another man or ourselves, as a "being" that is a consistent entity, reposing in itself and "occupying" a position in space as well as centralizing the passage of temporal phases of the past and future in a presence? We experience man, indeed, as the cornerstone of life and as continuously "present" in life's flux — not only participating in it, but, as it were, challenging it by his own life-directions, devices, etc. Hence we experience ourselves and others in what has always been considered a "substantial" persistence. The person representing the human being is then accountable for the ways in which he is experienced and manifests himself in the progress of life. He is credited then with accounting for *stability of self-enactment, and "substantiality" in manifestation*. These two attributes of the person manifest themselves through the body.

In principle, we distinguish in our experience of the body (1) the body as an object (whether it be someone else's or our own body); (2) our body as experienced by ourselves: the organs in their functioning that we experience as our own, e.g., sight, hearing, etc.;[84] (3) our body as "ourselves," that is, our originary (basic) feeling of ourselves as extending through our organs (e.g., movements which we command by *our* will, and which make us an integral segment of life in acting and "suffering"). Considered as such an experienced complex of functions, our body (or the body of another experienced through the impact of his bodily manifestation) as an automatized highly complex functional system "carries" the human person; the body is the "ground" in which the person lives and through which he manifests himself. How is this intimate interweaving of the "dumb" life-mechanism of Nature with the sentient expression of the psyche to be accounted for? In fact, the body as an organism is interwoven with the vital, psychic, "substantial" system of the soul.

(b) *Mute performance versus sentient interiorizing: The "voice" of the body and its elementary vital "sense"*

Not only do scientific observation of and experimentation on the way in which our body — the human body as such — is carried on by innumerable operational circuits show how the so-called "inorganic elements" take part in our organic life-carrying mechanisms and operations, but we experience it in direct observation (e.g., medicinal treatment of our vital organs by inorganic substances, etc.). This cooperative interplay of both occurs under the aegis of the individual's life-process.

The organic processes which carry out bodily stability and sustain us as an entity (in contrast to a process which consists merely of a series of transformations), are themselves so automatized — as Bergson already emphasized — that experiencing ourselves as "our body" we remain completely oblivious to them. Only when their automatic circuits break down (e.g., through illness or bodily injury) do we become aware of their role. And yet they seem to "carry" this being of ours and to establish and maintain in existence the outward appearance of ourselves, which we call "our body." They carry also the movements of our organs which we experience as ours and under our command; which organs themselves are established and carried on by these mute processes. Each and every one of these operations is "ours." In this sense, our body is a result of each and every operation, which constitutes an integral link in the circuits of a person's life and manifestation.

In fact, the functional circuits organize the vital operations and lead them to unfold organs; these latter play the role of establishing constructive centers. They all enter fully into the enactment of the life-process of the individual.

Contrary to misleading appearances, nothing just happens to us in an "anonymous" way; each functional segment participates fully in our progress and we, as a self-individualizing living beingness, stretch in it and through it. Here it suffices to note how some of the operations we remain totally unaware of, on breaking down in efficiency, disrupt our entire functional balance; we leave off our usual unawareness of our organs and feel a pain so acutely "localized" in one single area of our vital operations that we feel our entire being to be concentrated in this one segment, hitherto ignored (e.g., a toothache). We may distinguish, however, within a vast spectrum of their differentiation, "organically significant operations" and "vitally significant acts." The first ones are "mute." Their emergence and mechanical performance is so automatized and repetitive that they do not "stand out" to make themselves "seen," "heard," etc. They raise a "voice" only when regularity breaks down and upsets the entire system Their coming together occurs on the basis of a constructive need that "need" not affirm itself, i.e., make itself known. But in contrast with this type of operations, are the *vitally significant* acts which supplement them.

The life process in its spread calls for operations which release *vitally significant* reaction/responses to circumambient conditions. The release of the responses is not rigidly repetitive and uniformly established; they surge with respect to the ever-varying elements of the flux of life from which the human being differentiates his own course.

The operations surging "in response," in reaction, to the elements of circumambient conditions, emerge from the already established organs "on behalf of which" they "respond" by signals of alarm, signs of satisfaction, calls of need, etc. Thus, the nature of these operations is more complex; we call them in general "acts." Whether we speak of the most elementary "acts" (e.g., recoiling from a life-threatening contact, as in the lowest, multi-cellular organisms), or, within our more complex being, the pulsations of joy, forcefulness, like or dislike, etc., we mean operations endowed with expressiveness, standing out, attracting our attention; that is, "voicing" a cry. With the development of its expressiveness, the voice of vital acts intensifies into a coherent unity. The field upon which this unity of expression manifests itself — its ground — is what we experience as the "body." Indeed, what we experience as the body is the unity of a life-sustaining complex which spreads in space and time. As such it is the primary manifestation of the basic identity of man. It also maintains self-sameness. In its operation, as well as in its manifestation, the body establishes and sustains the spatio-temporal continuity of the "presence" of the human being within the world.

From the "substantial" but mute manifestation of the body in space, we have, with the vocal presence of the body, proceeded to its temporal spread. However, in moving from the mute organic operations to the "vocal" physiologico-psychic acts, we have almost imperceptibly penetrated into the middle-ground territory of sensing, feeling, desiring, etc., which the body shares with the psychic, or the passional, empirical realm of the soul.[85]

(c) *The body/soul manifestation of the person*

The body is indeed neither experienced nor externally manifested as a "neutral" or inanimate "thing." Unless we see it lifeless as a corpse (which does not maintain its form in space and time), the living body is not only "animated" in the sense of reacting, moving, but above all, it is "animated" as it expresses that it is more than what it merely appears to be. "Hidden" behind its frame appears an "invisible" concentrated "agency" which feels, desires, strives, decides, etc.[86] This hidden, invisible, and yet "substantial" complex of powers and forces constitutes a forceful "inward" presence. It is manifested by the bodily acts and motions as an equally, although differently "substantial," driving force. In fact, the human person is *experienced* most prominently in its "inward" presence. Our superficial experience of the overt activeness of the individual shows us already that it is organized and oriented from a "center." We become aware of the person through the experience of some or other strikingly individual act of a living being; this overt, bodily act enables us to glimpse the inward agency from which it stems; the act in its quality manifests the inwardness of the person. The multiplicity of acts sketches the field of this inwardness. With this we are moving upon the common territory of body and psyche.

To psyche, however, belongs also the "intimate" dominion of the soul, which constitutes the nature of this inwardness. We have now to describe the soul itself in its essential nature.

(d) *The essential nature of the soul*

Let us now consider the essential nature of the soul as it manifests itself.[87] Edmund Husserl, the founder of phenomenology, has explored in unparalleled depth the pre-eminent significance of the spirit in human life. He has also emphasized the crucial role of the soul in the mediation between the body complex and the spirit. There are in his thought three different functional realms that are interwoven but distinctive: the body, the soul and the spirit. At the borderline of the bodily functions emerge those of the soul, while at the borderline of the functions of the soul emerge those of the spirit. This diffusion of all three of them as if along one continuous axis occurs because Husserl (and later phenomenologists, e.g., Scheler) place themselves on one, single plane: that of the intellect and its ordering function. Although I fully recognize the indispensable role of the cognitive/constitutive apparatus (consciousness with its faculties), still I approach these functional complexes (including the rational apparatus) from a more fundamental point of view than that of rational ordering; namely, from the point of view of their role with respect to *man's unfolding from within the Human Condition*.[88] Only in its perspective may the nature of the soul appear in its fullness.

In agreement with Husserl, I see the soul, first, as the passional ground of forces nourishing the bodily mechanisms; second, as the center of the self-identity of the individual. I agree with Husserl, that the crucial role of the soul lies in being the middle ground between the body in its vital and passional (passions and strivings) resources and the spirit. Yet, I part radically with him. Although this natural, empirical wealth of the soul makes it the middle ground of the human make-up, its nature, its resources and its role have to be interpreted differently. Although Husserl is right in seeing in the soul the ground of the spirit, yet in contrast to his view, it is not at the *borderline* of the soul that the spirit originates; rather, it surges from its *center*.

(1) The soul gathers into itself, like into an experiential receptacle, all the life-operations of the living body, the organism; from the soul, as

from a center, spring the prompting forces and powers that galvanize the entire living psyche. In this fashion, the soul is the "substantial ground" of powers. Concretized in these powers, the soul reposes in itself; however, the soul is not — as Leibniz, Husserl, Ingarden, and others after them, thought — self-enclosed by its substantial content, like the Leibnizian "monad," which had "no windows" or "doors."

(2) On the contrary, just as the body is open to the influx of externally conditioned energies and substances, so the soul is open to stirrings, nostalgias, strivings, longings, revelations, which do not belong to its natural ground; they stem from the abysmal realms of pre-life-conditions. They do not remain encapsulated within the soul or merely pass through it. In fact, they galvanize and stir the most essential resources of the soul; through them they ignite the entire apparatus of man's functioning which is oriented rationally for the sole sake of survival — for the propagation of the designs of our animal nature — but is by their influence prompted to enter the workings of nature itself and to invent new avenues of life. This inventive work leads to the specifically human meaningfulness of life.

Indeed, it is through the crevasses of the otherwise opaque passional ground of the soul that there enters the "initial spontaneity" that has originated life as such, with all its resources.[89]

(3) It is with the Initial Spontaneity that there enter into the code of the natural life of the individual — its *entelechial* code of natural un-folding (to be rationally "deciphered") — the "virtualities of the Human Condition," of which the most significant for making life "human" — for endowing it with a "human significance" — is the *Moral Sense*.[90]

(4) The soul is the battlefield upon which, in the turmoil of life-energies and the influxes of the Initial Spontaneity, the Human Condition concretizes itself within an individual, concrete, living human being. Beyond that, the soul provides the ground and the field for an extraordinary, "extranatural" turn within the unfolding of the human condition: the turn toward the birth of the personal spirit.[91]

In fact, as I have attempted to show elsewhere, the life of the spirit, that is, of grace, is not offered ready-made, floating within the human cultural realm ready to be taught, absorbed, and participated in. On the contrary, as mystics have shown in their autobiographies, in order that it may emerge within a human psyche a tortuous and long road of a concrete, personal transformation is necessary.[92] This transformation occurs within the empirical soul as the response to its nostalgia, longings, stirrings, etc. prompting it to seek ways and means in order to surpass the aims of life. Furthermore, it is an outcome of a specific concentration of all the powers of the soul which occurs by its becoming progressively "disabused" of the natural life-values and of the "business" of life. The powers of the psyche/soul, so far engaged in the business of life, now turn back upon life's aims and their validity. There is initiated a *quest* oriented by the moral sense in which the soul calls for a "witness" of its plight of being "lost" in the vanities of life and seeks an "ultimate" evaluation of its earthly aims. In the moral-evaluative confrontation between the soul and its "inward witness" a thread is spun which is no longer conducted by life-subservient interests, but rather by the "Transnatural Significance of Life." If we follow the progress of this unfolding of the "life of grace" with Teresa of Avila (*The Mansions*), we see how the soul in its empirical, vital, and personal identity becomes the very substance from which is spun this thread of the Transnatural Destiny of man. In its moral evaluation vis-a-vis the "witness," the soul despoils itself of its earthly concerns like an artichoke, leaf by leaf. The "leaves" of the soul's concerns over the natural life all fall in succession until the very center of the soul is revealed, and the soul's thus liberated and purified dynamisms of grace are ready for a "radical leap" to meet the Divine Witness face to face. The soul is thus revealed as the inward receptacle of the unearthly significance of the sacred within which it meets face to face the Ultimate Witness.

This extra-ordinary role which the moral factor plays is beyond its life-oriented function, yet in such a way that it is through its entire life-involvement that the transnatural move of the soul may take off. It calls for a more detailed analysis of the way in which the moral sense is basically constitutive of the human person within her socio-cultural life-world. We will focus upon the exercise of the moral sense in and through the person in our next section. First we must draw conclusions from the presentation of its basic functional outlay.

To summarize: (1) The soul appears as an empirical life-promoting and sustaining factor. (2) The soul, which is orchestrated through the intellectual apparatus of intentional consciousness — with the self as its axis — appears as the factor of the self-identity of the human being. In this sense, we as human beings identify ourselves with the totality of our experience. (3) The soul appears with respect to the Human Condition as the "middle-ground" into which the decisive virtualities of man flow and within which their individualizing unfolding is generated and develops. That is, the soul appears as the soil for the origin of *all the types of meaning* by which man endows neutral and anonymous nature with *his own* meaningfulness, with *his own sense.* (4) Finally, although it seems that the soul extends and remains in an intimate interplay with the body, on the one hand, and with the life of the mind or intellect, on the other — articulating and animating the one, and being informed and processing its dynamisms through the filters of the other (thus encompassing the entire human person), it is far from enclosing it within itself. Although the human person might be self-enclosed like a "monad," the soul — contrary to the views of some phenomenologists — is not. It is, at one extreme, the recipient of the ungraspable, inexplicable Initial Spontaneity, and, at the other, the *processor of the existential thread breaking through all its natural frontiers toward the Transnatural.* In this crucial role it proceeds by the intermediary of the moral agent.

Now, it remains for us to bring together our presentation of the person in its substantial manifestation. It appears that the person is manifested: first, in the self-sustaining, "animated" body complex; second, through the substantial self-identity of the soul; and, third, as an agent presenting the person as we experience it in the "real" self; all three of these complexes are informed by the mind. This analysis of its modes of manifestations shows "what" and "how" the person is. Nevertheless, if we want both to understand what makes the individual specifically human and to account for humanity, we must approach the person from the point of view of the various types of *functioning through which he becomes and unfolds as a living being and accomplishes his human telos.* Advancing in degrees along the nature-spirit line he reaches his full dimension in his interplay with the Other.[93]

The reason for this priority is clear: the human being becomes human through the introduction of *his* type of meaningfulness of life into an otherwise anonymous, "pre-human," nature. He does it as the "Creator of his own Interpretation-in-Existence." The "sense" of this interpretation and of its unfolding emerge from and through his functional system. The modes of the manifestation of the person in reality, in life, and in the world are but the result of its meaning-unfolding functions.

Among them, the one which constitutes the instrument through which all lines of his constructive meaning-bestowing upon brute facts proceed is the moral sense.

It has to be emphasized at this point that the crux of the present conception of the human person lies in its being the moral agent. *Yet it is a moral agent only insofar as its life-enactment is, throughout all the "vocal" circuits of its functioning, informed by the moral sense.* The role of the moral sense in the creative orchestration of the human being has been already stated. Now let us trace its genesis in the constructive progress of life as it leads to the constituting of the human person.

PART II

THE MORAL SENSE OF LIFE AS CONSTITUTIVE
OF THE HUMAN PERSON

SECTION 1. THE PERSON AS THE SUBJECT/AGENT
WITHIN THE LIFE-WORLD

We have so far emphasized the role of the person in the living individual's organizing, articulating and acting; that is, in the functioning through which he unfolds by delineating his individual life-course. When it comes, however, to asserting the point at which this life-course takes a turn of a specifically human sort, it seems most difficult to single out from among the factors entering into human functioning an element that would account for the specificity of this turn which both differentiates man from other living beings and maintains the line of continuity with other functional circuits. When we ask what is it that accounts for the specificity of the human being, we cannot consider the human being as an abstract set of features by means of which he "presents" himself; we have to seek this specificity in the network of functioning by means of which his manifestations occur. That is, we have to seek it within the life-world which he establishes as the system of meaningfulness of his existence. We have to seek it in the various types of interrelations, meanings, and corresponding "languages" (e.g., the language of art, the moral language, the religious language, etc.) which serve as means of communication within the human world. Furthermore, as is obvious from the first two models of the person presented above, the person draws upon and participates in the entire system of life and nature. Unlike the notions of the "subject," "consciousness," or "ego," which stress the separation from concrete nature, the abstraction of human thought, the person emphasizes the *unity of all living factors within man.*

Although we could say that contemporary philosophy in general agrees that it is the ethical factor or the spirit that accounts for the specificity of the human manifestation (Husserl, Scheler, etc.), the problem is far from being solved in a satisfactory way. It depends on, first, how we conceive of the origin and nature of morality and, second, how much validity we attribute to it. The question of the specifically human factor within the life-world remains an open question. We have prepared the ground for taking it up afresh. First, we will pursue it as a question concerning the *origin and nature of the uniquely human meaningfulness of the human existence and of the world*. Second, we will approach it as a question concerning the *specific meaning-creating and meaning-bestowing function of the person as the subject/agent within the social world*. It will appear from our analysis that it is up to the human person to introduce the moral sense into the understanding of the *life-world* as the *social world*. Man's self-consciousness, thereby established, entails *consciousness of the conditions of its progress*, i.e., man's *responsibility for life's progress and survival*.

SECTION 2. MAN'S SELF-INTERPRETATIVE INDIVIDUALIZATION[94]

In fact, we may seek for the source of morality by retracing the phases of *man's self-interpretative individualizing life-course*. In my previous work on the self-individualizing (interpretative) progress of the real individual I have distinguished the following phases: (1) the "pre-life" virtualities coming together in the life-individualizing process; (2) the *entelechial-oriented organic/vital phase*; (3) the *vital sentient phase*; (4) the *sentient/psychic phase*; and (5) the *psychic/conscious phase*, initiated by the "source experience," which marks the onset of the creative orchestration in which *all* of the "virtualities" of the human condition unfold.[95] In each of these phases of the dynamic constructive progress of the individual, that is, in the unfolding complexity of the functional mechanisms and systems, the following crucial issues arise. First, there is that of the various types of way and means of coordinating the elements entering into the operative and generative systems; second, that of the principles of these coordinations; and third, that of the potentialities of the elements (and of the operational segments) to unfold their functioning and to assume their respective roles in the constructive advance of the self-interpretative process. I have maintained that it is by these various types of articulations of processes, by which the individual differentiates himself from the circumambient conditions — while benefitting from the otherwise neutral elements, but which he may turn into essential resources of his own progress — that he establishes the meaningfulness of this progress, and creates the meaningfulness of the circumambient conditions with respect to their relevance to his needs. It is the element of constructive differentiation from life-conditions while transforming them into *his conditions* of the "life-world." In the first phase of the pre-life conditions we may consider this coordination of needs and means as an automatic response of virtually loaded pre-life elements coming together in trial and error or seemingly haphazardly.[96] There is no valuation present there, not even in a germinal form.

We can, however, talk about a principle of "fitness" according to which the coordinates will occur. It begins, as it seems, with the origin of the individualizing process of beingness at its *organic vital* phase. There we are dealing with a solicitation response situation, in which the "need" of the emerging complex of living individualizing elements — under the aegis of the entelechial principle intrinsic to it — seeks and "solicits" other elements for its "satisfaction" toward the further progress of life in its unfolding.

With the phase of the *vital sentient* self-individualizing complex of processes there enters the acquiescence/rejection principle of the constructive discrimination of vitally significant elements — a far more complex significance. Here life's need for further life-prompting elements is not automatically and mechanically satisfied: it is qualified by sentient discrimination on the part of the individual, who qualifies the elements of his circumambient world by distinguishing those which may satisfy, or are congenial with, his needs, and those which are not. It is, however, only upon reaching the complexity of the *sentient/psychic* phase of man's self-differentiation in the constructing process that we witness a specific significance brought in by the *acquiescence/rejection* principle of articulation. Indeed, beyond the mechanical functionality present in the individual's sentient/vital seeking for, and "recognition of," the elements needed for his organic functions up to the point where satisfaction occurs — observed in the second and third phase of the constructive differentiation of life —, we find in the sentient/psychic functionality brought in by now a more complex existential interaction. It involves an evaluative complex of *recognition/estimation/appreciation* on the one hand, and a responsive acceptance or qualified refusal, on the other.

The discrimination/fitness system proceeds with a pluri-directional "sensitivity," and establishes "significance" consisting in "psychic" relations to elements of the virtual fulfillment of the individual's existential needs. This need/satisfaction system crystallizes in the network of existential gregariousness of the higher living beings. Its existential significance lies in communicating by protective reflexes, signals, single and chain-acts of care (belonging to the instinctual/psychic life-protective set) the existential "life-interests" shared by all individuals. It is rooted, however, exclusively in the *self-interest* of each member of the group, with the addition of an existential-affective reliance upon the affective presence of other individuals.

The above-mentioned types of coordination of life-promoting elements, operational segments and functions establish the distributing order of the individualizing progress. At each of the phases they establish the *meaningfulness* of the elements which enter into the individualizing process. Each type functions by establishing sense-giving. Yet, its sense comes from, first, the *vital*, and second, the *gregarious* life-significance of the life-serving process. In its coalescent/fusional/ organic way it functions as sense-giver; as vital sense-giver in the vital/psychic selecting mechanisms; as *vital/gregarious* sense-giver in sentient/psychic appreciative and interest-sharing selectiveness. At each of these phases there emerges an appropriate significant *novum* that is released from the progressing complexity in functioning, which stimulates the virtualities intrinsic to its components.

The previously enumerated coordination principles carry on the life-progress in all the types of selectiveness which they serve, whether by response, acquiescence, or even by an individual initiative. For their being they merely need to put into operation an *"exciting" reason*. But even the touching "devotion" to the care of little ones shown in animal behavior has its *reasons* in instinct and affectivity which *"excite"* the functional system and prompt its operations and direct the "actions" of the animal toward these goals. Exciting reason is applied in its full extent in the use of affectivity and instinct as specific life-prompting functional complexes.

With the emergence of the creative imagination, which does not simply enlarge the scope of relevances but, first of all, breaks out of their circumferences as they have been established by life's propagation interests, in the full-fledged conscious functioning of the individual, the exciting reason, which prompts his selective mechanism toward acquiescence or rejection, does not suffice by itself. Full consciousness, in its uniquely inventive projection, means not only the instinctive sharing of self-interest with other individuals, but also the propensity to *expand one's own individual meaningfulness into transactions with other individuals.* The dominant limitation by the *universal scheme of life* —

identical for each species — is broken down and recedes before the inventive function by which the individual devises his own way of existential self-expansion. This expansion may be accomplished only in transaction with others.

In *transactions* among individuals we deal with multiple and partly conflicting interests; each of them demands his own interest; each of them is prompted by *individual life-interests*; each of them seeks to promote the new significance of *his* devices for his own self-interpretation in existence; each of them is, by his own spontaneous impetus in this *existential expansiveness* — and even while encroaching upon those of others — going in directions that are naturally prompted to interpret the transactional components according to his own life-interest "carried" by his *expanding spontaneities*. Thus he is prompted to place his own significance upon the transactional network: the transindividual social world, which is nevertheless common to all. Were we left with the coordination principles of the exciting reason, hitherto valid, in which the decisive factor is the drive toward one's own life-interest — even already significantly expanded into that of sharing the *preservation* and *propagation-of-life-significance* with other individuals —, the expansiveness would have, in the first place, remained limited to the functional circumference of vital sensibility. The individual would share with the other beings the "law of the jungle," as penetratingly analyzed by Kipling. In his analysis the gregarious order appears partly as a "law" based upon the instinctive/vital/sentient/psychic/operational circuit, in which the sharing of common vital interests, survival and propagation instincts, affective needs, etc., establishes a vital-interest circuit which harmonizes with the overall system of life. With the advent of full-fledged conscious experience within which emerges the *intellectual sense*, marking a new individualizing phase of the individual life-progress, an *objective order* of the life-progress is released. The *inventive function* of consciousness — and cooperation with it — being added to it, a *communication* among individuals is instigated and spontaneously unfolds. The emergence into operation of the inventive function of the human being not only explodes the life-subservient directional scheme for the coordination of functional operations, but it gives them a new focus, an imaginatively *self-enlarging inventory of possible ways* to unfold and stretch *one's own meaningful existential script* over the intersubjective life network. The release of these factors would certainly prompt attempts at transactional undertakings by individuals in concert.

Yet, would the available coordination principles be adequate for such a common effort?

The operative-coordinating principles which give significance to the life-promoting operations — *organic, vital, gregarious* — are geared to the self-interest of each of them alone. They establish in the individual's self-interpretation its *vital sense.* Objectifying reason (intellect) releases a new sense — *the objective Sense.* This latter is altogether neutral to individual survival interests. The rational deliberation which it allows for the sake of estimating purposes, means, circumstances for action and undertakings in common appreciates the individual's approval of an "agreement" or an individual decision to commit oneself to its implementation. In such an agreement, the life-interest of the individual would be necessarily, as much satisfied as curbed or renounced. The "exciting reasons" which serve individual striving and express the needs recorded by instinct and affectivity for life-preservation would fall short of the mark. In the striving of individual interests could a transactional agreement ever take place? The "law" of the strong or of the cunning would prevail.

SECTION 3. THE MORAL SENSE IN THE INTERSUBJECTIVE
INTERPRETATION OF LIFE AFFAIRS

Seeking for a new factor which, in the face of the neutrality of the intellectual sense versus the individual aggressiveness of a pre-transactional situation, appears indispensable for entering upon a neutral deliberative analysis and for inspiring an interpretative turn toward mutual agreement, consensus, and commitment to implementing its terms, we discover the *Moral Sense.* In fact, the surging of the *Benevolent Sentiment* of the Moral Sense endows the interpretation of the transactional component variations with a *justifying reason.*[96a] Justifying reason, as Lord Shaftesbury so penetratingly saw, demands the "sense of right and wrong." This sense is presupposed by the cognitive function of deliberative operations; it is also independent of other extraneous sources (e.g., religious). It is by the working of the Moral Sense that the benevolent sentiment applies itself to the interpretation of conflictual situations. It surges from, and differentiates qualitatively in, the self-interpretative progress of the individual himself. Its effect manifests itself primordially on the significance of the transaction. The transactional self-interpretation goes together with the "neutral" informative and cognitively objectified set of elements for deliberation. The benevolent sentiment being brought in, the *value* of these elements for the significance of the purposive end of the transaction has to be established, not strictly individually but in common; and not for the sake of any one of the partners alone, but to transgress their strictly self-centered interests. This *value* resides in the threefold relevance of the transaction interests of the involved individuals. It resides, first, in the relevance of the given transaction to each unfolded individual interpretative script and in the prospect (with an implied necessity) of promoting in full or in part the life-significance of each individual. Secondly, it resides in the value of the elements of this expanding striving/adjusting/surrendering "negotiating" complex with reference to the given circumambient life-world situation (ecology, social system, etc.) of each partner in the negotiation. Lastly, it resides in the value of the elements for selection to the *universal life-system*, which the selection might serve, simply accommodate, or jeopardize in some respect.

However, the switch from the existentially significant coordination category of mere "fitness" in the automatic or "exciting" phases of the self-individualizing complexity, to that of valuative significance in the selective process of coordination is a further indication of the radical transformation within this process. Here we are hitting the threshold of the passage through which — as a discrete and progressively extended phase in the spontaneous self-interpretative progress of the living individual — from the merely life-promoting meaningfulness of self-individualizing life, we cross to the *human significance* of life. The sharpness of this threshold is marked by the question: On what basis does an individual make a deliberate selection of alternatives which are against, in conflict with, or simply a surrender of, his own *life-interests* for the sake of those of others? In other words, what gives "value" to the alternatives that oppose self-interest and in terms of what may we justify our selection? If the threshold to the human significance of life is marked by the new relevance of life-promoting deliberations to the significance-axis of "right" and "wrong," how does this axis originate in the Moral Sense? As the basic significant factor in the deliberation and valuation context, the right/wrong axis elevates this significance from the level of the strictly "exciting" mechanisms — serving the self-interest drive of the self-enclosed individual — to that of intersubjective "justification."

It is the Benevolent Sentiment at work, introducing the ultimately *moral* axis of *right/wrong*, that establishes the intersubjective life-sharing. It allows the balancing out of the conflicting self-interests.

The justifying reason which directs the decision of the transactive significance cannot indeed be founded on automatized relevancies; it is rather the result of, and a conclusive step in, a deliberative process. Although deliberation involves all of the conscious faculties — which have to be released in the source-experiences — none of them is capable of bringing in this *novum*. Where does it make its original appearance? I suggest that we discover its presence first in the *valuative process*. The principles of selection along the *valuable/unvaluable* line, operating in the valuation process with respect to the components of transactional deliberation — that is, concerning basically our relation to the Other — are conduits of the Moral Sentiment. The selective decision is not a mere calculus of convenience but conveys the moral sentiment by means of conscious moral acts of *approbation* or *disapprobation*.

Approbation/disapprobation, conscious acts that are the manifestations and carriers of this *significant novum* that we are concerned with, are neither based upon, nor consist in, an intuitive instance of the cognition of values. They are judgments which manifest the new uplifting sense-giving factor: the Moral Sense. This is the vehicle of man's significance, of his self-interpretation in existence: of the *social world*.

THE POETIC SENSE: THE AESTHETIC ENJOYMENT WHICH CARRIES THE LIVED FULLNESS OF CONSCIOUS ACTS

INTRODUCTION: THE PREDICAMENT OF VALUE-AESTHETICS AND OF LITERARY TEXT-BOUND THEORIES

It is now time to introduce the second primogenital sense virtually present in the Human Condition and actualized in the meaning-bestowing role of the human person: the poetic sense. It is best to bring it out as it emerges in the investigation of the literary work of art, where it crystallizes in its purest form. What is literary work? In contrast to the ontological stress upon the nature of the literary work itself, let us say that the literary work is *a specific type of result obtained by the creative activity of the human being*. It is "literary," first, insofar as it is "embodied" in the media of written (and spoken) language; it is a "literary creative result" insofar as this embodiment concerns the *poetic sense* brought to fruition through *aesthetic enjoyment*. In the exfoliation of this definition we must concern ourselves first with aesthetic enjoyment.

In every conception of the literary work we have to take into consideration its essential polarity: (a) there is aesthetic enjoyment by the reader which makes him acquainted with the literary work, but this enjoyment on the side of the experiencing subject is strictly bound up with (b) the nature of the literary work as an object, that is its availability in its own right. All depends now upon how we conceive of the *subjective experience of "enjoyment"* and of the *objective nature of the work*. Moritz Geiger, who stressed this polarity, initiated phenomenological aesthetics; but this polarity, first elaborated by Geiger and running through the entire line of phenomenological aesthetics, has yet to be developed far enough to yield crucially important results. The polarity between the objective and experiential dimensions in the approach to the literary work was accepted by Roman Ingarden — a student of Geiger in Göttingen — who pursued it to its furthest limit. Ingarden's aesthetic theory of the literary work follows two distinctive lines. Let us recall that, first, having stressed the ontological question,

405

"What type of object is the literary work?", Ingarden developed and ontology of the literary work. Second, faced with the question of how we experience the literary work, he proposed a systematic analysis of the ways of "cognition of the literary work." Lastly, he gave a culminating touch to this twofold investigation in the conception of the specifically "aesthetic object" understood as (1) the constitutive result of the cognitive process, which, however, (2) is supposed to be found in the aesthetic values inherent in the literary work itself. With such sharp differentiations as these, Ingarden's theory remains incapable of accounting for what makes the literary *work* aesthetic, or for resolving the question of what makes the *cognition* of the literary work aesthetic. We are referred from cognition to the values within the object and *vice versa*.

Neither the origin of supposedly aesthetic values, nor that of the retrieval (or crystallizing) of the aesthetic quality of these values in cognition is accounted for. If Ingarden is brought to the fore in the present argument it is not merely for historical reasons. I suggest in fact, that this predicament is unsolvable in any aesthetic theory that refers ultimately to aesthetic values. Yet how may one overcome the value approach?

These basic shortcomings of phenomenological aesthetics bring us back to its source: the Geigerian initial distinction between aesthetic enjoyment and the literary object. To investigate this distinction might reveal some important and hitherto unobserved features. Does not the original approach to the polarity of the literary work, as devised by Geiger, contain some basic hints missed by Ingarden, who accepted Geiger's views in a simplifed, approximate way? If Geiger himself did not exploit his conception fully, what can we find in it that may perhaps put us on the right track?

SECTION 1. THE CONCEPTION OF "AESTHETIC ENJOYMENT" IN MORITZ GEIGER'S AESTHETICS

It should be emphasized that, unlike Ingarden, it is from the reader's side that Geiger approaches the issue of literature: in discussing access to a literary work he begins with aesthetic enjoyment rather than ontological structure. In fact, he proposes aesthetic enjoyment as the Archimedean point for resolving questions concerning both the literary work's nature and the cognitive experiences in terms of which it is to be crystallized. To begin with, we have to distinguish between enjoyment as experience and enjoyment as a function. It is the experience of enjoyment that enters here into consideration. Experience as a function will be considered in the second part of this study.

(a) *Enjoyment differentiated from cognition*

Following Geiger, who focuses upon experience, we may differentiate from enjoyment in general the experience of enjoyment as a peculiar category understood as (1) an affective reverberation in our natural conscious acts — in contradistinction we may say to the "pure acts" of intellectual (transcendental) consciousness, and (2) as distinguished from enjoyment seen as a conscious dwelling upon experience itself, pleasurable or painful, or as a meditative inquiry. (3) He differentiates too from enjoyment seen in a more general sense as an emotive (affective) sensuous "thickness" of the experiences of natural conscious acts. (4) Being different from pleasure, enjoyment is also something other than *joy over* something. Joy over something is motivated objectively, whereas enjoyment does not extend "beyond" its object to anything else for motivation.[97] Yet enjoyment of a work of art has its *foundation* and a *cause*. What can be an object of enjoyment? Objects of enjoyment are numerous. We may enjoy our experiences, moods, etc.; a great many psychic experiences may become objects of enjoyment; situations may also be objects of enjoyment. But enjoyment must have an individual object (whether real or imaginary) and this object must have a "certain fullness."[98] So much for the differentiation of enjoyment with reference to its object.

(b) *Enjoyment distinguished from experiences*

But enjoyment should also be differentiated from cognitive and volitional experiences with respect to the way in which the experience of enjoyment constitutes its object. This question Geiger formulates by asking, how the experiencing self stands in relation to the experience of enjoyment, first, with respect to the act of enjoyment and, second, with respect to the act by which the object of enjoyment is constituted for the individual. We will here pursue the specific nature of the experience of enjoyment as a category of an intentional act.

Here, of course, it is the relation of the act of enjoyment to the object of enjoyment that is at stake. In contrast to cognitive acts which "strive for understanding of something," the act of enjoyment has a different direction. In cognitive instances the "movement" of the intentional act is to be grasped by going from the self to the object; in the act of enjoyment, Geiger emphasizes, the movement of the intention proceeds inversely, namely, *from the object to the self*. In addition, the act of joy consists in the movement of intention proceeding from the self, which "sends out a wave of joy." In contrast the act of enjoyment — even that most "active" in itself — is not a trap into which the object should fall, but is a "taking in" of what comes from the object. This latter is not grasped, structured, or constituted; it is "drunk up and absorbed."[98a] No matter how active, or intensely pronounced enjoying as a function is, the experience of enjoyment itself remains a "listening to the object."[99] It should be emphasized that intentional activity concerns only self-enjoyment but not the attitude of the self *in* the experience of enjoyment.

(c) *Enjoyment differentiated from the constitutive features of the will*

If we consider all manifestations of will, either direct as in desiring, willing, wishing, preferring, or indirect as present in every feeling (anger, satisfaction, etc.) involved in the turning of the subject "toward" or "against" an object — even in joy, if it is not the joyful state of the subject but "joy over" —, we see that in all of them a *position* is adopted by the self. In contrast, although desire, wishing, contentment may precede or follow the experience of enjoyment, the experience of enjoyment of a poem, music, or play does not give the enjoying subject the *distance* that is indispensable for taking a stand of any sort toward what he enjoys. In fact, he is not only absorbed by, but even merged in, what he experiences: poem, musical melody, drama. He no longer may hold a position toward it, not even that of pleasure or displeasure.

Hence it follows that enjoyment has no relation to will. To the contrary, enjoyment is an unreserved acceptance of, and an unconditional surrender to, its object.[100]

At the one extreme we see, then, the experience of enjoyment utterly suspended and drawing upon its object; at the other extreme, the experiencing act is conceived of as being free from all features of the constitutive/cognitive intention as well as of all strictly "subjective" volitive features. As such it appears to be utterly "free" from all subjective/empirical/constitutive contingencies, a type of "purist feeling" or "nothing but feeling."[101] But it is not an "unqualified" feeling: it is permeated by its object.

(d) *Enjoyment and the self*

Having thus freed the nature of the act of enjoyment from all dependency upon the constitutive functions of consciousness, both cognitive and volitive, on the one hand, and having previously distilled it from the empirical dependency upon the senses, emotions, and empirical feelings (even of pleasure and displeasure), on the other, we must now try to discover what this thus "purified" experience depends upon. There is only the self to which we may refer it.[102] We have, however, first to distinguish the self from the system of consciousness. Acts of consciousness may, according to Geiger's analysis, either just "happen in consciousness" as "something which happens to me" and impinges upon my conscious field even to the point of "taking possession of me" or they may be "self-centered," that is, arise from the self as the center of consciousness. In the first case, acts which just happen to me have not engaged my self. Anger, desire, or joy, for instance, may just happen in my consciousness whether I myself like it or not; they might be alien to myself; their source is the sentient context of my functions but not myself.[103] Enjoyment, however, never "happens" to me. It does not take possession of me — I am in it from the very beginning. While feelings, desires, etc. may happen in consciousness without or even against my consent, the consent of the self, I take the urge as *mine*. In the first case, the self does not participate in the "happenings" of consciousness, which burst out without my self-experience being engaged in them. In the second, the enjoyment is taken by myself as mine, as something which belongs to my self. In contradistinction to the experiences which appear at random within consciousness as superficial — even alien — to the self, enjoyment belongs to those experiences which proceed from the depth of the self.

We may then summarize the features of enjoyment with respect to the self: (1) it is always self-centered; (2) it is an experience of taking in; and (3) an experience of surrender to the object. These features presuppose that (4) the self-participation of enjoyment means experiencing by the self. In enjoyment we take what streams from the object but we do the enjoying (in contrast to all those experiences as well as simple feelings which do not include self-participation).

To conclude, the self might be more or less absorbed in enjoyment, which may be deeper or more superficial. Enjoyment even has the tendency to become our master. And yet enjoyment itself does not consist in these three features: self-centeredness, surrender, and acceptance. "Enjoyment itself is that which is conjoined with all those factors; it is a special way of being affected" — it itself "is an arousing of the self in which the self reacts to what flows into it."[104]

With Geiger we find a "series of properties which were shown to be characteristic of the essence of the phenomenon of enjoyment." They emphasize the kernel of experience which neither can be structured nor qualified.

Geiger concludes:

1. Enjoyment is motiveless.
2. The object of enjoyment has "fullness."
3. All enjoyment involves "participation" by the self.
4. Enjoyment is an experience of taking in.
5. Enjoyment contains no position toward the object, but is a surrender to the object.
6. Enjoyment is centered upon the self.
7. Enjoyment fills the self.
8. Enjoyment is an affect upon the self.
9. Enjoyment displays certain qualities and colorings, such as seriousness, light, and depth, which determine it more closely.[105]

(e) *The aesthetic specificity of aesthetic enjoyment*

Aesthetic enjoyment is surrendering to the object of art in contemplation/observation. In contemplation we accept the object — and yet hold ourselves open; we still keep a distance from it. In the enjoyment of observation the object takes possession of us, for it is neither the enjoyment of the *act* of observing nor the enjoyment of the act of painting an object, but of the *object* itself, which is being painted.

However, it must be emphasized, first, that following other thinkers who treated aesthetic enjoyment (Kant, Külpe, Edith Landmann, Lipps), Geiger's contemplation/observation of the work of art in enjoyment is not meant as an isolated or a particularized descriptive intention, but as the "designation of the total situation." Second, it is also significant — especially for what I intend to develop in the second part of this inquiry — that although strictly correlated with its object, the analysis of enjoyment does not begin from the object, but *from the experience of enjoyment itself.*

Geiger himself insists that what is understood by the aesthetic object is narrower than the field of objects which can be aesthetically enjoyed. Since such strong emphasis is laid upon the fact that it is the object which is the occasion of the "arousing of the self" and the "reaction" of the self with respect to what flows into it, we may now venture the question of whether in principle there is a restriction on objects which can be aesthetically enjoyed. Is it the object-side that determines the release of the subject's aesthetic enjoyment experience? Last, whence does the specifically aesthetic nature of aesthetic enjoyment arise? These questions gain all their interrogative significance when we consider two important points. The specific way of being aroused could be caused either (1) by specific features or intrinsic virtualities of the object which (a) may be *already* "aesthetic" and affect the self with direct impact upon its functioning, or (b) are *virtually* aesthetic, that is, within the contemplating/observing encounter between the object and the subject, these virtually aesthetic elements provoke enjoyment that is aesthetic and they themselves assume an aesthetic form within the object as concretized in the enjoyment. Or (2) the aestheticity of the enjoyment stems from the *specific affectivity of the self* for certain features of the object — this affectivity making the experience aesthetic and the object aesthetic.

Geiger's own answer to these questions is developed in a double line. On the one hand, he stresses the specific attitude of the subject: observation holding a distance, concentration (outer or inner), looking through the fullness of the object, excluding the self from it, etc. Furthermore, the aesthetic interest is characterized by the attitude of the subject; it is disinterested when the inner aesthetically enjoyed sympathy exceeds a certain minimum.[106] The attitude of the subject makes the aesthetic enjoyment the *enjoyment of the disinterested contemplation of the fullness of the object.*[107] Yet, on the other hand, there is a difference in the experience of enjoyment depending upon whether "it arises from aesthetic values or merely from objects which can be aesthetically enjoyable." The above-mentioned characteristics of aesthetic enjoyment depend upon the subject's *attitude*, but aesthetic enjoyment is still *more specifically determined* when the objects embody *aesthetic values.* That is, the aesthetic enjoyment is not only surrender to the object but to what Geiger calls "deep aesthetic values." Furthermore, this depends upon the "value" of the personality which is capable of experiencing such enjoyment.[108]

On this analysis there is only one step to be made, namely, to appreciate the value of aesthetic enjoyment itself in its depth, seriousness, intensity, etc. with reference to the aesthetic values of the object. Thus, even granting to the subjective attitude the capacity to be aesthetically aroused, the entire weight of aesthetic enjoyment may lean upon the aesthetic values supposedly intrinsic to the object. With this we naturally branch off into the aesthetics of values and objective structures that were first investigated by Ingarden, Hartmann, Bense, Dufrenne, and Wellek, and subsequently by others.

By including the factor of the author, Geiger has set the universal pattern for contemporary phenomenological aesthetics in its different variations. The pattern of the "aesthetic situation" is suspended upon three poles: the aesthetic enjoyment of the recipient (the reader or spectator), the work of art in its objective structure as embodying aesthetic values, and the writer who devised the structure of the work of art. Variants of this situation pattern can be detected in every phenomenologically inspired literary theory. Whether "aestheticity" as a quality of experience appears in the enjoyment itself or whether it is seen in the entire set-up of the aesthetic object as experientially concretized, it is brought down to values. Aesthetic values are assumed by its foundation. But the aestheticity of the values remains a well-sealed secret. No key to it is offered. Consequently within phenomenological aesthetics at large the aesthetic sensibility of the subject and his relation to values remain open questions.

Yet, Geiger's deepest intuitions have been ignored. I suggest that these crucial shortcomings do not compromise the question of aesthetic enjoyment, which he strongly emphasized lies at the origin of phenomenological interest in aesthetics and contains most precious indications worth pursuing further. I have indicated their direction by the above questions.

Now we should ask concretely, what is the specific affectivity of the self for a certain type of objective feature — whether of inner or outer concentration (objects or our moods) — that makes the experience *aesthetic*, or that makes us retrieve the *aesthetic* virtuality of the objects? Where does the aesthetic quality of values come from? What is the origin of aesthetic values? What, if any, is the relation of aesthetic values at their origin to this aesthetic affectivity of the self?

To these questions we will turn in what follows.

SECTION 2. AESTHETIC ENJOYMENT AND THE POETIC SENSE

I propose to go back to the seminal intuition which resides concealed in Geiger's emphasis upon enjoyment by exfoliating it in the line of my own thought. First, I propose to approach it as a unique moment present in all experiences: (a) insofar as they are concrete experiences; and (b) insofar as they are experiences in which the self "lives." This means that I will shift the emphasis from the experience of enjoyment to *enjoyment as a function*. Thus, the function of enjoying will appear first to express itself in the essential way of enacting the life of experiences and of the self and as the function which — to use Hölderlin's expression — manifests itself as a *vis viva* which discloses everything insofar as it is alive. Second, I raise the issue of the life-significance which this function entails. I propose to distinguish between the *vital* significance and the *poetic* significance of the enjoying function. Then, I will submit, that the function of enjoying brings into our meaning-bestowing the *poetic sense*. The *poetic sentiment, poetic feelings, poetic imagination*, etc., account within our language-forming for the "poetic language," which is the *basis for the aesthetic essence of all arts*.

(a) *The "poetic sense": Enjoyment in conscious experiences. The conscious act as an "act" versus the conscious act as an "operation"*

In the attempt to isolate in phenomenology the "pure" transcendental acts of intentionality from lived experiences, we simultaneously bring to light what we isolate it from; indeed, the strictly intentional skeleton of all our experiences (*Erlebnisse*) — that is, of our natural, empirical consciousness, to use Husserl's terms — are clad in a lived experiential pulp. While they concern the structurizing proficiency and order suspended upon this intentional schema, they are simultaneously, however, themselves manifestations of life consciousness. Intentional acts, which are "purified" in the phenomenological perspective from their expirical embodiment, manifest intentional operational order; in contrast, the experiential pulp, although far from being "formless," manifests in its complex net of intermotivations various types of human functioning which it establishes and by which it carries on the *vis viva*: the continuity of the living self.

    This concrete experiential pulp of sensing, feeling, and emotive stirrings is "conscious" not in virtue of its rational order, but in virtue of the "enjoyment" of its acts within which the self appears, first, as the one "who" enjoys them. Second, it is in virtue of the *enjoyment in the acts* that the subject is the center to which all of them — even the remotest simplest feelings — have some sort of relevant relation, are *my* experiences; not only are they "experiences" but they are *eo ipso* "mine" — as experiences of this specific self, uniquely his own.

(b) *The nature of enjoying*

It is in acts that the self lives. Without acts, which it either performs, or which are performed at the peripheries of the territory which the self unifies, the self would neither have the role of an ordering reference system with itself as the vortex, nor would it be "alive." The self does not control the acts in its spread of references. It *dwells* in what we could call a "fountain of enjoyment," from which the self-centered acts stream — or burst forth — and which is the core of the conscious network. It is not responsible for the quality or determination of the acts, nor for their emergence; but, on the one hand, it participates in the life of the acts (directly or remotely); and, on the other hand, as the representative of their unity it carries their virtual performance. Lastly, in the circumference of its direct reach and as the central factor of this ever-evolving/intermotivating unity the self is "clad" by the qualitative nature of the actual, as well as by the virtual content of the acts.

Yet, basically, it is not the qualitative feature of the content, nor the ordering proficiency, nor anything other than the enjoyment of the acts, which makes the self "alive." In the enjoyment of the acts the *self unites in one living system singular acts past, present, and virtual.* No matter how diversified, and in themselves isolated, the singular acts may be, or how close or remote from the self at the center they may emerge, and disregarding the divergent ordering networks of intentionality which bring them together, the crucial factor of the unity of this dispersed and discrete spread of acts, a factor which fills out all the crevasses of the structure and all the discontinuities, is the enjoyment of the acts. This enjoyment penetrates all of them in various degrees of intensity, vigor, etc., and yet carries on a continuing line of life, a line sustained by the self that comes to life with it. The self thus opens upon a *vis viva*, a living power, by which it "feels itself alive."

(c) *The enjoying function differentiated from the cognitive, volitive, or moral function*

Returning to our analysis of enjoyment, I must reaffirm that enjoyment (1) as the thread of *life-experience of being alive*, (2) as the *life-reverberation* effected by the acts, and (3) as the *filum Ariadne* of the labyrinth of the life of the self, is totally different from the *nature* of the acts. Although their very life sparkles, enjoyment is entirely "purified" of the willing, desiring, striving, and wishing features of *wilful acts*; nor do we see in enjoyment the features of cognitive acts which are empirical or purely intellectual. Nor do we mean by "enjoyment" anything that we could identify with the moral features of valuation or judgment. Lastly, inasmuch as we might be tempted to identify the life-dynamism of enjoyment with the exalting, elevating, energizing, aesthetic experience, we may not attach to enjoyment any of these energizing features. That is, leaving the experience of enjoyment aside, we move into analysis of the *function of enjoying* which manifests itself in the experience of enjoyment. Here we definitely part from Geiger's conception of enjoyment, for he considers it to be essentially object-bound. By the "self enjoying itself in the acts" and by the 'acts' reverberations in enjoyment," I mean the uniquely *subjective* nature of the enjoying function. In contrast to the intentional reaching-out of the volitive, cognitive, and aesthetic functions as such, *the enjoying function is self-consuming.* Enjoying as the function of the subject is a retreating, self-reposing state of the subject, who quivers *in* and *with enjoyment*. As such, it permeates all subjective functions or, rather, carries their manifestation. The subject, albeit in fractions of instants — if we may speak in temporal terms — reposes in itself in the "enjoyment" of the acts which *eo ipso* become his. Lastly, in its self-consuming nature, enjoying draws all the experiential tentacles which the subject extends into the life-world unto the subject itself. In enjoyment the subject exults in all its operations; it comes into its own. Although it ranges beyond intentional direction, in enjoyment it is self-absorbed; in enjoyment the subject becomes his own innermost foothold; he is the one who lives.

Does this mean, however, that enjoyment "energizes" so to speak the subject and is self-consumed in its performance, disappearing without a trace, without expanding in an expressive way? Or, to put it differently, is enjoyment self-consuming without being — as Geiger insists it is —

necessarily object-related? In what follows, I will try to show how the enjoyment of our acts — as the root-factor in our constructive self-interpretative progress — does not depend on already constituted objectivity nor upon qualitative meaningfulness borrowed elsewhere. To the contrary, in disagreement with Geiger, I propose that the *function of enjoyment is to contribute its own unique sense.*

(d) *The poetic sense of the enjoying function: The "vital sense" and the "aesthetic sense"*

Enjoyment of our acts varies along a widely differentiated range of intensities and degrees of self-absorption as well as extension within the circuits of our functioning. Thus, it varies in the nature of its *life-significance*. In fact, although a sharp demarcation line between the one and the other cannot be drawn because they are partly fused with each other, there are two senses involved in enjoyment. In their respectively pronounced visibility they stand out as being clearly different — as if we could switch one of them on or off. We distinguish one as the vital sense of our act-enjoyment function and the other as the aesthetic sense. Both of them are carried by the *root-factor of the enjoyment function*: the self living in his acts. And yet there is a special "qualitative" (still "pre-objective") *sense* which differentiates them. We may either emphatically experience our self vibrating with the richness of our life-potency — that is, in our *vital sense*, which endows all our individual enjoyments with a special vigorous sense of power — or that sense may be overshadowed by an emphasis in our experience on an imaginative "aesthetic" sense of our enjoyment within which the self finds something akin to a new dimension.

In fact, the innumerable acts which we perform and which carry our vital progress (for example, acts of pulsation, instinctual acts, acts of sensation, feelings, desires, volitions) and which express our vital or as it is usually said "animal" phase of existential progress, and express our specifically human circuit of experience as well, and which begins with the entrance into play of our cognitive, valuative, aesthetic, etc. faculties — that is, our fully developed human acts — are tempered in their respective intensities by the entire circuit within which they participate. To a certain degree they appear self-absorbing and subordinate to specific objectives (e.g., either as reactions "to . . . ," or as acts "of . . . ," directed toward objects). Consequently, they are extinguished or muted in their *own* "voice." The spans of our acts' extension over the entire circuit of functioning differ from each other, but their singular voices are coordinated with those of other acts within the constructive design which they unfold together, unless, that is, a particularly strong intensity disrupts the harmony of the entire circuit, resulting in one act — or a complex of acts — putting our entire being on alert for pain, anguish, pleasure, joy, expectation, etc. Nevertheless, their mode of performance, which is muted in the fulfillment of their specific role within a vast and self-ordering pattern, is not devoid of a specific *sense*. In fact, this sense is neither self-consumed without a trace in the performance of the act, nor is it "neutral" with respect to the specific and further extending role which it either performs or within which it at least participates. To the contrary, it endows this role with a specific *life-significance*.

It must be emphasized again that acts are neither neutral with respect to the individual progress which they carry, nor with respect to the self, whose "life" they are; they carry this progress as "ours"; they make this specific self "alive" inasmuch as they "live within the self." That is, our acts are neither neutrally mechanical, nor empty of a sense.

Here I must describe what I understand by "sense." In the first place, *sense is to be seen as prior to all structuralization of meaning as well as to the rules and principles of meaningfulness.* Consequently, it is also prior to quality, "quality" understood as the simplest structural unit (e.g., "pure red," "pure joyfulness," etc.). Hence, although sense acquires its meaningfulness from objectifying interrelations into which it fuses, yet within these relations it is a sense that plays the determining role: it infuses the virtual formal/qualitative moments with a "qualitative reverberation" of a certain modality. That is, although the sense in itself cannot be defined — it can be described only in the interrelations into which it spreads — yet we may say that it is an essential contribution to the modality of the experiences of the self. The function of enjoyment insofar as it carries a sense, bubbles with qualitative reverberations to be infused into, to spread through, to activate, to color, to tone, etc., the "contents of experience" which emerge. In this capacity the *function of enjoyment carries through its acts a life-significance*. It is with respect to the life-spread of the self and with respect to its spread of experiences that the qualitative reverberations of the enjoyment function live within its acts. Under the eye of attention there may be detected in every one of our acts a germinal qualitative complexity which is in a virtual state and only in the vaguest of forms, while virtually extending its tentacles into our entire living system. However, the qualitative virtuality of the enjoying function does not come forth, does not stand out in any qualitative fashion; it does not come to take voice. In their function of enjoyment, acts carry in their first, elementary role muted together *in unison, the vital significance of the life-progress.*

However, the vital significance, which finds its manifestation in our vital vigor, and which constantly vacillates between enthusiasm for and indifference to, even apathy toward, our undertakings and which spreads through an infinitely differentiated gamut between the two extremes, is not the only sense that the vibration of enjoyment carries. The vital sense of life, if it were our only sense, would confine our existence strictly to life-survival meaningfulness and its restricted scope. But our enjoying function carries still another sense. It must be pointed out that both of them are so closely interlaced within the Human Condition that we may draw a line between them only at the level of abstract thought. On the one hand, we experience our being in the vibrations of force, vigor, "faith in ourselves," and a feeling of completeness, fullness to the brim. On the other hand, those same vibrations are loaded with expectation of the unforeseeable, with longing for far-off, open, and limitless horizons, with foreboding of the unknown, the unseen, the marvellous as well as a subsequent compulsion to "leave it all" and go, undertake, and reach for the extraordinary and marvellous. This new sense "raises" our "vision" above the *hic et nunc* of life-concerns; they appear in contrast "pedestrian," "limited," etc. The new sphere of significance lifts us on the wings of the "elevated," the "sublime," the "beautiful."

Flowing into the source-experience from which human life originates, this new modality of our vibration stirs our inventive function which expands then into the *Imaginatio Creatrix*. Within the workings of their orchestration the new sense of life, the aesthetic sense, crystallizes. It creates its own, new vision within life but reaches beyond life's realities; it silences the hitherto captivating murmur of the life-necessities, speaking in its own voice; this voice makes our entire frame and our experiential compass reverberate with aesthetic significance.

SECTION 3. IMAGINATIO CREATRIX, "HOMO LUDENS" AND "HOMO CREATOR"

Since its basic role consists in energizing our entire system and prompting it toward manifestation, the vibration of enjoyment produces a state of special *life-exuberance* in our being. It does not need to reach any of the extravagant gestures, outcries, or acts with which we often associate exuberance. We are exuberant in an overall prompting to "get out of ourself" at every phase of our "healthy," that is "equilibriated," functioning. Life exuberance plays manifold, important roles in human existence, and in its progress, development, learning, capacity to overcome obstacles and, above all, in maintaining an equipoise in the struggles of life. Its meaningfulness is particularly strong at the crucial developmental phase of childhood. In fact, the childhood development/ learning phase is most vividly expressed by the activity of "play." The learning, experimentation with the surrounding world, and communicative experience involved in play is pointed out too often to require much attention. Play as learning about the world, as a means of unfolding skills and learning about our capacities, is something we have in common with other living beings, especially in the same initial phase of learning/experimenting with the world and forming skills to handle the elements of life. Yet it seems that the exuberance of life that prompts it does not lead much further than the fulfillment of these above-mentioned functions. As a matter of fact, as ingenious, complex, and fanciful as play might be, it is in its strict nature merely *experimental, not inventive.* This distinction is important: invention presupposes experimentation and play, but the converse does not hold.

The experimental moment of play does not entail an inventive turning point; it is restricted to the discovery of the rules of direct manipulation and to the acquisition of skills for manipulation. Young animals, and children, share this learning and acquiring of skills prompted by the exuberance of the enjoying function. They maintain it beyond this phase and throughout life in a narrower sense for the sake of alternating "work," which demands concentration, rigor, and purposeful orientation with "play," which is meant to be a spontaneous and therefore relaxing exercise of our vital forces in games (which refresh the psyche), in sports (which enable us to exercise our muscles and limbs), and in social or communal artistic activities (where we reorient our social relations which have been affected by the tensions of work). Play is meant as an outlet for our whimsical/spontaneous energies, in contrast to controlled, imposed work — as an outlet for our exuberance and a means of life-enjoyment.

Yet the same exuberance of our enjoyment-vibrations enters into the source-experience — which like a watershed gathers all our vital operations and functions, and, then, after these have been mixed, like a sieve filters them in a special proportion, stirring them all at once; doing so it releases the *inventive imaginary function*. It is here that from a mere exercise of fancy — which in agreement with Aristotle and with Husserl I believe to be one of the simplest vital-sense phenomena, one which allows for the most elementary functions of perception, flexibility, etc. — we move to the radically different level of *Imaginatio Creatrix*.

The same vibrations of enjoyment of our acts, which accompanied by fancy lead us to play, now, having released the inventive function, stir and carry the workings of the creative imagination. Imaginatio Creatrix proposes to us to "leave it all" behind and to create for ourselves wings and devices to explore the extraordinary and the marvellous, the unprecedented and the infinite. The individual armed with these becomes *homo creator*.

SECTION 4. THE AESTHETIC SENSE: ITS VOICE AND THE AESTHETIC LANGUAGE

As mentioned above, the exuberance of enjoyment releases its "voice" while it stirs the inventive imagination within the *source experience*,[108a] within which the specifically human faculties crystallize. By "voice" I do not mean an appeal, e.g., the "call of the wild." Exuberance prompts a "voice" expressive of its state — expression, which at the same time responds to a prompting to crystallize definitively some or other "mood" for our own completion, as well as for its communication to others. Under these promptings man hums, whistles, dances, jumps for joy, embraces others. In these gestures there vibrates a specifically "sounding" rhythm, pitch, cadence, "warmth" or "coolness," appeal or repulsion, "vibration with," or "distantiation"; finally, exuberance culminates by conveying a *sense*.

How can this sense be "read" from the gesture, the tune, the rhythm, the movement? Had they remained expressions of pure exuberance given a form by fancy, they would express a marginal outburst of undirected, spontaneous, whimsical, playful moods. As such they would take the place of a simply "pragmatically" oriented, life-carrying operation. However, once the entire system of source-experience brings about, under the direction of the creative imagination, the creative

orchestration of all human functioning, and the galvanizing and transforming of the entire experiential system, then man may go beyond
strictly life-subservient operations.[109] The function of enjoyment crystallizes indeed, within this orchestration, into the *poetic sentiment*,
which infiltrates the "neutral" voice of the enjoyment-vibrations. "Poetic"
and "aesthetic" mean at this stage two interchangeable notions. However, they direct different aspects of our sense-bestowing.

The *"aesthetic" significance of life* which enters into the *existential
self-interpretation of the human being is at its roots poetic.*[110] The poetic
sentiment calls all our noisy routine vital operations to pause, to silence
their beat in order to turn our attention away from their busy-ness and
toward the *inward spectacle.* If reveals within our entire experiential
system a dimension of the *sublime*, the *beautiful*, and opens it out to the
infinite. The reverberation-virtualities of our experiences respond within
the source experience to these three major lines of poetic sentiment.
They bring forth life-significant moments — which the vital current of
life left alone would not bring forth, but which are lying in waiting.
They do it in innumerable spectra of significance, encompassing entire
ranges of virtual qualitative evaluations inherent in our experience. In
contrast to the vital principle, the principle of life-significance given by
the poetic sense is not meant to promote life operations and growth but
to make it pleasurable. Thus emerges an infinitude of moments of
experience of the pleasurableness of life: its aesthetic significance, its
aesthetic enjoyment which lifts us out of pedestrian life-concerns to another plane.

The aesthetic sense invents significance and forms its own meanings
through the qualitative moments: aesthetic qualities, principles, values.

It brings forth a system of interconnectedness according to which it
functions as an *aesthetic language*, the language of elevated enjoyment
which — again contrasted with vitally oriented language — is not
directly life-action oriented but contemplative.

The formation of an aesthetic language culminates in artistic creation.
From there it pervades human communication. But *poetic language
lives on its own at the foothold of the artistic reaction proper, within the
orbit of the inventive imagination in relation to the elements of Nature,
life, and inward experience. In this phase it is, in fact, the foundation of
artistic creativity. The poetic sentiment endowed with voice and with
sense, uniquely its own, inventive and infinitely expanding, forms the
horizon of human life.*

It remains still to be seen how the "intellectual sense" brings the two primogenital sense giving factors, the moral and the poetic senses, into their innumerably varying formative molds in which they surge in experience in the way that accounts for the human life-world within and around us.

PART IV

THE INTELLIGIBLE SENSE
IN THE ARCHITECTONIC WORK OF THE INTELLECT

SECTION 1. INTRODUCING THE "INTELLIGIBLE SENSE" AND THE ROLE OF THE INTELLECT WITHIN THE NETWORK OF THE UNIVERSAL EXPANSION OF THE LOGOS

Having already introduced and discussed two of man's sense-giving virtualities, the moral sense and the aesthetic sense, a third is still to be acknowledged properly, and that is the sense which plays the most fundamental role in the human enterprise: the *intelligible sense*. The intelligible sense is a virtuality of the Human Condition which is unfolded in the work of the intellect as it accomplishes its task of setting up and maintaining patterns of ever recurrent order which, in our specifically human *self-individualizing* life progress, serve as a skeleton of order as much as the system of reference to be counted on in all the constructivity of human beingness. It sustains the mainstream of human *self-interpretation-in-existence*, and serves as a measuring stick for all the creative variations and imaginative projects of the human genius.

The work of the intellect, which essentially generates the intelligibility of Life's ways and means, culminates in bringing about the intelligibility of the human self in its expansion within a life-world that is equally intelligible and shared as such in *varying degrees* with other human beings and all living things in the *unity-of-everything-there-is-alive*. The stability of the human enterprise in its individual constructive endeavor, and the universal communicability that is indispensable for sharing with others the tasks of the business of life, is suspended upon its intelligibility and thus upon the intelligible sense.

In our foregoing analysis of the functional principles, regulations, and devices which are part of the creative process of man at its various junctions there lurked already the structurizing intellect, which serves as the reference system of that process. It appeared to be a rational mechanism that at some times underlies and at others is a full partner in our discriminating deliberations — as well as in our decision making — in the structurizing progress of the creative process. But even before the onset of the creative process it appeared to account for the standard

423

forms of the already established life-world which the creative mind challenges to begin with, and the principles, rules, and tendencies which it has to take into consideration when it reaches the final stage of bringing into being the creative product of its labors.

Furthermore, although creative imagination, in proposing ever new original and hitherto unknown forms and images, ways, etc., takes the lead, throughout even its most advanced and audacious, individual, and rare parturitions there runs a thread of "stereotypic" intelligibility, however thin. And can we forget that the constant analysis which sustains the formation of the creative object proceeds using the antennae which are projected by the mechanisms of the intellect, while the "inner eye" roves in all directions, scanning the creative elements in translucent intelligibility?

To say it succinctly, the previously differentiated faculties of imagination and memory will rely, for the exercise of their respective roles in man's self-interpretative life course, upon the faculty of the intellect which provides not only the skeleton for their constructive activity but, most significantly, the translucent presence of the creative system to the creative mind. It is through the unfolding and propagation of the entire schema of the intellect's functioning, principles, forms, rules, and categories in the *intelligible sense* that the intellect can account for the basic structuration of human life, as human and fully conscious existence within the full-fledged intelligibility of its exteriorization within the life-world.

The role and functioning of the intellect have been among the main subjects of philosophical inquiry in the history of Western philosophy, and in Kant and Husserl these investigations took on hitherto unprecedented dimensions. This is not the proper place to treat systematically this subject.[111] However, since we are proposing here a full-fledged critique of reason and the part the intellect plays in it, we will give briefly the main points to be considered in appreciating its role in the differentiation of the logos of life, marking its importance as well as its strict limits.

Our approach first situates the role of the human intellect within the complete schema of rationality, which orders life as such, and, second, views the intellect as merely one faculty within the foundational creative orchestration — but one which is coordinated with the other three faculties (imagination, memory, and will) in such a way that it (and this is the third characteristic of our approach) makes an essential contribution to the uniquely human task of the creative orchestration which releases the surge of the ever-renewing spectrum of inventive rationalities which differentiate *ad infinitum* the logos of life. This approach differs so drastically from those of Kant and Husserl that, although on many important points it confirms their insights, it still provides, as one may expect, new points of view on the workings of the intellect as well as on its role in the universal ordering of life, which consists mainly in the prolongation of the spontaneous direction of life's progress in the exceptional situation that the human situation is.[112]

Thus in what follows we will succinctly outline the ways in which the intellect acts on the promptings of the intelligible sense as that virtuality of the human condition which is crucially significant for the work of the creative orchestration, inasmuch as it allows for its full expansion in an explosion that opens out to the modality of the translucent intelligibility of the existence of man within his life-world.

SECTION 2. INTELLIGIBILITY'S EMERGENCE FROM THE
SUBJECT-OBJECT CORRELATION OF LIFE'S ORDERING

The essential task of the intellect consists in expanding life to its greatest reach. And, when we in retrospect follow the evolution of the forms taken by the progress of life, we will be struck by its constant effort at making the ordering links in forms, relations, principles ever more complex but also more concisely and clearly articulated. There is an ever-greater expansiveness of individual forms within their circumambient realm of existence, their world. The life of an individual in its genesis can be seen as convertible to the transformative "life" of the realm in which it proceeds. *Each living being is a beingness of his world of life* and, conversely, *the world is the world of life of some beingness.* This phenomenon of intrinsically motivated co-genesis, of the existential correlation of two distinctive and yet primogenitally intermotivated realms constituting ultimately *one unified complex of life's route,* a complex of life's ordering, acquires a unique position in the evolution phase of the human condition. It appears, indeed, that to attain the greatest reach of life these two correlated domains, that of the living individual and that of his life's realm, there had to be introduced a particular device within life which orders it, namely, one by which these networks of interactive involvement between self-individualizing beingness and the milieu within which it projects its tentacles come to acquire a uniquely efficient capacity by laying bare their rational linkages in all their modalities, types, etc. For the distance between the individual and his world, between the "inwardness" of the individual and all that is "external," is accentuated by his progress, and their correlation seemingly falls apart into what we call in modern philosophy "subjectivity" and "objectivity." Yet, *falling apart, subject and object become at the same time most intimately unified in the work of the human intellect*, which operates and completes this distinction between the inner and the outer of life's progress by internalizing and transforming this distinction into an agency of intelligibility.

By "intelligibility" we mean the *undefinable simplicity of the ordering articulations which are "transparent" or "open" to the subject who orders*, or acknowledges an ordering effect, and this in contrast to the impartial and "blind" operations of inorganic nature. Although we will situate this specific intelligible circuit of life's ordering within the entire system, yet we will here first focus upon the emergence of the intelligible sense in the subject-object correlation.[113]

As is common knowledge, Husserl particularly strongly pointed out and emphasized in numerous ways the role of the subject-object correlation within the constitutive system of intentional consciousness, which was conceived by him as the sole organ of meaning-bestowing, the sole instrument of reason. Rationality is within his schema of thought synonymous with the intentional character of the acts in which the constitution of the human beingness within its life-world proceeds as well as of the correlative objectivity in which it is presentified. It is the cognitive aspect of constitution which assumes the primary role.

It begins with sensory perception. Husserl describes how after the "naive," pre-reflective perception of an object the reflective attention initiates the hitherto "invisible" intentional ordering of both its content and its process, and establishing the apperceptive approach to this same perception, brings out this intentional ordering which is proper to both the perspective process and its correlative object.

The procedures of human intentional consciousness that bring about human objectivity — that is, man's life-world with his selfhood at its vortex — are grounded in the basic correlativity of subjectivity and its intentional object. Husserl distinguishes sensory perception as the groundwork of constitution or objectivization, the first stage of the objectivization of the human universe. In this primary perception the work of the "givenness" of the life-world begins. In this basic sphere is grounded the higher level of objectivization, which is the formation of universal objects, objects of thought (*Denkgegenstände*).[114]

It is strikingly significant that the role of attention, so crucial to the emergence of intentional consciousness within the sensory field, is coupled with the direction it takes, namely that of an *individual objectivity*. We find here in the focus upon the individual an important coincidence between the individualization, which is given absolute pride of place in our investigation of the constructive progress of life, and Husserl's conception of the intentional (conscious) constitution of "individual objectivities" assumed to ground the objective life-world.[115] In a way the process of the constitution of an object — individual objectivity — is analogous to the existential individualization in life's progressive enactment — only analogous, however.

In fact, the primordial directionality of constitutive attention (*Aufmerksamkeit*) toward the individual objectivity does not *construct* it as an individual in an originary (*ursprünglich*) way *in the sense that the "actual presence" of the individual's becoming is unfolded*, but merely identifies it "reproductively" as the already established intellectual, intentional, pattern of objectivity. Husserl's stress on the role of identification in the intentional process clarifies the course of this process adequately: identification in the first place, the directedness of an individuality in the second, which is essential but constitutively secondary. Here no individualization in the authentic sense is present in the originary perception of individual objectivities (*individuale Objektivität*). Moreover, the purely intentional character of the constitutive process separates the constitutive perception of an individual objectivity and the operation of the devices of identification from the continuing existential line of individualization which consists of a process-like life-enactment.

The way in which the perceptual genesis of an individual objectivity occurs differentiates it radically from *existential individualization*. This latter *in its progress individualizes life itself*; that of constitution puts the concrete progress of life to the side: it is merely intentional, apperceptive. Here we come back to the question of the subject-object correlation.

Within the Husserlian orbit of reflection the subject-object correlation in which the constitution-individualization of the object proceeds is already conceived of as being at the heart of the intentional ordering itself. That is, being directed toward the individuality of the object, the unifying orientation of constitutive acts, and the synthetic coalescence of the individualizing elements are all but the doings of intentional consciousness.[116] With this we come to the heart of the matter. Husserl distinguishes sharply the forms and structures of the acts and constitutive processes of intentional consciousness as such, on the one hand, and those of its correlative a priori universal forms of all the possible objects — objectivity as such — on the other hand; yet they possess an essential correspondence — one serves the other in the task of objectivization. It is this correspondence of the rules, principles, and structures of acts and processes with the objects that they are supposed to constitute that characterizes the nature of intentional consciousness, and its accomplishment of laying bare to itself its own workings and their fruits in infinite repetitive variations. In this correlation Husserl expects intentionality to reach "absolute rationality" in its ordering.[117] However, this is a *restriction to the intellectual type of rationality* — rational ordering alone. Envisaged in the limited field of its final accomplishment the subject-object differentiation of life's inner workings explains *neither its significance intelligibly nor its role and place within the universal ordering of life*. Neither does it put the work of intentional reason in its proper perspective. We must treat this differentiation within the progressive differentiation of the logos on its course through life.

SECTION 3. THE EMERGENCE OF THE INTELLIGIBLE SENSE
OF LIFE WITHIN THE SET OF THE THREE PHASES OF THE
SYNERGIES OF LIFE'S FORCES

When we focus upon the intelligible sense as a virtuality of the meaning-projecting Human Condition we distinguish it best, and first, in *the progressive stages of life's meaning-clarifying progress* and, secondly, in *the way in which it introduces intelligibility through the constructive workings of the intellectual faculty along its fully expanded subject-object axis of consciousness*. The intellect emerges in our perspective as the faculty which brings in the basic system with reference to which the establishment of the life order of the human individual proceeds. This life-order means, first, the manifold articulations of our vegetative, animal, and cultural unfolding and growth, and that together with the concurrent unfolding and expanding of our circumambient world. With the advent of the human condition within the evolutive gradation of living types, this life-order takes on a specific dimensional circuit, hitherto veiled in lower animals, and only progressively with the greater complexity of beingness does clarified intelligibility become in the highest type of human experience, namely, that of reflective apperception — which Husserl attributed to immanent phenomenological perception alone — "translucency."

From the central position that intelligibility acquires within the conscious life, we may, in one direction, retrace its genesis in its preceding stages back to its germinal emergence, as well as, in the other direction, acknowledge its fullest accomplishment.

To begin, life's progress marks each of its steps by bringing together, fusing, retaining, rejecting, and putting asunder, thereby constituting; that is, it articulates its progress by mixing the virtualities of the life forces which flow together. *It is this synergy of life's forces which promotes the various modes of fusing: it is through it that the initial spontaneity prompts the individualization of life.* And this individualizing process orders itself as it advances, carried on by the drive of its forces. We may say then that the ordering of life is carried on by the synergies of our vital forces, *while the principles of this ordering and the forms within which life advances belong to the system of life's progress and to its conditions.* Its rationality is the vehicle of life. The discovery of these principles and forms belongs to the metaphysics of life.

The surging of the human condition, with its unique self-ordering system, is an effect of the synergy of vital forces also. The intellectual ordering of life, which takes place in the full-fledged unfolding of the subject/object axis in our human individualizing progress and culminates in the subjectively operated constitution of an objective life-world which has the human subject as its vortex, is a special phase of the differentiation of the *logos of life* into life-serving rationalities. The progressive distantiation of the "inner" living agency and its "outer" field of life brings varying refinement in the evaluation of distinctiveness and in discernment to the composition of this outer field, and it institutes as well degrees of self-awareness in sensing and feeling — when standing before the threshold of the specifically human complexity, the human condition produces a *novum* through the synergy which realizes the "source-experience." Although the source-experience is the work of the synergy of life's forces, yet the "positional" function of consciousness is strengthened by the entry into play of the specific synchronizing tendency of the intellect; *intentional synchronization* leads to what Husserl calls naive, empirical "experience." The previously but vaguely sensed and felt complexes of feelings, stirrings, sensations, etc. have acquired a direction, an attentive focus upon an "object." From the "phantasma" of pre-experience, once synergized by the life-forces that brought them about, we have moved to a consistently *synchronized* complex of elements with a focus upon the objective, individual structure, which gives it all an objective unity. *We may see the placing of the implementation of full intelligibility along the axis of subject and object's mutual reflection in the source-experience.* It works like a watershed through which *the specific virtualities of the human condition* interlink and ignite with the life-forces bringing them together while differentiating the synergetic work of the second from the now emerging synchronizing work of the first, separating their impact without dividing their common task of promoting the drives of life. There it is, along the subject-object axis, that the four faculties constitutive of the specifically human life-world come together with the three meaning-bestowing senses, of which the intelligible sense is one; there "consciousness large as life" expands into intentional modalities. Our ever so object-geared experience is in fact constitutive of the object, so that it stands out there to be apprehended by the conscious reflective glance. It is due to the synchronizing function of intentional consciousness — which we, with Husserl, cannot fail to recognize as the primary and foundational performance of the faculty of the intellect — that the elements of an objective counterpart of conscious pre-experience, which lies in the complex of our feelings merely as a hazy phantasma, are due to the attentive direction of guiding intellect, brought appropriately together within relations which are neither willed nor fancifully imagined, but are carried and delivered through the entire pre-experiential complex of the individualization process. There it is that the objective forms, which we experience in the sensory perception that *reconstitutes their contours, are ingrained in the entire system of life-enactment.* Intentional consciousness under whose jurisdiction these relations fall — or that of the simpler functions of the intellect — has to bring them out giving them the constitutive shape of the clear INTELLIGIBLE structure of an object.

   We reach here the threshhold which the source-experience points to in our *pre-human ordering* and *human intelligible reconstruction* of life's individualizing progress, or the construction of the objectified life-forms, the groundwork which *the intellect lays down* while it engages *the intelligible sense* and makes the subject-object commerce "translucent," for the entire solidity and persistent universality of all the enterprises which man's creative striving may devise.

Henceforth, from attentiveness to the object to be constituted and from the concrete material produced by the vital synergies of forces, the intellect moves up the ladder to a translucent understanding of the world, "translucent" because it is free from its foundational concrete "material" and is "transparent" to the mind in its forms — the level of thought of universal objectivities. Here it is intelligibility *to* the mind, as such, that is the criterion of constitution. This higher sphere of the constitution of objectivity enjoys total flexibility and is — even though this intelligibility is ultimately based in the first sphere of perceptual constitution — open to the play of imagination. Also, *rather than have its ordering devices remain bound to data of the pre-experiential level, and calling for their synchronization*, here at the level of the constitution of universal objects and ideas, relations and thoughts *the intellect enjoys a new form of "autonomy."* It is its own function of what in agreement with Husserl we call "synthesis" which projects links, bindings, appreciative criteria, forms, and categories of its own. This is the intelligible sense at its acme. It is the faculty of the intellect which through its most complex mechanisms sets about the constitution of the fully intelligible — a project that makes manifest the intricate subject-object constitutive articulations of the life-world by calling on a specific sense of intelligibility *of . . . to . . . .* In short, the intelligible sense, once implemented as a rational linkage, makes the human self within his universe fully aware by "enlightening" both realms.

SECTION 4. THE FOUNDATIONAL POSITIONALITY OF
"CONSCIOUSNESS AS LARGE AS LIFE" AND OF "GIVENNESS"

The crucial question which is at stake here is: "What is this realm which life installs in its unfolding, for its expansion?" We, as living beings, exist as elements of it of a special sort; each of us experiences himself as the center of the world, "his" world; as the center to which this realm with which he deals and in which he occupies this central position is "given" inasmuch as he is within it "given" to himself. As an individual he performs all his living functions with its spread, spreading himself accordingly. The individualization of life calls first for this *distantiation* between the inner and outer, subject and object, myself and all else. That is, it proceeds by a distantiation which takes place already in the very functions which prompt life's process. That is, it installs a "spatial" spread just as it installs the vitally significant experience of time: successiveness, simultaneity and futurity. *Life as individualization installs the space-time axis of its progress.*

When we ask ourselves what is this *givenness* of the individualized life at its high human level of complexity we may, indeed, with Husserl, emphasize the presencing of things, beings, feelings, images, remembrances, etc. to us. This presencing of the world's elements to us (*Vergegenwärtigung*) occurs on the double axis of "spacing" and "timing," through which the life-functions punctuate themselves, throw themselves "ahead," "advance." It is, already at the initial, germinal circuit of life's functioning that the crucial distantiation inaugurating both of these dimensions occurs. The primeval principle of life appears to be differentiation, the distantiation between the inward/outward directedness, which unfolds a further differentiation between inner/outer, leading to that which in its full development becomes the threshhold of the human condition, namely, the subject/object differentiation. Although we may conjecture that at every phase of the complexity of life there occurs a givenness of the life-circumambient conditions in which the living individual works out its existential course, yet the human being seems to have *accomplished the fullest circuit of givenness* due first to the multi-dimensional objectivization of the elements of his life's circuit, and secondly due to the "clearest" intelligibility.[118]

The differentiation of the logos of life occurs along and through all the constructive functions beginning with the germinal distantiation and the coming together, mixing, and separating of the pre-life virtualities and the taking of its systematic course with the individualization of beingness. Yet it appears *that the creative orchestration is the peak, because there the human will, the measure of the givenness of life, is fulfilled.*

The very fact that we may "assert ourselves" in whatever activity, thought, experience, makes it manifest that we are "given" to ourselves in this self-assertion. It is manifest also that the objects of our experiencing — the very stirrings of our sensing, acting, or thinking — "are there for us" to "be ascertained" in our experience. The entire sphere within which we as a being are differentiated from the "rest," "distantiated" from it, and enabled to act, think, experience within it, and approach it, or join it, is given to us as a "being there" for us; the "rest" stands there having ourselves as its vortex. In this sense *givenness belongs to life's assertion and its very workings.* Yet with its complexities it assumes various forms. The givenness particular to man consists of an entire complex of *the human being given to himself* and spreading innumerable tentacles of distantiated and approximatable elements of a seemingly all-encompassing orbit around him within which his existence unfolds, his life-world of vital, societal, and cultural circuits of meaningfulness. This is the meaningfulness of an objective system of things, beings, relations, experiences, thought, feelings, etc. which stands there in front of us and simultaneously forms through its representational reflection "our" without as well as "our" within.

What is givenness for us as human beings is the givenness of an objective world paired with our subjective self. How does our givenness, which is the fruit as well as the vehicle of our existence, come about? It is certainly with the givenness of objects in sensory perception and of ourselves as we enact it that the specifically human givenness commences. "Perceiving" here signifies the basic work of human consciousness as the main functional complex which carries on the entire world of life's constructive endeavor at this phase of its complexity. It is consciousness as such that performs the foundational operations with the help of which the constructing faculties may begin their work.

Although it is the work of the faculties, in this case primarily of the intellect, to carry out the perceptual process, giving it its structural spread, objective relatedness and unifying links, etc., it is *consciousness which accounts for the springing forth of the acts* in which that process occurs; and for the *attentiveness* to which an objectifying focus and direction owes its inception; and for the *position-taking* with respect to the manner of attentiveness; lastly consciousness accounts for the experiential coalescence and unity of the continuum within which the process in its transformations proceeds. It is due to these three main performances of consciousness that givenness as *the presencing of "something" to "someone" as such is possible.*

Concurrently, there is also established the objectivity which is to be given as our "being there," as "our" standing before what is there in front of "us" — "we," who are simultaneously present to ourselves as we receive it.

This is the particular structurizing function of the intellectual faculty. However, this function could not unfold, if consciousness as such together with the intellectual operations which structurize the realm of objectivity, did not conjointly release the orderly successiveness in which the dynamic unfolding of the constitution of reality advances with the course of life's self-individualization: experiential, as well as conscious time. As Husserl himself emphasizes, consciousness, individuality, and time are inseparable notions. We would say in contrast that *life, individuality, and time* are inseparable; conscious time is but the special sphere of the specifically human life constitutive of objectivity.

This is so not simply due to some synergy of forces which carry out the articulation of life's processes, with their universal articulations, repetitive stages, and cycles of life's progress, which follow a pre-established schema, but due to a full-fledged expanded faculty of the intellect which, although grounded in the synergy of vital forces, sets about its structuring work prompted by the subject's will, imagination, and the urgency of a living present nourished by the memory of the past.

We must ask first how this intelligible sense is put into action.

SECTION 5. THE INTELLIGIBLE SENSE'S EXPANSION THROUGH THE PRINCIPLES AND CATEGORIES OF THE INTELLECTUAL STRUCTURATION OF OBJECTIVITY

We may, with Husserl, assume empirical, "naive" perception, on the one hand, and its counterpart, intentionally clarified apperception, on the other hand, to be the watershed, the threshhold, dividing the different workings of consciousness in which apperception, with its entrance into the play of intentional consciousness, would mark the borderline between animal consciousness and strictly human, intellectual consciousness and the awareness constitutive of full-fledged objectivity. Doing so, we may distinguish between the *principles of the basic constructive endeavor implemented spontaneously by our life functioning and which are inherent to life's constructive system* and the *principles and categories of the intellect according to which human objectivity is construed.*[119] When we acknowledge life's constructive spontaneous principles: distantiating and approximating, differentiating (inwardness/ outwardness) and unifying, prompting, differentiating and coalescing, mixing, fusing and diffusing, articulating, etc., as well as relevance and selectiveness, successiveness and multiple simultaneity, primogenital givenness, intertwining and our community-of-life-interests, etc., which account for the individualization of life in the course of time punctuated by its multiple unfolding and the simultaneous transformation of life's conditions, there is to be found a corresponding set of principles and categories according to which the intellectual consciousness establishes the full-fledged meaningfulness of the human objective life-world.

Husserl has himself recognized that it is individuality which plays the decisive role in the constitution of objectivity as such, beginning with the ground of the primary sensory perception (*Ursprüngliche Wahrnehmung*) and this at both of its levels, in empirical as well as in intentional perception. With the appearance of individuality time and space play basic roles in the constitution of the sensory object, albeit time is already basic to intentional consciousness as such insofar as it provides the elemental form of any possible object, of objectivity, as the successive steps of constitution order the flow of constitutive consciousness as such. Thus in the constitution of objectivity in Husserl's perspective the principle of individuality appears, first at the level of consciousness and, then at that of intellectual ordering. We reconfirm these views, emphasizing, however, that *individualizing at all levels is but the basic principle of life.*

In individuality-oriented constitution the referential categories of identity and diversity, difference, plurality, oneness, etc., enter in, under which categories the constitution of objectivity in its individual nature falls. However, we must also consider the categories of relations: compossibility and contrariness, equality and difference, similitude and divergence, positive and negative correlation, attraction and repulsion, congruity and incongruity, etc.

Naturally, these categorical forms correspond to the operations of *consciousness itself in its intellectual* (*intentional*) *role,* namely to the functions of identifying, distinguishing, separating and unifying, collecting and numbering, as well as to the relational operations of equating and diversifying, attracting and repelling, etc. In all these objectifying operations of the intellect it is the *unity of the object in formation* that is at stake. We may see the factors of this unity, first *in the fundamental operational tendency of consciousness as such.* At the *vital level,* consciousness manifests itself through (1) the *coalescence* of our complexes of feeling and sensing in their various levels of awareness. In the *perceptual, experiential circuit* of conscious functioning, the unifying tendency of consciousness, as such, works through (2) the *synchronization* of perceptual material with attentive directedness toward the object to be perceived at its center. In intellectual consciousness, however, we see the faculty of the intellect most strongly manifested in the autonomous power of (3) *synthesizing* elements which otherwise do not seem to indicate any congruence or affinities toward coalescence into the formations indicated by the deliberative activities of the intellect as it draws upon the works of memory, fantasy, and imagination.

At the threshhold at which the synchronizing activity of consciousness and the synthesizing, autonomous function of the intellect part ways, we have also the strict distinction between the constitution of individual sensory objects, on the one hand, and that of general objectivities and universal ideas as the forms of thought, on the other. Together they support the constructive works of the intellect establishing the specifically human universe of objectivity.

CONCLUDING BY WAY OF TRANSITION TO THE THIRD PANEL OF THE TRIPTYCH

The logos of life, like the sun, rises from the dark horizon of idle, lifeless, dormant existence and, as it spreads its rays, life awakens and the world of colors, sounds, shapes, living beings, plants and all things resplendent appears in its glory. We have seen in the preceding investigation how the human being, through his creative endeavor, brings the logos to its peak in the expansion of life, which culminates in the multiple rationalities which the genius of man invents and infinitely propagates. However, as life's striving carries its limits within itself, its emergence and growth foreshadows its inevitable decay and disapearance. So we have not yet, in our display of its glorious ascent to the zenith, witnessed the complete span of its course. Like life's phenomenal route, so the unfolding of the logos, which leads like a *filum Ariadne* from nowhere to fulfillment, will have to lead to its descent toward the opposite side of the firmament of existence, to the point where it vanishes. The descending route of the logos of life will constitute the subject of the subsequent third panel of this work. Indeed, to complete our critique of reason it remains still to be seen how, at its zenith, the power and expansiveness of reason effectuates its descent.

NOTES

FOREGROUND

[1] *Cf.* the present writer's monograph, "The First Principles of the Metaphysics of Life," *Analecta Husserliana, The Yearbook of Phenomenological Research*, D. Reidel, Dordrecht, 1987, Vol. XXI.

[2] Anna-Teresa Tymieniecka, *Why is there Something rather than Nothing, Prolegomena to the Phenomenology of Cosmic Creation*, Royal Van Gorcum, Assen (Humanities Press, New York), 1966, pp. 13—25.

[3] *Ibid.*, pp. 77—90.

[4] *Ibid.*, pp. 23—71, *loc. cit.*; also p. 95.

[5] *Ibid.*, pp. 33—34.

[6] *Ibid.*, p. 33.

[7] *Ibid.*, pp. 77—158.

[8] *Cf.* by the present writer, "Natural Spontaneity in the Translacing Continuity of Beingness," in *Analecta Husserliana*, Vol. XIV, 1982.

PANEL I

[1] We have examined this question in a specialized study: "Die phänomenologische Selbstbesinnung I: Der Leib und die Transzendentialität in der gegenwärtigen phänomenologischen und psychiatrischen Forschung," *Analecta Husserliana*, Vol. I, Dordrecht, D. Reidel, 1971.

[2] *Cf.* by the same author: *Why is there Something rather than Nothing: Prolegomena to the Phenomenology of Cosmic Creation*, Assen, Royal Van Gorcum, 1965; and the specialized study: "Cosmos, Nature, and Man, and the Foundations of Psychiatry," in *Heidegger and the Path of Thinking*, Pittsburgh, Duquesne University Press, 1970.

[3] *The Young Fate*, trans. David Paul, in Jackson Mathews, ed., *The Collected Works of Paul Valéry*, Vol. I, Princeton, N.J., Princeton University Press, 1971, p. 69.

[4] *Ibid.*, p. 71.

[5] *Ibid.*, p. 71.

[6] *Ibid.*, p. 87.

[7] *Loc. cit.*

[8] *Ibid.*, p. 97.

[9] *Ibid.*, p. 95.

[10] "The Philosopher and the Young Fate," trans. David Paul, in *The Collected Works of Paul Valéry*, Vol. I, *op. cit.*, p. 265.

[11] *The Young Fate, op. cit.*, p. 99.

[12] *Ibid.*, p. 103.

437

[13] *Loc. cit.*

[14] *Ibid.*, pp. 103—105.

[15] "Fragments of the Narcissus," *Charms*, trans. David Paul, in *The Collected Works of Paul Valéry*, Vol. I, *op. cit.*, p. 149.

[16] *Loc. cit.*

[17] *The Narcissus Cantata*, trans. David Paul and Robert Fitzgerald, in *The Collected Works of Paul Valéry, op. cit.*, Vol. III, *Plays*, p. 323. In French, the first line reads, "Cher *Corps*, je m'abandonne à ta seule puissance".

[18] "The Bee," *Charms*, trans. David Paul, *op. cit.*, p. 129.

[19] "Abundance of Evening," *Album of Early Verse*, trans. David Paul, in *The Collected Works of Paul Valéry*, Vol. I, *op. cit.*, p. 43.

[20] "The Plane Tree," *Charms*, trans. David Paul, *op. cit.*, p. 117.

[21] *Loc. cit.*

[22] *Loc. cit.*

[23] *Ibid.*, p. 119.

[24] *Loc. cit.*

[25] "Palm," *Charms*, trans. David Paul, *op. cit.*, pp. 231—233.

[26] *Ibid.*, p. 231.

[27] *Ibid.*, p. 233.

[28] *Ibid.*, p. 235.

[29] *Ibid.*, p. 233.

[30] *Loc. cit.*

[31] "Song of the Columns," *Charms*, trans. David Paul, *op. cit.*, p. 125.

[32] "Note and Digression," trans. Malcolm Cowley and James R. Lawler, in *The Collected Works of Paul Valéry*, Vol. VIII, *Leonardo, Poe, Mallarmé, op. cit.,* p. 83.

[33] "Anne," *An Album of Early Verse*, trans. David Paul, *op. cit.*, p. 51.

[34] *Ibid.*, p. 53.

[35] "Note and Digression," *op. cit.*, pp. 81—82. Day-laborers (in Italian in the original).

[36] *Loc. cit.*

[37] "The Young Fate," *op. cit.*, p. 73.

[38] *Semiramis*, trans. David Paul and Robert Fitzgerald, in *The Collected Works of Paul Valéry*, Vol. III, *op. cit.*, p. 301.

[39] *Ibid.*, p. 295.

[40] "The Caress," *Various Poems of All Periods*, trans. David Paul, in *The Collected Works of Paul Valéry*, Vol. I, *op. cit.*, p. 261.

[41] *Loc. cit.*

[42] *Loc. cit.*

[43] "The Sly One," *Charms, op. cit.*, p. 181.

[44] *Loc. cit.*

[45] *Loc. cit.*

[46] "The Footsteps," *Charms, op. cit.*, p. 135.

[47] "The Cruel Bird," *Various Poems of All Periods, op. cit.*, p. 253.

[48] "The Philosopher and the Young Fate," *op. cit.*, p. 265.

[49] *La Jeune Parque commentée par Alain*, Paris, N.R.F., 1953. Valéry wrote "The Philosopher and the Young Fate" in 1930 to serve as a prologue, or "preface," to Alain's commentary of *The Young Fate*. — Trans.

[50] *Loc. cit.*

[51] *Loc. cit.*

[52] *Note and Digression, op. cit.*, p. 83.

[53] *Ibid.*, p. 76.

[54] *Leonardo and the Philosophers*, trans. Malcolm Cowley and James R. Lawler, in *The Collected Works of Paul Valéry*, Vol. VIII, *op. cit.*, p. 137 (marginal note).

[55] *Notes and Digression, op. cit.*, p. 89.

[56] *Introduction to the Method of Leonardo da Vinci*, trans. Malcolm Cowley and James R. Lawler, in *The Collected Works of Paul Valéry*, Vol. VIII, *op. cit.*, p. 19.

[57] *Ibid.*, p. 20.

[58] *Loc. cit.*

[59] *Ibid.*, p. 19 (marginal note).

[60] *Ibid.*, p. 20 (marginal note).

[61] "The Young Fate," *op. cit.*, p. 75.

[62] *Ibid.*, p. 77.

[63] *Loc. cit.*

[64] This and the following citations are taken from *Note and Digression, op. cit.*, pp. 92—94.

[65] Unicity is the characteristic of the individual. In the framework of constitution, every individual is unique, but can never be "original." Originality is the property of a type. If the singular work is original, it is only because it has made a new type arise. The debate concerning the different prerogatives of constitution and creation is best expressed in this opposition: Constitution guarantees the *unicity* of the individual, but it belongs to creativity to produce *originality* in making a new system of meaning, supported by a new type, arise.

[66] *Variété*, Paris, N.R.F., Vol. I, p. 128; *cf.* L. Cain, *Trois Essais sur Valéry*, Paris, Gallimard, 1958.

[67] *Cahiers*, Vol. 5, p. 33.

[68] *Eupalinos, or The Architect*, trans. William McCausland Stewart, in *The Collected Works of Paul Valéry, op. cit.*, Vol. IV, *Dialogues*, pp. 90—91.

[69] "The Young Fate," *op. cit.*, pp. 103—105.

[70] *Ibid.*, p. 105.

[71] "Fragments of the Narcissus," *Charms, op. cit.*, p. 141.

[72] *Ibid.*, p. 143.

[73] *Leonardo and the Philosophers, op. cit.*, p. 137.

[74] *Ibid.*, pp. 136—137.

[75] *Ibid.*, p. 137.

[76] *Ibid.*, pp. 137—138.

[77] *Dance and the Soul*, trans. William McCausland Stewart, in *The Collected Works of Paul Valéry*, Vol. IV, *op. cit.*, p. 29.

[78] *Ibid.*, p. 28.

[79] *Ibid.*, p. 30.

[80] *Ibid.*, pp. 30—31.

[81] *Loc. cit.*

[82] *Ibid.*, pp. 31—32.

[83] Art is thus the point where the phenomena of the soul are translated into those of

the body, and vice-versa. In the secret of the dance, in the relations between the art and the body which exercises it, the pains of the body are exchanged for those of the soul. Sprains and bruises are exchanged, on the same plane, with phantasms, heartbreaks and various malaises and incidents like artistic or passionate jealousy, dreams, and day-dreams. The physician, by his art, discloses the precise relation they entertain with the soul, or with the body: "Do you know they have only to whisper to me some dream which torments them for me to conclude, for example, that some tooth is affected?" *Dance and the Soul, op. cit.*, p. 34.

[84] *Ibid.*, p. 34.

[85] *Ibid.*, p. 35.

[86] *Loc. cit.*

[87] *Ibid.*, p. 47.

[88] Cecil Hemley, "Euridice," *In the Midnight Wood*, New York, Noonday Press, 1957.

[89] "The man of today," says Valéry, "does not cultivate what cannot be abridged. One would say that the weakening in our minds of the idea of eternity coincides with our growing disgust with long tasks. We no longer tolerate forming values." *Prière sur l'art*, p. 24.

[90] *Note and Digression, op. cit.*, p. 66.

[91] *Cf. Why is there Something rather than Nothing?, op. cit.*

[92] This theme is found in the analyses of Chapter One.

[93] Our analyses in Chapter One relate to this.

[94] We are led to this conception in Chapter Two.

PANEL II

[1] Maurice Pradines, *Traité de Psychologie*, Presses Universitaire de France, 1943—1956, Paris.

[2] The main ideas of this section were already announced in the author's "Originality and Creative Perception," *Proceedings of the First International Congress of Aesthetics*, Amsterdam, 1964.

[3] *Cf. infra*, pp. 114—116; also the present writer's: "The Creative Self and the Other in Man's Self-Interpretation-in-Existence," *Analecta Husserliana*, Vol. VI, D. Reidel, Dordrecht, 1977.

[4] Jean Wahl, *Vers le concret*, Paris, Gallimard, 1962; *The Philosopher's Way*, Oxford University Press, New York, 1948; and *Traité de Métaphysique*, Payot, Paris, 1953.

[5] The idea of Initial Spontaneity was first presented by the present author in the study "Initial Spontaneity," *Analecta Husserliana*, Vol. V, 1976.

[6] *Cf.* the above-quoted, *The Philosopher's Way,* by Jean Wahl.

[7] *Cf. infra*, pp. 123—124.

[8] Etienne Souriau, "Du mode d'existence de l'oeuvre à faire," *Bulletin de la Societé Française de Philosophie*, Janvier—Mars, 1956.

[9] *Ibid.*

[10] The conception of the "creative vision" as the main point of reference for the intrinsic study of the work of art was first proposed by the present writer in the

Festschrift for Roman Ingarden indicating her radical opposition to the approach of her Master under the title, "*Nieboska Komedja*, Struktura a Wizja Poetycka."

[11] Tymieniecka, "Struktura a Wizja Poetycka," *op. cit.*

[12] *Ibid.*

[13] Samuel Taylor Coleridge, *Biographia Literaria*, Fol. 4a, *Archiv*, quoted by John Livingston Lowes in *The Road to Xanadu*, Vintage Books, New York, 1959.

[14] Henri Stendhal, *Pensées; La filosofia nova*, Le Divin Ed., Paris, 1931.

[15] *Cf.* Henri Poincaré, *The Foundations of Science*, trans. G. B. Halstead, Science Press, 1924, quoted in, *Creativity: Selected Readings*, P. E. Vernon, ed., p. 84, Penguin Books, Ltd., Harmandsworth, 1971.

[16] *Notebooks of Samuel Taylor Coleridge*, published by A. Brandl (in fragments) in 1896; also S. T. Coleridge, *Poems II*, 988—95, as quoted by John Livingston Lowes in *The Road to Xanadu*, Vintage Books, New York, 1959.

[17] John Livingston Lowes, *The Road to Xanadu, A Study in the Ways of Imagination*, Vintage Books, New York, 1959, pp. 35—49.

[18] *Ibid.*, pp. 49—55.

[19] Marcel Proust, *A la recherche du temps perdu*, Vol. I, Gallimard, Paris, 1954.

[20] Romain Roland, *Bethoven*, Ed. du Fablier, Paris, 1928.

[21] Lucien Rudrauf, *L'Annonciation, étude d'un thème plastique et de ses variations en peinture et sculpture*, Paris, Imprimerie Grou-Radenez, 1943, p. 145.

[22] *Ibid.*, pp. 15—122.

[23] *Ibid.*, p. 26.

[24] Virginia Woolf, *Diary*, The Hogarth Press, London, 1953, ed. L. Woolf entries quoted are respectively from pp. 101, 108, 137, 138, 144 and 145.

[25] Edmund Husserl, *Ideas*, Book II.

[26] Buckminster Fuller, in collaboration with E. J. Applewhite, *Synergetics II, Explorations in the Geometry of Thinking*, Macmillan Co., New York, 1979, pp. 25—57.

[27] Henri Stendahl, *Pensées: Filosofia nova*, Le Divan, Paris, 1931.

[28] Lev Tolstoi, *Anna Karenina*, Introduction by George Gibion, Harper and Row, New York, 1959.

[29] Ernst Kretschmer, *Körperbau und Charakter, Part II, Die Temperamente*, pp. 111—251, and *Theorie der Temperamente*, pp. 251—262, 3. Aufl. Berlin, J. Springer, 1922.

[30] Etienne Souriau, *Les grands problèmes de l'esthétique théatrale*, Les Cours de Sorbonne, p. 4, Centre de Documentation Universitaire, 1956.

[31] Anna-Teresa Tymieniecka, *Poetica Nova, At the Creative Crucibles, Analecta Husserliana*, Vol. XII, 1982.

[32] For the most penetrating study of the theater, *cf.* also Souriau's *Les deux mille situations dramatiques*, Paris, Flammarion, 1950.

[33] *Cf.* Denis Diderot, *Paradox sur le Comédien*, in transl. The Paradox of Acting, Hill and Wang, Inc., New York, 1951.

[34] Konstantin Sergeivich Stanislavskii, *An Actor Prepares*, trans. E. Reynolds, Hapgood, Theater Arts Inc., New York, 1936.

[35] For the question of the receptivity of the public as an influence essential to theater performance, *cf.* the particularly sensitive treatment of Allardyce Nicoll, *A History of the Restoration Drama* (1660—1770), Cambridge University Press, 1940. We quote the fragment of the poem above after Nicoll.

[36] *Ibid.*

[37] For the universal features of the theater with respect to the public, *cf.* Fortunat Strowski, *Le théatre et nous*, Ed. de la Nouvelle Revue Critique, Paris, 1934.

[38] Nicoll, *op. cit.*

[38a] *Ibid.*

[39] Tymieniecka, "Struktura a Wizja Poetycka," *op. cit.*

[40] *Cf.* by the present author: "Ideas as the Constitutive *a priori*," *Kant Studien*, 1959.

[41] *Ibid.*

[42] Edmund Husserl, *Analysen zur passiven Synthesis*, Nijhoff, The Hague, 1966, p. 319, footnote.

[43] *Ibid.*

[44] *Cf.* The First Panel of this Triptych.

[45] "... *je me concois capable de recevoir une infinité de semblables changements et je ne saurais néanmoins parcourir cette infinité par mon imagination et par conséquent cette conception que j'ai de la cire ne s'accomplit par la faculté d'imagination*," 2nd *Meditation*, 12, PUF, Paris, 1966, p. 47.

[46] *Cf.* Edmund Husserl: *Untersuchungen zur Phänomenologie des Inneren Zeitbewusstseins, Husserliana*, M. Nijhoff, The Hague, p. 232.

[47] From the many texts devoted to "free variation." *Cf. Ideas I*, pp. 223—224.

[48] *Cf.* Husserl, *Phänomenologie des Inneren Zeitbewusstseins, op. cit.*, pp. 10—38.

[49] *Ibid.*, p. 43.

[50] *Ibid.*, p. 51.

[51] *Ideen I*, p. 226.

[52] "*Näher ausgeführt ist das Phantasieren überhaupt die Neutralitätsmodifikation der 'setzenden' Vergegenwärtigung, also der Erinnerung im denkbar weitesten Sinne.*" *Ideen I*, p. 224. *Cf.* also *Analysen zur Passiven Synthesis*, pp. 322—330.

[53] *Cf. supra*, pp. 121—125.

[54] Husserl, *Phänomenologie des Inneren Zeitbewusstseins, op. cit.*, Appendix I, p. 108.

[55] "*Die Eigentümlichkeit dieser Bewusstseinsspontaneität aber ist dass sie nur Urerzeugtes zum Wachstum, zur Entfaltung bringt, aber nichts 'Neues' schaft.*", *ibid.*, p. 100.

[56] Immanuel Kant, *Kritik der reinen Vernunft*, A50, B74/R. Schmidt (ed.), Felix Meiner, Hamburg, 1956.

[57] *Ibid.*, B103, p. 116.

[58] *Ibid.*, Para. 24. *Von der Anwendung der Kategorien auf Gegenstände der Sinne überhaupt*, 1646, 10, B/198.

[59] *Ibid.*, 178a.

[60] *Ibid., Elementarlehre II, Teil I. Abt. II. Buch.* p. 193/A132/20.

[61] *Ibid.*, pp. 197—199.

[62] *Ibid.*, p. 200/A142/20.

[63] *Ibid.*, p. 200, 10/B181.

[64] *Analysen zur Passiven Synthesis*, Vorlesungen, pp. 275—276.

[65] Such a reaching to the depths is for Kant possible although it was not for Husserl because he — as has been pointed out by A. Gurwitsch and M. Merleau-Ponty — abandoned the "hypothesis of constancy" between the "impressional consciousness" and a possible "external" agent supposed to produce the impression.

[66] Husserl himself seems to see these points of analogy. *Cf. Analysen zur Passiven Synthesis*, p. 126.

67 *Kritik der Urteilskraft, Introduktion.*
68 *Ibid.,* p. 189.
69 *Ibid.,* p. 205.
70 *Ibid.,* p. 292.
71 *Ibid.,* p. 286.
72 "*Die Kunst des Genies besteht darin, das freie Spiel der Erkenntniskräfte mittelbar zu machen.*" H. G. Gadamer, *Wahrheit und Methode,* I., C. B. Mohr, Tübingen, 1960, p. 50.
73 *Cf.* Anna-Teresa Tymieniecka, *Why is There Something Rather than Nothing, Prolegomena to the Phenomenology of Cosmic Creation,* Van Gorcum, Assen, 1964, and the above-quoted "Ideas as the Constitutive *a priori.*"
74 *Cf.* the section on Karl Jaspers and Gabriel Marcel, as well as the entire part on phenomenological psychiatry, in my book *Phenomenology and Science in Contemporary European Thought,* Farrar, Straus, and Giroux, New York, 1961.
75 By "political" is meant here, in the Greek tradition, the specific feature of man's social nature consisting of constructing a "polis," a state orchestration of social life.
76 *Cf.* Calvin S. Hall and Gardner Lindzey, *Theories of Personality* 3d ed (New York: John Wiley, 1978).
77 *Cf.* Ludwig Binswanger, *Grundformen und Erkenntnis menschlichen Daseins* (Zurich: Nichans, 1953). Ludwig Binswanger, the celebrated Swiss psychiatrist inspired by Husserl and Heidegger, has developed a psychiatric conception of the human being within the "life-world" in which, in contrast to Freudian views, no priority is attributed to a unique driving force within man. Rather, man's entire experiential system as expanded by his interactions with other men within the world becomes the pattern with reference to which psychiatric methods are devised. Binswanger has found numerous followers in several branches of what has become known as "phenomenological psychiatry."
78 In recent times, a highly developed conception of the specifically human person has come from the famous French psychiatrist Henri Ey. Ey and his school have brought to a culminating point the phenomenological tendency of Binswanger, Buytendyk, E. Minkowski, E. Straus and many others, in vindication of the belief that psychiatric diagnosis and therapy should deal with human nature as a whole. In his famous book, *Consciousness, a Phenomenological Study of Being Conscious and Becoming Conscious,* translated by John H. Flodstrom (Bloomington: Indiana University Press, 1978), Henri Ey presents, in its full expanse, the source and the experiential compass of the uniquely human conscious self as a person. Ey, and following him, Lanteri Laura, devise methods of psychiatric diagnosis with reference to the "disintegration of consciousness," i.e., of the person.
79 It is Max Scheler who has stressed particularly the significance of acting in the understanding of the human person. While emphasizing the autonomy of the person and the differentiation of the person from the individual, Scheler has highlighted particularly the social participation of the "intimate person," endowing it with a specific form of the "social person." *Cf.* Max Scheler, *Gesamtwerke,* Bd. 2, *Der Formalismus in der Ethik und die Materiale Wertethik* (Bern: Franke Verlag, 1966), and by the same author, Bd. 8, *Erkenntnis und Arbeit* (Bern: Franke Verlag, 1960).
80 In this perspective the "autonomy" versus the "conditioning" of the person is the center of the controversy.
81 Although Max Scheler attempts an inversion of this approach by seeking to show

the origin of values in emotions, nevertheless values ultimately emerge in an already constituted form; this could not have occurred without the work of the intellect. *Cf.* the present writer's monograph, "The Moral Sense at the Foundations of the Social World," in *Foundations of Morality, Human Rights and the Human Sciences, Analecta Husserliana*, Vol. XV, 1983.

[82] By "sense" is meant here that which "infuses" the linguistic forms with significance so that they may present meanings (it should not be understood in relation to senses, sensory, sensuous etc. referring to sensory organs).

[83] By "substantial persistence" is meant here the way in which the living being "appears" to our senses as a cogent, self-reposing, stable and perduring factor of life and to our actions as a responsive and autonomous partner.

[84] *Cf.* Anna-Teresa Tymieniecka, "Die phänomenologische Selbstbesinnung, Der Leib and die Transzendentalität in der gegenwärtigen phänomenologischen und psychiatrischen Forschung," *Analecta Husserliana*, Vol. I (Dordrecht/Boston: D. Reidel, 1971).

[85] The distinction between our body as an object and our body as experienced stems from Edmund Husserl. *Cf.* his *Ideas Pertaining to a Pure Phenomenology and a Phenomenological Philosophy*, Book II (Martinus Nijhoff, 1982), Part I.

[86] For Husserl's most careful and masterful analysis of the relationship between our body as experienced and the psyche (or empirical soul), *cf. ibid.*, Part I.

[87] I have attempted an investigation of the soul in its "essential manifestation" in the third part of my book, *The Three Movements of the Soul*, to appear in Vol. XXV of *Analecta Husserliana*.

[88] Regarding the concept of the "human condition," *cf.* the present author's monograph, *Poetica Nova . . . a Treatise in the Metaphysics of the Human Condition and of Art, Analecta Husserliana*, Vol. XII (Dordrecht/Boston: D. Reidel, 1982).

[89] *Cf.* Anna-Teresa Tymieniecka, "The Initial Spontaneity," *Analecta Husserliana*, Vol. V (Dordrecht/Boston: D. Reidel, 1976).

[90] In the above study, I have also indicated that from the very beginning of the individual unfolding of the human being, moral "virtualities" are present.

[91] I have succinctly analyzed this progress, terming it the forging of the "Transnatural Destiny of the Soul" in several of my writings. *Cf.* "Hope and the Present Instant," in S. Matczak, ed., *God in Contemporary Thought* (New York/Louvain: Learned Publications/Nauvelearts, 1977).

[92] This progress of spiritual unfolding with reference to the Other, the other self — the "inward witness" will be the subject of the third panel of our triptych: *The Three Movements of the Soul*, which will appear as *Analecta Husserliana*, Vol. XXV.

[93] The specific "mechanism" of this quest for the ultimate significance of human existence, as conducted with respect to another self, has been shown by the present writer in "Man the Creator and His Threefold Telos," *Analecta Husserliana*, Vol. IX (Dordrecht/Boston: D. Reidel Publ. Co., 1979). It appears that whoever the Other is, the concrete "encounter" with him or her *in* the significance of life is ever-elusive, because the Other functions merely as a concrete reference point, while it is the "inward witness" that is being consulted by the soul in its innermost depths. I show in this study how this comes to light when every supposed "communication" between the soul and the other self necessarily breaks down. With this break, however, the soul is ready for the face-to-face meting with the Ultimate Witness, who "has been there hidden in the intimate center of the soul all along" (as Teresa of Avila shows also).

[94] The following analyses have appeared in my monograph, "The Moral Sense at the Foundation of the Social World," cited in note 81.

[95] The term "source-experience" — in contradistinction to the classic phenomenological term "originary experience" — has been introduced by the present author precisely to pinpoint the crucial moment within the unfolding of individualizing life at which from the animal action/reaction agency a transition occurs to the specifically human experience that simultaneously originates the human subject.

[96] I have outlined the life-progress from the pre-life conditions accomplished by means of the individualization of the living being in "Natural Spontaneity in the Translacing Continuity of Beingness," in *The Phenomenology of Man and of the Human Condition: The Individualization of Nature and the Human Being, Analecta Husserliana*, Vol. XIV (Dordrecht/Boston: D. Reidel, 1982); and in "Spontaneity, Individualization and Life," in *Phenomenology of Life: A Dialogue between Chinese and Occidental Philosophy, Analecta Husserliana*, Vol. XVII, 1983.

[96a] *Cf.* my monograph, "The Moral Sense," *Analecta Husserliana*, Vol. XV.

[97] Moritz Geiger, *Beiträge zur Phänomenologie des ästhetischen Genusses*, 2, unveränderte Auflage, Tübingen: Max Niemeyer, 1974, pp. 21—31.

[98] *Ibid.*, pp. 35—47.

[98a] *Ibid.*

[99] *Ibid.*, pp. 40—45.

[100] *Ibid.*, pp. 39—40.

[101] *Ibid.*, p. 45.

[102] Geiger means not the "phenomenal self" which accounts for the fact that all contents of consciousness are to be characterized as "mine": "That everything that I experience belongs to my individual consciousness and never to another's". He speaks rather about the experience of the self as the self (*Icherleben*). *Ibid.*, p. 45.

[103] *Ibid.*, p. 175.

[104] *Ibid.*, p. 180.

[105] *Ibid.*, p. 61.

[106] *Ibid.*, pp. 95—96.

[107] *Ibid.*, p. 97.

[108] *Ibid.*, pp. 103—104.

[108a] *Cf.* footnote 95, *supra*.

[109] *Cf.* the present writer's "Natural Spontaneity in the Translacing Continuity of Beingness," *Analecta Husserliana*, Vol. XIV, 1983, pp. 125—151.

[110] *Cf.* the present writer's "*Poetica Nova*," *Analecta Husserliana*, Vol. XII, 1982, pp. 1—93.

[111] Edmund Husserl has left us a vast investigation of the ways in which givenness as such and then in its full-fledged construction of the life-world occurs in the processes of intentional consciousness — as well as in some pre-intentional circuits. The Husserlian corpus gives us a most detailed analysis of the ways in which the specifically human world is constituted in intentional consciousness. Husserl proposed intentional consciousness as the factor *par excellence* of the *unique* type of rationality which is characteristic of the human life-world and proposed from the beginning as an "ideal of absolute rationality" to strive for in human life.

The human life-world, of which the human individual is the vortex, is, indeed, in the Husserlian schema, a meaningful system established by the structurizing workings of intentional consciousness. In early lectures (1906—07), given between his *Logical Investigations* and *Ideas I,* Husserl gives us, although in fragments, an outline of his proposal to elaborate a groundwork for all the human sciences in a theory of the rational structuration of this meaningful system of the life-world which has man at its vortex, through the investigation of ways in which its intentional constitution, that is, its objectivization, occurs.

[112] We are here concerned with the ontic, that is the sense-giving, function of the Human Condition and not with the universal order of the individualization of life. That is, we outline here an "ontology of the Human Condition" but do not treat *in extenso* the "metaphysics of life" in which it is embedded. *Cf.* my "The First Principles of the Metaphysics of Life, *Tractatus Brevis*," in *Analecta Husserliana,* Vol. XXI, 1987.

[113] Between *Logical Investigations* and *Ideas I* Husserl, in his efforts to establish phenomenology as the foundation of all rationality, gave in his lectures of 1906—07, albeit in fragments, an outline of his theory of reason. The "absoluteness" of intentional consciousness is particularly emphasized by Husserl in these lectures (published recently under the title *Einleitung in die Logik und Erkenntnistheorie*, Bd. XIV *Husserliana,* The Hague: Martinus Nijhoff, 1984). This absoluteness is here related to the "ideal of absolute rationality" as the aim of phenomenology. (*Cf.* pp. 236—242 and 243—358.) In our present discussion we refer to this period in Husserl's thought because in these lectures Husserl's discussion of objectivization led him to an outline of a theory of the intellect, the subject with which we are here concerned. These lectures, situated histori-cally between *Logical Investigations* and *Ideas I,* give a succinct outline — although only in fragments — of Husserl's basic views concerning the intentional constitution of the objective world, views which departed sharply from those of empirical conscious-ness. Although his views underwent several stages of transformation in detail, the main ideas persisted throughout these stages. The intentional ordering, that is the process of constitution, is sharply distinguished from the complexes of feeling, emotion, sensory stirrings, etc. which also represent consciousness — but merely empirical, psychological consciousness. Consciousness as "experience" appears only when in the experiencing process it enters the maw of the function of attention (*Aufmerksamkeit*), which is directed at something distinctive, on an individual object. *Ibid.,* Chapter "Die Niederen Objektivationsformen," pp. 242—252.

[114] Husserl emphasizes the "apperceptive" character of constitutive individualization. Even though the lower level of objectivization, it is yet strictly rational, the work of intellectual reason (*Vernunft*). With this work the givenness of the life-world, according to Husserl, begins. The level of primary perception offers the sphere that grounds the higher level of objectivization which Husserl considers to be the formation of the objects of thought (*Denkgegenstände*), grounded and analogical to the first level. And bringing forth a number of a priori principles and categories according to which constitution proceeds, he outlines a theory of the intellect. *Ibid.,* p. 274.

[115] Subjectivity as an intentional agency, being the *absolute* source of rationality, and objectivity as such (*Objektivität überhaupt*) share essential formal principles: the objectivity of the life-world constitutes itself in forms corresponding to those of the objectifying experience in which the constitution takes place; they share the categorical principles of constitution.

[116] Husserl brings forth individuality as the absolutely basic principle of constitution, that is, that of objectivity as such. It is, in fact, with respect to the principle of individ-uality that the objectivization of the world begins. *Ibid.,* pp. 271—274.

[117] Husserl's early ideal of "absolute rationality" which is the task proposed to pheno-menology is strongly stated in the above-quoted lectures. *Cf.* pp. 236—240.

[118] I introduce here a conception of consciousness that covers all the pulsations of individualizing life.

[119] Husserl and followers, such as Scheler, Patocka, Pacci, Merleau-Ponty, and Gerd Brand have offered a wealth of insights into the constitution of the life-world and aired a great many issues concerning it.

Although our succinct account of the work of the intellect in the various phases of its setting up the multi-dimensional life-world of which we are the center and vortex agrees with and confirms many Husserlian observations concerning the workings of consciousness and reason (*Vernunft*), and although we will frequently use his terminology, this will serve only to indicate how far his ideas prove themselves in our new perspective and how far they undergo transformation.

INDEX OF NAMES

ANALYTICAL INDEX OF SELECTED SUBJECTS

TABLE OF CONTENTS OF BOOK 2

457